The Family
with a
Handicapped
Child

THE FAMILY WITH A HANDICAPPED CHILD

Second Edition

Edited by

MILTON SELIGMAN, Ph.D.

Professor, Department of Psychology in Education
University of Pittsburgh
Pittsburgh, Pennsylvania

ALLYN AND BACON
Boston   London   Toronto   Sydney   Tokyo   Singapore

Copyright © 1991, 1983 by Allyn and Bacon
A Division of Simon & Schuster, Inc.
160 Gould Street
Needham Heights, Massachusetts 02194

Library of Congress Cataloging-in-Publication Data

The Family with a handicapped child
 edited by Milton Seligman. — 2nd ed.
  p. cm.
 ISBN 0-205-12524-7
  1. Handicapped children — United States — Family
relationships. 2. Handicapped children — Care —
United States. I. Seligman, Milton, 1937–0000.
  [DNLM: 1. Child, Exceptional — psychology.
2. Family — psychology. 3. Family Therapy.
4. Handicapped — psychology. 5. Interpersonal
Relations. WS 105.5.H2 F198]
HV888.5.F35 1990
362.4'083 — dc20
DNLM/DLC
for Library of Congress   90-544
              CIP

Printed in the United States of America

10 9 8 7 6 5 4 3 2 1   95 94 93 92 91 90

To Lisa for her spunk, intelligence, creativity, and caring

To Lori for her motivation, initiative, and courage

Contents

CHAPTER **Three**

Initial and Continuing Adaptation to the
Birth of a Disabled Child   55
Rosalyn Benjamin Darling

CHAPTER **Four**

Families and the Community
Service Maze   91
Carole Christofk Upshur

CHAPTER **Five**

Parent-Professional Interaction: The
Roots of Misunderstanding   119
Rosalyn Benjamin Darling

CHAPTER **Six**

CHAPTER **Seven**

CHAPTER **Eight**

CHAPTER **Nine**

Collaboration with Families of Persons with Severe Disabilities   **237**

Steven R. Lyon and Grace A. Lyon

CHAPTER **Ten**

The Family with an Autistic Child   **269**

Sandra L. Harris, Mary Jane Gill,
and *Michael Allesandri*

CHAPTER **Eleven**

Pediatric Chronic Illness: Cystic Fibrosis and Parental Adjustment   **295**

Ginny Poole Brinthaupt

Preface

In the preface to the first edition of *The Family with a Handicapped Child,* I wrote "the 1960s and especially the 1970s heralded a period of increased parent involvement and advocacy, signified not only by the passage of landmark legislation, but also by the publication by parents of their own experiences with their handicapped sons and daughters. A considerable amount of interest in exceptional families marked the 1970s as a number of books and articles appeared in the professional literature" (p. vii).

As the 1970s merged into the 1980s and as we stand on the threshold of another decade, interest in childhood disability and the impact it has on family functioning continues to capture the interest of researchers, service providers, and even the general public. Through creative media programming our society is being better informed about disabilities and family members' response to them through television productions and movies like *The Rain Man.*

The major focus in the 1980s and of this book is the family and how it copes with a child who has a disability. Research has concentrated on the relationship of childhood disability and stress in the family and how stress can be ameliorated through social and other means of support. In the 1980s, there was a major effort to integrate knowledge about disability in the family and family systems theory. This *marriage* provided some needed conceptual clarity. Furthermore, there was an increased awareness that families reside within larger systems, and that they must also cope with events far removed that affect the family such as economic crises and political changes.

In terms of individual family members, fathers and siblings of disabled children received increased, yet still modest, attention in the professional literature. Furthermore, we became increasingly aware in the

1980s that intergenerational relationships must be taken into account when studying the nuclear family with a disabled child and that we must also attend to the grandparent/disabled grandchild relationship.

Recent legislation (P.L. 99–457) focuses on disabled newborns and their families' instrumental and psychological needs. This legislation makes it incumbent upon service providers to consider family needs at an early stage, birth through 3 years of age. The reasoning is that if services are provided early, the child and the family will experience fewer problems in the future.

Concomitant with the focus on the first years of life is a more recent surge of interest in the family's later adjustment. As the child develops and as the other family members proceed through various life stages and transitions, different problems emerge and other coping strategies must be learned. As the family encounters disability and copes with it over many years, there may be a need for appropriate interventions. Thus, there is a need to consider interventions that can increase coping behaviors and reduce stress.

In my role as editor of the second edition, it was my intention to include content that reflects recent areas of endeavor, such as those mentioned previously. However, I am also committed to retaining subjects that reflect ongoing research and clinical concerns. Thus, this second edition of *The Family with a Handicapped Child* reflects both recent advances and retains core areas that were identified in the first edition.

Joseph Newman, in chapter 1, describes the philosophical and historical antecedents to the present-day interest in families with disabled children. Chapters 2 and 3, by Seligman and Darling, are new and present a conceptual framework and a developmental perspective on families. Chapter 4, by Upshur, speaks to the interplay between families and the service delivery system.

Darling, in chapter 5, discusses family/professional relationships and examines why they are too often marked by conflict. Important, but sometimes forgotten members of the family, siblings and fathers are addressed by Lamb, Meyer, and Seligman, in chapters 6 and 7. Acknowledging that children with chronic disabilities resemble each other in some ways and, yet, are remarkably different in others is the subject matter of chapters 8 and 9 by Fewell, Lyon, and Lyon. In particular, the severity of a child's disability and the impact this may have on the family is examined in these chapters.

With considerable attention being paid to some childhood disabilities (such as retardation and physical disability) and not to others, Harris, Gill, and Alessandri in chapter 10 provide insight into the family that is coping with autism. Their chapter is a new one in this edition as well as chapter 11 by Brinthaupt which focuses on chronic pediatric illness with particular attention to families coping with cystic fibrosis, a chronic and lethal childhood disease. And finally, specific therapeutic interventions are presented in chapters 12 and 13 by Laborde, Seligman, and Elman. Practical, individual counseling, and family therapy strategies are presented as they relate to families with disabled children.

There are extensive changes in this edition. Chapters 2, 3, 10, 12, and a portion of chapter 7 are entirely new contributions. The other chapters have all been revised and updated.

This book should provide useful insights into exceptional families for professionals working in mental health, educational, and medical settings. It is also a useful text in graduate courses in family therapy, disability and the family, and on chronic childhood disability in the family. It is hoped that by informing professionals, this book will make a contribution to the lives of family members who have a child with a disability. The well-being of families who are attempting to cope with their disabled children is in the hands of educational institutions, medical, and social service agencies and the professionals who populate them.

University of Pittsburgh
May 1990

Contributors

Michael Alessandri
Doctoral student in Clinical Psychology, Rutgers — The State University of
New Jersey and Classroom Supervisor at the Douglass Developmental
Disabilities Center of Rutgers, New Brunswick, New Jersey

Ginny Poole Brinthaupt, Ph.D.
Murfreesboro, Tennessee

Rosalyn Benjamin Darling, Ph.D.
Executive Director, Beginning Early Intervention Services of Cambria
County, Inc., Johnstown, Pennsylvania

Nancy S. Elman, Ph.D.
Associate Professor, Department of Psychology in Education
University of Pittsburgh, Pittsburgh, Pennsylvania

Rebecca R. Fewell, Ph.D.
Karen Gore Professor of Special Education, School of Education
Tulane University, New Orleans, Louisiana

Mary Jane Gill, Ph.D.
Eden II Institute, Staten Island, New York

Sandra L. Harris, Ph.D.
Professor of Psychology and Clinical Psychology
Rutgers — The State University of New Jersey, and Director of the Douglass
Developmental Disabilities Center of Rutgers, New Brunswick, New Jersey

Peter Randell Laborde, M.Ed.
Director of Core Team Services for Hall-Mercer Community Mental Health/Mental Retardation Center of Pennsylvania Hospital, Philadelphia, Pennsylvania

Michael E. Lamb, Ph.D.
Research Scientist and Chief, Section on Social and Emotional Development, National Institutes of Health, Bethesda, Maryland

Grace A. Lyon, M.A.
Research Associate, Program in Severe Disabilities, Department of Instruction and Learning, School of Education, University of Pittsburgh, Pittsburgh, Pennsylvania

Steven R. Lyon, Ph.D.
Associate Professor and Coordinator of the Program in Severe Disabilities, Department of Instruction and Learning, School of Education, University of Pittsburgh, Pittsburgh, Pennsylvania

Donald J. Meyer
Coordinator, Early Childhood Education
Children's Hospital and Medical Center, Seattle, Washington

Joseph Newman, Ph.D.
Professor Emeritus, Department of Psychology in Education
University of Pittsburgh, Pittsburgh, Pennsylvania

Milton Seligman, Ph.D.
Professor, Department of Psychology in Education
University of Pittsburgh, Pittsburgh, Pennsylvania.

Carol Christofk Upshur, Ed.D.
Associate Professor, University of Massachusetts, Boston, associate in Pediatrics and Senior Research Associate on the Early Intervention Collaborative Study at the University of Massachusetts Medical School

The Family
with a
Handicapped
Child

CHAPTER ONE

Handicapped Persons and Their Families

Historical, Legislative, and Philosophical Perspectives

Joseph Newman

Joseph Newman is Professor Emeritus in the School of Education, University of Pittsburgh. He pursued doctoral studies in psychology at the University of Syracuse. He has devoted virtually his entire professional career to the field of rehabilitation as a clinician and as a teacher in programs preparing personnel for careers in rehabilitation. He is active in community groups concerned with the problems created by handicapping conditions. He has contributed to numerous professional journals and books in the field.

INTRODUCTION

After a history of parents slowly relinquishing the care, treatment, and education of their handicapped children to institutions, professionals, and schools, that process is being reversed.[1] On every level, parents are becom-

---

[1]In practice, the care, treatment, and education of handicapped children frequently cannot be separated into these three components; usually any intervention involves elements of all

1

ing active participants in programs involving their handicapped children. In fact, parental participation is regarded as so fundamental a component of these programs, that parental participation was mandated by federal legislation in the Education for All Handicapped Children Act (P.L. 94–142, 1975).

But the shift back to family involvement does not represent a return to the time when family bore the entire burden of the disabled member with virtually no available resources for help. When such help was developed beginning in the 19th century, parents were passive recipients of whatever assistance was offered. These services resulted from the efforts not only of the parents of disabled persons but of public-spirited individuals working through charitable and voluntary organizations. During the 20th century, parents began to join these organizations, eventually becoming their chief supporters and workers. These groups have become the leading advocates for the initiation, improvement, and extension of services for disabled persons. Moreover, because it is now recognized that it is necessary to plan for the lives of disabled people beyond childhood, these organizations extend their concerns to individuals of all age groups.

Over the years, the activities of these essentially humanitarian movements have been important forces in the development and wide acceptance of two basic concepts crucial to the support of programs for disabled persons: societal responsibility and the recognition and extension of disabled persons' constitutional rights. As acceptance of these concepts has increased, so has the scrutiny of existing programs, and essential services that have been missing are being pressed for. Of necessity, these measures involve litigation and political activism. Ineluctably, the organizations are drawn into confrontation with those who control budgets, which in times of economic cutbacks present serious problems, namely, the threat of curtailment of services. In these circumstances, the role of government in providing for disabled persons is prominently questioned. These and other issues have their roots in earlier centuries, and a brief review of these backgrounds provide a clarifying perspective.

THREE GUIDING PHILOSOPHIES

The treatment society accords its handicapped members is determined by philosophies that reflect the historical period and circumstances of that so-

---

three. For this reason, the three terms will be used as being virtually synonymous in this discussion. Also, the term handicapped will refer to persons of all ages to reflect the current philosophy that treatment should include attention to future as well as to present problems. Additionally, the terms handicapped and disabled are treated as synonymous.

ciety. The first philosophy to function was probably an early form of what came to be known as *utilitarianism*. Its central doctrine is that usefulness determines the value of some thing or person to society. This concept differs among societies and eras, but its primary tenet remains: usefulness to society is the criterion for value (Windelband, 1958).

Among many primitive and ancient societies, usefulness took on a direct meaning: usefulness in the struggle for survival. That struggle was constant and intense in an environment that was hostile and filled with dangers. Diseased and disabled persons were seen as burdens to the group because they could not contribute significantly to the group's welfare. Similarly, children and the aged only contributed to the group in negligible ways. When times were hard, these weaker individuals became burdens the group could not bear and had to dispose of. The result was abandonment, being cast off, or being killed. Infants were particularly low on the scale of human value since they were most helpless; female infants had a usefulness potential that was even lower than male infants and were the *most* frequently disposed of. Hence the expression of the utilitarian philosophy among many primitive and ancient cultures was barbaric and cruel but was seen by those cultures as necessary (Abt, 1965).

With the advent of Christianity, a more humane view toward society's unwanted took hold. All human life was regarded as sacred and compassion was stressed as a moral force. Nevertheless, the principal focus of early Christian doctrines was on a future heavenly life rather than on a present earthly one, and this emphasis did not lead to significant change in the treatment of human "burdens." Although infanticide was interdicted, the Church was indifferent to the lot of children. Nascent forces of change had been created, however, and in time, new ideas developed, culminating with the philosophy of humanism during the Renaissance. This philosophy attached primary importance to human beings and their conditions, affairs, aspirations, and well-being. Life before death became the focus as opposed to the ecclesiastical view of the importance of existence after death. Each individual had personal worth, and was not to be subordinated to political and biological theories. These ideas formed the basis of *humanitarianism,* the second of the philosophies guiding society's treatment of the disabled (Salt, 1914).

Although humanitarianism permitted benevolent and charitable deeds, changes toward more benign treatment evolved slowly. Nevertheless, the climate for change was developing, as is inferred from the art of the Renaissance, during which time motherhood and infancy was exalted, particularly through the depiction of the Madonna and the Christ Child. The work of St. Vincent de Paul in the 17th century also signaled change. He established homes and hospices for abandoned children, which were early expressions of societal concern about child abuse. However, for the masses of the impoverished and outcasts, utilitarian considerations remained dominant. Life was hard, and in such straitened circumstances, children were burdens and were frequently abandoned or sold (Abt, 1965).

At the same time, the arts and literature flourished, and the foundations of the modern thought, especially of modern science and medicine, were laid. The scientific status of medicine affects in a fundamental way the treatment of disability and the diseases which lead to disability. As advances in science and medicine took hold and people with disabilities and diseases survived, society began to alter its negative views toward handicapped persons.

Scientific progress in the Renaissance led to the development of technology, which in turn affected the production of goods. This marked the beginning of the Industrial Revolution. Concurrently, social and political changes ensued — the factory system developed, cities grew as the population moved from rural to urban areas, and new ideas about political relationships and authority changed. As humanistic theories flourished (e.g., natural rights and social contract), traditional theories were questioned. Existing religious doctrines were challenged, and many new religious groups came into existence. The New World was colonized, and the gradual unfolding of a democratic philosophy had a significant impact on societal institutions and, in particular, on the family.

However, improvements in social and economic conditions lagged, and poverty and wretched living circumstances persisted. The new factory system made exploitative use of child labor and the low wages and long hours of work brought a welter of public health problems, which led to disease and disability among the populace. The terrible living conditions created by the Industrial Revolution attracted the attention of persons with humanistic beliefs and led to efforts to alleviate social distress. The humanitarian movement grew and reached its peak during the 19th century. Its first efforts led to the establishment of places of refuge, hospices, and hospitals to shelter and care for society's castoffs — the sick, the disabled, the disturbed, the retarded, and the abandoned. Numerous charitable, benevolent, philanthropic, and reform groups came into existence, and some pioneered the improvement in the treatment of the handicapped (Kauffman, 1981).

The third philosophy, the concept of *rights* (Lowell & Schiavoni, 1980), is based directly on law. In the United States, it rests on the Constitution and the Bill of Rights, as well as on the 5th and 14th Amendments with their guarantees of rights, equal protection, and due process (fair and proper legal procedures). To be sure, the rights philosophy has elements of humanism in that it emphasizes the intrinsic value of the individual. However, it moves beyond humanism in its insistence that individuals exercise active roles in reaching decisions on matters that affect them, which is a realization of the democratic ideal. The movement to gain these rights for the handicapped began in the 1950s and developed rapidly in the ensuing years, culminating in legislation enacted in the 1970s in which the rights of the handicapped were further spelled out (Bateman & Herr, 1981; Cavan, 1963).

Three pieces of legislation form the core of this thrust. In addition to the Education for All Handicapped Children Act (P.L. 94-142), the others are Title V (Section 504) of the Rehabilitation Amendments of 1973 (P.L. 93-112) and the Developmentally Disabled Assistance and Bill of Rights Act (P.L. 94-103, 1975). Essentially, the legislation provide statutory safeguards in (a) protection against discrimination in federally assisted programs, (b) accessibility to facilities and programs supported or operated by the federal government, and (c) the rights to a free, appropriate education. Further legislation was enacted in 1980 that permitted the Federal government to initiate civil suits against states to protect the rights of the mentally retarded and other institutionalized individuals (see the "Summary of Existing Legislation Relating to the Handicapped," U.S. Department of Education, 1980).

The rights movement has been influenced by a number of allied and related movements: civil and minority rights, women's rights, children's rights, and consumer rights. The spheres of activities are in the courts and the legislatures, and the objectives are to bring the governmental apparatus into a protagonist role in establishing and protecting the rights of aggrieved groups. This role of the government is one that is under continual challenge, and that challenge, if successful, could radically affect the entire structure of how human services are delivered, including services to the handicapped.

The three major philosophies function and interact concurrently in present-day endeavors and proposals to initiate and guide plans for the handicapped. For example, the utilitarian approach has constituted the strongest and most productive argument for programs for handicapped persons. Ideally, such programs would help handicapped persons become taxpayers instead of remaining tax consumers so that eventually they would repay many times over the costs of their rehabilitation. Similarly, the deinstitutionalization drive was fueled by the promise to reduce the mounting costs of operating large public institutions. Consistently, no matter how desirable the goal, it must be practicable and cost-effective.

Additionally, the argument for support includes the humanitarian pleas about the essential worth of the individual and the need for compassion for the less fortunate. Also at work is the plea to rise above materialistic considerations, because helping people cannot be measured in such terms. The philosophy fueling the rights movement is directly related to the issue of social responsibility, as expressed through the governmental structure. It starts with the position that handicapped persons have not received the same rights that are extended to nonhandicapped individuals. It is the responsibility of the state to affirm or reaffirm those rights through judicial and legislative actions. But utilitarian factors (i.e., money) often play major roles, such as is the case of attempting to provide handicapped citizens with access to public buildings and transportation. The crucial terms used are *reasonable costs* and *budgetary restraints.* It must be recognized that these utilitarian concerns are cogent and must be taken into account. Also implicated in the problem of access are political values and philosophies, liberal versus conservative positions on the role of the state, the role of the private sector, and the role of volunteerism.

The potency of utilitarian arguments is seen in the continuing spate of budgetary reductions for human service programs. It has been observed that conservatives usually subscribe to the utilitarian philosophy, as was evident by the Reagan administration.

FORCES FOR CHANGE IN THE TREATMENT OF HANDICAPPED PERSONS

The advances in productivity, and the improvements in living conditions and in health have, in effect, ensured that disabled persons will at least survive—if not thrive—in society. Improved living conditions has made it possible to tolerate and pursue more benign practices with them; because merely surviving was no longer the crucial force at work, humanitarian principles had an opportunity to take hold and the rights philosophy to develop. The emphasis on utilitarianism became limited to financial or cost-benefit factors.

Astounding advances were made in medical sciences as well. Progress in the treatment and understanding of disease and disability changed the epidemiological picture of human disease and disability. Rates of survival and longevity increased; for example, in 1900, life expectancy in this country was 48 years, three quarters of a century later it became over 74 years (*The World Almanac,* 1987). Dramatic reductions were achieved in infant and maternal mortality rates. At the same time survival rates increased for persons with congenital defects and birth injuries, and for those disabled by disease and accidents. Prior to the 20th century, few disabled persons survived until adulthood. The establishment of pediatrics as a medical specialty in the late 1800s, closely followed by a similar specialty for obstetrics, signified the rising medical recognition that children required special attention (Abt, 1965). But this recognition extended only to healthy or intact children; the medical profession did not as yet display any great interest in the care of those who were not. However as medical science acquired the capability for effective intervention and alleviation of disabling conditions, the medical profession began to take note of handicapped children and handicapped adults. But it was the humanitarian movement that first raised social consciousness about the need to care for the disabled. It was the impact of the humanitarian movement that induced public acceptance of this responsibility (Bremner, 1970).

The lack of significant public attention to and interest in handicapped children until this century can be attributed also to the persistence of naive, superstitious, and animistic beliefs about handicaps. In earlier societies, illness and disability were seen as the work of demons and supernatural forces. These occult powers controlled life and intervened in the birth process. These supernatural powers could substitute one of their own as a changeling and thus create a defective infant or monster. If more than one baby was born, the infants were frequently killed, because they were perceived to be unnatural, uncanny, or the result of adulterous intercourse. If a child was born on an "unlucky" day, it might be killed, as might a child born with an abnormality. Witches and sorcerers were believed to cast spells, or the child was subjected to the "evil eye." When the child was not killed or abandoned, the treatments pursued were in accord with such bizarre beliefs. Shamans or their equivalents administered prayers, incantations, exorcisms, and ritualistic sacrifices along with the use of "holy relics" and amulets. These practices extended well into the Middle Ages in Western societies. Magic was still widely used. For instance, a sick or rachitic child would be passed through clefts or arching roots of trees, holes in large stones, ladders, and the like (Abt, 1965). Nevertheless, it was during the Middle Ages that religious orders in Switzerland and in France began to sporadically use more humane treatment (Juul, 1981).

The medieval church, however, did little to advance medical science (Abt, 1965). As in the Judaic and the Islamic faiths, Christianity saw disease and disability as the scourges of God, as punishment for sin, or as disciplines to be endured. In some orders, priests and monks were forbidden to study medicine or even to see doctors and take medicine. At the same time, the Church opposed the magic practiced by witches, and it is believed that witches by the thousands were put to death. The authority followed in these actions was the "Malleus Maleficarum" (The Witches Hammer), a compendium of "clinical" procedures to detect and defeat the demons that were the presumed causes of disease and disturbed human conditions.

Even well into the Renaissance, progress toward scientific treatment methods was slow in coming. By the 18th century, although a good many of the superstitious ideas had changed, treatment had not. Individuals with ailments were abandoned or cast out, which along with high mortality rates from disease reduced survival rates. The 18th century, called the Age of Enlightenment, saw the blossoming of scientific thought and reason and the quickening of the forces of change. Increasingly, steps were taken to help the disabled, particularly the deaf, the retarded, the blind, and also the abused. Help came in the form of the establishment of institutions, a movement that proliferated during the 19th century and that, as it expanded, provided for sick and dependent children. It was later, in the decades around the turn of the 20th century, when schools became involved in the care and treatment of handicapped children that the concept of special education was formulated (LaVor, 1976).

RISE OF INSTITUTIONS

The close of the Middle Ages saw profound changes in English society. People moved from rural areas in increasing numbers to settle in the growing towns and cities. For most people, their labor became a commodity, and many began to live apart from their families in order to make a living. The indigent sought refuge through the church and the institutions operated by the church. Because the power of the church became increasingly restricted as that of the state grew, laws were passed making families financially responsible for their indigent members. When the families were unable to provide support, that obligation was assumed by the state. In England the obligation was legalized with the promulgation of the Poor Laws in 1601. The Poor Laws marked the entrance of the government into a field that previously was the exclusive responsibility of the family. As the burden of support was placed on the local government, compulsory taxes were levied. The local communities observed these levies reluctantly and sought to control the numbers of their poor through the use of settlement laws, which restricted movement of the populace among communities. Poorhouses were established for the aged, the disabled, and the mentally disturbed among the poor of the community. Later, workhouses were created through which the able-bodied among the indigent were required to work and contribute to their support. In time, other institutions came into being that provided services for the sick of the communities. These various institutions became the chief providers of care for the socially dependent and disabled and remained so for generations. As the humanitarian movement expanded in the 19th century, so did the number of institutions, but with a significant change: the establishment of special institutions such as hospitals and schools for certain disabilities (the blind, the deaf, the retarded). The growth in the variety of institutions was the work of social reform groups, which were usually privately supported. The institutionalization drive was extended in particular to handicapped children, which was a recognition of the failure of public education systems to serve the handicapped. It was this concern that led to the beginnings of special education—the first forms of which were special classes. In a sense, the special education classes were small institutions within schools and hospitals. In time, most of these institutions and special classes were taken over by the state and public schools in the larger cities (Weintraub, Abeson, & Braddock, 1971).

Institutionalization was seen as the answer to the care of society's dependent and unwanted members. The institutions were invariably established in rural areas and placement in them was seen as beneficial. Because of their likely remote locations, these institutions rarely came under scrutiny as to their effectiveness. Generally, it was assumed that a placement would be permanent. The legal basis for placement in an institution were the doctrines of *parens patriae* and *police power. Parens patriae* enables the state to act in the interest of the child to protect his or her welfare, whereas the *police power* doctrine enables the state to act to protect the safety and well-being of society.

Although medical knowledge and psychological interest in handicapped children advanced rapidly in the first half of the 20th century, institutionalization remained the primary treatment of the disabled. However, as pediatrics became an accepted medical specialty, hospitals for children were founded. These hospitals drew attention to the problems of handicapped children. Public schools also came to share the responsibilities for the care and treatment of fragile, sickly, and disabled children; special education classes were created in greater numbers. An awareness grew of the crucial role of the family in health matters and in the care and education of the handicapped. The same years—the 1930s—saw the foundations laid for a national social security system to which, in time, was added health care.

These events did not take place without opposition—opposition that sprang from radical interpretations of the utilitarian philosophy, ranging from Social Darwinism to budgetary preoccupations to outright rejection of the programs as not being the business of the state. This opposition denounced social legislation as being socialistic, unconstitutional, and in violation of states' rights. Moreover, they were seen as destructive invasions of the privacy of family life, as the meddlesome preoccupations of "bleeding hearts," and as encouraging the perpetuation of "inferior stock." Underlying these attitudes was a continuing apprehension of creating a permanent dependent underclass of citizens receiving various types of governmental assistance. In times of economic hardship, these arguments, which are always present, become more forcefully asserted and more widely accepted. Moreover, these arguments are used by individuals and groups who are seeking to find ways to curtail, close, or otherwise limit institutions for the disabled. Paradoxically, opposition to institutions has also been voiced by groups known for their strong support of programs for the disabled. To be sure, their opposition is based not on the existence of institutions, as such, but rather on the limitations of institutions as part of treatment, training, and educational programs.

Changes in views toward institutions were stimulated by the developments of new concepts in special education. Questions began to be raised about the practice of routinely placing handicapped children in institutions. The challenges became widespread after the 1950s. Although the prime targets were institutions for the retarded, the same accusations were leveled at the institutions for the mentally disturbed. These institutions were thought of as human warehouses, incapable of providing decent treatment, and as places that robbed its residents of dignity and independent will. It was also charged that the institutions were perpetuated by the state governments because of the great economic and political stakes involved. To be sure, as already stated, some critics disapproved of institutions as being increasingly expensive to maintain, and they questioned their value especially when the necessity of making costly capital improvements arose. However, more fundamentally, criticism was evoked through the theoretical concepts that emerged during those years. These concepts took a more constructive view of exceptionality — away from hopelessness, labeling, and categorizing, and toward an emphasis on behavioral, developmental, and adaptive outlooks. The guiding concept was *normalization,* and it was obvious that institutions did not provide the conditions in which normal living could occur. This rationale flowed directly from the landmark civil rights Supreme Court decision, *Brown vs. Board of Education* (1954), which established the rights of blacks, and of all minority groups, to an equal education. Thus, this case may be regarded as the first legal action to promote normalization. Once the *Brown vs. Board of Education* decision had taken effect in the schools, the legal approach to making changes became the model. Literally hundreds of cases appeared in the courts demanding equal rights for minority groups — including the handicapped.

Several guiding principles that serve as precedents emerged through these lawsuits. One is that of *the least restrictive alternative.* This principle is derived from the premise that, because the state is making decisions for others that restrict their personal freedom, it was obligated to provide living circumstances that restrict the individuals concerned as little as possible. The suits involving this principle were generally successful and resulted in improving living conditions for many individuals. The principle has been applied in cases dealing with treatment and educational placements, deinstitutionalization, and commitment procedures.

Usually the suits were argued in conjunction with the *due process right* to treatment and habilitation. This procedure resulted in individualized study of each child for whom a decision was being sought. However, despite the success in establishing the legal basis for improvement of services to the handicapped, the desired changes were slow in coming. In most instances the suits involved retarded individuals who had been placed in institutions that required massive allocations of resources. It became clear that continued monitoring and vigilance were necessary to obtain implementation of court decisions (Children's Legal Rights Journal, 1982; Addison, 1976).

It also became evident that the needed oversight would have to be exercised by the reform groups, given the default of the public officials. The path followed was to seek court action but legal suits required expert representation. Fortunately, many communities began to establish public interest law centers whose lawyers would pursue the suits to force the public officials to act. Again these efforts were limited by a lack of adequate funds. Increasingly, it was becoming clear that the state's greater resources were needed to augment the meager resources of private and voluntary groups in order to advance the existing programs for the handicapped.

THE ROLE OF THE STATE

The role of government, the state, in the affairs of the handicapped has evolved over many years. We have discussed how the status of any individual in earlier Western cultures was contingent on that individual's value to the survival of his or her society. Intact male adults had high value because they could make fundamental contributions, economically and militarily. In contrast, those who could make little or no contributions—the handicapped, the infirm, the aged, children, and infants—were expendable in terms of their utilitarian values. In times of hardship they became threats to survival and were subject to elimination. This practice had the sanction of the "government" or leadership of the society. Moreover, the child was not regarded as a person and therefore had no rights. Children could achieve personhood and move directly into adult society only when they began to be able to perform adult tasks. Essentially, the child was viewed as chattel, as an economic resource (Aries, 1962). Handicapped children were worth little as a resource. It is doubtful that disabled children survived to any significant extent in early societies, given the primitive and superstitious medical understanding and treatments and the high rates of infant and child mortality. Some ancient cultures, however, such as those of Egypt, Babylon, Israel, and Athens, did not treat their children harshly.

Whatever were the practices pursued with children, they must have had the direct or indirect sanction of what constituted the government. As societies became more organized, intervention became more direct and formal as in Egypt, Israel, and Athens, which established schools for governmental, military, or religious purposes. In Sparta and Rome, a form of eugenics was widely pursued in order to produce vigorous offspring for the military. All puny, sickly, and deformed children as well as "excess" female children were abandoned or killed. Although this policy was eventually abolished, unwanted children continued to be exposed, abandoned, or sold into slavery through the Middle Ages (Abt, 1965). During this period, the state did not directly intervene in the care of children; the state's involvement was essentially passive.

The child, as chattel, could be dealt with as any piece of property might be, and hence the custodial rights of the parents included the right to transfer and sale. The right to custody appeared to have had an economic basis, and custodial right was mainly a property right. As economic objects, children were open to abuse. With the continuing influence of the Church and the rise of more humane ideas, the state was induced to act when it was deemed necessary to protect the child. The development of the 17th-century English doctrine of *parens patriae* has been referred to. This doctrine provided the basis for the power to intervene to protect children, but only under unusual circumstances. Parents were recognized as having the "right to custody" unless shown to be unfit. With time, the emphasis of the doctrine shifted from the property theory of custody to the personal status theory, which held that the parents, because of their relationship to the child, were the custodians best suited to serve the child's needs (Katz, 1971). This change contained the incipient view of the child as a person, out of which grew the rights philosophy.

Although humanizing forces became manifest during the Renaissance, there were marked social class differences in how the influences of these forces took effect. They mainly affected the upper social strata, and indeed these are the population groups about whom information in this respect exists. The lives of the lower classes, such as the artisans and peasants, were apparently not changed in any meaningful way. Life for them was wrought with the same poverty, ignorance, callousness, and cruelty that was common during the Middle Ages.

The first evidences, then, of change in the treatment of children were found among the literate and economically favored classes. Also, the aristocracy, as the ruling class, did have a tradition of protecting their "subjects" and of acting in accordance with the doctrine of *parens patriae* (Katz, 1971). The state also acted out of concern for certain other special groups of subjects. In the England of the 15th and 16th centuries, when seapower was fundamental to its economy, the government took steps to ensure an adequate supply of manpower for the dangerous and unattractive occupation of seaman by establishing a program, in contemporary terms, of compulsory health and disability insurance for the men of the Royal Navy and the merchant fleet. The men and their families would be provided for, should the men be disabled or killed in the course of duty. Later, marine hospitals were established, and other seapowers followed suit. The new American nation also established marine hospitals soon after the United States was founded. These early expressions of societal acceptance of responsibility for certain groups were seen as being in accordance with the utilitarian philosophy and therefore were deemed to be proper governmental expenditures (Straus, 1965).

The protective role of the state slowly expanded, as the idea of the child being the private property of parents and under their exclusive control weakened. Generally, intervention by the government in family life has been viewed as benevolent. In England, intervention was practiced for dependent, abused, and neglected children of incompetent parents. Such children were bound out in the community, that is, placed with families with whom they lived and worked for a specified period. Although this practice relieved the authorities of the need to support these children, benefits presumably accrued to the children in terms of stability in living conditions. There are, however, records of proceedings against masters who abused their charges. Nonetheless, the entire practice was an illustration of the subordination of the authority of the natural parents to that of the state when the welfare of the child and the good of the community were threatened. The same policies were followed in the colonial life of America (Bremner, 1970).

The great flowering of humanitarianism in the 19th century in Europe was reflected in the young American republic where it was marked by an acceleration of philanthropic and social reform activities. The reformers came from the dominant groups in the United States, the middle and upper classes, who were persons with ties to influential societal circles. Attention was directed to the unfortunate souls of society, and increasingly the state was induced to bring neglected, abused, and handicapped children under the protection of the public authorities. The state began to intervene more frequently on behalf of such children. Legislation was passed for compulsory school attendance, moral education, prohibition of physical abuse, and age restrictions in child labor. This legislation advanced governmental authority, and, in general, the authority of parents and guardians was reduced, albeit only in specific areas of social concern. To be sure, these developments aroused the opposition of conservative and traditional groups, particularly among those who adhered to the notion that personal misfortune was the consequence of defects in the individual rather than in society.

Nonetheless, significant steps to protect children continued to be made. One such step came in 1912 when the U.S. Children's Bureau was created. Bremner (1971) regards this event as the single most important development in child and maternal health and welfare in the early 20th century, for it signified the acceptance by the federal authorities of the responsibility for promoting the health and welfare of the young. The Children's Bureau grew from being a research and information center to one that was charged with the administration of laws relating to child labor, child health, and child welfare. Beginning in those years and continuing to the present, a series of social legislative measures were promulgated that directly affected disabled persons and their families. Among these measures were legislation for workmen's compensation, health insurance, equal opportunity, rehabilitation of the handicapped, and education of handicapped children.

In the United States, the active role of the state in the affairs of families was neither sought nor encouraged by public authorities. However, its evolution was inherent in society's growing acceptance of responsibility for children in trouble. Because the necessity to intervene arose when a home was deemed unfit, intervention usually meant removal of the child from that home. That step was taken with hesitation because of the prevailing belief that the poorest home was superior to the best surrogate one. However, the suitability of a home was judged by economic and moral standards, which were found to be applied in highly discretionary fashion (Katz, 1971). The decision to remove a child from his or her home followed social class biases, because most of the children involved came from the lower social classes and those who made the judgments were from a higher social class. Intervention was practiced, therefore, almost exclusively when the families were politically, economically, and psychologically powerless (Rodham, 1974).

Institutions were established for the care of children removed from homes deemed to be unsuitable. Eventually these institutions were found wanting and the concept of the suitable home prevailed (Katz, 1971). Controversy had also arisen over whether or not foster homes were superior to institutions, and in time the value of the institution itself was questioned.

Society expects parents to fulfill certain fundamental obligations. These include financial security, maintenance of a child's health, obtaining necessary medical treatment, ensurance of education, and inculcation of values such as morality and respect for authority. Failure in any of these areas constitutes neglect and may create a basis for state intervention. Beyond these obligations, there is no comprehensive statement in law concerning the full range of responsibilities of parents to children or even in the special case of the handicapped child. Neglect and abuse have been, historically, the predominant grounds for state intervention.

However, over the years, the ability of the state to be an adequate substitute parent has come under question. Opposition to the role of the state as a parent has emerged as parents and advocates have asserted their rights. In addition, there has been greater recognition that the prevailing assumption that a child's interests were identical to those of parents did not hold (Rodham, 1974). One outcome of this recognition has been the rise of the advocacy movement for the rights of children, and this has led to more litigation and greater focus on the political aspects of child care issues. ("Baby Doe revisited," Children's Legal Rights Journal, 1982).

Children's rights advocates raise questions about the traditional parent-child relationships, such as the issue of parental dominance, and these advocates insist that children have essentially the same rights as do adults. However, the advocates do recognize that there are reality considerations and that children's participation in making decisions affecting their lives be followed appropriately. They recognize that because of their dependency, children are not capable of fulfilling responsibilities that go hand-in-hand with rights (Worsfold, 1974).

The concept of children's rights emerged, to a large extent, from the White House Conferences on Children, which began in 1909. It was the conference of 1930 that drew up a children's charter that spoke of "the rights of the child as the first rights of citizenship." Subsequent White House conferences issued similar pronouncements. In 1959, the United Nations promulgated a Declaration of the Rights of the Child, which was followed by a White House Conference endorsement of a Children's Bill of Rights in 1970. That year the report of the Joint Commission on Mental Health of Children emphasized family life as being crucial to the fulfillment of the rights of children. Furthermore, it advanced the conviction that the quality of parental care had important mental health consequences. The report further marked the emergence of a unique concept of present-day Western culture: Children form a distinct group of citizens (Aries, 1962; Bremner, 1974).

The White House conferences were discontinued in 1981, but their historical influence remains—that is, that it is essential to improve family life in the attack on the problems facing children and youth, both nondisabled and disabled. This emphasis on the family inevitably casts the mother in a major role in the home, is often true in homes with disabled members. Mothers are encouraged to become more active and even to become leaders in the efforts to overcome the myriad problems involved in programs for disabled children. This elevated position of the mother is closely linked to the contemporary trend toward equal partnership in family life (Cavan, 1963). Thus, the intertwining of children's rights with women's rights form the background for disabled children's rights. Ultimately, all rights movements are linked by their efforts to overcome discriminative minority status, and they have all made ready use of litigation. Traditionally, parent-child relationships have been regarded as being beyond the jurisdiction of laws except for violations that involve serious criminal charges. Since the 1950s, however, most states have promulgated legislation that brought parents, in general, within the jurisdiction of the law. During this period, there was tremendous growth in the juvenile court system in the country. The judiciary has moved with caution in its rulings involving disabled children in order to avoid charges of unreasonable interference in family life. There have been numerous court decisions affirming the need to recognize the integrity and security of the family.

Children's rights moved along two major paths: the right to education/treatment and the right to deinstitutionalization (mainstreaming or normalization). We have already referred to the 1954 Brown decision and the fact that it established the legal entitlement to equal educational opportunity for racial minorities. This became a pivotal ruling behind the concept of later decisions of the lower federal courts extending similar rights to handicapped children. The successful use of courts for the advancement of children's rights signaled a shift in the role schools came to play in American society. Education became the vehicle with which individuals could share in the principles of individual liberty, social equality, and personal fulfillment, as well as become active participants in the development of a common outlook. We have referred previously to the role schools came to play in health and welfare matters. Schools could not avoid becoming involved in the broad social problems of the post-World War II decades. *Brown vs. Board of Education* thrust schools into the midst of the on-going rights movements.

DEINSTITUTIONALIZATION

The constitutional issues raised by the school desegregation movement focused attention on the most segregated of society's handicapped—the institutionalized. The state, in placing handicapped persons in institutions, relied either upon the *parens patriae* doctrine—which enables the state to act in the interest of an individual—or on the *police power* doctrine—which enables the state to act in order to protect the safety and well-being of society in general. The court decisions that were handed down limited both doctrines in accordance with the due process clause of the 14th Amendment. These two principles guided institutionalization decisions: the least restrictive environmental alternative and the right to treatment (Soskin, 1980).

Deinstitutionalization came into full force in the 1970s. Until then, meager attention had been paid to the problems and needs of thousands of mentally or emotionally disabled persons confined in public institutions.

Federal and state legislation by and large did not protect the rights of those institutionalized persons, if indeed they had rights. Institutions had been established with virtually no questions raised about them for over 100 years. However, modern social and psychological theories do not view mental and emotional disabilities as static and hopeless conditions; much progress and change could occur given treatment and normal living circumstances — conditions usually lacking in institutions. Federal courts have ruled that residents of institutions suffer "an extraordinary deprivation of liberty" despite the fact they have committed no crime against society. The courts have also held that the residents of institutions have a "constitutional right to treatment." Both of these principles have not been determined as yet by the U.S. Supreme Court. The judiciary, moreover, have become increasingly reluctant to commit persons to institutions. The conviction has developed that large institutions do not provide viable means for treating disabled people. The speed with which the deinstitutionalization drive took hold was fueled by utilitarian motives as well as by the children's rights advocacy movement. The mounting costs of maintaining institutions made them attractive targets for budget-cutting legislatures, which is what occurred in California, beginning in 1969, and in other states.

Unfortunately, effective means to achieve deinstitutionalization and the establishment of community alternatives did not readily come into being. Closing institutions or discharging residents did not ensure better care or services. These realizations thrust parents and families into the deinstitutionalization fray. It became apparent that there were many legal issues to be clarified as well as guiding principles to be fully accepted and expressed in court decisions. A host of community zoning, licensing, and other regulatory measures had to be enacted, and funds appropriated, before a stable and adequate system of community services could be created.

Critics of deinstitutionalization point to these problems as justification for a more deliberate and considered course of action. They emphasize that certain groups of handicapped persons are not capable of benefitting from the treatment necessary for living in the community and that they require continued institutional life. The problems, issues, and controversies surrounding deinstitutionalization directly affect parents and families, as do the many similar issues and problems confronting mainstreaming in special education.

THE FAMILY AND THE HANDICAPPED CHILD

We now turn to the central concern of this work — the contemporary American family and the treatment of the handicapped child. We have identified and traced the important forces, concepts, and trends that have shaped the present-day societal attitude to these children. We have delineated the major philosophies that have guided society. We shall now examine the family's role, and record some of the changes that have occurred in that role over time.

Today's American family is not the family of its European forebearers, nor is it the family of the early years of the nation. As a social institution, the family is molded by the culture in which it exists, and as that culture changes, so does the family. The changes that have occurred in the family have been quite varied: For most families they were fundamental, for others they were moderate or fragmentary, and for some they were minimal or nonexistent. In contrast to European families, the American family changed at a faster rate. Although we can speak generally of an American family, the changing and pluralistic nature of American society leads to a variety of family life patterns. Change puts stress on a family as it strives to maintain old values and functions, a task complicated by the similar process facing other societal institutions undergoing change as well. Many traditional family functions have been disturbed or destroyed, creating a process of social disintegration (Cavan, 1963).

Essentially, the original American colonies abided by English customs and institutions. Thus, the English patriarchal family, in which the father was the master predominated. Women and children occupied subordinate positions, and discipline was stern and harsh. Because information about colonial life derives mainly from middle class sources, there is little information about families on lower socioeconomic levels. The early settlers came to the New World primarily as individuals rather than as families. Thus, as communities were established there were organized efforts to promote the formation of families. Life for the settlers was filled with hardships, and most people had a low standard of living. It was necessary that everyone in a family contribute to its economic upkeep, mainly in the form of physical work. Moreover, work was seen to have both religious and moral values as well.

There existed in the colonies a large floating population composed mainly of persons in a lower socioeconomic status. Included in this population were numerous children and youth who, for one reason or another, became separated from their families. The communities saw these individuals as social dependents and undertook to control the problem. They were assigned to families, following the English practice of "binding out." As in England, the youngsters received their maintenance, and performed work or chores in the colonies and were provided at least a minimal education. By binding out the youngsters, communities were relieved of the necessity to support these dependents. Binding out was also used with children of parents deemed to be incompetent, thus following the *parens patriae* doctrine.

Although the governmental bodies in the colonies set about to oversee the moral and ethical behavior of the members of the communities, families carried this basic responsibility. This was only one of the social and economic functions they performed. Families were not only responsible for raising literate children, but ethical individuals who had respect for public laws and domestic manners. In the home strong discipline and an authoritarian atmosphere prevailed, which led many young people to flee from this environment, usually joining the floating population. There was a constant temptation to escape the rigidly controlled atmosphere of the established Eastern towns for the freedom of the frontier to the West. This influence and the migration it stimulated were some of the forces in American life that led to changes in the family. Indeed, change in the New World was inevitable when we consider that so many people had originally left the onerous social, economic, political, and religious circumstances that existed in the Old World in the hope of improving their situations.

In those years, the 18th and early 19th centuries, no reference could yet be made to a "typical" American family. The family varied greatly according to religious affiliation, social class, ethnic identity, and economic character. However, certain forces for change can be identified. Clearly, the family began to be influenced by the philosophies and attitudes of an individualistic, laissez-faire, white democracy. As the hierarchical family was slowly leveled culturally by democratic social principles, children assumed a more favored role in the family. Children became increasingly independent, individualistic, assertive, and challenging. These traits were strengthened by several influences. From the frontier came aggressive individualism, a desire for independence, egalitarianism, the elevation of the status of women, and an emphasis on physical and moral qualities. Doctrines of human improvement and perfectibility were current, especially among the young. For a time there was a sense, derived from evangelistic Calvinism, that people attain "heaven or hell" through their decisions and actions. Although in time, as the urban and industrial development of the 19th century took hold, this religious orientation eroded, and more materialistic views of life came to prevail. However, the basic aspirations of the frontier and of these early religious doctrines survived in modified form (Burgess & Locke, 1953).

The factory system brought women and children into the industrial work force. From the point of view of Puritan ideology this was not radically different from colonial practices. Work in both settings had the encouragement of the religious doctrine of the sanctity of work and the fear of idleness as the Devil's opportunity. Two systems of factory employment prevailed: one in which entire families—mainly rural—worked, and the other in which children—mainly girls—worked in textile factories, and the parents continued to live on the farm. The working hours were alike regardless of setting; every member of the family above the age of 7 years worked from sunrise to sunset.

The effects of working in factories were drastic for the family. It was no longer a self-contained economic unit. Children were paid, albeit exploited, at the rate of 25 to 50 cents a day, which was different from being bound out: They were not protected by the traditional rules of apprenticeship. There were no controls over abuse and the only source of protection, if it existed at all, was the paternalism of the employer. The child now had two masters—the father and the foreman. The long working day left little time for school or recreation. By 1830 the use of children in factories was common and continued through the middle of the century (Bremner, 1970).

During these years, child labor was not a major concern of humanitarian reformers. Children were expected to work, and their labor was viewed as being socially productive and individually beneficial. Reformers, however, were concerned about the lack of education for working children, and some states passed compulsory school attendance laws, as did Massachusetts in 1857. However, these laws were widely ignored. The factory system bred other social ills as well, mainly disease and public health problems.

By the turn of the century many reform movements existed and they influenced change toward improving the economic, health, welfare, and educational status of the family. Especially fundamental was the government's acceptance of responsibility in these matters, which established a precondition for social legislation—an undertaking that was to increase in momentum during the 20th century and to eventually affect the disabled (Bremner, 1971).

Improved recognition of the problems of the handicapped and the development of services for them came slowly. Special education began to exert influence in school systems. For adults, legislation was enacted for the vocational rehabilitation of handicapped soldiers in 1918. This was followed in 1920 by legislation that created a system of vocational rehabilitation for handicapped civilians. Further developments were minimal until the 1930s when the foundations of the present social security system were established. In the 1940s, rehabilitation made significant advances in providing services to the nonphysically handicapped. Under the impact of the experiences of World War II, the present veterans and civilian rehabilitation programs were formed (Sussman, 1965).

Although similar reforms in services to handicapped children lagged somewhat, attention to their needs continued to be focused on through the activities of interest groups, such as the National Association for Retarded Children and its affiliates. These groups and analogous groups for other types of handicapped children were the direct results of the transformations that had occurred in the family and in the role of the parents in the handicapped children movement since the beginning of the 20th century.

The English family and the family of the continental European settlers became altered in America; they were no longer predominately patriarchal, authoritarian, and duty-bound with an overriding economic preoccupation. They became more democratic and emphasized relationships characterized by companionship, affection, and decision making by consensus. The child was no longer looked upon as chattel, but rather, assumed a central place in the family with unique characteristics and needs. Increasingly expressed was the recognition of the child's rights as a citizen in a democratic society possessing freedom of expression, assembly, petition, and conscience (Burgess & Locke, 1953).

The process of social change for the family took on momentum in the years following World War I. Women were employed in increasing numbers, a development that accelerated change in the traditional, patriarchal family and that especially affected the position of the husband and father as the primary supporter and head of the family. The women's rights movement, and later, the feminist movement were significant elements in the changes that have occurred in the family. These movements have played significant roles in the development of the present-day family, in which the concept of partnership prevails — that is, the concept in which husband and wife share equally in rights and responsibilities. These processes of disintegration and reintegration are gradual and ongoing. They are not neat and precise affairs; the old exists with the new, and there is more change in some aspects and relatively little in others (Cavan, 1963). Nevertheless, they are the forces that have led the mother to assume a greater voice in the fate of her disabled child.

We also note the change in the class characteristic of the reform movements. Traditionally, what had mainly been the domain of the middle and upper classes began to embrace families from lower social-cultural classes. This democratic orientation tended to provide families with a greater sense of control over their lives and to instill in them a sense of hope for the future of their handicapped children. In their first active roles, parents were directly involved in programs for their own handicapped children. For instance, parents participated in classes that focused on the problems of families with children in special education. As these parents assumed progressively more active roles, they served in home training and group training projects and as classroom helpers. It has been observed that any degree of parental involvement enhances a child's developmental progress and that parent involvement helps meet the family's emotional needs. In addition, parents have become involved at the policy-making level.

However, parental involvement in programs for handicapped children has raised a number of questions. The underlying assumption that parental involvement is beneficial has been established. However, there are professional versus parental problems, or status considerations. Some feel that if parents become too closely aligned with school systems, this would interfere with their roles as parents. Others believe that parents need a respite from the strains of difficult parenting, and hence they should not be involved in classroom activities or home instruction. Nevertheless, the prevailing opinion appears to be that parental involvement has been a positive factor in terms of child performance, parent satisfaction, and program effectiveness. If parental involvement leads to the kinds of already mentioned problems, this would be indicative not so much of the inherent deficiencies of this involvement as of its developing nature.

Although there has been progress in providing facilities for the treatment and education of handicapped children and in improving the psychological climate in which they live, there remain many controversial issues that hinder further progress such as the provision of additional programs for mainstreaming. The reasons for the present regressive period for programs for the disabled are not only budgetary; they are predominantly political and philosophical positions that flow from a conservative utilitarian ideology. Thus, "big government" is to be reduced and "local government" is to be promoted, regardless of the fact that programs for the handicapped are a national concern. Also to be encouraged is voluntarism despite its inability, historically, to meet a complex, continuing national problem such as disability. Underlying these political positions are vestiges of prejudice (Gellman, 1959). The consequences of these forces are loss or reduction in budgetary support.

Illustrative of the uncertainties created by such strongly held controversial convictions is the case of Baby Doe, a newborn defective infant, now deceased. Baby Doe suffered from Down syndrome and intestinal blockage; she required surgery in order to survive. The parents, after consulting with their physicians, came to the conclusion that the prognosis for a meaningful life for Baby Doe was hopeless. Hence they decided that treatment should be withheld, and the baby died as a consequence. The case and the death aroused strong public reactions, particularly since Baby Doe was not an isolated incident but one of a succession of such cases in which treatment was withheld—treatment that could have sustained life ("Baby Doe revisited," 1982).

To be sure, the Baby Doe case involved not only medical issues but moral ones as well—both the right to life and abortion rights are relevant here. Moreover, the publicity created by the case stirred political interest. The federal government entered the fray through the Department of Health and Human Services (HHS). The HHS charged that the hospitals involved in Baby Doe had denied treatment to a handicapped person and were in violation of federal law, Section 504 of the 1973 Rehabilitation Act. The consequence of the violation was loss of federal funds. The HHS argued, before the Federal District Court, that much progress had been made in the treatment of handicapped newborn babies, thus improving their chances for survival. In addition, a number of corrective and rehabilitative facilities to provide continued treatment had been created. The Federal Court did not uphold the HHS arguments, ruling that the HHS actions were capricious and arbitrary and that they interfered with treatment. Moreover, the HHS did not give consideration to the judgments of the parents. The Court's decision was that the application of Section 504 to Baby Doe was inappropriate and not justified.

Needless to say, the Baby Doe decision did not solve the ethical and moral issues that were raised. These issues will undoubtedly appear again. In particular, they are appearing in controversies involving teenagers' rights to abortions, privacy, and contraception. These matters are intrinsic to the fundamental question of the relationship between children's rights and parental rights. Is conflict necessarily involved? Are children's rights coterminous with parental rights?

These issues are being presented in the courts, continuing the pattern of instituting lawsuits that began with the *Brown vs. Board of Education* suit. This procedure will be strengthened by the movement of parents assuming active roles in pressing for improvements in programs for the handicapped. These developments signify the introduction of political factors in the handicapped children's movement. The family is no longer a private, non-political unit (Bohrer, Breedon, & Weikert, 1974). Advocates of the rights of handicapped persons recognize that the existence of legislation does not necessarily ensure that these rights are secure. Laws do not enforce themselves, and implementation of legislative and judicial mandates requires persistent monitoring (Soskin, 1980). It is not likely that parents will readily relinquish their current role, given its evolution out of several historical influences: cultural, economic, medical and political-legislative. In particular the political-legislative emphasis has been effective, forming the core of present-day strategies on behalf of handicapped people. Indeed the power of the approach is illustrated in recent legislation, Public Law 99–457, which extends services to handicapped children ages birth to five years, thus providing a long sought remedy for a service deficiency made prominent by Baby Doe. Moreover, this legislation also continues and extends the fundamental role of the family in programs for the handicapped. The achievement of such legislation in a period of budgetary retrenchment that has contracted programs and services for handicapped persons validates the legislative strategy and further strengthens the role of the family in programs for the handicapped.

REFERENCES

Abt, A. F. (1965). *Abt–Garrison history of pediatrics.* Philadelphia: W. B. Saunders.

Addison, M. R. (1976). Citizen advocacy. *Amicus, 1*(4), pp. 9–10.

Aries, P. (1962). *Centuries of childhood.* New York: Knopf.

Baby Doe revisited. (1982). *Children's Legal Rights Journal, 4* (4), pp. 13–23.

Bateman, B. D., & Herr, C. M. (1981). *Law and special education.* In J. M. Kauffman & D. P. Hallahan (Eds.), *Handbook of special education.* Englewood Cliffs, NJ: Prentice-Hall.

Becker, G. S. (1981). *A treatise on the family.* Cambridge, MA: Harvard University Press.

Bohrer, T. S., Breedon, L., & Weikert, R. J. (1974). On lay advocacy. *Amicus, 4,* pp. 82–85.

Bremner, R. H. (Ed.). (1970–1974). *Children and youth in America: A documentary history* (Vols. 1–3). Cambridge, MA: Harvard University Press.

Brothwell, D., & Sandison, A. T. (Eds.). (1967). *Diseases in antiquity.* Springfield, IL: Charles C Thomas.

Burgdorf, Jr., R. L., & Burgdorf, M. P. (1977). The wicked witch is almost dead: Buck *v.* Bell and the sterilization of handicapped persons. *Temple Law Quarterly, 50,* (4), pp. 995–1034.

Burgess, E. W., & Locke, H. J. (1953). *The family* (2nd ed.). New York: American Book.

Juul, K. D. (1981). Special education in Europe. In J. M. Kauffman & D. P. Hallahan (Eds.), *Handbook of special education.* Englewood Cliffs, NJ: Prentice-Hall.

Katz, S. N. (1971). *When parents fail.* Boston: Beacon Press.

Kauffman, J. M. (1981). Introduction: Historical trends and contemporary issues in special education. In J. M. Kauffman & D. P. Hallahan (Eds.), *Handbook of special education* Englewood Cliffs, NJ: Prentice-Hall.

LaVor, M. L. (1976). Federal legislation for exceptional persons: A history. In F. J. Weintraub, A. Abeson, J. Ballard, & M. L. LaVor (Eds.), *Pub-*

lic policy and the education of exceptional children (pp. 96–102). Reston, VA: The Council for Exceptional Children.

Legal issues for the 80's. (1980). *Children's Legal Rights Journal, 2*(5), pp. 23–31.

Lowell, H. D., & Schiavoni, T. F. (1980). Can the handicapped child survive another fall through the cracks? *Children's Legal Rights Journal, 1*(5), pp. 20–26.

Rodham, H. (1974). Children under the law. *Harvard Educational Review.* (Reprint Series No. 9), pp. 1–28.

Ryan, W. (1971). *Blaming the victim.* New York: Vintage Books.

Salt, H. S. (1914). Humanitarianism. In J. Hastings (Ed.), *Encyclopedia of religion and ethics* (Vol. 6, pp. 636–640). New York: Scribner.

Siller, J. (1976). Attitudes toward disability. In H. Rusalem & D. Malikin (Eds.), *Contemporary vocational rehabilitation* (pp. 67–80). New York: New York University Press.

Skolnick, A. S., & Skolnick, J. H. (1971). *Family in transition.* Boston: Little, Brown.

Soskin, R. M. (1980). Handicapped advocacy: A last hurrah. *Amicus, 5*(3) pp. 69–71.

Straus, R. (1965). *Sociology and rehabilitation.* Washington, DC: American Sociological Association.

Streib, G. F. (Ed.). (1973). The changing family: *Adaptation and diversity.* Reading, MA: Addison Wesley.

Sussman, M. B. (Ed.). (1965). *Sociology and rehabilitation.* Washington, DC: American Sociological Association.

The Family Protection Act. (1981). *Children's Legal Rights Journal, 3*(2), pp. 15–23.

The guardian *ad litem.* (1979). *Children's Legal Rights Journal, 1*(1), pp. 10–47.

The rights of children. (1974). *Harvard Educational Review.* (Reprint Series No. 9), pp. 1–379.

The right to an abortion revisited. (1984). *Children's Legal Rights Journal, 5*(1), pp. 20–22.

Thorne, B., & Yalom, M. (1982). *Rethinking the family.* New York: Longman.

U.S. Department of Education, Office for Handicapped Individuals. (1980). *Summary of existing legislation relating to the handicapped* (Publication No. E-80-22014). Washington, DC: U.S. Government Printing Office.

Weintraub, F. J., Abeson, A., Ballard, J., & LaVor, M. L. (Eds.). (1976). *Public policy and the education of exceptional children.* Reston, VA: The Council for Exceptional Children.

Weintraub, F. J., Abeson, A. R., Braddock, D. L. (1971). *State law and education of handicapped children: Issues and recommendations.* Reston, VA: The Council for Exceptional Children.

When can the state cut the parental bond? (1982). *Children's Legal Rights Journal, 4*(1), pp. 4–8.

Winch, R. F. (1977). *Familial organization.* New York: Free Press.

Windelband, W. (1958). *A history of philosophy* (Vol. 2). New York: Harper & Row.

The World Almanac (1987). New York: World Almanac.

Worsfold, V. L. (1974). A philosophical justification for children's rights. *Harvard Educational Review.* (Reprint Series No. 9), pp. 29–44.

CHAPTER TWO

Family Systems and Beyond
Conceptual Issues

Milton Seligman

Milton Seligman, Ph.D. is professor in the Counseling Psychology Program, Department of Psychology in Education, at the University of Pittsburgh. He has edited and authored books and articles in the area of group psychotherapy and in the area of childhood disability and the family.

Dr. Seligman teaches courses in individual and group therapy, clinical supervision, and disability in the family. He maintains a private practice in Pittsburgh.

A focus on children with disabilities ignores other family members who may be affected by the presence of the child. In addition, focusing on the disabled child is short-sighted because it neglects the dynamic nature of family functioning. A disability in one family member affects the entire system and in turn affects the disabled person.

The hesitancy to consider a perspective grounded in ecological principles may have been partially caused by the reign of psychoanalysis where the focus was on intrapsychic rather than interpersonal processes. Similarly, psychoanalytic theory focused almost exclusively on the mother/child relationship. Parke (1981) noted that fathers, for example, were ignored purposely because of the assumption that they were less important than were mothers in influencing the developing child. In fact, the father was considered to be peripheral. Bowlby (1951) also stressed that the mother is the first and most important object of infant attachment and that fathers play a supporting role for the mother. Another contributing factor may be that, with few exceptions (Minuchin, 1978), family theorists and family therapists did not show particular interest in chronically disabled persons within the context of the family. Whatever the reasons for this heretofore narrow perspective, there is currently considerable interest in integrating theories of family systems with the available information about chronically disabled persons and their families (see, e.g., Chapter 12, "Family Therapy" by Elman; Berger & Foster, 1986; Blacher, 1984; Crnic, Friedrick, & Greenberg, 1983; Seligman, 1983; Turk & Kerns, 1985; Turnbull & Turnbull, 1986). The remainder of this chapter will attempt to reflect this integration.

FAMILY SYSTEMS THEORY

Minuchin (1974) captured the essence of the interactive nature of the family:

> The individual influences his context and is influenced by it in constantly recurring sequences of interaction. The individual who lives within a family is a member of a social system to which he must adapt. His actions are governed by the characteristics of the systems and these characteristics include the effects of his own past actions. The individual responds to stresses in other parts of the system to which he adapts; and he may contribute significantly to stressing other members of the system. The individual can be approached as a subsystem, or part of the system, but the whole must be taken into account (p. 9).

Minuchin proposed, then, that the family operates as an interactive unit and that what affects one member affects all members. Relatedly, and before Minuchin, Von Bertalanffy (1968) observed that all living systems are composed of interdependent parts and that the interaction of these parts creates characteristics not contained in the separate entities. McGoldrick and Gerson (1985) agreed with Minuchin when they asserted that:

> The physical, social and emotional functioning of family members is profoundly interdependent, with changes in one part of the system reverberating in other parts of the system. In addition, family interactions and relationships tend to be highly reciprocal, patterned and repetitive (p. 5).

However, before one can grasp the dynamic nature of family functioning, it is imperative to have an understanding of the characteristics, both static and dynamic, that comprise family units. The following sections present such concepts, which are derived from family systems theory.

FAMILY STRUCTURE

Family structure refers to the variety of membership characteristics that make families unique. This "input" factor includes membership characteristics, cultural style, and ideological style.

Membership Characteristics

As Turnbull, Summers, and Brotherson (1986) noted, much of the literature on families with disabled members is based on the assumption behind family homogeneity. Families differ with regard to numerous membership characteristics, such as (a) extended family members who may either reside in the household or are geographically separated, (b) single parent families, (c) families with an unemployed bread winner or one who has a major psychiatric disorder, and (d) a deceased family member whose influence continues to assert itself on the family.

Although membership characteristics of families with disabled members have been studied, little has been done to investigate the relationship of these attributes to either successful or unsuccessful family interaction. Turnbull and Turnbull (1986) reminded us that membership characteristics change as the family members' life cycles proceed from infancy through old age. For example, the exiting of a family member will precipitate different communication and relationship patterns. The inclusion of grandparents into the family unit can also influence family dynamics.

Cultural Style

A family's cultural beliefs are possibly the most static component of the family and can play an important role in shaping its ideological style, interactional patterns, and functional priorities (Turnbull et al., 1986). Cultural style may be influenced by ethnic, racial, or religious factors or by socioeconomic status. In her extensive review of the literature, Schorr-Ribera (1987) pointed out that culturally based beliefs affect the manner in which families adapt to a child with a disability. In addition, it can influence their ability to request help and the level of trust given to caregivers and caregiving institutions.

Ideological style

Ideological style is based on a family's beliefs, values, and coping behaviors — and is influenced by cultural beliefs. For example, McGoldrick, Pearce, and Giordano (1982) noted that Jewish families place a great deal of importance on intellectual achievement. Academic achievement may be stressed by Jewish families, in part, to enable a family member to pursue professional opportunities designed to escape the repercussions of discrimination. Therefore, attending college in these families is strongly urged. Italian families tend to emphasize family closeness and affection; thus, college attendance may be viewed as a threat to family cohesiveness. Other beliefs and values may be handed down from generation to generation and influence how family members interact with one another and with other families and other systems (such as schools and governmental agencies). It is important to be reminded here that families from the same culture can differ significantly.

Although the responses of the family to a disabled child is influenced by ideological style, the reverse may also be true — that is, that a child may influence a family's values. For example, when a child with disabilities is born, the parents must both respond to the birth and confront their beliefs about disabled persons. Chronic childhood disability does not discriminate, therefore, a disabled child may be born to a family that is dogmatic and prejudiced. When that occurs, the family must come to terms with what this event means to them psychologically and practically, but they must also confront their beliefs about persons who are deviant according to culturally derived values. The family must then cope with this new addition to their family and they must also confront their life-long values and beliefs.

Ideological style influences the coping mechanisms of families. Turnbull et al. (1986) defined coping as any response designed to reduce stress. Coping behaviors can motivate the family to change the situation or change the perceived meaning of the situation. An illustration of a potentially dysfunctional coping strategy comes from a recent study that revealed that fathers of mentally retarded adolescents, compared with a matched control group of fathers with nondisabled adolescents, reported high levels of stress and employed significantly more withdrawal and avoidance behavior to cope with their anxiety (Houser, 1987).

McCubbin and Patterson (1981) classified coping styles into internal and external strategies that included, for *internal:* passive appraisal (problems will resolve themselves over time), and reframing (making attitudinal adjustments to live with the situation constructively); and *external:* social support (ability to use family and extra familial resources), spiritual support (use of spiritual interpretations, advice from clergy), and formal support (use of community and professional resources).

FAMILY INTERACTION

It is important for professionals to realize that children with disabilities do not function in isolation but that they live within a context — the family — and that when something happens to one member of the family, everyone is affected.

To say that a family is a unit composed of a particular number of individuals who function in dynamic interrelationships provides only a partial picture of how a family operates. Turnbull et al. (1986) elaborated on the four components of the interactional system: subsystems, cohesion, adaptability, and communication.

Subsystems

Within a family there are four subsystems:

- Marital — husband and wife
- Parental — parent and child
- Sibling — child and child
- Extra familial — interaction with extended family, friends, professionals, and others.

The makeup of subsystems is affected by the structural characteristics of families (e.g., size of extra familial network, single mother or father, number of children) and by the current life-cycle state (e.g., a family with school-age children or one with children ready to leave home).

Professionals need to be cautious when they intervene in a subsystem. For example, an intervention designed to strengthen the bond between a mother and her disabled child will affect that mother's relationship with her husband and other children. Strategies need to be considered within the context of the other subsystems so that the resolution of one problem does not bring about the emergence of others. Elman discusses useful family therapy strategies designed to avoid such problems in Chapter 12.

Cohesion and Adaptability

The subsystems describe *who* in the family will interact, whereas cohesion and adaptability account for *how* family members interact.

Cohesion can be characterized by referring to the concepts of *enmeshment* and *disengagement*. Minuchin (1974) observed that highly enmeshed families have weak boundaries between subsystems and can be characterized as overinvolved and overprotective. Such families have difficulty allowing individuality to thrive among the members. Overly protective families can have deleterious effects on their disabled children. Such families experience considerable anxiety in letting go of their child and hence may keep them from participating in activities that would promote independence.

Conversely, disengaged families have rigid subsystem boundaries (Minuchin, 1974). With regard to a family with a disabled child, interactions may be characterized by minimal involvement. A disengaged family member can be a father who denies the disability and withdraws from both marital and parental interactions.

Well-functioning families are characterized by a balance between enmeshment and disengagement. Boundaries between subsystems are clearly defined and individuals within a family feel both a close bonding and a sense of autonomy. Thus, enmeshment and disengagement represent the outer boundaries of a continuum; the approximate middle of the continuum is where well-functioning families are found.

Adaptability refers to a family's ability to change in response to a stressful situation (Olson, Russell, & Sprenkle, 1980). Whereas rigid families do not bend in response to stress, chaotic families are characterized by instability and inconsistent change. A rigid family would have difficulty adjusting to the demands of caring for a significantly impaired child. A father's rigid breadwinner role, for example, would not allow him to help with domestic chores or to assist with the child (i.e., to help with "woman's work"), thereby placing an inordinate burden on the mother. The mother, therefore, would have to put all of her energies into caretaking responsibilities, leaving little time for the other children in the family or for other people. This family would be in jeopardy of becoming dysfunctional.

A chaotic family has few rules to live by, and those rules that do exist often change. There is no family leader and there may be endless negotiations and frequent role changes (Turnbull & Turnbull, 1986). Chaotic families seem to move frequently from a sense of closeness or enmeshment to one of distance, hostility, and disengagement. Families who interact in a functional way maintain a balance when change occurs between emotional unity and autonomy, between reacting to change and holding on to a sense of stability, and between having closed and random communication (Turnbull et al., 1986).

Communication

Communication problems reside in the interactions between people, not within people (Turnbull & Turnbull, 1986). The systems perspective places emphasis on changing patterns of interaction and not changing individuals. The professional avoids placing blame on any one family member and instead tries to assess which factors have contributed to dysfunctional communication patterns. It is not unusual for family members to single out an individual (e.g., disabled child) as the source of their problems in an effort to lessen their own anxiety. Families shouldn't be blamed for using this tactic but should be helped to understand that problems are not caused by linear and simple cause and effect factors.

Family Functions

In order to carry out functions successfully, considerable interdependence between the family and its extrafamilial network is required. Also, families differ with regard to the priorities they attach to different functions, and they differ in regard to who will carry out these functions.

According to Turnbull and Turnbull (1986), the following characteristics reflect typical family functions:

1. Economic (e.g., generating income, paying bills, and banking)
2. Domestic/health care (e.g., providing transportation, purchasing and preparing food, visiting doctors when necessary)
3. Recreational (e.g., enjoying hobbies and activities, both for the family and for the individual)
4. Socialization (e.g., developing social skills and interpersonal relationships)
5. Self-identity (e.g., recognizing strengths and weaknesses, developing a sense of belonging)
6. Affection (e.g., working on intimacy and the capacity to nurture)
7. Educational/vocational (e.g., completing homework, making career choice, developing a work ethic).

Turnbull et al. (1986) reported that a disabled child in the family, especially a severely disabled child, can increase consumptive demands without proportionately increasing its productive capability. These authors noted that a child residing in the least restrictive environment — namely, in the family — may create the unintended consequence of generating a restrictive environment for family members in carrying out their functions. Furthermore, it is conceivable that a disabled child can, among other things, change the family's self-identity, reduce its earning capacity, and constrict its recreational and social activities.

Some would question the emphasis placed on the role of parents as teachers of their child (Seligman, 1979; Turnbull et al., 1986). It is important to remember that the educational function is only one of several family functions. Parents have many roles and functions to perform, and it is important to be concerned about how the overburdening of one role or function affects the others. In addition, when asking parents to assume an educational function it is important to find out whether the parents wish to take on that role and whether they are prepared to assume it. Family members are sometimes asked to do more at home with their child than the family system can tolerate. Too much stress can be placed on the family when professionals fail to coordinate the activities they ask the family to assume. With certain types of childhood impairments, a family may be given assignments to be carried out at home by numerous professionals, all of whom wish to help but who inadvertently add to the family's stress. Activities that professionals ask family members to carry out should be monitored, and they should recognize that the overburdening of one family function can affect the successful functioning of others. Families would benefit by having a coordinator of services who could help monitor conflicting and/or excessive demands.

Family Life Cycle

The structure and function of any family changes over time. These changes affect the way the family interacts. A family's life cycle involves a series of developmental stages in which, during a particular stage, the family's lifestyle is relatively stable and each member is engaged in developmental tasks related to that individual's period of life (Duvall, 1957). For example, a family with two children in late adolescence must cope with the usual intensity and ambivalence of adolescent life as well as with the concerns facing adult (i.e., the parents') mid-life. Change occurs for this family when one of the children leaves home, which affects the family structure (e.g., where there were four persons, there are now three) and may affect other aspects of family life, such as interactions between members. With regard to families of children with life-threatening illnesses like cystic fibrosis, the death of the child may precipitate several crises. The parents have to cope with the loss of their child and they must also contend with interactional patterns that will change after the child's death. The physical management of a child with CF is so demanding that a family's attention during the child's life centers around the physical requirements of the disease. After the child's death, the parents must come to terms with their loss and their relationship and communication patterns now that they are not preoccupied by their child's physical care.

With regard to the developmental changes characteristic of families, Olson, McCubbin, Barnes, Larsen, Muxen, and Wilson (1984) identified the following seven stages: couple, childbearing, school age, adolescence, launching, postparenting, and aging. Each stage involves its own developmental tasks. Such functions are highly age related. For example, providing physical care by parents is essential during infancy, and education and vocational guidance is important when children are in high school and college. Where bonding and attachment is vital during infancy, the ability and willingness to let go is important when children reach late adolescence. Thus, a key aspect of life-cycle stages is the change in function required of family members over time. Developmental transitions (moving from one stage to another) can be a primary source of stress and even of family dysfunction.

Turnbull et al. (1986) related the developmental stages derived from systems theory to the stress that families with disabled children experience. The following are five stages and their associated stress factors identified by Olson et al. (1984):

1. Childbearing period — Getting an accurate diagnosis, making emotional adjustments, and informing other family members.
2. School age — Clarifying personal views regarding mainstreaming versus segregated placements, dealing with the reactions of the child's peer group, and arranging for child care and extracurricular activities.
3. Adolescence — Adjusting to the chronic nature of the child's disability; dealing with issues of sexuality, peer isolation, and rejection; and planning for the child's vocational future.
4. Launching period — Recognizing and adjusting to the family's continuing responsibility, deciding on appropriate residential placement, and dealing with the paucity of socialization opportunities for the disabled family member.
5. Postparental period — Reestablishing relationship with a spouse (i.e., if the child has been successfully launched) and interacting with disabled members' residential service providers.

These family systems concepts provide a fundamental framework for understanding families with children who have disabilities. Although it is essential to understand the dynamics of the nuclear family, it is not enough. In order to grasp an objective perspective of the situation, influences beyond the immediate family must be considered.

THE SOCIAL ECOLOGY MODEL

The consideration of the family as a dynamic interdependent unit, as already discussed, was a major step forward. However, according to some theorists, there continued to be a flaw in the conceptualization of family life. We know that young children with disabilities do not live in isolation. They reside within the family and the family as well lives in a broader context. The formulation of the family within a social ecological framework has been discussed extensively by Bronfenbrenner (1979) and has more recently been discussed in relation to families and childhood disability by Mitchell (1983) and by Bubolz and Whiren (1984).

Bubolz and Whiren (1984) characterized an ecological approach as the biological and physical properties of the organism and environment as well as psychosocial characteristics and interactions. Similar to what occurs within the family (and as delineated by the family systems model), the basic tenet of the ecological model is that a change in any part of the ecological system affects subparts of the system, creating the need for system adaptation, that is, for equilibrium. The ecological environments for the family furnish the resources necessary for life — and make up the life support and social support systems.

Similar to boundary concerns in the family systems model, the ecological model is also concerned with the permeability of the family in interacting with other systems. An example is a situation in which a family with a disabled child is or is not open to support from other similarly situated families (e.g., support groups) or whether they are willing to accept assistance from social agencies or other sources of help.

Bronfenbrenner (1977) described an elaborate theory in which the family is viewed as a system nested within a number of other societal systems (see Figure 2-1). A key tenet of the social ecological point of view is that if a person wishes to change behavior, he or she needs to change environments. The social ecological view further asserts that a child or family can be affected by events occurring in settings in which the person is not even present. An illustration of this phenomenon is one in which a young child can be affected by the conditions of parental employment. Furthermore, conditions of employment can be influenced by the strength of the economy. And whether a local economy is healthy can, in turn, be affected by events occurring on a national or even international level. Thus, the behavior of a child or a family unit can be influenced by a variety of seemingly remote events. This view encourages a broad conceptualization of the forces that impinge on the family.

According to Figure 2-1, Bronfenbrenner's (1979) subsystems include the microsystem, mesosystem, exosystem, and macrosystem. Mitchell (1983) applied Bronfenbrenner's concepts to the study of families with disabled children. A discussion of Mitchell's adaptation follows.

Microsystem

The microsystem constitutes the pattern of activities, roles, and interpersonal relationships experienced by the family. In it, the following components are found: mother/father, mother/disabled child, mother/

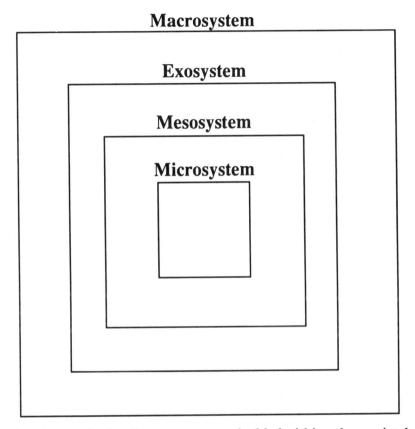

Figure 2-1. The family as a system embedded within other societal systems. Adapted from Bronfenbrenner (1979).

nondisabled child, father/disabled child, father/nondisabled child, disabled child/nondisabled child (similar to family systems theory). Some of the problems facing families with a disabled child that fall under each of these components of the microsystem are:

1. Mother/father
   The problems facing parents concern how well they cope individually and as a couple before the birth of a disabled child; after the birth, how well they accept their child's disabilities.
2. Mother/disabled child
   The mother must deal with depression, guilt, and self blame.

3. Mother/nondisabled child
   The mother must become aware of how much attention her nondisabled children receive, she must guard against giving the nondisabled child excessive caretaking responsibility for the disabled child.

4. Father/disabled child
   The issue here is whether the father withdraws or is psychologically and instrumentally present for the disabled child and the family.

5. Father/nondisabled child
   The potential problems here are similar to those faced by the mother/nondisabled child (see No. 3).

6. Disabled child/nondisabled child
   Siblings must deal with feelings of guilt, shame, and fear of catching the disability; the tendency of disabled sibling to "enslave" nondisabled brother/sister; normal siblings' ambivalence toward their disabled brother/sister.

Mesosystem

The microsystem functions in a mesosystem comprising a wide range of settings in which a family actively participates. The following individuals and services comprise the mesosystem:

1. Medical and health care workers
   The following issues involving professionals' interactions with the disabled child often crop up: how diagnosis is handled; professionals' depth of knowledge and accessibility; attitudes of professionals toward families with chronically disabled children; professionals' skill in being honest and forthright with parents but also kind, humane, and helpful.

2. Extended family
   Grandparents' and other extended family members must grapple with their acceptance/rejection of the disabled grandchild; these extended family members can relieve parental stress by helping with certain family functions or add to stress by rejecting the child.

3. Friends/neighbors
   Community acceptance and support help parents cope with their feelings of shame, embarrassment, and stigma.

4. Work/recreation associates
   It is helpful for family members to be treated, not as extensions of a child's disabilities, but as normally as possible.

5. Early intervention programs
   There has been high praise for early intervention programs, but because of high costs and other factors, they are not always available for many families.
6. Other parents
   Considerable social, psychological, and practical help is available from support groups for parents and siblings; these groups serve an advocacy function affecting social policy through legislative initiatives.
7. Local community
   Although community assistance is invaluable, availability of services tend to differ markedly in urban versus rural communities and in poor versus affluent communities.

Exosystem

In the exosystem there are influences and settings in which the family is not actively involved yet which can affect the family, such as:

1. Mass media
   The media can affect attitudes about disabled persons; for example, disabled individuals can be portrayed as pittiable souls, incapable and undesirable, or they can be portrayed as competent, likeable, and reliable individuals.
2. Health
   Families of severely physically impaired children in particular are dependent on health care systems.
3. Social welfare
   For some families financial and other governmental support are essential.
4. Education
   The implications of the Education for All Handicapped Children Act and its amendments, the sometimes adversarial relationship between parents and schools; the degree to which the schools help families achieve independence and respite from their disabled child are all affected by the educational institutions.

Macrosystem

Finally, there is the macrosystem, which is the ideology or belief systems inherent in our social institutions:

1. Ethnic/cultural, religious, and socioeconomic
   Ethnic/cultural and religious values can affect how the disability is viewed by family members. These values also play a role in how a family chooses to interact with the service-delivery system. In addition, socioeconomic status may determine or reflect the availability of a family's instrumental resources.

2. Economic and political
   The health of the economy and the political atmosphere invariably have an important impact on programs for disabled persons and their families.

Bronfenbrenner (1979) asserted that the core of an ecological orientation—and that which distinguishes it from other models—is the concern with the progressive accommodation between a growing organism and its immediate environment and the way this relationship is mediated by forces from more remote regions in the larger social and physical milieu. Thus, a major shift in governmental philosophy can, when the philosophy is translated into legislation, affect the availability of funds for social programs designed to help disabled persons and their families.

Although Bronfenbrenner (1979), Bubolz and Whiren (1984), Mitchell (1983), and more recently Imber-Black (1988), complemented our knowledge of systems that surround the family, it may have been Kurt Lewin in the 1930s and 1940s that laid the groundwork for a social ecology point of view (see Hall and Lindzey, 1978). Influenced by Gestalt psychology which held that behavior is determined by the psychophysical field consisting of a system of external forces, Lewin developed Field Theory. Field Theory posited that the adaptation of an object (a person) is determined by the total field in which the object is embedded.

Lewin viewed the person surrounded by forces that were perceived as having positive or negative valences and where the interaction between the person and the environment depended on the permeability between the subject and other events of systems. He felt that language was too imprecise and ambiguous to communicate psychological reality so he constructed a typological system (See figure 2-2), where P, the person is embedded in E, the psychological environment which is surrounded by the foreign hull.

The person's psychological environment might include peers, family, community, social-medical resources, etc. The foreign hull has social, political, and economic factors and catastrophic events among others in it. The person, then, is influenced by a multitude of adjacent and distant factors and may be drawn to or repelled by an object depending upon the value (valence) some factors may have (positive/negative) and their permeability.

In a similiar vein, Hartman (1978) developed a diagrammatic assessment of family and community interactions which is called an ECO-MAP

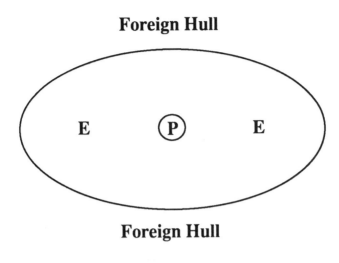

P + E = Life Space

Figure 2-2.   Lewin's Field Theory

(see Figure 2-3). She felt that a graphic representation of the family's reality would avoid simplistic reductionistic cause and effect relationships. "Such linear views reflect the limitations of thought and language rather than the nature of the real world, where human events are the result of transactions among multiple variables" (p. 466).

The ECO-MAP is a simple paper and pencil simulation that demonstrates the existence and flow of resources. According to Hartman, the ECO-MAP "highlights the nature of the interfaces and points to conflicts to be mediated, bridges to be built, and resources to be sought and mobilized (p. 467). Figure 2-3 provides the basic schema of the ECO-MAP and Figure 2-4 illustrates the case of "Jim," his family, and their present reality. Like a genogram, the ECO-MAP can help the professional conceptualize a family's circumstance and consider appropriate intervention strategies. Hartman recommends that a copy of the ECO-MAP be given to family members so that they can see themselves in relation to factors outside of the nuclear family. It can also be used in a pre-post fashion to determine the effectiveness of a particular intervention.

In understanding and helping families with disabled children, one cannot only focus on the child, nor the child and the mother, nor the dynamics occurring within the family. Rather, it is becoming increasingly crucial to examine the family within the context of larger social, economic, and political realities.

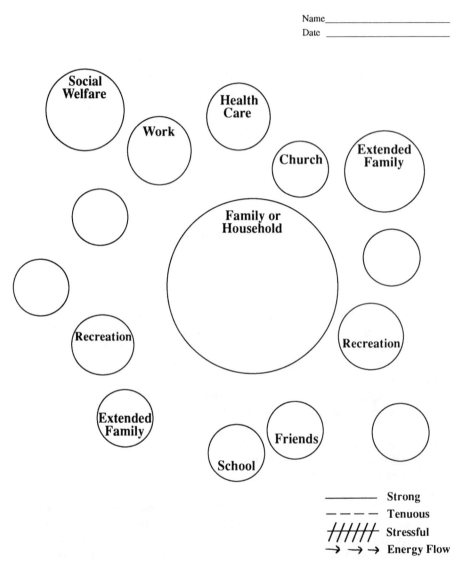

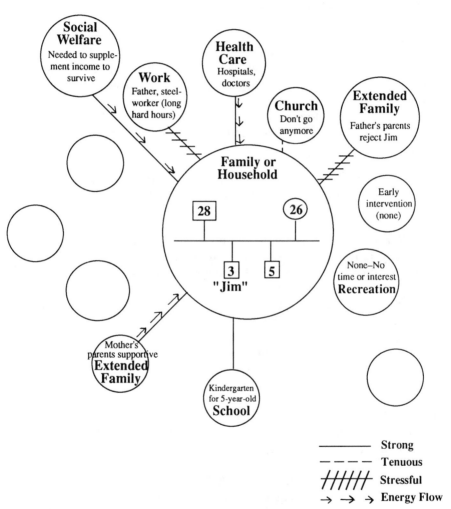

Figure 2-4. ECO-MAP Illustration of "Jim."

RELATED CONCEPTS

A number of contributors to the professional literature have concentrated on particular aspects of family adaptation. The following discussion centers on several key concepts that are often cited in the literature and relate directly to families with disabled children.

Stress

The notion of stress has already been touched on. Stress has been mentioned in relation to life-cycle changes and is implicated also in events occurring within the family's social ecology.

Hill (1949) developed a theoretical model of stress that is often cited in the family literature and that has been designated as the ABCX family crises model:

> *A* (the stressor event) — interacting with *B* (the family's crisis meeting resources) — interacting with *C* (the definition the family makes of the event) — produce *X* (the crisis).

The A factor (the stressor) is a life event that can produce change in the family system. The family's boundaries, goals, patterns of interaction, roles, or values may be threatened by change caused by a stressor (McCubbin & Patterson, 1983). A stressor event, for example, may be the family's need to generate more income because of the economic burdens brought on by the realities of having a child with disabilities. This hardship can place demands on the roles and functions of family members, alter their collective goals, and affect the family's interaction.

The B factor (family resources) is the family's ability to prevent an event or change in the family from causing a crisis (McCubbin & Patterson, 1983). The B factor is the family's capacity to meet obstacles and shift its course of action. This factor relates directly to the notion that the family's flexibility and quality of relationships prior to the birth of a disabled child may be an important predictor of its ability to adapt. It may also reflect how the parents' family of origin coped with stressful events.

The C factor is the definition the family makes of the seriousness of the experienced stressor. The C factor reflects the family's values and their previous experience in dealing with change and meeting crises. This factor is reminiscent of Ellis's (1958) theory of rational-emotive psychotherapy. He asserted that it is not the event itself that is disturbing to an individual but the meaning attributed to the event that causes neurotic thinking and behavior.

Taken together the three factors all influence the family's ability to prevent the stressor event from creating a crisis (the X factor). A crisis reflects the family's inability to restore balance and stability. It is important to note that an event may never become a crisis if the family is able to use existing resources and defines the situation as a manageable event.

Family Adjustment and Adaptation

Patterson (1988) describes the Family Adjustment and Adaptation Response Model (FAAR) which asserts that families attempt to maintain balanced functioning by using its *capacities* to meet its *demands*. A critical factor is the *meaning* the family gives to a situation (demands) and what they have to cope with in the situation (capabilities). A crisis happens when demands exceed existing capabilities and an imbalance occurs. Balance can be restored by (a) acquiring new resources or learning new coping behaviors, (b) reducing the demands that confront the family, and/or (c) changing the way the situation is viewed.

In illustrating how symptoms or behavioral patterns serve as feedback mechanisms that become part of the pile-up of demands, Patterson describes the reciprocity between a diabetic child and his family:

> . . . hyperglycemia in a diabetic child may contribute to his or her emotional lability and thus to a greater incidence of conflict with siblings or parents. Conversely, parental conflict may contribute to internalized tension on the part of the diabetic child and a neuroendocrine response leading to hyperglycemia (p. 79).

Social Support

Social support is often viewed as a mediating or buffering factor in meeting the demands of a stressful event (Cobb, 1976; Crnic, Greenberg, Ragozin, Robinson, & Basham, 1983). The presence of a disabled child is considered to be a stressful event (Crnic et al., 1983) and one which is considered chronic in nature (Olshansky, 1962).

Researchers such as Crnic et al. (1983) have examined social support in terms of three ecological levels: (a) intimate relationships (e.g., spousal), (b) friendships, and (c) neighborhood or community support. For example, in their study designed to assess the relationship of maternal stress and social support, they found that mothers with greater social support were more positive in their behavior and attitudes toward their infants. Intimate (spousal) support proved to have the most positive effects.

Kazak and Marvin (1984) and Kazak and Wilcox (1984) developed a conceptualization of social support networks and applied this model to the study of families with disabled children. Kazak and Marvin (1984) elaborated on three components of social networks: network size, network density, and boundary density.

Kazak and Marvin defined *network size* as the number of persons perceived as offering different types of support such as spiritual, medical, psychological, or instrumental support. These authors contend that, in general, the larger the social network, the greater the possibility of successful adaptation. However, perceived high quality social support albeit small in quantity can enhance adaptation.

Network density refers to the extent to which members of an individual's social network know each other, independent of the focal person. Density provides an indication of the interrelatedness of the social network. In their study of families with spina bifida children, Kazak and Wilcox (1984) found that the social networks of these families were comparatively dense, which suggests that the people from whom help was sought knew and interacted with one another.

The third characteristic of social networks is *boundary density,* which is a measure of that portion of the network membership that is shared by the individuals involved. That is, the boundary density is determined by the number of network members that both parents know and use. One method of determining boundary density is to ascertain to what extent spouses list the same network members. Kazak and Wilcox (1984) reported that network overlap (high boundary density) tends to be associated with marital stability.

These authors assert that there are three areas of concern relevant to understanding the ecological context of families with disabled children. These points relate directly to the notion of social networks. First, it is important to specify the precise nature of existing stresses and to integrate this knowledge into a family model. The implication is that an examination of the social support network needs to be undertaken by professionals and factored into existing models of family functioning. Second, although these families are sometimes characterized as socially isolated, greater specification is needed in terms of the nature, extent, and consequences of this isolation. An assessment instrument like Hartman's (1978) ECO-MAP can facilitate one's understanding of family isolation in relationship to support networks. Third, the dissatisfaction families express regarding their relationships with professional personnel (see Chapter 5, "Parent-Professional Interaction: The Roots of Misunderstanding"), on whom they are often dependent, underscores the importance of examining more closely the availability of informal sources of support.

Generally, the quantity and especially the quality of formal and informal sources of social support bear a relationship to the family's ability to cope and adapt. To clarify the relationship between social support and families, researchers are seeking to determine more specifically which aspects of social support are more helpful to families and how (Dunst, 1990; Dyson & Fewell, 1986; Kazak & Marvin, 1984; Kazak & Wilson, 1984).

DEVELOPMENTAL MILESTONES

The family life cycle has been discussed as a component of family systems theory. Basically, the family life-cycle refers to the following six life stages described by Olson et al. (1984): couple, childbearing, school age, adolescence, launching, postparental, and aging. Because of the nature and severity of a child's disabilities and the family's response to them, families must prepare for a series of stages that, at least to some extent, are unique to these families. For some families it is not possible to apply any type of developmental or stage-theory model because of events that continue to occur throughout the child's lifetime. This may be true, for example, in a family with a hemophilic child where periodic "bleeds" can cause considerable ongoing stress. Such events trigger a new cycle of upset, changing demands, and new adaptations. Furthermore, the availability and quality of social support can exacerbate or buffer the effects of a difficult situation.

Farber (1975) and Fewell (1986) noted that children with disabilities will be slower accomplishing certain life-cycle or developmental milestones, and some may never achieve them. As a disabled child approaches critical periods, parents may experience renewed anxiety or sadness. Fewell (1986) described six periods that are particularly stressful to these parents:

1. Encountering the disability
   The nature of a child's disability generally determines when the parents learn about it. Genetic disabilities, such as Down syndrome, are apparent soon after birth; therefore, parents become aware of their child's condition early. Conditions such as deafness, or language and learning disabilities may not be discovered until the child is older and diagnosis may be delayed due to the existence of a rare disease. Also, families may be confronted with disability when the youngster is older that results from an accident or illness. The confirmation of a serious and chronic problem generally precipitates a crisis which creates demands on the family system to call upon their available capacities (Patterson, 1988). Immediate reactions may be those of shock, disappointment, and depression, and the family follows a fairly predictable series of stages of adjust-

ment (see Chapter 3 by Darling). Contact with physicians and health care workers is particularly intense at this stage. Also during this period, the reactions of others, especially grandparents, is particularly important (Seligman & Darling, 1989).

2. Early childhood
The early childhood years can be difficult ones for the family as they anxiously watch for their child to achieve certain developmental milestones. The chronicity or episodic nature of a child's disabilities and what it means to the family is a major part of the early childhood years. The nature and severity of the disability may play a key role in the family's perception and behavior (see Chapter 8 by Fewell and Chapter 9 by Lyon and Lyon). With regard to a child's developmental delay, Fewell (1986) observed that,

> The task of diapering a three-year old is simply not as easy as it was when the child was one year old. The larger and heavier child requires more energy to lift and carry. The emotional burden is also great: parents anticipate the end of diapers and two o'clock bottles, and when these things don't end, it can shatter dreams and invite questions about the future (pp. 16–17).

Although early intervention programs are generally applauded (Dunst, 1990), Fewell (1986) noted that a crisis may develop when a child enters an early intervention program, for the following reasons:

- Families see older children with a similar condition and wonder whether their child will resemble them as he or she develops.
- Families become aware that the services their child needs can represent a significant financial drain on them as well as be a burden on their available time.
- Families who share their experiences with other families realize that they may need to fight for the services their child needs, further draining the family's resources.
- Families learn that they are often expected to be their child's primary caregivers and teachers over many years.

3. School entry
Parents may experience another setback or period of adjustment when they realize that their child fails to fit into the mainstream of the traditional educational system and may require special education classes. As more of their schoolmates learn that they have a disabled brother or sister, siblings may find this a particularly diffi-

cult period. This stage can be characterized as the period when the family "goes public," because it is the time when the disabled child ventures beyond the boundaries of the family. And finally, parents, if they have not done so already, must modify and come to grips with the educational and vocational goals they had envisioned for their child.

It is important to note that the difficulties parents experience depends on the nature of the child's disability (e.g., there may be relatively few adjustments if the child is moderately physically disabled) and the degree to which the school system is prepared to provide adequate educational and adjunct services for special needs children. Also, during this period, parents may debate the merits of a segregated versus a mainstreamed educational setting for their child. Family tensions may arise if there are major differences in the parents' views on this issue.

4. Adolescence

Adolescence marks the period when children begin to separate from their parents. This period also reflects the time when adolescent children experience considerable change, turmoil, and ambivalence (Marshak, 1982). For families of children with disabilities this stage can be a painful reminder of their child's failure to successfully traverse this life-cycle stage, because they continue to remain dependent.

Peer acceptance or the lack of it may be particularly painful for the entire family during the adolescent years. Peer acceptance may determine the degree to which the child feels rejected and isolated. This, in turn, may contribute to the stress parents and siblings experience.

5. Beginning adult life

Public education offers both children and parents several benefits. It helps the child gain important educational and vocational skills, as well as a sense of independence. For the parents, it offers them respite. As a child's education draws to an end parents must make some difficult choices. Because of limited vocational opportunities and inadequate community living arrangements, families may be left with few viable choices. This is a particularly stressful period because the spectre of the child's future looms and can cause considerable concern and anxiety.

A parent's concern about the future is vividly portrayed by educator and parent Helen Featherstone (1980):

I remember, during the early months of Jody's life, the anguish with which I contemplated the distant future. Jody cried constantly, not irritable, hungry cries, but heartrending shrieks of pain. Vain efforts to comfort him filled my nights and days. One evening when nothing seemed to help, I went outside, intending to escape his misery for a moment, hoping that without me he might finally fall asleep. Walking in summer darkness, I imagined myself at seventy, bent and wrinkled, hobbling up the stairs to minister to Jody, now over forty, but still crying and helpless (p. 19).

6. Maintaining adult life
   Where a disabled person will live and the level of care he or she will require characterize the family's concerns at this stage. A major concern for parents is the future care of their adult child. They worry about the years when they may not be able to actively oversee the care of their child or about when they are deceased. Mental health professionals become particularly important at this stage, in that they can help families plan for their child's future in terms of his or her vocational options, leisure time activities, and living arrangements. Adult siblings as well as other extended family members may be a useful resource and should be approached as potential helpers during this period. Although community support services are always needed, their availability and accessibility become crucial at this point.

In a fitting conclusion to her discussion of the aforementioned stages, Fewell (1986) noted that:

> When a family has a disabled child, all the actors in this support network must adapt to the extended needs of the disabled member. The adaptations family members make are often significant, and individual destinies may be determined by the experience. Family adaptations change as the child matures; the stress at various periods may affect family members differently, for much depends on the familial and environmental contributions to the dynamic interactions of adaptation at a given point in time (p. 19).

SUMMARY

This chapter has presented several conceptual perspectives of the family with a disabled child. Perhaps key to this chapter is the notion that families are remarkably complex and dynamic because there are many factors that contribute to and impinge on family life. The family does not remain static but changes as new events occur and as family members progress through the life cycle. In our interventions with families with disabled children we must be well grounded in the static and dynamic features of families if we expect to work successfully with them. We must also be cognizant of the factors outside of the nuclear family that influence its functioning.

REFERENCES

Berger, M., & Foster, M. (1986). Applications of family therapy theory to research and interventions with families with mentally retarded children. In J. J. Gallagher & P. M. Vietze (Eds.), *Families of handicapped persons*. Baltimore: Brookes.

Blacher, J. (Ed.). (1984). *Severely handicapped young children and their families: Research in review*. Orlando, FL: Academic Press.

Bowlby, J. (1951). *Maternal care and mental health*. Geneva, Switzerland: World Health Organization.

Bronfenbrenner, U. (1979). *The ecology of human development*. Cambridge, MA: Harvard University Press.

Bubolz, M. M., & Whiren, A. P. (1984). The family of the handicapped: An ecological model for policy and practice. *Family Relations, 33,* 5–12.

Cobb, S. (1976). Social support as a moderator of life stress. *Psychosomatic Medicine, 38,* 300–314.

Crnic, K. A., Friedrick, W. N., & Greenberg, M. T. (1983). Adaptation of families with mentally retarded children: A model of stress, coping and family ecology. *American Journal of Mental Deficiency, 88,* 125–138.

Crnic, K. A., Greenberg, M. T., Ragozin, A. S., Robinson, N. M., & Basham, R. B. (1983). Effects of stress and social support on mothers and premature and full-term infants. *Child Development, 54,* 209–217.

Darling, R. B. (1979). *Families against society: A study of reactions to children with birth defects*. Beverly Hills, CA: Sage.

Dunst, C. J. (1990). Discerning the implications and future of early intervention efficacy research. Paper presented at the "Students at Risk" seminars, University of Pittsburgh, Jan. 1990.

Duvall, E. (1957). *Family development*. Philadelphia: Lippincott.

Dyson, L. & Fewell, R. R. (1986). *Sources of stress and adaptation of parents of young handicapped children*. Unpublished manuscript, University of Washington, Seattle.

Ellis, A. (1958). Rational psychotherapy. *Journal of General Psychology, 59,* 34–49.

Farber, B. (1975). Family adaptations to severely mentally retarded children.

In M. J. Begab & S. A. Richardson (Eds.), *The mentally retarded child and society: A social science perspective.* Baltimore, MD: University Park Press.

Featherstone, H. (1980). *A difference in the family.* New York: Basic Books.

Fewell, R. (1986). A handicapped child in the family. In R. R. Fewell & P. F. Vadasy (Eds.), *Families of handicapped children* (pp. 3–34). Austin, TX: Pro-Ed.

Grossman, F. K. (1972). *Brothers and sisters of retarded children.* Syracuse, New York: Syracuse University Press.

Hartman, A. (1978). Diagramatic assessment of family relationships. *Social Casework,* Oct., pp. 465–476.

Hill, R. (1949). *Families under stress.* New York: Free Press.

Houser, R. (1987). *A comparison of stress and coping by fathers of mentally retarded and non-retarded adolescents.* Unpublished doctoral dissertation, University of Pittsburgh, Pennsylvania.

Imber-Black, E. (1988). *Families and larger systems: A family therapists guide through the labyrinth.* New York: Guilford.

Kazak, A. E., & Marvin, R. S. (1984). Differences, difficulties and adaptation: Stress and social networks in families with a handicapped child. *Family Relations, 33,* 67–77.

Kazak, A. E., & Wilcox, B. L. (1984). The structure and function of social support networks in families with handicapped children. *American Journal of Community Psychology, 12,* 645–661.

Lyon, S., & Preis, A. (1983). Working with families of severely handicapped persons. In M. Seligman (Ed.), *The family with a handicapped child* (pp. 203–232). Orlando, FL: Grune & Stratton.

Marshak, L. (1982). Group therapy with adolescents. In M. Seligman (Ed.), *Group psychotherapy and counseling with special populations* (pp. 185–213). Baltimore, MD: University Park Press.

McCubbin, H. I., & Patterson, J. M. (1981). *Systematic assessment of family stress, resources, and coping: Tools for research, education, and clinical intervention.* St. Paul: University of Minnesota, Department of Family Social Science, Family Stress and Coping Project.

McCubbin, H. I., & Patterson, J. M. (1983). The family stress process: The double ABCX model of adjustment and adaptation. *Marriage and Family Review, 6,* 7–37.

McGoldrick, M., & Gerson, R. (1985). *Genograms in family assessment.* New York: Norton.

McGoldrick, M., Pearce, J. K., & Giordano, J. (1982). *Ethnicity and family therapy.* New York: Guilford Press.

Minuchin, S. (1974). *Families and family therapy.* Cambridge, MA: Harvard University Press.

Minuchin, S. (1978). *Psychosomatic families.* Cambridge, MA: Harvard University Press.

Mitchell, D. (1983). Guidance needs and counseling of parents of mentally retarded persons. In N. N. Singh & K. M. Wilton (Eds.), *Mental retardation: Research and services in New Zealand,* Christchurch, New Zealand: Whitoculls.

Olshansky, S. (1962). Chronic sorrow: A response to having a mentally defective child. *Social Casework, 43,* 190–193.

Olson, D. H., Russell, C. S., & Sprenkle, D. H. (1980). Circumplex Model of Marital and Family Systems II: Empirical studies and clinical intervention. In J. P. Vincent (Ed.), *Advances in family intervention assessment and theory* (Vol. 1, pp. 129–179). Greenwich, CT: JAI Press.

Olson, D. H., McCubbin, H. I., Barnes, H., Larsen, A., Muxen, M., & Wilson, M. (1984). *One thousand families: A national survey.* Beverly Hills, CA: Sage.

Parke, R. D. (1981). *Fathers.* Cambridge, MA: Harvard University Press.

Patterson, J. M. (1988). Chronic illness in children and the impact on families. In Chilman, C. S., Nunally, E. W., & Cox, F. M. (Eds.) *Chronic illness and disability.* Beverly Hills: Sage, pp. 69–107.

Schorr-Ribera, H. K. (1987). *Ethnicity and culture as relevant rehabilitation factors in families with children with disabilities.* Comprehensive paper. University of Pittsburgh.

Seligman, M. (1979). *Strategies for helping parents of exceptional children: A guide for teachers.* New York: Free Press.

Seligman, M. (Ed.). (1983). *The family with a handicapped child: Understanding and treatment.* Orlando, FL: Grune & Straton.

Seligman, M. (1985). Handicapped children and their families. *Journal of Counseling and Development, 64,* 274–277.

Turk, D. C. & Kerns, R. D. (1985). *Health, illness and families: A life-span perspective.* New York: Wiley.

Turnbull, A. P., Summers, J. A., & Brotherson, M. J. (1986). Family life cycle: Theoretical and empirical implications and future directions for families with mentally retarded members. In J. J. Gallagher & P. M. Vietze (Eds.), *Families of handicapped persons.* Baltimore, MD: Brookes.

Turnbull, A. P., & Turnbull, H. R. (1986). *Families, professionals, and exceptionality.* Columbus, OH: Merrill.

Von Bertalanffy, L. (1968). *General systems theory.* New York: George Braziller.

Wikler, L. (1981). Chronic stresses of families of mentally retarded children. *Family Relations, 30,* 281–288.

CHAPTER THREE

Initial and Continuing Adaptation to the Birth of a Disabled Child

Rosalyn Benjamin Darling

Rosalyn Benjamin Darling, Ph.D., is Director of Beginning Early Intervention Services in Johnstown, Pennsylvania, and is an adjunct faculty member at the University of Pittsburgh at Johnstown, where she teaches courses in medical sociology and the sociology of disability. She is also the immediate past president of the Early Intervention Providers Association of Pennsylvania.

Dr. Darling is the author of three books, Ordinary Families, Special Children: A Systems Approach to Childhood Disability *(with Milton Seligman),* Children Who Are Different: Meeting the Challenges of Birth Defects in Society *(with husband, Jon), and* Families Against Society: A Study of Reactions to Children with Birth Defects, *as well as various articles and chapters on sociological aspects of disabling conditions in children.*

The father of a disabled child wrote,

> No event in your entire babyhood could rival the despair of its first day. That, in itself, is consolation for parents who find out the worst right at the start. There is no lower depression than the day of being told (Abraham, 1958, p. 64).

Various writers have suggested that certain crisis periods are especially traumatic for parents of children with disabilities (e.g., MacKeith, 1973), including when parents first learn or suspect that their child has a disability, when a child with a disability enters school or is ready to leave school, and when parents become older and worry about their child's welfare. This chapter reviews some popular theories about family reactions to news of a child's disability and adaptations during the childhood years. In addition, a model of family reactions using an interactionist perspective is suggested.

APPROACHES TO UNDERSTANDING FAMILY REACTIONS

Stage Theory

Many writers have suggested that parents pass through a series of stages before they accept a diagnosis of disability in their child. Blacher (1984) listed 24 studies that present some variant of stage theory as part of their conclusions about parent reactions. Many writers have suggested a similarity between the sequence of stages in the acceptance of death and dying and the sequence found in parents of children with disabilities. Solnit and Stark (1961) argued that parents must mourn the loss of their wished-for normal child before they can accept their disabled child.

In a typical study concluding with a stage model, Drotar, Baskiewicz, Irvin, Kennell, and Klaus (1975) looked at the parents of 20 children with congenital malformations and found a common sequence of reactions:

- Shock. Most parents' initial reaction to their child's diagnosis was overwhelming shock because they had anticipated a normal baby.
- Denial. Parents tried to escape from their shock by disbelieving the diagnosis.
- Sadness, Anger, Anxiety. The most common reaction was intense sadness, which accompanied or followed denial.
- Adaptation. Eventually, intense feelings subsided, and parents were able to care for their children.

- Reorganization. Positive, long-term acceptance finally developed. Guilt also tended to lessen with time.

Chronic Sorrow and Nonsequential "Stage" Theories

A number of studies (see, e.g., Wikler, Wasow, & Hatfield, 1981) have suggested that, although the reactions described by the stage theorists may be present in parents of disabled children, these reactions are not necessarily experienced sequentially. The reactions may, in fact, occur repeatedly, precipitated by various life crises and turning points.

Olshansky (1962) argued that parents of mentally retarded children do not ever completely abandon the grief process. Rather, he suggested, that the *normal* reaction to the birth of a child with a disability is *chronic sorrow:*

> The permanent, day-by-day dependence of the child, the interminable frustrations resulting from the child's relative changelessness, the unesthetic quality of mental defectiveness, the deep symbolism buried in the process of giving birth to a defective child, all these join together to produce the parent's chronic sorrow (p. 192).

In this view, chronic sorrow is a natural reaction, and its continued presence many years after a child's birth is not pathological. In fact, chronic sorrow and acceptance of a child's disability may coexist as part of the normal, long-term process of parental adjustment.

"Kinds of Families/Kinds of Children" Theories

"Kinds of families/kinds of children" theorists do not necessarily reject stage theory or any of its variants. Rather, they suggest that whether a family will pass through certain stages or have specific reactions will vary according to a number of factors:

(a)   socioeconomic status,

(b)   support services (or lack of them),

(c)   physician attitude,

(d)   presence of other children and spouse in the home,

(e)   prior information,

(f)   availability of support persons in the community,

(g)   single- versus two-parent homes,

(h)   religiosity,

(i)   previous births of nondisabled children, and

(j)   actual physical appearance of the child.

In addition, Schell and Marion (reported in Mori, 1983) included the severity and social acceptability of the child's disability. Mori (1983) added the manner in which parents are informed of the diagnosis, the age of onset or age of the child when the diagnosis is made, and the sex of the parent involved. Other factors, noted by Collins-Moore (1984), include

(a)   general emotional maturity of the parent,

(b)   cultural attitudes,

(c)   education,

(d)   parent's age,

(e)   birth order,

(f)   child's sex,

(g)   child's ability to respond to the parent,

(h)   etiology of the disability, and

(i)   prognosis.

Because of the great diversity among families, no single reaction or sequence of reactions can be found in all parents of children with disabilities. In addition to predisposing characteristics that shape parental reactions, situational contingencies play an important role in parental response. These contingencies are discussed in the next section.

Interactionist Perspective

The symbolic interactionist view of human behavior focuses on social process rather than on static characteristics of individuals such as sex, ethnicity, or personality type. When applied to families of children with disabilities, parental reactions can be interpreted within the context of the parents' interactional histories prior to their child's birth and their experiences afterward. Parents attach meanings to their experiences as a result of definitions they have encountered in their interactions with others.

Not all interactions are equally important. Among the most important are those with *significant others,* usually close family members and friends. When significant others define the parents' situation positively, parents are likely to define it positively as well. The effects of interactions with significant others, along with the broader interactional context, is explored in the next section.

AN INTERACTIONIST APPROACH TO UNDERSTANDING PARENTS' INITIAL REACTIONS

The Prenatal Period

Prior Knowledge About Disability   Prior to their child's birth, most parents have had only limited experience with individuals with disabilities. In general, they have been exposed primarily to the stereotypes and stigmatizing attitudes toward the disabled that pervade our culture. Richardson (1970) and others have shown that almost all groups in the population have negative attitudes toward the physically disabled, and Gottlieb (1975) and others have shown that the mentally disabled are also negatively labeled in our society. During the prenatal period, then, most parents dread the possibility of giving birth to a disabled child. As one mother of a Down syndrome child said, "I remember thinking, before I got married, it would be the worst thing that could ever happen to me" (Darling, 1979, p. 124).

When parents express concerns about the health of their unborn child, these concerns are usually discounted by friends, relatives, and others. Even a mother who had *four* children with the same genetic disorder managed to rationalize her fears during each successive pregnancy with the help of physicians who assured her that her bad luck was not likely to recur. With regard to her third pregnancy, she said, "I was unrealistic. I said, 'He's going to be a Christmas baby. There won't be anything wrong with him' " (Darling, 1979, p. 143). In general, then, parents' fears about the health of their unborn baby are usually neutralized through interactions with others, and most approach the birth situation anticipating a healthy child.

Most parents, then, are poorly prepared for the birth of a child with a disability. In some cases, parents are not even aware of the existence of their child's disability prior to the baby's birth. As one parent said, "I never heard of Down's . . . Mental retardation wasn't something you talked about in the house . . . There wasn't much exposure" (Darling, 1979, p. 124). In other cases, parents can recall having heard of a defect, but only in a limited, and typically negative, way: "I'd heard of it from a book. It was just a terrible picture on a certain page of an abnormal psych book that I can still sort of picture" (Darling, 1979, p. 125).

With the advent of modern technology, some childhood disabilities are being diagnosed prenatally. Through techniques such as amniocentesis, ultrasound, and maternal serum testing, parents are able to learn of problems prior to their child's birth. In cases of prenatal diagnosis, anticipatory grieving may be tempered by the hope that "maybe they made a mistake," and the baby will be all right after all. One mother, who was told after an ultrasound screening late in her pregnancy that her baby had hydrocephalus, said she was "shocked, sad, and depressed" after hearing the news but "hoped they were wrong" at the same time (Darling & Darling, 1982, p. 98). After she saw the baby's enlarged head in the delivery room, she no longer doubted the diagnosis.

Pregnancy as a Social Role: Expectations and Dreams   Attitudes toward pregnancy and birth vary among cultures and subcultures. In a culture in which familism is highly valued, as in some Italian-Americans, for example, pregnancy is also likely to be highly valued, and the pregnant woman is likely to occupy an esteemed status. In other cultural contexts, such as that segment of the urban American middle class in which one-child or two-child families are the norm, some pregnancies may even be disvalued. Certainly, whether a pregnancy is planned or unplanned, whether the parents are married or not, and other circumstances surrounding the pregnancy and birth situations will shape parental reactions, regardless of whether the child is born with a disability.

Expectant parents typically fantasize about their unborn baby. They may imagine the baby's sex, appearance, personality, or other attributes. Interactions with friends and relatives help to shape parents' fantasies. Folk wisdom sometimes plays a role when the pregnant woman's shape or size or the baby's prenatal movements are interpreted as indicative of the child's sex, size, or temperament.

Parents enter the birth situation, then, with a particular base of knowledge, attitudes, expectations, and hopes. They possess varying degrees of knowledge about disabilities, various attitudes toward people with disabilities and toward their status as expectant parents, differing expectations about the birth situation, parenthood, and the attributes of their unborn child, as well as hopes and wishes relating to those attributes.

The Birth Situation

A number of studies (see, e.g., Doering, Entwisle, & Quinlan, 1980; Norr, Block, Charles, Meyering, & Meyers, 1977) have suggested that parents who have taken childbirth classes are more likely to define the birth situation in a positive manner. The more prepared that parents are, the more likely it is that they will be aware of deviations in routine that might occur in the delivery room in the case of the birth of a baby with a problem.

Typically, concerns about a baby are not revealed directly to parents in the delivery room. Rather, parents become suspicious as a result of unintentional clues given by physicians and nurses. D'Arcy (1968) and Walker (1971) noted that clues include such things as "the look on the nurse's face," consultations between nurses in hushed voices, and nurses who "looked at each other and pointed at something."

In rarer cases, the clues are not so subtle:

> When the baby was born, they said, "Oh my God, put her out." That's the first thing they said, "Oh my God, put her out" . . . and the next thing I remember was waking up in the recovery room . . . I had my priest on my left hand and my pediatrician on my right hand . . . and they were trying to get me to sign a piece of paper. . . . I just couldn't believe that this was happening to me and I said to my priest, "Father, what's the matter?" and he said, "You have to sign this release. Your daughter is very sick," and I said to the pediatrician, "What's the matter with her?" and he said . . . she had something that was too much to talk about, that I shouldn't worry myself . . . Nobody was telling me what this was. . . . I was very depressed. (Darling, 1979, p. 130)

Parental reactions in the immediate postpartum situation, then, may be best characterized by the sociological concept of *anomie* or normlessness. Because even prepared parents are unable to make sense of atypical events in the delivery room, the birth experience is stressful for almost all parents of children whose disabilities can be detected immediately by medical personnel. McHugh (1968) showed that the components of anomie are *meaninglessness* and *powerlessness,* and both are commonly experienced by parents of disabled newborns.

The Postpartum Period

The Establishment of Parent-Child Bonding As many studies have shown, parents' initial reaction to the news that their child has a disability is likely to be negative. Rejection of the baby during the early postpartum period is common, as these statements illustrate,

> I was kind of turned off. I didn't want to go near her. It was like she had a disease or something, and I didn't want to catch it. I didn't want to touch her (Mother of a child with Down syndrome).
> ***
> I saw her for the first time when she was 10 days old. . . . She was much more deformed than I had been told. At the time, I thought, "Oh my God, what have I done?" (Mother of a child with spina bifida) (Darling, 1979, pp. 135, 136).

Even when a baby has no disability, however, bonding between parent and child is not always immediate. LeMasters (1957) found that most of the parents of normal infants in his study had little effective preparation for parental roles and had romanticized views of parenthood. Similarly, Dyer (1963) noted that 80 percent of the parents he studied "admitted that things were not as they expected them after the child was born" (p. 200).

With any baby, disabled or not, bonding grows out of the process of parent-child interaction. When babies respond to parental attempts to feed and cuddle them, parents feel rewarded. Bonding is further enhanced when babies begin smiling and making sounds in response to parental gestures. Infants with disabilities, however, may not be able to respond to their parents' efforts.

Bailey and Wolery (1984), Blacher (1984b), Collins-Moore (1984), Robson and Moss (1970), Waechter (1977), and others have suggested that the following characteristics of some childhood disabilities may impede the formation of parent-child attachment:

(a) the child's appearance, especially facial disfigurement,
(b) negative response to being handled (stiffening, tenseness, limpness, lack of responsiveness),
(c) unpleasant crying,
(d) atypical activity level — either lowered activity or hyperactivity,
(e) high threshold for arousal,
(f) no response to communication,
(g) delayed smiling,
(h) feeding difficulties,
(i) medical fragility,
(j) presence of medical equipment, such as feeding tubes or oxygen supplies,
(k) life-threatening conditions,
(l) prolonged hospitalization and consequent separation,
(m) impaired ability to vocalize,
(n) inability to maintain eye contact, and
(o) unpleasant behaviors, such as frequent seizures.

Abnormal response patterns in infants may result in withdrawal by parents. As Stone and Chesney (1978, p. 11) wrote, "The failure of the handicapped infant to stimulate the mother leads to failure of the mother to interact with the infant."

The tremendous adaptive capacity of families is evidenced by the fact that, given all of the obstacles to parent-child bonding present in the case of childhood disability, the vast majority of parents *do* form strong attachments to their disabled infants. In general, all but the most severely disabled children are able to respond to their parents to some extent, by sound, gesture, or other indication of recognition. In addition, bonding is usually encouraged by supportive interactions with other people.

The mother of the Down syndrome infant quoted earlier explained,

> I talked to a nurse and then I felt less resentment. I said I was afraid, and she helped me feed the baby. . . . Then my girlfriend came to see me. She had just lost her husband, and we sort of supported each other. . . .By the time she came home I loved her. When I held her the first time I felt love and I worried if she'd live (Darling, 1979, p. 136).

Similarly, the mother of the child with spina bifida reported,

> As time goes on, you fall in love. You think, "This kid's mine, and nobody's gonna take her away from me." I think by the time she was two weeks old I wasn't appalled by her anymore (Darling, 1979, p. 136).

Various situational contingencies may also affect bonding. As Waechter (1977) and others have noted, the timing of the baby's birth in relation to other family events is important. Another member of the family may be ill, the family may be experiencing financial difficulties, or the parents may be having marital problems. The amount of time and energy available to parents for the new baby will depend on these contingencies. Professionals need to be aware of a family's situation when they look at parenting practices and parent-child relationships so that expectations are not unrealistic.

The Case of Delayed Diagnosis   Not all disabilities are diagnosed in the immediate postpartum period. Some developmental disabilities such as cerebral palsy or mental retardation may not be readily apparent shortly after birth. Other disabilities occur as a result of accidents or illness later in infancy or childhood. In still other cases, professionals delay communicating a known diagnosis to parents for a variety of reasons. (These reasons are discussed in greater detail in Chapter 5, "Parent-Professional Interaction: The Roots of Misunderstanding.") In general, parents have said that they were better able to adjust when they were aware of their child's diagnosis from the beginning.

Most of the time, parents suspect that a problem exists before they receive a diagnosis, and diagnostic delay only protracts the period of suspicion and its attendant stress. In such cases, parents tend to be relieved rather than shocked when they finally receive a diagnosis. This reaction is apparent in these families of mentally retarded children quoted by Dickman and Gordon (1985, pp. 31, 32):

> When the doctor told us, he couldn't believe how well we accepted the diagnosis. All I can say is that it was such a relief to have someone finally just come out and say what we had feared for so long! We felt that now we could move ahead and do the best we could for Timmy.
>
> ***
>
> When James turned six months old, my husband and I decided to change pediatricians. The second doctor was an angel in disguise. She spotted the problem immediately. . . . The reason I called her an angel was that she finally put an end to the unknown. The not knowing exactly what was wrong was driving me crazy.

The Post-Diagnosis Experience

Although a diagnosis may relieve the stress associated with meaninglessness, parents generally continue to experience anomie to some extent until issues surrounding prognosis have been resolved and until the child is enrolled in a treatment program.

The Need for Prognostic Information   A father who had been told that his son would be "a slow learner" expressed the following concerns:

> [I was most worried about] how he would develop. It was the uncertainty of not knowing whether he'd be able to go to school and get a job or whether he'd always be dependent on us. It was just not knowing what was likely to happen and what the future held for him and for us (Baxter, 1986, p. 85).

When parents receive only a diagnostic label or limited information from professionals, they generally continue to wonder — and worry — about what their child will be like in the future. Most parents are especially concerned about whether the child will be able to walk and talk, go to school, or play normal adult occupational and marital roles. Baxter (1986) noted that the basic underlying factor in all expressions of parental worry is uncertainty. Parents of disabled children experience an ongoing need for information about the meaning of their child's condition — a need that professionals must meet. The parents in Baxter's study indicated that the most important type of help they had received from professionals was *information,* and that this help was more important than sympathy and emotional support.

The Quest for Treatment   In addition to providing information, professionals are also able to provide therapeutic intervention that will minimize the effects of a child's disability. Once they learn that their child has a disability, virtually all parents are eager to begin a program of treatment.

When they receive diagnostic information, parents are relieved of the stress of meaninglessness; until they begin to *do* something about their child's condition, however, they may continue to experience anomie in the form of powerlessness.

As early intervention programs have become more widespread and publicity about them has increased, parents' quests for services have become shorter. Yet, most continue to search until they are satisfied with their children's medical care and have secured needed services such as physical therapy or special stimulation programs. The extent of parents' quests for services will be based on the resources available to them. Most families have geographical and financial limitations that prevent them from searching endlessly for the best program for their child. Competing needs, such as the welfare of other children at home, may also prevent parents from enrolling their child in a time-consuming program or one far from home.

The Need for Emotional Support   One mother said,

> I met other parents of the retarded after we moved here. I felt that made the biggest difference in my life. . . . Down there [where we lived before], with my husband working so much and no other families with retarded children, I felt that I was just singled out for something, that I was weird. I felt a lot of isolation and bitterness (Darling, 1979, pp. 162–163).

The parental need that professionals are probably least able to fill is the need for social support. The importance of social support in alleviating stress in families with disabled children has been well documented (see, e.g., Dyson & Fewell, 1986; Trivette & Dunst, in press). Trivette and Dunst recently showed that parents' personal well-being, perceptions of child functioning, and family integration were positively influenced by a family's informal social support network. They concluded that "the negative consequences often associated with the birth and rearing of a child with developmental problems can be lessened or even alleviated to the extent that the members of a family's informal support network are mobilized to strengthen personal and familial well-being and buffer negative effects." In some cases the birth of a disabled child creates a rift in a family's relationship with former friends and family members. In other cases, even though friends and family are supportive, parents still need the special kind of support offered by others with children like their own.

Support Within the Family and Other Existing Networks.   One of the most difficult tasks facing new parents of children with disabilities is telling other family members and friends about their child's problem for the first time. Many have said that they "just didn't want to explain." In some cases, parents are afraid of upsetting elderly relatives or family members who are pregnant.

Receiving the support of family members may be more important among rural and small-town families, where extended family members tend to live in close proximity and serve as significant others for one another. Heller, Quesada, Harvey, and Warner (1981) found, for example, that among families living in the Blue Ridge Mountains of Virginia, the identities of nuclear and extended families were fused. Kin were the major source of social support, and involvement with relatives was obligatory. Urban middle-American families, on the other hand, were more primary-kin oriented, and the opinions of extended family members were not as important to them.

Support Groups.   When friends and family react negatively, parents must look elsewhere for support. Even when members of existing social networks try to be helpful, parents may still feel that they do not *really* understand the parents' situation. Meeting other parents of disabled children thus becomes very important to many parents after they learn about their child's disability.

Support groups composed of parents of disabled children and disabled adults serve a number of functions including

(a)   alleviating loneliness and isolation,
(b)   providing information,
(c)   providing role models, and
(d)   providing a basis for comparison.

As the mother quoted earlier said, before she became involved with a support group, she felt as though she was "singled out for something." Another mother said, "I was in a once-a-week mothers' group, and it was very helpful. You find out you're not the only person with this problem" (Darling, 1979, p. 161).

When they meet other families, parents discover not only those who are coping successfully, but also those whose children's problems are worse than theirs. Most develop a greater appreciation of their own situation as a result:

> You don't feel sorry for yourself when you see some children that are just vegetables.

***

> We went to a couples' group where we saw that other children were a lot
> worse than Peter (Darling, 1979, p. 161).

Providing support is important during infancy. Suelzle and Keenan (1981) found, however, that reliance on personal support networks tended to decline over the life cycle, as did "rap sessions" with other parents. Parents tend to become involved in more normalized routines as their children grow out of infancy, and interests shift from involvement in segregated peer groups to immersion in the more integrated structures of the larger society.

Interactions with Strangers   After they have told friends and family members about their child's problem, parents must deal with encountering strangers on the street, in restaurants, and in shopping malls. Most parents have said that taking their child out in public was very difficult for them at the beginning. These reports illustrate the difficulty:

> We took her to a store downtown, and she had a hat. . . . I wanted to
> make sure that hat would stay on so no one would see her ears. . . . We
> didn't want people to look at her. We didn't want to explain.
>
> ***
>
> I used to go to the laundromat . . . and so many people would say,
> "Your little girl is *so* good to sit there so quietly in the stroller." . . . I
> would just like, sit there, and my insides were like knots, and I would
> think, "Oh no, do I have to tell them about the cerebral palsy? Should I
> or shouldn't I? Should I just let it pass?. . ." All this is going through
> my mind. . . . I never told anybody (Darling, 1979, pp. 155, 156).

Eventually, most parents become more comfortable explaining to strangers about their children's disabilities. Professionals can help them develop explanations they can use in these situations; support groups can also be helpful in that parents can share the explanations they have used.

Leaving Infancy: Moving Toward Normalization

Parents' reactions to the news that their child has a disability, then, will vary according to their interactions with other people—before, during, and after the time that the news is received. The meanings they attach to their child's disability will continue to change as the child grows and they encounter new interaction situations.

The ability of an individual to cope with any situation depends on that person's definition of the situation. Defining the situation is one of the most difficult tasks facing new parents because of the degree of meaninglessness and powerlessness usually present. Because the birth of a child with a disability is generally an unanticipated event, parents must rely on other people to establish meaning for them. Professionals play an important role by providing parents with diagnostic, prognostic, and treatment information.

NORMALIZATION: THE GOAL OF THE CHILDHOOD YEARS

By the end of the infancy period, the resolution of anomie is complete for most families. As their children move through the preschool years, parents generally try to resume activities that were disrupted by their child's birth and the period of anomie that followed. The mother who has left a job may wish to return to work; the parents may resume social activities; the family may want to take a vacation or pursue other recreational activities.

Parents are encouraged to maintain a "normal-appearing round of life" (Birenbaum, 1970, 1971) by other parents, friends, and professionals. Voysey (1975) argued that parents have a normality perspective because they are *expected* to be normal by other agencies in society: Parents' associations, magazine articles, clergy, and various helping professionals. These agencies help parents rationalize their situation and teach them that they are *supposed* to be "coping splendidly" with their child's disability.

Although the components of normalization vary by social class and other subcultural factors, in general, a normalized lifestyle for families with school-aged children in American society includes the following components: (a) employment for either or both parents, (b) appropriate educational placement for children, (c) access to appropriate medical care, (d) adequate housing, (e) social relationships with family and friends, (f) leisure time, (g) freedom of movement in public places, and (h) sufficient financial resources to maintain a basic lifestyle. The presence of a child with a disability in the home can prevent a family from attaining any or all of these components.

The ability of families to achieve a normalized lifestyle will often be determined by their opportunity structure, that is, their access to resources. Society provides a variety of resources, ranging from financial aid to respite care for disabled children. These resources are not equally distributed in the population, however, and for many families, life is a constant struggle. Regardless of the nature of a child's disability or of the personality or coping ability of the parents, the most important determinant of normalization for most families of disabled children will be the availability of supportive resources in the community.

OBSTACLES TO NORMALIZATION

In a study of 330 parents of retarded children, Suelzle and Keenan (1981) found that perceptions of unmet needs varied over the life cycle. Perceived needs for family support, respite care, and counseling services were highest among parents of preschoolers and young adults and lowest among parents of school-aged children. In general, as children grow older, parents' primary concern seems to shift from coping difficulties to more practical concerns. These include additional financial hardships; stigma; extraordinary demands on time; difficulties in caregiver tasks such as feeding; diminished time for sleeping; social isolation; less time for recreational pursuits; difficulties managing behavior; and difficulties performing routine household chores (Moroney, reported in Mori, 1983). A discussion of these and other problems, which serve as barriers to normalization, follows.

Continuing Medical Needs

Children with disabilities generally require more specialized medical care and more frequent hospitalizations than do other children. In addition, these children may need medically-related services, such as physical, occupational and speech therapy. The availability of these services varies from one geographic location to another. Butler, Rosenbaum, and Palfrey (1987) wrote that "where a child lives has become more than ever a predictor of the affordability and accessibility of care" (p. 163). Furthermore, their study showed that use of health care services was related to access and ability to pay: "Even for the most severely impaired group, the likelihood of seeing a physician was 3.5 times higher if the child had insurance coverage."

Even in areas where health care is readily available, parents may have difficulty locating a physician who is interested in treating children with disabilities. Pediatricians especially tend to prefer treating nondisabled children with acute, curable diseases (Darling, 1979). As a result, parents of children with disabilities may engage in lengthy searches before they find a physician with whom they are satisfied. As one disgruntled father of a severely disabled youngster commented, "It's like when you take your dog to the vet. . . . Not many doctors pick him up and try to communicate with him as a child" (Darling, 1979, p. 151). Eventually, most parents do obtain satisfactory health care for their child.

Special Educational Needs

Although the quest for medical services may become less of a priority as children approach school age, the search for appropriate educational programs often becomes more important at that time.

Preschool Education   For the disabled child, formal education may begin shortly after birth. With the proliferation of early intervention programs in recent years, many children have begun receiving services soon after they are diagnosed. These programs may be either home-based or center-based, although the best programs almost always involve parents as teachers for their own children. Some programs include specialists such as physical or speech therapists in addition to specially trained teachers.

In some cases, however, parents do not discover early intervention programs until well into their children's preschool years. As one mother said,

> [The doctor] said, "Just take him home and love him." . . . I wondered, "Isn't there anything more?" . . . When he was 2 and a half, I read in the newspaper about a preschool program for retarded children (Darling & Darling, 1982, p. 133).

Some parents engage in extensive searches to find a preschool program that is appropriate for their child.

Generally, by the end of the preschool years, parents have found a satisfactory program for their children. However, concerns about the quality of available educational programs are likely to arise again when children reach school age. Parents of nondisabled children may take for granted the fact that the school system will provide an appropriate education for their children; parents of children with special needs who have similar assumptions often learn that local programs do not meet those needs.

The School Years   Prior to the passage of Public Law 94–142 in 1975, guidelines for the education of children with disabilities were vague, and parents' rights were not clearly stated. Because of the difficulties they had in obtaining an appropriate education for their children, many parents of teenage and young adult children now feel bitter and resentful toward the school system and, in some cases, even toward parents of younger children who have benefited from more recent legislation and programs.

Special education legislation of the 1970s and 1980s (P.L. 94–142, P.L. 98–199, and P.L. 99–457) mandated that children with disabilities receive a free and appropriate public education in the "least restrictive environment." However, for a number of reasons, including ignorance, fear, and the limited resources of school districts, the promise of the legislation has not been realized for many children. Because of poor knowledge about their legal rights, many parents have not challenged their children's educational placements. Public awareness has been growing, however, and more and more parents are questioning educators about their children's programs.

Parents may challenge their children's educational plans for a variety of reasons. One common complaint involves placement in an inappropriate setting. Parents may wish to have their child placed in an integrated setting rather than in a special school or classroom; in other cases, they want more special programming for their children. The former case is illustrated by this experience, related by the mother of a child with spina bifida:

> When Ellen entered kindergarten, she was in a special needs class in the morning and mainstreamed in the afternoon. . . . [In the special needs class], she was with children whose needs were much more demanding than Ellen's. . . . Some were retarded. . . . At the end of the year we had a meeting. The first grade was on the second floor . . .[Ellen was in a wheelchair]. They said we should keep her in the special needs class. I was furious. . . . She had done so well in the mainstreaming class. . . . I wanted her in a regular first grade and I suggested moving the class downstairs. . . . They wanted Ellen in the special needs class because it was easier for *them,* not for any other reason (Darling & Darling, 1982, p. 140).

Behavior Problems

Baxter (1986) found, in a study of families with retarded children, that the major stressors associated with the care and management of the child were behavior-management problems and the child's continued dependence. The first stressor will be discussed here, and the second in the next section.

Baxter found that although concern about the child's physical needs tended to decrease with the age of the child, worry about the child's behavior in public increased over time. Behavior-management problems commonly occur in conjunction with disabilities such as mental retardation. The following description of a deaf-blind child illustrated some of the forms that these problems take:

> When he gets off the bus Friday afternoon after a week at the residential school for the blind, he lies on the sidewalk kicking and screaming while his mother runs frantically to and from the house with various foods which might appease his anger. Over the weekend no one in the household is permitted to make program selections on the television because Johnny takes charge of the dial. Most of the night the family lies awake to the sound of ear-piercing screams, and the hours of quiet when they at last lapse into grateful sleep bring the morning rewards of ransacked kitchen shelves and mutilated books (Klein, 1977, p. 310).

Such nonnormative, disruptive behavior may limit the family's opportunities for social participation.

Baxter (1986) found that certain social situations produced considerable stress:

(a)   formal social occasions when the child does not conform to norms,

(b)   other persons' homes where coping with the child's behavior is difficult,

(c)   public settings where behavior management is a problem,

(d)   restrictive settings that do not readily allow parents to withdraw from the situation, and

(e)   social situations where the child engages in deviant forms of interaction with other people.

Parents feel stress when their child's behavior calls attention to the family. Although most try to explain the child's disability to friends or strangers, some simply control their feelings and say nothing or move away from the distressing encounter. Birenbaum (1970) showed that some parents may try to hide their children's behavior problems by cleaning the house before guests arrive or by controlling the interaction setting in other ways.

Although the extent of a child's behavior problems may be related to the nature of the child's disability, even families with severely involved children may be able to achieve some degree of normalization if they have adequate social support. Bristol and Schopler (1984) showed that, in the case of autistic children, family adaptation is more closely related to perceived adequacy of informal support than to the severity of the child's disability, and families without support may suffer considerable social isolation as a result of their child's behavior. Baxter (1986) showed, too, that small families tend to experience greater stress in care and management than do larger families.

Continuing Dependence

As nondisabled childen grow older they become less dependent on their parents. By the end of the preschool years, they are able to feed and dress themselves and take care of their toileting needs. Later, they become able to go about the neighborhood without supervision, and eventually, they can stay home alone, without the need for babysitters. Demands on parents' time thus decrease. Disabilities may limit the ability of children to achieve such increasing independence, however.

Even families with highly dependent children can achieve normalization if they have access to good support services such as low-cost, specially trained babysitters or respite care. A special camp in Arkansas, for example, cares for school-aged children with disabilities 48 weekends a year in order to provide relief for families.

> Julie Mills, a severely mentally handicapped 10-year-old with a speech impairment, attends the camp.
>
> "It allows us to be together the whole weekend, to go shopping at our will or just sit around and watch television," Julie's mother, Sherry Mills, said of time alone with her husband, Carl. "We become a little closer, get to know each other. It's almost like a date."
>
> Susan and Mike Walker send their 7-year-old daughter Rachel to the camp so they can spend time with their 9-year-old daughter Dawn.
>
> Rachel suffers from seizure disorders and mental and physical disabilities, Mrs. Walker said, and caring for her can deprive Dawn of attention ("Camp Cares for Handicapped Kids," 1986).

When such resources are not available, maintaining a normalized lifestyle can be difficult.

Financial Burden

Childhood disabilities have an economic impact on families in addition to their psychosocial "costs." This impact includes both direct costs, such as expenses for child care, medical care, therapy, and special equipment, and indirect costs, such as lost work time, special residential needs, and interference with career advancement.

Direct Costs   In a nationwide survey of 1,709 families with physically disabled children, Harbaugh (1984) found that the largest single out-of-popcket expense was for babysitting. This finding is not surprising, considering the continued dependence of children with disabilities (discussed in the last section). However, because of the costs involved, some parents of disabled children may actually use babysitters less than do parents of non-disabled children, even though their needs are greater.

Physician visits, hospitalizations, and other medically-related services are also expensive for these families, especially when they are not covered by private health insurance or Medical Assistance (Medicaid). In one study (Butler et al., 1987), only 22 percent of privately insured disabled children had all their visits to physicians paid by their insurance plans. Another study (Select Committee on Children, Youth and Families reported in Morris, 1987) estimated that 10.3 percent of disabled children and 19.5 percent of disabled children in poverty have no health insurance. In addition, 40 percent of all disabled children below the federal poverty level are not covered by Medicaid.

Although medically-related costs will vary by disability, two recent studies found medically-related total expense cost of raising a child of this nature to age 18 was over $100,000. In a study of families of spina bifida children, the total cost of medical care and equipment from birth to age 18 was $108,000 to $192,000 in 1982 dollars (Lipscomb, Kolimaga, Sperduto, Minnich, & Fontenot, 1983). Similarly, a study of families of children with cerebral palsy (Morris, 1987) found an average cost of $126,631 for disability-related expenses over the same time period.

Other Direct Costs   A child's disability may also require housing or vehicle modifications, such as ramps, lifts, or widened doorways to accommodate a wheelchair. Klein (1977) noted, too, that a family often needs items such as locks for cabinets and bars for windows in the case of deaf-blind children. Additional items are noted by the father of four teenagers with a cerebral-palsy-like syndrome:

> Our kids have a phone. It's essential. Other kids can go out and play. We can't afford it but we have it. . . . We also can't afford the swimming pool, but water's the best therapy. . . . Where else can they go and swim almost every day in the summer? The city don't have it, so I have it (Darling, 1979, p. 180).

Indirect Costs   Other hidden, costs are sometimes also associated with childhood disability. Because these children require access to services and greater commitments of their parents' time than do other children, the family's overall economic situation may be adversely affected.

Some parents may reject opportunities for career advancement, because services for their children may not be as good in a new location. The amount of parents' time required by a child's special needs may also interfere with career advancement or a parent's having a job at all. Lipscomb et al. (1983) found that the average weekly work reduction among parents of children with spina bifida was 5 hours for fathers and 14 hours for mothers. In 1982 dollars, the resulting average annual income loss for these families ranged from $8,000 to $17,000.

Stigma and its Consequences

As children get older, their disabilities generally become more visible and, thus, more stigmatizing. Baxter (1986) found that the attribute most likely to attract attention to a disabled child was speech, rather than appearance or behavior. Parental stress was also related to the quality of their child's speech. In order to prevent stigma-producing encounters, then, families may have to structure their lives to avoid social situations that would require their children to speak or perform roles that would otherwise call attention to their disabilities. Lifestyles may be limited as a result.

Physical Barriers

A final obstacle to normalization involves physical barriers in the environment. Individuals with disabilities and their families may be prevented from full social participation because of stairs, narrow doorways, and hilly terrain. Our society is structured, both socially and physically, to meet the needs of the nondisabled. Although accessibility has been increasing in recent years, families with disabled children are still limited in their housing choices, vacation destinations, and general freedom of movement.

CATALYSTS TO NORMALIZATION

The strength of families is demonstrated by the fact that, given the many obstacles that exist, most are still able to achieve a close-to-normal lifestyle; normalization is in fact the most common mode of adaptation found among families of children with disabilities in our society. Achievement of a normalized lifestyle is related less to the degree of a child's disability or parents' coping abilities than to the *opportunity structure* within which the family resides.

Opportunity Structures

All families do not have equal access to opportunities for normalization. These opportunities include

(a)   access to satisfactory medical care and medically-related services,

(b)   availability of appropriate educational programs,

(c)   supportive relatives and friends,

(d)   access to respite care and day care if needed,

(e)   adequacy of financial resources,

(f)   presence of accepting neighbors,

(g)   quantity and quality of household help,

(h)   access to behavior-management programs if needed,

(i)   availability of appropriate recreational programs,

(j)   access to special equipment if needed,

(k)   presence of friends and social opportunities for the disabled child, and

(l)   adequacy of available transportation.

Families' opportunity structures can be changed. Such changes may occur when a family moves to a new neighborhood or encounters a helpful professional. Opportunity structures are also changed by new laws and court decisions and through parental activism and disability rights movements. Professionals can play an important role in working with families to change their access to existing opportunities and to create opportunities where none exists.

Changes in Support Networks

As noted earlier, parents commonly become immersed in support groups of others like themselves when their children are young and newly diagnosed. Continued immersion in such homogeneous groups can eventually become an obstacle to normalization, however. As a result, parents often decrease their involvement in segregated support networks as their children get older.

Parents may also decrease their involvement with other families of the disabled by encouraging their children's friendships with nondisabled children in the neighborhood or at school. As one mother of a child with spina bifida explained, her daughter has some friends at "myelo" clinic but she does not see them elsewhere. "They live too far away," and the mother will not go out of her way because she wants her daughter to be "as normal as possible" (Darling, 1979, p. 193). Although parents may choose to become integrated into "normal" society, their success will depend on their opportunity structures — "normal" society must accept them.

Placement Out of the Home: A Form of Normalization

In writing about families of severely retarded children, Farber (1975) described a "principle of minimal adaptation." He argued that families disrupt their patterns of living as little as possible to adjust to a problem situation and that parents who have difficulty living with a severely retarded child move through a progression of minimal adaptations:

(a) the labeling phase — the bases for existing role arrangements are removed,

(b) the normalization phase — based on pretense of maintaining normal roles (most families remain in this phase and do not proceed further)

(c) the mobilization phase — normality claims become difficult to maintain,

(d) the revisionist phase — involves isolation from community involvements and role renegotiation,

(e) the polarization phase — parents attempt to locate the source of their difficulty within the family, and

(f) the elimination phase — normality is maintained by excluding the offending person. Farber noted that parent-oriented families are more likely than child-oriented families to reach the elimination phase, as are families that were weak prior to the birth of the child. Movement through phases is also influenced by social and cultural expectations and not only by internal family dynamics.

Movement from one phase to another may occur more frequently at turning points in family life. If a mother becomes chronically ill, for example, she may not be able to continue caring for a disabled child at home. Similarly, if a family's support network changes (as, for example, in the case of the death of a grandparent who helped with child care), the parents will be more likely to move toward the elimination phase, opting for an alternative such as institutionalization of the disabled child.

Changes in the child can also lead to placement out of the home. As nonambulatory children grow and become heavier, caring for them at home becomes more difficult. Some severely retarded children also become more difficult to handle as they grow and become more mobile. In some cases, parents may come to believe that a child's special needs can be better met in a residential treatment facility than at home. Meyers et al. (reported in Blacher, 1984b) noted that the proportion of severely and profoundly mentally retarded children residing in their natural home drops sharply at school age.

Residential placement enables some families to achieve normalization when alternatives are not available or acceptable. Through some means, then — social support, access to resources, or removal of the disabled child from the home — most families are able to have a normalized lifestyle. *Normalization is the most common mode of adaptation among families with disabled children during the childhood years.* The next section examines other adaptations and presents a typology of family adaptations based on a model of differential opportunity structures.

A TYPOLOGY OF ADAPTATIONS

The Crusadership Mode

Although normalization is the most common parental adaptation through most of the childhood years, for some parents normalized routines remain elusive. In particular, parents whose children have unusual disabilities, ongoing medical problems, or unresolved behavior problems may have difficulty finding the social supports necessary for normalization. Some of these families adopt a *crusadership* mode of adjustment in an attempt to bring about social change.

Unlike parents who have achieved normalization, these parents may become *more* involved in disability associations and segregated support groups as their children get older. Parents' associations tend to draw their active membership from parents of younger children (who have not yet achieved normalization) and (though their number is smaller) parents of older children with unresolved problems. When normalization cannot be attained, associations and the activities they provide may fill important needs.

The goal of crusadership is normalization, and families who adopt this mode strive to achieve that goal in a variety of ways. Some become involved in campaigns to increase public awareness of their child's disability. Others testify before congressional committees in an attempt to promote legislation favorable to the disabled. Still others wage legal battles or challenge the school system to establish new programs. (For a further discussion of crusadership and parent activism, see Darling, 1988.) Some crusaders eventually achieve normalization and withdraw from involvement in advocacy groups and roles; a few, however, may continue to advocate on behalf of others in an altruistic mode.

Altruism

Because the ultimate goal of most parents is normalization, altruism is not common. As noted above, parents generally decrease their involvement in organizations and activities that emphasize their stigmatized status in society as their children get older. The departure of families who have achieved normalization from these organizations is unfortunate for the parents of younger children in need of successful role models. Not all such families abandon organizational activity, however.

A few families who have achieved normalization remain active in segregated groups for the sake of others, and individuals from such families often assume leadership roles in national disability associations. Their motivations vary: some are truly caring, humanistic people; some have a strong sense of justice; some are applying the principles of their religion, and others simply enjoy the social aspects of participation or the prestige resulting from their leadership roles. Altruists, then, are those who *choose,* for whatever reason, to associate with the disabled even though they have access to opportunities for integration in "normal" society.

Resignation

At the opposite pole from the altruists are the families who, despite their inability to achieve normalization, never become involved in crusadership activity at all. Such parents are doubly isolated: They are stigmatized by "normal" society, and yet they never become integrated into alternative support groups. Some may become fatalistic, whereas others may have mental health problems resulting from stress.

Parents who become resigned to their problematic existence may lack access to supportive resources for a number of reasons. Some may live in isolated rural areas where no parent groups exist. Other may not be able to search for support because of poor health, lack of transportation, or family problems that are separate from the disabled child. In the lower socioeconomic classes, especially, the burdens of daily life—of simple survival—may take precedence over concerns relating to a child's disability. Families who are isolated from the mainstream of society because they do not speak English or because the parents are themselves disabled may not have access to the lay or professional referral networks that provide information on available resources. Crusadership and altruism are luxuries that presuppose some free time, making those modes of adaptation most appropriate for middle- and upper-class families.

A Model of Modes of Adaptation

By the time their children have entered adolescence, then, most parents have adopted a characteristic mode of adaptation to their children's disabilities. These modes are shown in Table 3.1. The reader should keep in mind that these modes are "ideal types" that are only approximated by real families. Some families move back and forth between modes as their needs and opportunities change. Ideal types help us understand family lifestyles, but they should not be used to stereotype families or to predict their responses in any given situation.

TABLE 3-1 Modes of Adaptation Among Parents of Children with Disabilities

| | Type of Integration | |
Mode of Adaptation	Normal Society	Alternative Subculture (Disability as a "career")
Altruism	+	+
Normalization	+	−
Crusadership	−	+
Resignation	−	−

NOTE: + = Integration achieved
    − = Integration withdrawn or not achieved

All parents, then, have different levels of access to two opportunity structures: (a) "Normal" or mainstream society and (b) the smaller subculture of the disabled, consisting of parent support groups, advocacy organizations, special-needs media, and state and national associations. In general, parents who have equal access to both structures will choose a normalization mode rather than the segregated mode of altruism. Parents who do not have equal access to both structures will choose crusadership if their access to normalized structures is severely restricted, or they will choose resignation if their access to the subculture of the disabled is restricted as well.

As children with disabilities approach adolescence, the adjustment strategies adopted by their families during the childhood years may become problematic. When children leave school, parents are faced with planning for the future and confronting questions about whether their children will be able to play adult roles. These concerns are discussed in the next section.

APPROACHING ADULTHOOD: A THREAT TO NORMALIZATION

Adolescence is a stressful time for most families, whether the children are disabled or not. Blumberg, Lewis, and Susman (1984) identified a number of tasks that adolescents must accomplish:

(a) establish identity,
(b) achieve independence,
(c) adjust to sexual maturation,
(d) prepare for the future,
(e) develop mature relationships with peers, and
(f) develop a positive self-image and body image.

In addition, Brotherson, Backus, Summers, and Turnbull (1986) noted some tasks that are unique to families with developmentally disabled young adults:

(a) adjusting to the adult implications of disability,
(b) deciding on an appropriate residence,
(c) initiating vocational involvement,
(d) dealing with issues of sexuality,
(e) recognizing needs for continuing family responsibility,

(f) dealing with continued financial implications of dependency,

(g) dealing with a lack of socialization opportunities for the disabled outside of the family, and

(h) planning for guardianship.

Continuing Dependence

Clemens and Axelson (1985) noted that in families with *nondisabled* children, the continued presence of adult children in the home can be stressful because it violates social expectations. Parents of disabled children may find themselves in a similar situation as their children approach adulthood. As one father said,

> We'll never reach the stage that other people reach when their children leave home, and that's depressing. . . . I also wonder what will happen to Brian when he no longer looks like a child (Darling, 1979, p. 184).

Although some disabled children of normal or close-to-normal intelligence, whose physical problems are not too severe, *do* achieve independence during later adolescence and adulthood, many are not able to do so. The mentally retarded and those with physical problems that prevent the mastery of self-help skills will continue to be dependent on others to some extent for the rest of their lives.

Most parents of disabled children begin to have concerns about the future from the day they suspect that something is wrong with the child. During the infancy and childhood periods, however, they develop rationalizations that enable them to see the future in positive terms or push it out of their minds. Until their children reach middle adolescence, parents of disabled children almost universally seem to adopt an ideology of "living one day at a time."

As a child moves through adolescence and approaches adulthood, parents are forced to begin thinking seriously about the future. Some parents who had hoped that their child would be independent someday, may have to reassess their situation at this time and come to realize that independence is an unrealistic goal. The parents of a 15-year-old expressed these concerns:

> We've been a little down . . . in the past year. . . . He's getting to be an adult. . . . He's never going to make it on his own. . . . The present is fine. We can manage it. . . . Our basic concern is the future. . . . We are getting older. We need babysitters constantly. . . . Joe really can't be

left alone. . . . What if something happens to us? That's our basic fear (Darling & Darling, 1982, p. 156).

Parents such as these typically embark on a search for solutions to their worries that is reminiscent in some ways to the searches undertaken by younger parents whose children have just been diagnosed. They search for such things as appropriate living and enployment arrangements, financial and legal advice, and social, recreational, and, when deemed appropriate, sexual opportunities for their children.

Exploring Alternatives for the Future

Living Arrangements Although physically disabled, many mentally normal adults are able to live independently with supports such as modified housing, equipment, or vehicles. These individuals need to be included in planning for their own futures, and some may become involved, like their parents, in crusadership to make normalized ways of life more accessible to them.

For the adult who cannot achieve true independence, a number of alternatives may be available, depending on where they live and their financial resources. At one end of the spectrum is institutionalization; at the other are various forms of community living arrangements. Although residential alternatives have continued to grow during the last decade, studies indicate most disabled adults still reside in relatively large settings (Krauss & Giele, 1987). Waiting lists for group homes and other, smaller, community-based programs are often long. In more rural areas, such facilities may not exist at all.

Employment Opportunities Normalization for adults in most segments of society includes independent employment. Yet, individuals with disabilities may be limited, either by their disabilities or by employer attitudes, in their quest for jobs. Parents' concerns about their children's ability to achieve independence include issues of employment, as evidenced by these comments from the mother of a young adult with spina bifida:

> Right now we're not sure what he'll be able to do and what's available for him to do. . . . I've thought for years, "What will Paul do?" His father and I won't always be around to take care of him. Paul's got to have a reason to get up in the morning . . .
>
> Eighteen seemed like a long time away when he was four years old. . . . Now he doesn't have any inkling as to the value of a

> dollar. . . . I'm concerned about what he will do. . . . Sometimes, I get
> so angry at Paul. . . . He's waiting for me to come up with an answer
> (Darling & Darling, 1982, p. 162).

Some disabled individuals may not be able to achieve competitive employment at all but may be able to work in a sheltered or supported employment situation. Still others may not be capable of any kind of work. Being able to work for a living is a basic expectation deeply rooted in the American way of life. The capitalist ethic suggests that those who do not work are in some way morally inferior to those who are employed. Consequently, the realization that a severely disabled child might not ever be able to do any productive work is a difficult one for parents to accept.

Social Opportunities   Parents' concerns about their children's social acceptance include a variety of interactional issues: friendship, dating, marriage, recreational opportunities, and opportunities for sexual expression. Questions of normalization arise when disabled adolescents attempt to establish heterosexual relationships with their nondisabled peers:

> Like most teenagers, I became very self-conscious about my appearance
> and physical state. In childhood, my family and others had accepted my
> physical limitations with little or nothing said; in my teens, these same
> limitations started cutting me off from the world. I think the first boy-
> girl parties that my age group started having were probably the begin-
> ning of the social and emotional difficulties that have been greater than
> my physical ones (Kiser, 1974, p. 54).
>
> *   *   *
>
> My cousin and Judy's steady egged me to ask her for a date. I told them
> I didn't think it was right for me to ask a non-handicapped girl to go on
> a date because I was in a wheelchair (Chinn, 1976, p. 75).

Legal/Financial Needs   When parents realize that their disabled children may outlive them, they usually become concerned about providing for their children's future legal and financial security. Finding an estate-planning specialist who can help them plan for the future is not always easy.

Beyer (1986) noted that if parents leave their assets directly to their disabled child, the child may not be eligible for benefits such as Supplemental Security Income or Medicaid. He recommends instead that parents establish a trust for the child, naming a sibling or other person as the trustee. A recent alternative to family or public guardianship of the disabled individual is corporate guardianship (Appolloni, 1987).

FAMILY CAREERS IN PROCESS: AN OVERVIEW OF EMERGENT PATTERNS

Several consistent patterns or styles of adaptation emerge from a review of the lifestyles over time, or careers, of many families with disabled children. The major determinant of the career path that any given family will follow is the social opportunity structure. When supportive resources and services are available to parents, they are most likely to choose a lifestyle based on normalization. When the opportunity structure is limited, on the other hand, they may engage in various forms of seekership or crusadership in an attempt to achieve normalization. The modes of adaptation that families adopt commonly change in a patterned sequence over the course of a child's lifecycle. These career changes are shown in Figure 3-1.

Therefore, as noted earlier, parents are generally in a state of anomie immediately after a diagnosis has been issued; that is, they feel both meaninglessness and powerlessness in relation to their situation. Human beings constantly strive to make sense of their experiences. When events seem random and individuals feel out of control, most try to rationalize their experiences and reestablish order in their lives. Consequently, when parents feel anomic, they are likely to engage in behaviors that will restore their sense of meaning and purpose. During their children's infancy, then, most of these parents become engaged in a process of *seekership* — they read books, consult experts, write letters, and make telephone calls — in an attempt to find answers to their questions and alleviate the anomie that they feel.

Most parents find the answers they are seeking. As a result, most parental quests end in *normalization.* By the time their children reach school age, most parents have obtained an accurate diagnosis, found an acceptable pediatrician, and enrolled their child in an appropriate education or training program. Most parents, then, are able to achieve a close-to-normal style of life during the childhood years. Although the majority of parents choose normalization when it is available to them, a few remain active in parent groups or other advocacy organizations in an attempt to help other parents achieve normalization. Such parents forego the comforts of a normalized routine and adopt an *altruistic* mode of adaptation.

Because of a limited opportunity structure, some families are unable to achieve normalization. When parents do not have access to good medical care, appropriate educational programs, or other services, they may adopt a mode of prolonged seekership, or *crusadership,* and attempt to change the opportunity structure. Finally, some parents who do not have access to services for their children may also not have access to the means for bringing about change. These parents who are doubly isolated adopt a mode of *resignation.* They struggle alone with difficulties created by the disabled child and often with other problems as well.

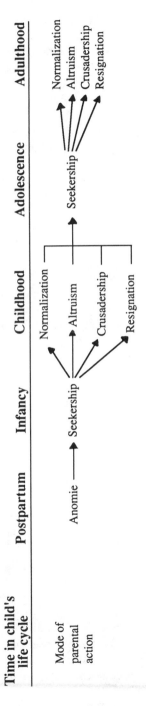

Figure 3-1. Career paths of parents of disabled children

When the disabled child reaches adolescence, normalization is likely to be threatened. During the childhood years, most parents adopt an ideology of "living one day at a time." Once a child approaches adulthood, however, problems raised by the child's continuing dependence must be faced. Regardless of the adaptations they made during the childhood years, then, all parents must eventually make decisions about their child's future. At this time, seekership commonly resumes as parents search for living arrangements, employment opportunities, or other services that their children will need when the parents are no longer willing or able to care for them.

Finally, for some parents, the normalization equilibrium will be reestablished after they have located a satisfactory residential placement for their adult child. Other parents may choose to continue in an altruistic mode and remain active in organizations for the disabled even after they have found a place for their own child. Some parents may not be able to locate a satisfactory placement at all and may keep their adult child with them while they adopt a crusadership or resignation mode.

Normalization *should* be available to all families. Social change in the form of more and better services for the disabled could bring normalization to the crusaders and to those who are resigned to their fate. Altruism would, consequently, be eliminated as well for lack of need. Professionals should help families explore ways to expand their opportunity structure and to achieve the normalization they seek.

REFERENCES

Abraham, W. (1958). *Barbara: A prologue.* New York: Rinehart.

Appolloni, T. (1987, November/December). Guardianship: new options for parents. *The Exceptional Parent,* pp. 24–28.

Bailey, D. B., & Wolery, M. R. (1984). *Teaching infants and preschoolers with handicaps.* Columbus, OH: Merrill.

Baxter, C. (1986). *Intellectual disability: Parental perceptions and stigma as stress.* Unpublished doctoral dissertation, Monash University, Clayton, Victoria, Australia.

Beyer, H. A. (December 1986). Estate planning: Providing for your child's future. *The Exceptional Parent,* pp. 12–18.

Birenbaum, A. (1970). On managing a courtesy stigma. *Journal of Health and Social Behavior, 11,* pp. 196–206.

Birenbaum, A. (1971). The mentally retarded child in the home and the family cycle. *Journal of Health and Social Behavior, 12,* pp. 55–65.

Blacher, J. (1984a). Sequential stages of parental adjustment to the birth of a child with handicaps: Fact or artifact? *Mental Retardation, 22,* pp. 55–68.

Blacher, J. (1984b). *Severely handicapped young children and their families: Research in review.* Orlando, FL: Academic Press.

Blumberg, B. D., Lewis, M. J., & Susman, E. J. (1984). Adolescence: A time of transition. In M. G. Eisenberg, L. C. Sutkin, & M. A. Jansen (Eds.), *Chronic illness and disability through the life span: Effects on self and family* (pp. 133–149). New York: Springer.

Bristol, M. M., & Schopler, E. (1984). A developmental perspective on stress and coping in families of autistic children. In J. Blacher (Ed.), *Severely handicapped young children and their families* (pp. 91–141). Orlando, FL: Academic Press.

Brotherson, M. J., Backus, L. H., Summers, J. A., & Turnbull, A. P. (1986). Transition to adulthood. In J. A. Summers (Ed.), *The right to grow up: An introduction to adults with developmental disabilities.* Baltimore, MD: Paul H. Brookes.

Butler, J. A., Rosenbaum, S., & Palfrey, J. S. (1987). Ensuring access to health care for children with disabilities. *New England Journal of Medicine, 317,* pp. 162–165.

Camp care for handicapped kids. (April 18, 1986). *Johnstown Tribune-Democrat,* p. 5C.

Chinn, H., Jr. (1976). *Each step of the way.* Johnstown, PA: Mafex Associates.

Clemens, A. W., & Axelson, L. J. (1985). The not-so-empty nest: The return of the fledgling adult. *Family Relations, 34,* pp. 259–264.

Collins-Moore, M. S. (1984). Birth and diagnosis: A family crisis. In M. C. Eisenberg, L.C. Sutkin, & M. A. Jansen (Eds.), *Chronic illness and disability through the life span: Effects on self and family* (pp. 39–46). New York: Springer.

D'Arcy, E. (1968). Congenital defects: Mothers' reactions to first information. *British Medical Journal, 3,* pp. 796–798.

Darling, R. B. (1979). *Families against society: A study of reactions to children with birth defects.* Beverly Hills, CA: Sage.

Darling, R. B. (1987). The economic and psycho-social consequences of disability: Family-society relationships. In M. Ferrari & M. B. Sussman (Eds.), *Childhood disability and family systems* (pp. 46–61). New York: Haworth Press.

Darling, R. B. (1988). Parental entrepreneurship: A consumerist response to professional dominance *Journal of Social Issues.*

Darling, R. B., & Darling, J. (1982). *Children who are different: Meeting the challenges of birth defects in society.* St. Louis, MO: Mosby.

Dickman, I., & Gordon, S. (1985). *One miracle at a time: How to get help for your disabled child—From the experience of other parents.* New York: Simon & Schuster.

Doering, S. G., Entwisle, D. R., & Quinlan, D. (1980). Modeling the quality of women's birth experience. *Journal of Health and Social Behavior, 21,* pp. 12–21.

Drotar, D., Baskiewicz, A., Irvin, A., Kennell, J., & Klaus, M. (1975). The adaptation of parents to the birth of an infant with a congenital malformation: A hypothetical model. *Pediatrics, 56,* pp. 710–717.

Dyer, E. D. (1963). Parenthood as crisis: A re-study. *Marriage and Family Living, 25,* pp. 196–201.

Dyson, L., & Fewell, R. R. (1986). Stress and adaptation in parents of young handicapped and nonhandicapped children: A comparative study. *Journal of the Division for Early Childhood,* 10, pp. 25–35.

Farber, B. (1975). Family adaptations to severely mentally retarded children. In M. J. Begab & S. A. Richardson (Eds.), *The mentally retarded and society: A social science perspective* (pp. 247–266). Baltimore, MD: University Park Press.

Gottlieb, J. (1975). Public, peer, and professional attitudes toward mentally retarded persons. In M. J. Begab & S. A. Richardson (Eds.), *The mentally retarded and society: A social science perspective* (pp. 99–125). Baltimore, MD: University Park Press.

Harbaugh, G. R. (1984). *Costs and "out of pocket" costs of rearing the handicapped child.* Unpublished manuscript.

Heller, P. G., Quesada, G. M., Harvey, D. L., & Warner, L. G. (1981). Familism in rural and urban America: Critique and reformulation of a construct. *Rural Sociology, 46,* pp. 446–464.

Kiser, B. (1974). *New light of hope.* New Canaan, CT: Keats Publishing.

Klein, C. (1977). Coping patterns of parents of deaf-blind children. *American Annals of the Deaf, 122,* pp. 310–312.

Krauss, M. W., & Giele, J. Z. (1987). Services to families during three stages of a handicapped person's life. In M. Ferrari & M. B. Sussman (Eds.), *Childhood disability and family systems* (pp. 213–229). New York: Haworth Press.

LeMasters, E. E. (1957). Parenthood as crisis. *Marriage and Family Living 19,* pp. 352–355.

Lipscomb, J., Kolimaga, J. T., Sperduto, P. W., Minnich, J. K., & Fontenot, K. J. (1983). *Cost-benefit and cost-effectiveness analyses of screening for neural tube defects in North Carolina.* Unpublished manuscript, Duke University, Institute for Policy Sciences, Durham, NC.

MacKeith, R. (1973). The feelings and behaviour of parents of handicapped children. *Developmental Medicine and Child Neurology, 25,* pp. 524–527.

McHugh, P. (1968). *Defining the situation.* Indianapolis, IN: Bobbs-Merrill.

Mori, A. A. (1983). *Families of children with special needs: Early intervention techniques for the practitioner.* Rockville, MD: Aspen Systems.

Morris, M. M. (1987, July). Health care: Who pays the bills? *The Exceptional Parent,* pp. 38–42.

Norr, K. L., Block, C. R., Charles, A., Meyering, S., & Meyers, E. (1977). Explaining pain and enjoyment in childbirth. *Journal of Health and Social Behavior, 18,* pp. 260–275.

Olshansky, S. (1962). Chronic sorrow: A response to having a mentally defective child. *Social Casework, 43,* pp. 190–193.

Richardson, S. A. (1970). Age and sex differences in values toward physical handicaps. *Journal of Health and Social Behavior, 11,* pp. 207–214.

Robson, K. S., & Moss, H. A. (1970). Patterns and determinants of maternal attachment. *Journal of Pediatrics, 77,* pp. 976–985.

Solnit, A. J., & Stark, M. H. (1961). Mourning and the birth of a defective child. *The Psychoanalytic Study of the Child, 16,* pp. 523–537.

Stone, N. W., & Chesney, B. H. (1978). Attachment behaviors in handicapped infants. *Mental Retardation, 16,* pp. 8-12.

Suelzle, M., & Keenan, V. (1981). Changes in family support networks over the life cycle of mentally retarded persons. *American Journal of Mental Deficiency, 86,* pp. 267–274.

Trivette, C. M., & Dunst. C. J. (in press). Proactive influences of social support in families of handicapped children. In N. Stinnet et al. (Eds.), *Family strengths (Vol. B): Positive and preventive measures,* Lincoln: University of Nebraska Press.

Voysey, M. (1975). *A constant burden: The reconstitution of family life.* London: Routledge & Kegan Paul.

Waechter, E. H. (1977). Bonding problems of infants with congenital anomalies. *Nursing Forum, 16,* pp. 299–318.

Walker, J. H. (1971). Spina bifida — and the parents. *Developmental Medicine and Child Neurology, 13,* pp. 462–476.

Wikler, L., Wasow, M., & Hatfield, E. (1981). Chronic sorrow revisited: Parent vs. professional depiction of the adjustment of parents of mentally retarded children. *American Journal of Orthopsychiatry, 51,* pp. 63–70.

CHAPTER FOUR

Families and the Community Service Maze

Carole Christofk Upshur

Carole Christofk Upshur, Ed.D., is an Associate Professor of Community Planning at the University of Massachusetts at Boston. She is also an Associate in Pediatrics and Senior Research Associate on the Early Intervention Collaborative Study at the University of Massachusetts Medical School and is affiliated with the Training Program in Mental Retardation and Developmental Disabilities at the Florence Heller School for Social Welfare at Brandeis University. She has written extensively and provided consultation on the development of community service systems, especially in the areas of respite care and early intervention services.

This chapter focuses on the roles families play in providing and brokering services for their children with developmental disabilities. Many persons have stereotyped views concerning the availability of services for developmentally disabled children, adolescents, and adults. These stereotypes carry over into the ways in which families respond to the challenges of raising a child who has special needs. As an attempt to understand families and the special delivery system, this chapter provides an historical overview of care for this population. Some common assumptions concerning the service needs of families with a disabled child are explored. The status of national policies and programs that provide support for all families are described as a context that makes the service system for families with disabled children fragmented and confusing to access. The discussion of family policy issues is followed by a brief review of the current service system for the developmentally disabled and their families. Finally, the problems and stresses in the dynamic relationship between parents and professionals are examined.

HISTORICAL OVERVIEW OF SERVICES FOR THE DEVELOPMENTALLY DISABLED

Despite the fact that much of the research and publicity concerning developmentally disabled individuals over the past two decades has focused almost exclusively on institutional care and deinstitutionalization, only about 5% of the total population of individuals with such disabilities has ever been cared for in institutional settings (Vitello & Soskin, 1985). Between 1967 and 1982, institutional populations declined by 40% (Rotegard, Bruiniks, & Krantz, 1984). Many of those individuals leaving institutions returned home (Gollay, Freedman, Wyngaarden, & Kurtz, 1978; Scheerenberger, 1983). Moroney (1980) indicated that about 165,000 severely mentally retarded children are cared for at home, whereas Hauber, Bruininks, Hill, Lakin, Scheerenberger, and White (1984) pointed out that of the approximately 2.5 million developmentally disabled individuals in the U.S., only 243,669 are in out-of-home community placements (including foster family care and community-based group homes, but excluding institutions). This means that around 86% of individuals with developmental disabilities are living in families that are in potential need of services.

Historically, families have been the primary source of care for disabled family members. The emphasis on professional care evolved in the middle to late 19th century. The family was seen as an economic unit and the disabled member needed to be "trained" to be a productive member of society (Faber, 1986). Changes in the nature and place of work (i.e., from rural to urban settings) and the growth of the medical model of care led to the prevailing theory of the first half of the 20th century that providing specialized, segregated services was the most appropriate way to meet the needs of individuals with disabilities. This was true even though, as already noted, only a small number of disabled individuals have typically been served in settings outside of the home.

During the 1960s, the conceptualization of the service needs of the disabled changed. This was due to a combination of factors, including the presidency of John Kennedy (whose sister, Rosemary, is mentally retarded), the cumulative research on the negative effects of institutional care, and the revelation of the scandalous conditions in the majority of institutions (Blatt & Kaplan, 1966; Braddock, 1986; Butterfield, 1967; Kauffman, 1966). Several landmark court cases during the 1970s further fueled the community care movement, because the type of care provided by the institutions was demonstrated to lack adequate habilitative elements (*New York State Association for Retarded Children and Parisi v. Rockefeller,* 1973; *Pennsylvania Association for Retarded Citizens v. Commonwealth of Pennsylvania,* 1971; *Wyatt v. Stickney,* 1972).

A new theoretical concept, normalization, was also taking hold at this time. This concept was brought to the United States from Scandinavia (Nirje, 1969; Wolfensberger, 1972). Normalization suggests that the mentally retarded (as well as other individuals with disabilities or unique problems) deserve to be treated as normally as possible. This does not mean that individuals with handicaps can be "made normal," but rather that, as much as possible, such individuals must be allowed to participate in regular, age-appropriate activities common to the general population. Treatment and education for the disabled, according to the principle of normalization, should include teaching functional skills that are necessary for successful participation in the community. The most appropriate and "normative" living arrangement for handicapped children, accordingly, is with their own families. Segregation into institutions and lack of opportunities for participation in normal family life, daily routines, education, recreation, work, and leisure activities denies individuals access to the principle of normalization.

Furthermore, normalization requires that the community and specialized services provided to individuals with disabilities adapt their resources so that handicapped persons can participate as equally as possible with non-handicapped peers. Making buildings accessible to handicapped persons and providing sign language interpreters for those with hearing impairments are examples of adaptations society must make to implement normalization. Normalization has become the accepted standard by which services for individuals with disabilities are judged. As we shall see, however, the concept of normalization also poses some difficult dilemmas for assuring that the disabled have opportunities for the broadest possible participation in community life. In addition, it is one of the reasons why families have difficulties carrying out the primary service-provider role for their handicapped children.

This brief description of the history of the philosophy of care for the developmentally disabled in this country emphasizes that families have always provided most of the care for their children. In addition, the current philosophy of caring for disabled individuals, at least as far as children and adolescents are concerned, proposes that the most appropriate and humane place for care is in the context of the family (biological or adoptive). It is clear, however, that individuals with handicaps do have special care-giving needs, especially those who are severely disabled, and that families cannot provide for all their needs without outside assistance.

SERVICE NEEDS OF FAMILIES

There are three major misconceptions among professionals about the needs of families with a handicapped member: (a) that the quality of family life is permanently and pervasively damaged by the presence of a handicapped member; (b) that all families with handicapped members are alike; and (c) that social policy designed for families with handicapped members should be different than that directed toward other families.

The Deficit Versus Difference View of Families With Handicapped Members

Professionals have long assumed that the presence of a handicapped person in a family creates an abnormal stressor that makes normal family life impossible. These families are assumed to be quite different from families without handicapped members. As a result, a number of research studies on families with handicapped or chronically ill children during the past two decades have focused on the presumed difficulties these families face in carrying out normative tasks. Increased family stress affecting both the parents and siblings has been reported (Featerstone, 1980; Friedrich & Friedrich, 1981). Other studies also have reported high divorce rates (Love, 1973), high child maltreatment rates (Schilling & Schinke, 1984), and more depression among both mothers and fathers (Crnic, Friedrich & Greenberg, 1983; Cummings, 1976).

Some studies, however, have found that there are more modest effects on family functioning. For example, the Philadelphia Association for Retarded Citizens' evaluation of family support groups found that family resources and coping skills were not reported differently by families with handicapped members compared with families who did not have a handicapped member (Association for Retarded Citizens, 1983). Kazak and Marvin (1984) found that mothers of children with spina bifida reported no difference in marital satisfaction compared with mothers of nonhandicapped children, and for some subscales, mothers of the handicapped children reported *more* satisfaction. Mothers with handicapped children, however, did experience more stress, but they appear to adapt to this by having more intense contacts with extended family members, although less with friends. Kazak and Marvin make the cogent observation that the differences in social contacts of mothers with and without handicapped children represent *differences,* not *deviances,* on the part of families with handicapped children.

Salisbury (1986) reported that mothers of severely handicapped children spent more time taking care of the handicapped child than other children in the family; the higher amount of time these mothers spent in child care was associated with higher stress and less coping ability compared with mothers of mildly handicapped and nonhandicapped children. However, there were no differences found in perceived quality of life or time used for leisure and housekeeping activities. In comparing parental reports of stress across several groups, Salisbury also found that mothers and fathers of young handicapped children reported more stress than did parents of nonhandicapped children, with single parents of both groups reporting higher stress than did married parents. However, single parents of handicapped children reported higher stress only if their child's caregiving needs were excessive. Most notable, there were no differences found in this study between parents of handicapped children and those of nonhandicapped children on measures of marital integration or personal well-being.

A recent study by Erickson and Upshur (1989) reported similarly mixed findings from mothers' ratings of difficulty of caregiving and time. In an age matched analysis of mothers of very young children with three types of disability and mothers of infants without disabilities, few mothers reported high difficulty of care ratings. However, mothers of children with Down syndrome and developmental delay (but not mothers of children with motor impairment) reported more difficulty in bathing, feeding and dressing than mothers of children without disabilities. Mothers of children with Down syndrome and motor impairment (but not mothers of children with developmental delay) also reported more caretaking time due to providing special home activities for their child, but only mothers of children with Down syndrome reported less time for themselves.

Although this discussion has reviewed only a few of the research studies on families with handicapped children (others are discussed elsewhere in this volume), it is clear that some families function quite normally and their service needs are not noticeably different from those of families with nonhandicapped children. The assumption that families with handicapped members must be overly stressed and cope poorly is inaccurate and misleading. This is not to say that families do not need services. The point is that families are not all alike, and careful examination of the variability among families is essential in order to understand and predict their service needs.

All Families Are Not Alike   Because of a variety of factors, families react differently and cope differently to the birth and rearing of a child with disabilities. Not the least of these factors is the reality that each child has a unique set of abilities and disabilities and an individual personality and temperament that place different demands on the family. Furthermore, there are differences in personal coping styles of parents, differences in the level of marital satisfaction and adjustment, and differences in the availability of support. As both the child and the family ages, there are also predictable life cycle changes that result in family needs changing over time (Turnbull, Summers, & Brotherson, 1986). For example, even the same family may function quite differently and need different types of help in the face of caring for a preschool handicapped child as opposed to planning for the long-term needs of a 30-year-old adult in the face of the failing health of the parents.

Studies that attempt to predict family functioning from specific child characteristics are not numerous. However, those that have been conducted provide us with important reminders that we should not expect that all families will have the same responses or needs, given that disabilities vary tremendously. For example, Goldberg, Marcovitch, MacGregor, and Lojkasek (1986) investigated stress, social support, and locus of control among three groups of families: those with children with Down syndrome, with neurological impairments, and with disabilities of unknown etiology. Families with a child with Down syndrome reported less stress, more social support, and more control over their lives than did families with children with other disabilities. Beavers, Hampson, Hulgus, and Beavers (1986) also reported more stress in families whose mentally retarded children had been given unclear diagnoses and prognoses.

The Beavers et al. (1986) study further described characteristics of families who seem to be functioning well and those who were rated as functioning poorly. The ability of the parents to accept the handicapped child as *one* family member with needs, rather than the *only* family member with needs, was an important distinguishing factor. In other words, families functioned well when family dynamics were not entirely fueled by the child's handicap and caretaking needs and when other family members needs were not neglected. Families who have flexible ways of coping with their child's handicap will have quite different ways of interacting with the service system. Beavers et al. (1986) described poorly functioning families in their study as being overly rigid in complying with professional directions. Weyling (1983) indicated that as a parent, she had to come to a reasonable accommodation about what suggestions of professionals she and her husband could implement; they also gave up the notion of being perfect parents.

In another study, Friedrich, Wilturner, and Cohen (1985) noted that marital satisfaction is the single best predictor of adjustment in families with mentally retarded children. However, the absence of maternal depression, type of locus of control, and quality of family social climate also contributed to adjustment. Factors that were found to assist in coping were utilitarian resources (e.g., financial, specific services), energy/morale (e.g., absence of maternal depression), beliefs (e.g., whether parents felt they had control over their lives), and social support. Clearly, families have different access to these types of resources as well as different views of life, and therefore each family will function idiosyncratically in response to a similar constellation of child needs.

The area of social support is one that has recently been investigated more thoroughly in differentiating functioning among families who have disabled children. The definition of social support varies across research studies. However, it generally refers to the degree to which other family members, friends, or professional services are available to assist the family in coping with problems or stresses. The Beavers et al. (1986) study noted that the presence of more than one adult caretaker (whether a spouse, a grandparent, or other family member) was significantly related to more positive family functioning. Thus, for example, it cannot be assumed that all single parents of handicapped children experience the same level of stress and service needs. One must examine the family's entire constellation of caregivers to determine an accurate assessment of family needs. In fact, Erickson and Upshur (1989) have reported that mothers of infants with disabilities rated their satisfaction with social support from community groups as higher than mothers of infants without disabilities. Thus, only some families with children with disabilities may need extraordinary support services.

In another study, Dunst and Trivette (1986) reported results of interviews with 96 mothers and 41 fathers of at-risk, mentally retarded, and physically handicapped young children. They found that higher satisfaction with social support, and not just larger network size, was related to the child's developmental gain, to better physical and emotional health for the parents, to a lack of overprotection of the child, and to positive parent perceptions of the child. However, Dunst and Leit (1986) and Trivette and Dunst (in press) pointed out that a broad range of family resources as well as child characteristics also influence family integrity and personal, emotional, and physical well-being of parents of handicapped children.

A final point in this discussion of why "all families are not alike" is that family needs change over time as a child grows. No family is the same today as it was yesterday or will be tomorrow. This is particularly evident when the basic family constellation changes (e.g., through birth, adoption, divorce, or the death of a family member), but it is even true during times when such major events do not occur. As family members age, the family experiences developmental transitions defined in terms of the oldest child's age. These transitions require changes in family roles and resources and often are points when a family experiences increased stress (Turnbull et al., 1986).

Wikler (1981) and Turnbull et al. (1986) described major crises for families of handicapped children, starting with the diagnosis of the condition to the time when parents must plan for their child's survival beyond their own deaths. Other significant periods include times when the child would have reached normal developmental milestones (e.g., beginning to walk, entering school, graduating from high school, 21st birthday), when a younger sibling's abilities surpass those of the handicapped child, or when behavior or health problems of the handicapped child dramatically worsen. At each of these points, Wikler noted that the family must face feelings concerning the possibility that their child and family will be stigmatized, the burden of prolonged dependency of the child, the lack of adequate information on how to make decisions across the life span about a handicapped child, and the reawakening of grief over the loss of a normal child.

Other researchers (Bristol & Schopler, 1983; Byrne & Cunningham, 1985; Suelzle & Keenan, 1981) also reported that the handicapped child's age has a differential impact on family life, with the presence of older disabled children and adolescents correlated with fewer personal supports, fewer services, and more stress for families. This research points to the misconception that the highest stress in families with handicapped children occurs around the original diagnosis and early childhood years. Indeed, a study by Wikler, Wascow, and Hatfield (1981) found that, compared to parental reports, social workers overestimated early stressors and underemphasized stress as the child grew older.

It can be seen that there is an abundance of variability among families with handicapped members. This variability is due to the child's characteristics (including age), family patterns of coping, the types of both formal and informal resources available to the family, and the family life cycle stage. Thus families with handicapped members differ for a number of reasons, and one would expect that service needs would be as variable as these multiple family structures, adaptations, and coping strategies.

Social Policy Toward Families With Handicapped Members Should Be Different   The third major misconception concerning families with handicapped members is to assume that they have unique needs from other families, limited primarily to directly caring for their handicapped member. Failure to conceptualize family needs in the broadest of terms is one major cause of inadequate family support services. This failure is based on the view that public institutions should not have a role in family life and that families do not want assistance from the public sector (Agosta & Bradley, 1985).

The view of the self-sufficient extended family, which has adequate "helping hands" for caregiving for children and other dependent members, is, however, one that does not reflect current sociodemographic patterns. In the past 20 years the trends toward higher divorce rates, decreased family size, high geographic mobility and increased labor market participation of women because of both economic necessity and self-fulfillment have resulted in significantly less ability of families to care for their members without community supports (Bronfenbrenner & Weiss, 1983; Kagan, Klugman & Zigler, 1983). As Moroney (1983) indicated, our ideology has not yet caught up with empirical reality. Thus, rather than starting from a broad view of the needs of families, policymakers identify specific interventions that are responsive to a particular problem, overlooking the larger context. For example, specialized early intervention services are available from birth in some states only for deaf and blind children, although children with many types of disabilities and their families can benefit from early support and therapy. Indeed, it has been recognized that many families need support when a child is born, even if the child has no special care needs. However, instead of broadly available services, only limited services are available to a few families with the most disabled infants.

Another example of narrow service policy is the provision of respite care services (relief care for parents of disabled children and adults). In many areas respite care is only available in an emergency situation (i.e., hospitalization of the primary caregiver) rather than on a routine basis. Routine access to respite care would help prevent the build up of stress and the need for the family to seek out-of-home placement. Furthermore, program guidelines, such as limiting services to families with retarded children, often arbitrarily exclude families with children with other equally difficult care needs (e.g., degenerative neurological disorders or cancer).

In the current policy/program delivery context, families with handicapped members usually have access to some services not available to other families. However, these services often are not comprehensive and coordinated, and they fail to take into account the environment in which the family functions. For example, a mother with several young children at home could not take her child with a disability to a center-based early intervention program because she had no child care for the other two children. Some money for a babysitter would have been most helpful to this family, but since the other children did not qualify for services, such funds were not available. As a result, the child with a disability received fewer services through infrequent home visits.

Clearly, many families juggle impossible situations because the system cannot adapt to some of the real needs of families.

The problem of organizing community services for families with handicapped members is thus not one that can focus exclusively on the specific needs of the handicapped family member. The needs of other family members and the ways in which the family as a whole must work to appropriately support each other and the handicapped member must be considered. In addition, the problems and stresses of families with severely handicapped members must be seen as merely part of a continuum of family needs. Because specific disability or income categories are required for service eligibility, some needy families are automatically excluded, and distinctions among families with varying needs become entirely arbitrary. For example, one mother is forced to stay on welfare because private health insurers will not cover the extensive health problems of her young son who requires kidney dialysis. Another family cannot bring their critically ill infant with Down syndrome home from the hospital because they make $3000 over the limit to qualify for federal support that would help pay for home health aides, special equipment, and medication. This situation continues because of the lack of adequate social policy that should recognize that local and national government must play a more flexible role in family support services for all families.

Conclusion: What We Know About the Needs of Families With Handicapped Members   There is no simple answer to the question of what type of community services families with handicapped members need. However, it seems clear that a range of services are needed, that individual families will have differing needs, and that, over time, family service needs will change.

Only a few studies have surveyed families directly about their needs. Kornblatt and Heinrich (1985) interviewed 24 families and found that the most frequent area of need was information about their child's condition. The second highest category was "family living patterns," which included such issues as transportation, finances, and help with personal and family problems. Studies of respite care services have indicated that agency policies usually set priorities for providing emergency care, whereas families most often cite vacations and free time away from caregiving responsibilities as their reasons for needing respite (Upshur, 1982). A survey of 400 families by Dunlap and Hollinsworth (1977) found similar needs expressed, such as concerns about the inability to take trips or vacations, as well as restrictions on shopping and other recreational activities. These findings have important implications for how policy is set for service delivery.

A survey of families who use Department of Public Health Services in Massachusetts (Project Serve, 1985) found that families needed case management, advocacy, assistance in accessing services, information on availability and eligibility of services, financial counseling, parent groups, sibling groups, specialized equipment, and housing adaptations (e.g., wheelchair ramps). Furthermore, problems involving a paucity of third-party insurance coverage for many of these services and large out-of-pocket expenses for medically related, but not insurance-eligible expenses were noted (e.g., transportation to medical appointments, medications, adaptive equipment, special clothing). Many families, although they had medical insurance, were also limited in their ability to change jobs because of the possible loss of coverage in switching from one medical plan to another.

The Massachusetts study and others (e.g., Healy, Keesee & Smith, 1985) also indicated that families have particular needs during transition periods. When a child exits one service system and enters a new system as they age or their abilities change, information needs become acute and stress increases because the family experiences the pressure to make appropriate choices. Particularly stressful transitions occur when children enter public school special education programs and when they leave school and must have access to the adult service system. Increasingly, aging parents, whose disabled children have always resided at home, are having to make long-term plans for their adult disabled children who will survive them. Such planning in families with developmentally disabled members parallels the needs of middle-aged couples who may be caring for their own aging and disabled parents.

Lack of planning, information and referral, and financial assistance for long-term care are issues of general public concern. These issues have recently been heightened by Stone and Newcomer (1985), who described the drawbacks of current services for the aged in this country. They question whether the underdeveloped existing elder service system can meet the needs of aging developmentally disabled persons, and suggest that specialized services be funded in order to assure appropriate care for elders with developmental disabilities.

A final note concerning the needs of families harkens back to the concept of normalization. Although it is clear that family care of handicapped individuals is expected during infancy, childhood, and adolescence, the assumption that families should provide lifetime care for handicapped individuals places a particular burden on families and denies them normative experiences characteristic of middle and later adulthood. Indeed, once a child reaches the age of majority, families are not legally and financially responsible for his or her care (Harris, 1985). At this point, a family should petition a court to determine their child's competency to carry out adult decision-making roles, such as signing a lease, agreeing to a rehabilitation or service plan, or consenting to medical care. If the ruling establishes the inability of the individual to handle some or all of his or her own affairs, a limited or full guardianship will be established. The guardian may be a biological parent or sibling but can be any other competent adult willing to undertake this role. Often, during this transitional process, the disabled adult will have his or her own advocate or legal representation, separate from the family's.

Many families are unaware of these legal issues, and service providers are slow to initiate guardianship proceedings until a crisis arises in which an important decision must be made about an individual's care. In the meantime, families continue to provide comprehensive care for many of their disabled adult members. There are limited opportunities for young adults with disabilities to experience the normative separation and independence from their families at this stage of the life cycle. The quality of family life for many families is thus also highly restrictive (Turnbull et al., 1985). These quality of life issues are rarely raised in the policy arena because they tend to encroach on the dominant philosophy that government should intervene in family life as little as possible. However, the notion of shared responsibility between the state and the family for the provision of care is one that makes sense in preserving an adequate quality of life, productivity, and self-sufficiency for both the family unit and the individual with disabilities. The service needs of families and of their handicapped members must thus be looked at from several perspectives. What may be a normalizing experience for one party may be highly stigmatizing or restrictive for another.

ORGANIZATION OF THE SERVICE SYSTEM

Accessing services and finding the particular combination of services that fit a family's needs pose the greatest challenges for families with handicapped members. There are two major constraints of the social service delivery system: (a) inadequate funding and (b) lack of coordination of services. This section reviews some of the problems inherent in the service delivery system.

Funding of Community/Family Support Services

Over the past 10 years, there has been considerable growth in financial support for community-based services for individuals with developmental disabilities. State funding for community services topped funding for institutional services for the first time in 1983 (Braddock & Fujiura, 1987). However, a large portion of the community services budgets fund residential services for a small number of individuals rather than funding a wide array of different services that a disabled child or adult living at home needs. Agosta and Bradley (1985) noted that a disproportionate amount of state and federal dollars for the developmentally disabled are still spent on institutional care instead of community services, although the ratio has improved since 1977. (It has decreased for 3.5 times more to 1.5 times more spent for institutional services.)

Unfortunately, few of these dollars are spent on family support services. For example, in a review of case-management services in the state of New York, MacEachron, Pensky, and Hawes (1986) found that only 26% of the clients receiving case-management services lived with their families, whereas the remainder lived in group homes or other residential programs. Thus there has been growth in the absolute amount of resources available for community services but not nearly enough to meet the needs of the majority of individuals with disabilities who live outside of institutions and the families who care for them.

A review of state-sponsored family support programs conducted in 1984 (Agosta & Bradley, 1985), found that 49 states had some type of family support programs, but only 25 had statewide services, and states with services "on-paper" serve very few families (e.g., only 15 families were served in both Connecticut and South Carolina). Other states, however, have broader programs. California reports serving 35,000 individuals. Agosta and Bradley estimate that about 62,000 families nationwide receive family support services, or about 2.5% of families nationwide who have a handicapped member living at home. Furthermore, most states have policies that seek to limit use of services by defining income, disability level, age, or type of disability as eligibility requirements (Krauss, 1986). Thus lip service is paid to the notion of family support, but in reality, few services are available. Unfortunately, this means that it is difficult for families to have access to services even if they are eligible to receive them.

Problems With Coordination of Services   Given the array of actual services, a major issue for families with handicapped members is that there is no coordinated system for delivery of services. Boggs (1984) noted that there are eight distinct federal agencies involved with handicapped children. This means that parents may have to rely on different offices and programs to piece together the services that their child needs. Braddock (1987), in a review of federal policy toward mental retardation and developmental disabilities, had to cover 28 statutes and 82 programs directed to this group.

Each of the federal programs has different eligibility requirements, different application processes, and different (although also frequently overlapping) services. The complexity of the federal programs is further compounded at the state and local level — where different state agencies administered some of the federal programs as well as provide supplementary services through their own system.

Comparability of services across states is nonexistent. For example, Agosta and Bradley (1985) found that two states offered as many as 14 different family support services, whereas others offered as little as three. Twenty-one states offered respite care, however, and 20 states provided adaptive equipment. A total of 35 different services were identified as family support services by the different states.

Comparability even within states in terms of available services is often inconsistent. A study by Castellani, Downey, Tausig, and Bird (1986), which reviewed family support programs of 135 agencies in 12 counties in New York, found a widely varying distribution of services, with as few as 11% of agencies providing in-home respite care but 87% providing information and referral. Often, however, support services were not separately budgeted or planned for and were offered only to families already receiving other services from the agency.

The lack of adequate funding available to meet community service needs for families, the uneven distribution of services, the difficulty in locating services, and the priority in providing services to those already institutionalized are the elements that represent the service maze referred to in the title of this chapter. As Schalock (1985) described, the current human service system is so duplicative and fragmented that multilevel efforts to coordinate and collaborate need to be implemented in order to effect a comprehensive system of services for individuals and families.

As professional thinking has moved from segregated toward more integrated care for handicapped persons, families have been encouraged to use services from the generic service system (e.g., local recreational facilities, doctors, churches). In many communities, the generic service system is not generally equipped to serve handicapped individuals. Physical accommodations and necessary support services (such as building special ramps for community swimming pools or having a sign language interpreters at church) are often not in place. Physicians who are not familiar with caring for handicapped individuals often have difficulty communicating with them and may believe that the handicapping condition precludes the necessity to offer elective treatments — which might improve the quality of life of the individual, but which are not medically necessary (Darling, 1979). The need for families to seek services from a combination of the generic service system and from programs specifically designed for individuals with handicapping conditions contributes to the confusion and stress. Despite the compelling problems created by limited funding and lack of coordination, however, there is a range of services available in every state. A brief review of these programs and how families can have access to them follows.

Services Available to Families   The most widely available services are those established by federal statute. These include medical care, vocational rehabilitation, and special education. In addition, there are three major sources of financial support for individuals with handicaps. These are Supplemental Security Income (SSI), Social Security Disability Income (SSDI) and Social Security Disability Insurance/Adult Disabled Child Program (SSDI/ADC). The SSI program was implemented in 1972 and provides support for elderly adults, as well as blind and disabled individuals who are unable to obtain gainful employment and who meet the standards of financial need established by federal regulation. Children under 18 with severe disabilities are eligible if the family meets income guidelines. Food stamps are also available to persons receiving SSI.

The SSDI program is an insurance program, which means that a worker who becomes disabled and has paid into social security through employment is eligible for benefits. The SSDI/Adult Disabled Child program provides benefits for disabled children (age 18 or older) of a retired, disabled, or deceased worker who qualified for social security benefits.

Individuals who qualify for SSI also qualify for Medicaid, the health care program for low-income individuals and families. Those who qualify for the SSDI/Adult Disabled Child Program can qualify for Medicare after two years. All states also receive Public Health Services funding for "crippled children's programs." States use these funds to provide special medical care to children under age 21 who have a broad range of handicapping conditions.

Vocational rehabilitation services provide a range of employment-related programs for individuals with developmental disabilities. These include (a) supported work programs, where a staff person assists the handicapped individual to learn and perform a job in a regular job site, (b) enclave models, where a group of disabled workers is supervised on a daily, long-term basis on a job site; (c) work crew models, where a group of disabled workers with a supervisor perform jobs such as gardening, maintenance, or janitorial services; and (d) benchwork, where disabled workers at a segregated job site take on contract work for an industry. Services for disabled persons through state vocational rehabilitation agencies have recently been expanded. However, resistance to planning employment services for individuals with severe handicaps persists because of the traditional belief that these individuals cannot engage in economically productive functions.

A major issue that accompanies these innovative employment opportunities (which enable disabled individuals to earn higher salaries than they do in sheltered workshops) is the possibility of losing income support and medical benefits. Federal regulations dictate a formula for subtracting part of earned income from benefits and a fairly low limit beyond which all benefits cease, which results in a disincentive to participate in the work force. Although productive work at modest wages may greatly enhance the life of an individual with disabilities, most can ill afford to pay for the minimal necessities of life with such incomes and would have great difficulty obtaining medical care. Currently there are attempts being made to solve this problem, but for the moment, the complicated formulas may prove difficult for families to decipher.

Perhaps the most well-known and accessible service for families with handicapped children is special education. Public Law 94–142 was enacted in 1975 to guarantee a public education to all handicapped children. This law provides safeguards for parents to obtain appropriate educational and ancillary services by requiring individual evaluation and planning for each child's needs, transportation, and placement in the "least restrictive setting" possible to achieve educational goals. Parents have rights to appeal decisions by local schools if they disagree with the services offered. Under this law, public schools can provide a variety of services to assist a child to meet the individual education plan (i.e., IEP). Home visiting, family counseling, summer programming, physical, occupational, and speech therapy can be provided, as well as placement in private day and residential schools paid for at public expense.

Because the services are administered by local authorities, there is great variability in what services are available and offered to individual children and families across school systems. Currently, services must be provided at age of school entry (5 or 6 years). However, PL 99–457, which passed in 1986 will require that by 1991, services begin at age 3. Additional (but discretionary) funding has also been allocated by PL 99–457 for states to plan for and expand services for handicapped children starting from birth. Services are required to be provided through age 18, but states that choose to extend services to handicapped children through age 21 also will receive federal reimbursements. Many states have additional state-level legislation that reinforce the federal statute and supplement funding for special education.

Other services such as case management, housing modifications, adaptive equipment, transportation, respite care, parent training, early intervention, and homemaker/home health aide visits are available to varying degrees, depending on the states and localities. Access to services and facilities available to the general public (e.g., public transportation, universities, public buildings) is also guaranteed for handicapped individuals by Section 504 of the Vocational Rehabilitation Act of 1973.

Accessing Services It can be a challenge for families to find their way through the community service maze. Many families go without existing and needed services because they do not know what services are available to them or how to find out about these services. There are three key ways to start the search for services that may expedite a family's mission.

First, families who have been informed during the neonatal period that their child will have disabilities or may be at risk can turn to hospital social workers for assistance. Second, each state has a developmental disabilities agency funded by the federal government to plan and coordinate services for individuals with disabilities. Locating this agency — perhaps with the help of a professional — within the state government bureaucracy may be the first difficult but manageable task. This central coordinating unit can guide a family to appropriate local agencies. Local Social Security Offices are excellent sources of information about income support programs offered by the federal government. In "Counseling Parents With Children With Disabilities" (Chapter 11 of this volume), Labore and Seligman discuss how professionals can assist parents in their search for services.

Third, perhaps the most valuable resource for families with handicapped members comes from other families who have already been through the service system. Many groups and parent associations have been formed around specific disabilities, such as the Association for Retarded Citizens, the Epilepsy Association, and the March of Dimes. These groups are often run by parent volunteers or by paid staff who are also parents or family members of handicapped persons. Many times these groups also administer some of the federal and state-funded programs for the handicapped on a contract basis; thus they are not only a source of support and information, but also of direct services. Locating services is, however, only one of the difficulties that parents of children with disabilities face. Another major hurdle for parents is establishing working relationships with professionals as they negotiate the service maze. This issue is addressed in the next section.

PARENT-PROFESSIONAL RELATIONSHIPS

The literature written by parent authors is replete with stories about difficult relationships with professionals (see, e.g., Chapter 5, "Parent-Professional Interaction: The Roots of Misunderstandings" by Darling). From the parents' point of view, professionals almost universally treat them as part of the child's problem, rather than as partners on the professional team. Furthermore, parents often encounter professionals who have little empathy or patience for the daily difficulties of living with a mentally handicapped or chronically ill child; professionals often discount the parent's role as an accurate observer of the child's developmental skills, problems, and needs (Darling, 1979; Featerstone, 1980; Turnbull & Turnbull, 1985). On the other hand, professionals often see parents as resisting recommendations that are in the best interest of the child and as failing to carry out programs at home that would provide continuity and more consistent developmental progress. They also see parents "shopping" for other opinions and feel that their professional expertise and credentials are being questioned (Mulich & Pueschel, 1983). When parent-professional relationships are strained, it is likely that neither the family nor the handicapped child will be well served by the service system.

The Parent's Point of View

Parent's first experiences with professionals concerning their handicapped child occur at the time of the initial diagnosis. A recurring theme reported by parents is the difficulty professionals seem to experience in informing them of their child's disabilities. When the presence of an infant's handicapping condition is communicated to parents shortly after birth, there is almost universal anger directed at physicians, in particular, for being evasive, for not providing enough information, for hiding behind technical language, and for making prognoses that are too optimistic or too pessimistic (Darling, 1979; Featerstone, 1980). Nurses and other hospital staff also feel awkward in interacting with parents and often isolate them from other parents who are celebrating the birth of a healthy child. Although the frequent recommendation of 15 or 20 years ago to immediately institutionalize an infant with handicaps is no longer as common, pediatricians still often know little about community resources for assisting families in caring for their child. Parents also report being given little accurate information about their child's disabilities and the possible course of development or even practical suggestions for home management. From their perspective, parents find it much more helpful for a professional to admit that they do not know an answer to a parent's question rather than provide evasive or inaccurate responses (Akerley, 1985).

For parents who leave the hospital with a healthy appearing neonate, the gradual discovery and final confirmation of developmental problems typically produces even more negative reactions toward professionals. There are many accounts of parents who long suspected developmental problems, but whose pediatricians insisted "she'll grow out of it" (Darling, 1979; Turnbull & Turnbull, 1985). One parent reports that her pediatrician denied the disabilities of her infant son for a full year before referring the child for special evaluation, and once a diagnosis of mental retardation had been established, it took four more years of requests before suspected cerebral palsy was also confirmed (The Hesel Family, 1985). Other parents report that only after seeking the opinion of several professionals, including psychologists, psychiatrists, neurologists, and other medical specialists, was an accurate diagnosis determined.

Subsequent to the initial diagnosis, parents must confront a long and rocky road of interaction with professionals. Many feel they have a constant battle to receive the best medical care from physicians who find it difficult to treat patients who are not curable (Ford, 1967) and who unconsciously blame families for trying to maintain severely handicapped children at home (Darling, 1979). Some parents have disagreements with teachers regarding the appropriateness of a curriculum that focuses on academic skills rather than functional skills (Bernheimer, Young, & Winton, 1983; Roos, 1985). Other parents disagree with the types of services professionals recommend, because parents feel that they know their child best (Schulz, 1985).

Another major tension for parents of handicapped children is the constant reminder of the differences in their family life. Although many families cope well, some families feel isolated, confused, and ashamed about their child, and these feelings may persist for years. They note that they feel quite different when the special van pulls up to take their preschooler to classes, while other parents are worrying about nursery school car pools (Michaelis, 1981). Some feel embarrassed by having to accept government help when no one in their family has ever done so before. They also worry about friends and neighbors resenting that they receive services, paid for by tax dollars, which are not available to other families. They point out that this resentment from their peers is coupled with professional attitudes that they should feel grateful for whatever special services are received, even when services are inadequate. These professional attitudes also convey impatience with special requests and carry with them subtle anger and lack of cooperation if the parent disagrees with a professional about programs or goals for their child. The consequences of these professional attitudes are often feelings of guilt and self-blame on the part of the parents.

Still other parents resent the constant prying of professionals into their daily lives, the lack of privacy that frequent contact with professionals brings, and the amount of personal information that must be shared. They note that professionals who have not themselves lived on a daily basis with a handicapped child often have unrealistic notions about parents carrying out home therapies and programs (Featherstone, 1980; Weyling, 1983). Professionals often contribute to parental guilt if the parents do not carry out all recommended programs and if they take time for their own needs. However, parents point out that most families have a compelling need to strive to create a normal family life in which the entire identity of the parents and siblings is not tied to the handicapped child (Bennett, 1985; Darling, 1979).

Finally, parents need professionals to see them as individuals and to view family needs as discrete and variable. As one parent and professional social worker points out, the "end of the rope" comes at different times and in different forms for different families (Avis, 1985). Parents also point out that not all families benefit equally from typically available services. For example, it may be that parent support groups can create stress for parents with more mildly delayed/disabled children. They may feel guilty for seeking help when others have more problems to deal with (Bernheimer et al., 1983). Parents whose children have a known syndrome find it hard to deal with parents who are in constant search for the cause of their child's disability, whereas other parents want a respite from constant and intense involvement with their child (Winton & Turnbull, 1981). These parent views of the service system must be heeded by professionals if appropriate partnerships in meeting child and family needs are to be fostered. As the following section demonstrates, professionals also have views about parents that are not always complimentary.

The Professional's Point of View

There are three important points to highlight concerning parent-professional relationships from the professional point of view. These are (a) the professional's ability to understand and successfully cope with parental anger, hostility, and deliberate or unconscious noncompliance with recommendations, (b) the professional's need to recognize his or her own feelings of anger, grief, and frustration, and (c) the lack of adequate training and practice in assuming collaborative roles with parents.

The professional's understanding of parental behavior is crucial to healthy partnerships. However, professionals are not always able to accurately interpret parental behavior that seems to be, from a professional viewpoint, contraindicated. One of the first reactions of parents to the doctor—the bearer of bad news—is anger. This anger is sometimes a displacement from generalized anger about the difficult situation parents are confronting. It can also be anger displaced from earlier, negative encounters with professionals, or genuine anger concerning how insensitively the message is being communicated. Professionals need to recognize the source of parental anger and realize the normality of their reaction to a crisis (Moses, 1983).

Often, in addition to anger, parents will go through a stage of denial. This may result in parents' refusing to acknowledge the existence, permanence, or impact of the child's handicap, which can interfere with planning necessary services. Professionals view parents' missed appointments, a refusal to listen to suggestions, and the search for other opinions as problem behavior rather than as necessary coping mechanisms (Moses, 1983). In an attempt to deal with their own feelings, parents may also react by being overprotective or extrapunitive toward the child. These reactions need to be understood by the professional rather than perceived only as negative parental behaviors requiring change. They should also not be used as an excuse to withdraw from the relationship (i.e., "The parents don't really want help, so we'll stay away"). Thus, professionals must learn to deal with and understand the cause of parental reactions rather than blame them for having abnormal or resistant behaviors.

Professionals must also recognize feelings of anger, grief, and frustration that they may experience because of the difficulty of finding answers for the cause of a disabling condition or the lack of clear remedies. Doctors, social workers, nurses, teachers, and school administrators who do not have extensive experience with handicapped children have their own, often inaccurate, views of the place of children with disabilities in society (Darling, 1979; Featherstone, 1980). They may experience the stigma associated with disabled individuals in the same way families sometimes do. For a doctor who knows the family well, the unanticipated arrival of a severely impaired infant may attack the professional's sense of competence and expertise, much as the family may question what they did wrong during the prenatal period to cause the disability.

As indicated by Darling in Chapter 5, doctors are taught to find cures. Many indicate that they do not like to provide care to chronic patients because there is no hope for recovery (Ford, 1967). Similarly, teachers define their own self-worth on the basis of the progress their students make. The need for professionals to experience positive effects of their work can result in their becoming overly invested in a child and competing with parents about who is best able to facilitate the child's development. When progress is slow and answers are not forthcoming, feelings of professional inadequacy arise and discomfort increases in interacting with parents who want to see improvements (Featherstone, 1980).

More than ever before children are surviving physical conditions that previously would have resulted in death in early infancy. Improvements in medical care have accompanied innovations in teaching technologies and adaptive equipment. It is not surprising that it is difficult to predict the course of development or how much progress disabled children may make. Professionals need to come to terms with the realization that they will not always have answers. They may wish to share these occasional feelings with families as a means of emphathizing with the dilemmas of trying to serve a child with many needs. Being compassionate and honest helps overcome the traditionally adversarial relationship that can develop when both parties are frustrated.

Finally, professionals need to develop better ways of collaborating with parents. All too commonly, the professional dominates and gives directions to the family and the parents follow the directive without giving input. Public Law 94–142 was designed to clearly establish parental rights and participation in planning special education services for children with disabilities. In some surveys, parental attendance at meetings in which a child's Individual Educational Plan is developed ranges from 65% to 85%. However, actual decision making and parental participation in developing the IEP is much lower, suggesting that parent views are often ignored (Turnbull & Winton, 1983). Often the plan is already drawn up when the meeting is called, and thus from the parents' point of view, their input is not taken seriously. Any changes requested by the parent at this point in the process are viewed negatively by teachers, and thus parents are made to feel that they have to fight to be heard. Using parents as a primary source of information about the child, and involving them in the planning process, would help diffuse parent-professional antagonisms.

Another model of collaboration is the use of parent training. Although not all parents are able to or want to assume a primary teaching responsibility with their handicapped child, some skills such as feeding, dressing, and toileting can be most effectively learned at home. Also, parents often want suggestions about behavior problems that may be major irritants at home. Opportunities for group instruction and self-instruction using clearly written and illustrated materials have been shown to lead to increased self-confidence and optimism in parents (Baker, 1983). This model requires that the parents be the primary expert, from diagnosing the problem to recording behavioral data, devising a solution, and implementing an intervention program. The professional acts as a consultant but does not dominate the relationship. Professional training at the college level and in graduate schools should encourage exposure to and practice with models of collaborative relationships. In addition, professionals in training should become familiar with the feelings and needs of parents and they should explore, in-depth, their own reactions to individuals with disabilities. The burden is clearly on the professional community to change the prevailing mode of interaction with parents from an adversarial one to a cooperative one.

CONCLUSION

The primacy of the family's role as the major provider of social services for handicapped individuals has been reasserted just at the time when trends in national policy reflect restrictions and cutbacks in services. In addition, this role is being asserted at a time when the demographic characteristics of families (divorce rates, mobility, working mothers) make it more difficult for families to provide the caregiving that many individuals with handicapping conditions require. This chapter has explored some of the needs of families with handicapped members. It has noted policy shortcomings and service barriers, and described some of the available services and the problems in relationships between parents and professionals.

It is clear from this review of family needs and the existing service system that although a range of innovative ideas and services are developing, better information about the variability in family needs is essential, and significant efforts must be made to coordinate existing services. Furthermore, we must work toward eliminating the wide geographic inequities in availability of services. And finally, both professionals with specialized training in disabilities and those in the broader service system need to recognize the past history of difficult relationships between families and professionals. They must strive to create collaborative partnerships rather than create adversarial situations.

REFERENCES

Akerley, A. S. (1985). False gods and angry prophets: The loneliness of the long distance swimmer. In H. R. Turnbull & A. P. Turnbull (Eds.), *Parents speak out: Then and now* (2nd ed.) Columbus, OH: Merrill, pp. 23–37.

Agosta, J. M., & Bradley, V. J. (1985). (Eds.). *Family care and persons with developmental disabilities: A growing commitment.* Boston: Human Services Resource Institute.

Association for Retarded Citizens. (1983). *Developing family support networks research report.* Philadelphia, PA: Author.

Avis, D. W. (1985). Deinstitutionalization jet lag. In A. P. Turnbull & H. R. Turnbull (Eds.), *Parents speak out: Then and now* (2nd ed.) Columbus, OH: Merrill, pp. 185–199.

Baker, B. L. (1983). Parents as teachers: Issues in training. In J. A. Mulich & S. M. Pueschel (Eds.), *Parent professional partnerships in developmental disability services.* Cambridge, MA: Ware, pp. 55–74.

Beavers, J., Hampson, R. B., Hulgus, Y. F., & Beavers, W. R. (1986). Coping in families with a retarded child. *Family Process, 25,* pp. 365–378.

Bennett, J. M. (1985). Company halt. In A. P. Turnbull & H. R. Turnbull (Eds.), *Parents speak out: Then and now* (2nd ed.) Columbus, OH: Merrill, pp. 159–183.

Bernheimer, L.P., Young, M. S., & Winton, P. J. (1983). Stress over time:

Parents with young handicapped children. *Journal of Developmental and Behavioral Pediatrics, 3,* pp. 177-181.

Blatt, B., & Kaplan, F. (1966). *Christmas in purgatory: A photographic essay on mental retardation.* Boston: Allyn & Bacon.

Boggs, E. M. (1984). Feds and families: Some observations on the impact of federal economic policies on families with children who have disabilities. In M. A. Slater & P. Mitchell (Eds.), *Family support services: A parent professional partnership.* Stillwater, OK: National Clearinghouse of Rehabilitation Training Materials, pp. 65-78.

Braddock, D. (1986). Federal assistance for mental retardation and developmental disabilities I: A review through 1961. *Mental Retardation, 24,* pp. 175-182.

Braddock, D. (1987). *Federal policy toward mental retardation and developmental disabilities.* Baltimore, MD: Paul H. Brookes.

Braddock, D., & Fujiura, G. (1987). State government financial effort in mental retardation. *American Journal of Mental Deficiency, 91,* pp. 450-459.

Bristol, M. M., & Schopler, E. (1983). Stress and coping in families of autistic adolescents. In E. Schopler & G. B. Mesibov (Eds.), *Autism in adolescents and adults* (pp. 251-278). New York: Plenum Press.

Bronfenbrenner, U., & Weiss, H. B. (1983). Beyond policies without people: An ecological perspective on child and family policy. In S. Kagan & T. Klugman (Eds.,), *Children, families and government: Perspectives on American family policy.* Cambridge, England: Cambridge University Press, pp. 393-413.

Butterfield, E. C. (1967). The role of environmental factors in the treatment of institutionalized mental retardates. In A. A. Baumeister (Ed.), *Mental retardation: Appraisal, education and rehabilitation.* Chicago: Aldine, pp. 120-137.

Byrne, E. A., & Cunningham, C. C. (1985). The effects of mentally handicapped children on families: A conceptual review. *Journal of Child Psychology and Psychiatry, 26,* pp. 847-864.

Castellani, P. J., Downey, N. A., Tausig, M. D., & Bird, W. S. (1986). Availability and accessibility of family support services. *Mental Retardation, 24,* pp. 71-79.

Crnic, K., Friedrich, W. N., & Greenberg, M. T. (1983). Adaptation of families with mentally retarded children: A model of stress, coping and family ecology. *American Journal of Mental Deficiency, 88,* pp. 125-138.

Cummings, S. T. (1976). Impact of the child's deficiency on the father: A study of fathers of mentally ill and chronically ill children. *American Journal of Orthopsychiatry, 46,* pp. 246-255.

Darling, R. B. (1979). *Families against society: A study of reaction to children with birth defects.* Beverly Hills, CA: Sage.

Dunlap, W. R., & Hollinsworth, J. B. (1977). How does a handicapped child affect the family?: Implications for practitioners. *The Family Coordinator, 26,* pp. 286–293.

Dunst, C. J., & Leit, H. E. (1986). *Family resources, personal well being and early intervention.* Morganton, NC: Human Development Research and Training Institute, West Carolina Center.

Dunst, C. J., & Trivette, C. M. (1986). Mediating influences of social support: Personal, family and child outcomes. *American Journal of Mental Deficiency, 90,* pp. 403–417.

Erickson, M. & Upshur, C. C. (1989). Caretaking burden and social support: Comparison of mothers of infants with and without disabilities. *American Journal of Mental Retardation, 94,* pp. 250–258.

Faber, B. (1986). Historical contexts of research on families with mentally retarded members. In J. J. Gallagher, & P. M. Vietze (Eds.), *Families of handicapped persons* Baltimore, MD: Paul H. Brookes, pp. 3–23.

Featherstone, H. (1980). *A difference in the family.* New York: Basic Books.

Ford, A. B. (1967). *The doctor's perspective: Physicians' view of their patients and practice.* Cleveland, OH: Case Western Reserve University Press.

Friedrich, W., & Friedrich, N. (1981). Psychosocial assets of parents of handicapped and nonhandicapped children. *American Journal of Mental Deficiency, 86,* pp. 551–553.

Friedrich, W., Wilturner, L. T., & Cohen, D. S. (1985). Coping resources and parenting mentally retarded children. *American Journal of Mental Deficiency, 90,* pp. 130–139.

Goldberg, S., Marcovitch, S., MacGregor, D., & Lojkasek, M. (1986). Family responses to developmentally delayed preschoolers: Etiology and the father's role. *American Journal of Mental Deficiency, 90,* pp. 610–617.

Gollay, E., Freedman, R., Wyngaarden, M., & Kurtz, N. (1978). *Coming back: The community experience of deinstitutionalized mentally retarded people.* Cambridge, MA: Abt Books.

Harris, G. A. (1985). Fairy tales, Beatlemania and a handicapped child. In A. P. Turnbull & H. R. Turnbull (Eds.), *Parents speak out: Then and now* (2nd ed.), Columbus, OH: Merrill, pp. 261–268.

Hauber, F. A., Bruininks, R. H., Hill, B. K., Lakin, K. C., Scheerenberger, R. C., & White, C. C. (1984). National census of residential facilities: A 1982 profile of facilities and residents. *American Journal of Mental Deficiency, 82,* pp. 236–245.

Healy, A., Keesee, P. D., & Smith, B. S. (1985). *Early services for children with special needs: Transactions for family support.* Iowa City, IA: University Hospital School.

The Hesel Family. (1985). Story of Robin. In A. P. Turnbull & H. R. Turnbull (Eds.), *Parents speak out: Then and now* (2nd ed.), Columbus, OH: Merrill, pp. 81–106.

Kagan, S. I., Klugman, E., & Zigler, E. (1983). Shaping child and family policies: Criteria and strategies for a new decade. In S. L. Kagan & E. Klugman (Eds.), *Children, families and government: Perspectives on American social policy.* Cambridge, England: Cambridge University Press, pp. 415–438.

Kauffman, M. E. (1966). The effects of institutionalization on development of stereotyped and social behavior in mental retardation. *American Journal of Mental Deficiency, 71,* pp., 581–585.

Kazak, A. E., & Marvin, R. S. (1984). Differences, difficulties and adaptations: Stress and social networks in families with a handicapped child. *Family Relations, 33,* pp. 67–77.

Kornblatt, E. S., & Heinrich, J. (1985). Needs and coping abilities of children with developmental disabilities. *Mental Retardation, 20,* pp. 2–6.

Krauss, M. W. (1986). Patterns and trends in public services to families with a mentally retarded member. In J. L. Gallagher & P. M. Vietze (Eds.), *Families of handicapped persons.* Baltimore, MD: Paul H. Brookes, pp. 237–248.

Love, H. (1973). *The mentally retarded child and his family.* Springfield, IL: Charles C. Thomas.

MacEachron, A. E., Pensky, D., & Hawes, B. (1986). Case management for families of developmentally disabled clients. In J. J. Gallagher & P. M. Vietze (Eds.), *Families of handicapped persons.* Baltimore, MD: Paul H. Brookes, pp. 273–287.

Michaelis, C. T. (1981). Mainstreaming: A mother's perspective. *Topics in Early Childhood Special Education, 2,* pp. 11–16.

Moroney, R. M. (1980). *Families, social services and social policy: The issues of shared responsibility.* Washington, DC: U. S. Government Printing Office.

Moroney, R. M. (1983). Families, care of the handicapped and public policy. In R. Perlman (Ed.), *Family home care: Critical issues for services and policies.* New York: Haworth Press, pp. 118–212.

Moses, K. L. (1983). The impact of initial diagnosis: Mobilizing family resources. In J. A. Mulich & S. M. Pueschel (Eds.), *Parent professional partnerships in developmental disability service.* Cambridge, MA: Ware, pp. 11–39.

Mulich, J. A., & Pueschel, S. M. (Eds.) (1983). *Parent professional partnerships in developmental disability services.* Cambridge, MA: Ware.

New York State Association for Retarded Citizens and Parisi v. Rockefeller, 357 F. Supp: 752 (E.D.N.Y. 1973).

Nirje B. (1969). A Scandinavian visitor looks at U.S. institutions. In R. B. Kugel & W. Wolfensberger (Eds.), *Changing patterns in residential services for the mentally retarded*. Washington, DC: President's Commission on Mental Retardation.

Pennsylvania Association for Retarded Citizens v. Commonwealth of Pennsylvania, 324 F. Supp. 1257 (E.D. Pa. 1971).

Project Serve. (1985). *New directions: Serving children with special health care needs in Massachusetts*. Boston, MA: Massachusetts Health Research Institute.

Roos, P. (1985). Parents of mentally retarded children: Misunderstood and mistreated. In A. P. Turnbull & H. R. Turnbull (Eds.), *Parents speak out: Then and now* (2nd ed.), Columbus, OH: Merrill, pp. 245–257.

Rotegard, L. L., Bruninks, R. H. & Krantz, G. C. (1984). State operated residential facilities for people with mental retardation, July 1, 1978–June 30, 1982. *Mental Retardation, 22,* pp. 69–74.

Salisbury, C. L. (1986). Parenthood and the need for respite. In C. L. Salisbury & J. Incagliata (Eds.), *Respite care: Support for persons with developmental disabilities and their families*. Baltimore, MD: Paul H. Brookes, pp. 3–28.

Schalock, R. L. (1985). Comprehensive community services. In R. H. Bruininks & K. C. Lakin (Eds.), *Living and learning in the least restrictive environment*. Baltimore, MD: Paul H. Brookes, pp. 37–63.

Scheerenberger, R. C. (1983). *Deinstitutionalized residential services for the mentally retarded: 1982*. Washington, DC: National Association of Superintendents of Public Residential Facilities for the Mentally Retarded.

Schilling, R. F., & Schinke, S. P. (1984). Personal coping and social support for parents of handicapped children. *Children and Youth Services Review, 33,* pp. 47–54.

Schulz, J. B. (1985). The parent-professional conflict. In A. P. Turnbull & H. R. Turnbull (Eds.), *Parents speak out: Then and now* (2nd ed.), Columbus, OH: Merrill, pp. 3–20.

Stone, R., & Newcomer, R. (1985). Health and social services policy and the disabled who have become old. In M. P. Janicki & H. M. Wisinewski (Eds.), *Aging and developmental disabilities: Issues and approaches*. Baltimore, MD: Paul H. Brookes, pp. 27–39.

Suelzle, M., & Keenan V. (1981). Changes in family support networks over the life cycle of mentally retarded persons. *American Journal of Mental Deficiency, 86,* pp. 267–274.

Trivette, C., & Dunst, C. J. (in press). Proactive influences of social support in families of handicapped children. In N. Stinnet (Ed.), *Family strengths: Vol. 8. Positive and preventive measures.* Lincoln, NE: University of Nebraska Press.

Turnbull, A. P., Brotherson, M J., & Summers, J. A. (1985). The impact of deinstitutionalization on families. In R. H. Bruininks & K. C. Lakin (Eds.), *Living and learning in the least restrictive environment.* Baltimore, MD: Paul H. Brookes, pp. 115–140.

Turnbull, A. P., Summers, J. A., & Brotherson, M. J. (1986). Family life cycle: Theoretical and empirical implications and future directions for families with mentally retarded members. In J. J. Gallagher & P. M. Vietze (Eds.), *Families of handicapped persons: Research, programs and policy issues.* Baltimore, MD: Paul H. Brookes, pp. 45–65.

Turnbull, A. P., & Turnbull, H. R. (Eds.). (1985). *Parents speak out: Then and now.* Columbus, OH: Merrill.

Turnbull, A. P., & Winton, P. (1983). A comparison of specialized and mainstreamed preschools from the perspective of parents of handicapped children. *Journal of Pediatric Psychology, 8,* pp. 57–71.

Upshur, C. C. (1982). Respite care for mentally retarded and other disabled populations: Program models and family needs. *Mental Retardation, 20,* pp. 2–6.

Vitello, S. J., & Soskin, R. M. (1985). *Mental retardation: Its social and legal context.* Englewood Cliffs, NJ: Prentice Hall.

Weyling, M. C. (1983). Parent reactions to handicapped children and familial adjustment to routines of care. In J. A. Mulick & S. M. Pueschel (Eds.), *Parent professional partnerships in developmental disability services.* Cambridge, MA: Ware, pp. 125–138.

Wikler, L. (1981). Chronic stresses of families of mentally retarded children. *Family Relations, 30,* pp. 281–288.

Wikler, L., Wasow, M., & Hatfield, E. (1981). Chronic sorrow revisited: Attitude of parents and professionals about adjustment to mental retardation. *American Journal of Orthopsychiatry, 51,* pp. 63–70.

Winton, P. J., & Turnbull, A. P. (1981). Parent involvement as viewed by parents of preschool handicapped children. *Topics in Early Childhood Special Education, 1,* pp. 11–19.

Wolfensberger, W. (1972). *The principle of normalization in human services.* Toronto: National Institute on Mental Retardation.

Wyatt v. Stickney, 344 F. Supp. 387 (M.D. Ala. 1972).

CHAPTER FIVE

Parent-Professional Interaction
The Roots of Misunderstanding

Rosalyn Benjamin Darling, Ph.D.

Rosalyn Benjamin Darling, Ph.D., is Executive Director of Beginning Early Intervention Services in Johnstown, Pennsylvania, and is an adjunct faculty member at the University of Pittsburgh at Johnstown, where she teaches courses in medical sociology and the sociology of disability. She is the immediate past president of the Early Intervention Providers Association of Pennsylvania.

Dr. Darling is the author of three books, Ordinary Families, Special Children: A Systems Approach to Childhood Disability *(with Milton Seligman, the editor of this volume),* Children Who Are Different: Meeting the Challenges of Birth Defects in Society *(with husband, Jon) and* Families Against Society: A Study of Reactins to Children with Birth Defects, *as well as various articles and chapters on sociological aspects of disabling conditions in children.*

It's somebody's tragedy. I can find good things in practically everything — even dying — but birth defects are roaring tragedies. . . . There's nothing interesting about it. . . . Death doesn't bother me, but the living do.*

—a pediatrician

They told me it would be a long, hard road with nothing but heartaches. . . . It hasn't been that way at all. . . . She's my baby, and I love her and I wouldn't trade her for another child.*

—the parent of a child with Down syndrome

WORLDVIEWS AND THEIR SOURCES

Sociologists use the concept of worldview to describe the way individuals and groups perceive and define the events they encounter in everyday life. Members of the same cultural group tend to have similar worldviews. However, to the extent that their life experiences differ, individuals may have views that diverge markedly from those of others. The quotes above illustrate such divergent views in the case of disabled children. Because their life experiences and consequent expectations differ, parents and professionals often approach children with disability from different perspectives. As a result, parent-professional interactions are strained, and conflict is a common outcome. As Friedson (1961) wrote, "the separate worlds of experience and reference of the layman and the professional worker are always in potential conflict with each other" (p. 175).

Knowledge, beliefs, attitudes, and opinions about a subject are learned through experience — at home, at school, on the job. Many parents have little knowledge of children before they have children of their own. The parenting experience is a powerful means of socialization that shapes parents' views of child development and appropriate parental behavior. Similarly, physicians and other professionals acquire their views from their educational training and subsequent professional experience, as well as from their day-to-day experiences. A professional who is not a parent cannot understand parenthood from the same perspective that the parent of five children has. Similarly, a parent of a typical child cannot understand the experience of parenting a child with a disability in the same way as can the disabled child's parent.

The differing worlds of experience of parents and professionals is illustrated by the following account related by the mother of four multiply handicapped children.

*Reported in Darling, 1979, pp. 166, 169, 215.

> I told my doctor I was always tired, and he said, "It's your nerves." . . .
> It got to the point where I thought, "Nobody wants to help me." . . . I
> saw a psychologist on TV and I called him. He said, "Don't you think
> someone else could take care of your children as well as you can?" I
> said, "It's not a matter of someone else. It's a matter of being able to
> pay somebody." He said, "Go to work." . . . I'm not qualified. I've been
> home for 20 years. . . . I'm seeing someone else now. He's kind of giv-
> ing me the blame for the way I am: "It's your fault you feel the way you
> do about things." I don't *want* to feel this way. . . . He says, "You cre-
> ate your own problems." My problem is that I have four handicapped
> children, and that has nothing to do with the fact that I had an unhappy
> childhood. . . . I'm nervous because I have reason to be nervous. . . .
> That night we were supposed to go someplace, and the van at the CP
> center broke down, so suddenly we had four kids to worry about. . . .
> We had to change our plans. . . . *That's the problem with these profes-
> sionals. . . . They have a job . . . They don't live with the parents 24
> hours a day.* What sounds nice at the office just doesn't work in real life
> [emphasis added] (Darling, 1979, pp. 179–180).

Similarly, a mother of a spina bifida child explained,

> The doctor says "Don't put her in diapers," and comes down hard on
> me when I do. . . . The last time I tried [putting her in panties], we
> both ended up being embarrassed in public. . . . Medical professionals
> see things only one way. They have no idea how the problem affects the
> family (Spina Bifida Association of America, 1982).

In one study (Wolraich, 1980), a majority of pediatric practitioners reported
no nonprofessional contact with developmentally disabled individuals, and
in another small sample of pediatricians (Darling, 1979), less than 7 percent
had an immediate family member who had a disability.

In this chapter the differing worldviews of parents of disabled children
and professionals who work with them are examined. The sources of both
parental and professional attitudes and behavior are explored, and strategies for reconciliation are suggested, with the aim of improving the treatment of the disabled child.

THE PROFESSIONAL (CLINICAL) WORLDVIEW

Many different professionals are involved with families of disabled children.
Depending on the child's disability, treatment professionals may include primary care and special physicians, nurses, and other medical personnel, educators, various therapists, social workers, psychologists or other

counselors, among others. Each of these professionals has a unique world-view associated with professional training and practice as well as with every-day social experience. In the past, the primary shapers of the professional worldview have been (a) socialization in a stigmatizing society and (b) train-ing in the clinical perspective. Each of these forces is discussed in turn.

Social Stigma

Professionals are, first of all, people. As a result, they are exposed to the same social influences as others in society. From the time they are small they see uncomplimentary images of disabled people on television or read uncomplimentary accounts in books (literary villains, such as Long John Silver, have been classically depicted as disabled or disfigured), they hear unfavorable epithets, such as "retard" or "crip," and most have little infor-mal, direct social contact with disabled individuals. Media images *are* slowly changing, and the disabled *are* becoming a more vocal and visible minority in American society. Most professionals practicing today, however, have grown up with negative images of the disabled that are not easy to change.

As Goffman (1963) stated in his classic work on the subject, the pre-dominant social attitude toward those who are "different" is one of *stigma,* and stigmatized individuals are regarded as morally inferior to those who are "normal." Goffman's observations have been supported by a number of studies, which found that persons with various disabilities were not ac-cepted by "normals." (See, for example, Kleck, Ono, & Hastorf, 1966; Rich-ardson, 1970; Richardson, Goodman, Hastorf, & Dornbusch, 1961.) Discrimination against the disabled has been well documented in educa-tional, occupational, recreational, and other settings.

Most of the public's exposure to disabling conditions is negative. Even when the disabled are shown in a positive light, they are typically depicted as objects of pity rather than as happy, fulfilled human beings. Considering such exposure, one pediatrician's view of disabled children is not surprising.

> There are personal hang-ups. You go home and see three beautiful, per-fect children; then you see this "dud." You can relate more easily to those with three beautiful, perfect kids. . . . If somebody comes in with a cerebral palsy or a Down's, I'm not comfortable. . . . It's hard to find much happiness in this area. The subject of deformed children is de-pressing. Other problems I can be philosophic about. As far as having a Mongoloid child, I can't come up with anything good it does. There's nothing fun or pleasant (Darling, 1979, pp. 214–215).

Some professionals may have more negative views of families than families have of themselves. One study (Blackard & Barsh, 1982) found significant differences between parents' and professionals' responses to a questionnaire about the impact of the disabled child on the family. As compared with parents' responses, the professionals tended to overestimate the negative impact of the child on family relationships. The professionals overestimated the extent to which parents reported community rejection and lack of support and underestimated parents' ability to use appropriate teaching and behavior management techniques.

Such negative attitudes could be counteracted by professional training. However, as the following section shows, stigma may actually be reinforced by education in medical schools and other professional training programs.

The Clinical Perspective

The clinical perspective is shared by a variety of professionals, including physicians, social workers, and psychologists. Not all professionals are exposed, to the same extent, to the clinical perspective, and many changes are taking place in professional education. A majority of the professionals practicing today, however, have had some exposure to this perspective, and their attitudes and behavior have been shaped by it as a result.

The clinical perspective has a number of components, including

(a) a belief in psychologistic theories of human behavior that traces the causes of problems within the victim's personality or other individual traits,

(b) the medicalization of all human problems based on an acute infectious disease model,

(c) a belief in the need for professional dominance, and

(d) a tendency to accept the restrictions imposed by the bureaucratic context of clinical work.

These components are learned both formally and informally in the course of professional education and in professional practice. Each component is discussed separately.

Blaming the Victim   Much clinical work involves changing the individual who has a problem. In the traditional medical model, the physician examines the patient, but not the patient's environment, to locate the cause of an illness. Similarly, when a child performs poorly in school, the child is often evaluated by an educational psychologist to determine the cause of the problem. Not many would suggest that the school or teacher be evaluated instead of the child. In the same way, a juvenile convicted of theft is sent to a training school to be rehabilitated; the juvenile's parents are not usually sent to prison. Education for clinical work, thus, tends to focus on the patient or client to the exclusion of the social framework within which the client operates.

The behavioral science training that is part of many professional education programs often has an individualistic focus as well. Training in the psychoanalytic perspective in particular emphasizes that the source of most human problems is within an individual's (or his or her parents') psyche. Subconscious motives are sought as explanations for pathologic behavior and, in some cases, *all* behavior is attributed to subconscious motives.

The clinical literature regarding parents of children with disabilities is replete with such psychologistic interpretations. The major motivational force in these cases is believed to be parental guilt over having given birth to an imperfect child (see, e.g., Forrer, 1959; Powell, 1975, Zuk, 1959). When such an interpretive framework is used, expressions of parental love are sometimes defined as "idealization," attention to a child's needs becomes "overprotection," and treating a child as normal is seen as "denial." Regardless of whether parents apparently accept or reject their children, their actions are believed to stem from a similar guilt-based source.

In some cases, parents are directly blamed for their children's disabilities. In instances of fetal drug and alcohol syndromes, for example, parents may be scorned by professionals for their direct role in causing their children's problems. Certain disabilities tend to be more stigmatizing than others. Wasow and Wikler (1983) found, for example, that professionals tended to react more positively toward parents of mentally retarded children than toward parents of children who were mentally ill, because these parents were believed to be responsible for their children's disabilities.

Professionals who accept victim-blaming explanations seem to have difficulty believing that parents of disabled children can *really* love their offspring in the same way as do parents of typical children. Yet at the same time parents are expected to cope with their situation, regardless of the availability of physical, social, or financial supports to help them. When parents fail to cope, then, their failure is blamed on a supposed neurotic inability to accept their child. *Real* needs for financial aid, help with child care, or medical or educational services tend to be discounted and attributed to parental inadequacy rather than to a lack of societal resources.

Although some parents certainly *do* have neurotic tendencies, the victim-blaming model is inadequate to account for the many problems faced by parents of children with disabilities. These problems stem largely from the fact that society is structured for typical families, and goods and services for the disabled are usually difficult, if not impossible, to find. Parental counseling does little to relieve parents of the burdens of daily care associated with having a disabled child in the home. Yet many textbooks in the field persist in stressing guilt-based theories of parental behavior, and many new professionals come away from their training with the belief that the parents of children with disabilities are responsible for their own problems.

The Medical Model   The primary focus of medical education is curing. Diseases that are readily amenable to cure provide the greatest rewards for medical students and physicians and enhance the physicians' feelings of self-worth and success. When physicians in one study (Mawardi, 1965) were asked which aspects of their careers they found most satisfying, they typically said "good therapeutic results or a large percentage of successful cases." Similarly, in a study of medical students, Ford (1967) found that the students had unfavorable attitudes toward "severely disabled" and "hopelessly ill" patients.

Pediatricians, in particular, have been trained to cure the acute illnesses of childhood, and most have chosen their specialty because of an appreciation for the qualities of typical, healthy children. As one pediatrician said, "our business is a pleasant business — going into the hospital to see a mother who has just had a [normal] baby" (Darling, 1979, p. 211). In one study of a small group of practicing pediatricians, Ford (1967) found that none of the respondents especially liked chronically ill patients and 46 percent definitely disliked the chronic cases.

The character of pediatric practice has changed over the years with the advent of modern antibiotics and immunizations techniques. The emphasis on the curable has consequently shifted from severe infectious illnesses to high technology management of life-threatening situations. The neonatal intensive care unit marks this shift. The ultimate goal, however, remains *the maintenance or restoration of normalcy of function.* This goal does not take into account the child who cannot be made "normal."

Because of its emphasis on the typical child, pediatric education has traditionally neglected the area of developmental disabilities. One study of pediatricians (Powers & Rickert, 1979) found that only 27 percent felt that medical school and residency training had prepared them adequately to work with disabled children. Similarly, Wolraich (1980) found that pediatric practitioners had less knowledge of developmental disabilities than did residents with 1 month of special training in this area. Finally, Kelly and Menolascino (reported in Wolraich, 1982) found that most physicians were unaware of associations of parents of disabled children, and many were unfamiliar with mental retardation services. Thus, most physicians complete their training with little knowledge of developmental disabilities and with the idea that permanently disabling conditions are not interesting, not important, or too depressing for further involvement. As one pediatrician (reported in Darling, 1979) said,

> I don't enjoy it. . . . I don't really enjoy a really handicapped child who comes in drooling, can't walk, and so forth. . . . Medicine is geared to the perfect human body. Something you can't do anything about challenges the doctor and reminds him of his own inabilities (p. 215).

Sometimes the emphasis on curing has even led physicians to refuse to treat children with severe, permanent disabilities (U.S. Commission on Civil Rights, 1986). Lorber (1971) and Duff and Campbell (1973) have presented strong arguments for nontreatment in some cases, and Todres, Krane, Howell, and Shannon (1977) have reported that more than half of the pediatricians they studied felt that newborns with Down syndrome should not receive lifesaving surgery. Similarly, two-thirds of the surgeons in another study (Shaw, Randolph, & Manard, 1977) would not consent to surgery for intestinal obstruction if their own child had Down syndrome. The argument for nontreatment is the ultimate natural outcome of a model that stresses curing when curing is defined as making perfect.

Some have suggested the need for a new model in pediatric practice. Those who cannot be cured can still be treated. Treatment methods go beyond traditional medical practice and include educational and advocacy techniques. Pediatrics *is* slowly coming to recognize the need for more and better education in this area (Guralnick, 1981; Guralnick & Richardson, 1980). Bennet (1982) suggested that the pediatrician's role in the future will involve being "an active advocate for the 'whole' child in the family, community, and society." Recent trends in pediatric education are discussed later in this chapter.

Professional Dominance   The professional-client relationship involves power and subordination. Traditionally, the professional's expertise has created a situation of professional dominance (Freidson, 1970), in which the "helpless" client or patient accepts whatever treatment the professional prescribes. Examples of professional dominance can be found in all fields. Most parents sign without question the individual education plans presented by their children's teachers, and most patients do not question their physician's diagnoses (at least not while they are still in the doctor's office).

Professional dominance does differ somewhat among professional fields. By virtue of their education and training and their high social status in the community, physicians have greater dominance than other professionals. Teachers are more vulnerable and more likely to feel threatened by parents. As Lortie (reported in Seligman, 1979) noted, parents in America enjoy considerable rights in controlling their children's education. The enhancement of these rights by recent legislation (P.L. 94–142 and its amendments) is regarded by many teachers to be a challenge to their professional expertise. On the other hand, some studies (Barsch; Shapiro, reported in Seligman, 1979) indicate that parents may be more positively predisposed toward teachers than other professionals.

Professional dominance serves to enhance a professional's self-esteem at the expense of the client's. As Slack (1977) has written, "For centuries, the medical profession has perpetrated paternalism as an essential component of medical care and thereby deprived patients of the self-esteem that comes from self-reliance." In order to maintain their self-esteem, professionals have traditionally felt a need to be in control of the interaction situation. Such control is enhanced by the settings in which such interactions generally occur—in the professional's office, school, hospital, or clinic—and only rarely in the client's home or office. Even in home-based programs, though, parents may feel a need to impress the teacher or therapist with the cleanliness of their house, the way their child is dressed, or their statements about having worked on program activities.

Professional dominance is learned in the process of professional education. As Haug and Lavin (1981) noted, "the training of physicians lays heavy stress on their taking responsibility for their patients, which would seem to require the authority to be in charge and, if necessary, to take control in order to carry out that responsibility despite patient objections" (p. 218). Furthermore, Wolraich (1982) has written, "Medical training often neglects to teach physicians how to say 'I don't know' in a manner that will not reflect poorly on their competence. In fact, during medical school and residency training any lack of knowledge is frequently viewed as poor performance" (p. 325). Thus, the physician (and other professionals) learns to speak authoritatively as a mark of responsibility, competence, and expertise.

One way that professionals can maintain their dominance is to control the amount of information that the client receives. As Crozier (reported in Waitzkin & Stoeckle, 1976) wrote, "A physician's ability to preserve his or her own power over the doctor-patient relationship depends largely on the ability to control the patient's uncertainty." Numerous examples exist in the literature of physicians' withholding information about prognosis in the case of serious, permanent, or terminal conditions (see, e.g., Darling, 1979; Davis, 1960; Glaser & Strauss, 1965; Quint, 1965). When curing is not possible, the professional's dominance is threatened, and power is maintained only as long as the client or patient does not recognize the professional's inability to control or change the prognosis.

In the case of permanent birth defects, for example, physicians commonly engage in stalling techniques such as avoidance, hinting, mystification, or passing the buck (see Darling, 1979, pp. 212–213, for a further explanation of these terms) in order to delay informing the parents. These techniques are usually rationalized with statements about parents' inability to handle emotion-laden information, as seen in these pediatricians' remarks (Darling, 1979):

> Birth is a traumatic experience. For 24 to 48 hours after birth the mother has not returned to a normal psychological state, so I just say everything is O.K., even if it isn't.
>
> It's not wise to go into all sorts of possibilities. I don't want to raise anxiety. Emotionally, they're in shock. They're really not listening.
>
> With cerebral palsy, I sort of lead them into it. I say, "Wait and see." I hedge. Usually I don't call in specialists for two or three months. It depends on parental pressure.
>
> I go slowly. . . . I don't seek a consultation right away. Usually the mothers want to see a specialist right away. They want the uncertainty removed (pp. 205, 208).

Sosnowitz (1984) has shown, too, how the control of information was used as a patient-management technique in a neonatal intensive care unit: "The staff wanted a chance to observe how the parents would react to the crisis. When staff was unable to predict the parents' reactions, they usually gave just enough information to keep the parents involved" (Sosnowitz, 1984, p. 396). Freidson (1970) argued that the client is believed to be "too ignorant to be able to comprehend what information he gets and . . . is, in any case, too upset at being ill to be able to use the information he does get in a manner that is rational and responsible" (p. 42). Although information control is deliberately used to maintain professional dominance, in some cases, it does seem to result from misperceptions by professionals. Waitzkin (1985) found, for example, in an analysis of 336 outpatient encounters, that physicians overestimated the time they spent in information-giving and underestimated patients' desires for information.

Gliedman and Roth (1980) noted that parents of disabled children are typically caught between victim-blaming and professional dominance: "As for the parent . . . he finds himself in a double bind: Either submit to professional dominance (and be operationally defined as a patient) or stand up for one's rights and risk being labeled emotionally maladjusted (and therefore patientlike)" (p. 150). The clinical perspective is thus difficult to escape.

The Bureaucratic Context Professional-client relationships reflect their societal context. The traditional model of the country doctor who makes house calls to a patient who is an old friend is no longer valid. As Bloom and Summey (1978) and others have noted, the patient today engages the services of a professional institution rather than a professional person. Increasing bureaucratization has diminished the interpersonal bond between the professional and client. The bureaucratic context is apparent in this mother's report (Darling, 1979): "We went to the clinic at _____ Children's Hospital. . . . We saw a different doctor every time and we always had to wait a long time. One time, Kathy was so fussy by the time they got around to examining her, they couldn't even examine her. . . . The doctors treated her like a 'thing' " (p. 152).

The professional sees many clients with similar problems, and individual clients are only rarely regarded as special or unique. As Freidson (1961) has written, "The routine of practice not only makes varied elements of experience equivalent — it also makes them *ordinary*" (p. 176). With regard to teachers, Waller (reported in Seligman, 1979) noted that the child is just one member of the category "student," and parents' requests for special treatment are regarded as presumptuous because their child is no different from the other pupils in the class. Gliedman and Roth (1980) noted, similarly, that although an appointment with a professional may be the highlight of a parent's day, for the professional, it is routine.

Although the parent sees the child in many different contexts (homes, school, neighborhood, etc.), the professional looks at the child only within the context of a particular specialty, such as medicine or education. According to Roth (1962): "The goals of the professional in his relationship to the client tend to be highly specialized . . . whereas the goals of the client include goals generated by all of his roles in addition to that of client of a given professional person" (p. 577).

Professional training teaches the student to see the client as a "case" rather than as a person. With regard to medical education, Straus (1978) has written,

> In [medical education] . . . a preoccupation with the intensely gratifying rewards associated with modern medical miracles has tended to focus values on impersonal techniques, substances, organs, systems, and procedures and to obscure the continuing importance of knowledge about the patient and the vital need for effective personal relationships with the patient (p. 416).

Wolraich (1982) noted, too, that communication skills have traditionally been regarded to be part of the "art" of medicine and consequently have not been stressed in medical education.

As part of increasing bureaucratization, our professional care system has been marked by increasing specialization. Thus, as Pratt (1978) noted, although the client may expect total care from a given professional, the professional's expectations may include only limited involvement with the client. A physician, for example, may have little or no interest in a child's school adjustment or even in the child's medical problems that fall outside his or her field of specialization. Parents are not always aware of these distinctions between specialists.

The professional worldview is an ideal type. Not all professionals necessarily accept all of its tenets; in fact, many would reject some or all of them. Haug and Lavin (1981) have shown, for example that some physicians do try to accommodate their patient's wishes rather than play a dominant role, and even within the bureaucratic context, a few professionals do develop close, personal relationships with their clients.

Although the ideal type may not fit any given professional individual, it describes the subculture or norms, values, attitudes, and beliefs to which most professionals are exposed in the course of their training, practice, and collegial associations. The professional worldview characterizes the *professional community as a whole* but allows for variation within the whole. The worldview thus describes what parents may encounter when they interact with professionals concerning their disabled children.

THE PARENT WORLDVIEW

Parents' worldviews generally change over time. Before their children are born, most parents of disabled children hold the same stigmatizing views of the disabled that others in society hold. The experience of giving birth to and parenting a child who is "different," however, usually has a profound effect on parents' beliefs, values, and attitudes. Changing parental worldviews over a course of the following four time periods are discussed:

(a)   prenatal,
(b)   infancy,
(c)   childhood, and
(d)   adolescence.

These periods describe stages in the lives of parents of congenitally disabled children. Although parental reactions may be the same, these time periods will differ in the cases of disabilities that occur later in childhood or in later-appearing birth defects.

Prenatal Views

Most parents anticipate the birth of a healthy newborn. Although many do express concerns about the health of their unborn offspring, these concerns are generally rationalized away by the time the birth is imminent. Obstetricians and childbirth education classes usually assume that the baby will be normal, and the possibility of birth defects is not mentioned.

Parents enter the delivery room, then, with a set of expectations revolving around the birth of a normal baby. In the case of obvious birth defects, these expectations are not fulfilled. Although few physicians tell parents about a defect immediately, many physicians arouse suspicion by their behavior:

> The doctor did not say anything at all when the baby was born. Then he said, "It's a boy," and the way he hesitated, I immediately said, "Is he all right?" And he said, "He has ten fingers and ten toes," so in the back of my mind I knew there was something wrong (mother of a Down syndrome child, reported in Darling, 1979, p. 129).

Sometimes, parents' suspicions continue to be aroused well into the postpartum period when physicians continue to deny the existence of a problem. Most parents are aware of an abnormality before they are informed by their pediatrician. However, as noted in the last section, physicians generally use various stalling techniques before acknowledging that parents' suspicions are correct. The result is bitterness toward the physician:

> I always thought they told you the truth in the hospital and if you wanted to know anything you should ask. I really thought her ears looked funny and I had this funny feeling, so I asked the doctor, "Is there anything wrong?" and he looked right at me and said, "No." . . . The next morning he told me she was retarded. . . . I was very bitter about it (mother of a Down syndrome child, reported in Darling, 1979, p. 131).
>
> [The neurologist said] "I think I know what's wrong with your son but I'm not going to tell you because I don't want to frighten you." Well, I think that's about the worst thing anyone could say. . . . We didn't go back to him. . . . We insisted that our doctor refer us to Children's Hospital, but the doctor said, "He's little. Why don't you wait? You don't need to take him there yet." . . . Everyone was pablum-feeding us, and we wanted the truth (mother of a child with cerebral palsy, reported in Darling, 1979, p. 147).

Before they are given a truthful diagnosis, then, many parents of children with congenital disabilities feel a great deal of *anomie* in the form of meaninglessness. They know that *something* is wrong with their baby and they fear the worst. When professionals refuse to confirm their suspicions, parents sometimes develop pathologic reactions, such as blaming the baby's delayed development on their own inadequacies. They rarely challenge their physicians directly because they have been socialized to respect the physician's professional dominance. In the end, however, parents' confidence in their physician is likely to be eroded.

Infancy

When parents are first informed about their children's disabilities they are likely to feel shock, disappointment, grief, sorrow, and remorse. Such reactions are understandable in light of the fact that, typically, parents' only prior exposure to disabling conditions has been negative. As one mother said, "I was thinking of all the retarded people I'd seen. I wasn't thinking about my little girl anymore" (Darling, 1979, p. 135). Another mother said, "I remember thinking, before I got married, [having a disabled child] would be the worst thing that could ever happen to me" (Darling, 1979, p. 124).

Strongly negative reactions are usually short-lived, however. Most parents receive encouragement and support from close friends and family members, but the strongest shaper of parental feelings is usually the infant itself. As parents live with their children, they learn to love them. Most parents leave the postpartum period with the desire to do all they can for their children, because, like parents of nondisabled children, their self-esteem as parents is based in some measure on their children's accomplishments. Although parents' goals may have to be adjusted (the physically disabled child may not become a star athlete, and the mentally disabled child will not become a great scientist), most parents are able to find meaning and pleasure in the goals their children *can* accomplish, no matter how small.

In our society, "good" parents do all they can for their children. As a result, most parents are strongly motivated to find appropriate treatment programs that will maximize their children's achievements. Parents' quests, however, are sometimes thwarted by professionals who see little merit in training disabled children who will never be "normal" to achieve small objectives. Consequently, meaninglessness is replaced by feelings of powerlessness, and parents continue to feel anomie because they are not in control of their children's lives and have no definite plan of action.

Because some pediatricians are not aware of services for disabled children even when they do see the value of such services, parents sometimes embark on long and elaborate searches to find information about their children's problems, infant stimulation and preschool training programs, physical therapy, special equipment, and community resources of various kinds.

As one mother said, "I was looking for a door at that point — somebody who could give us any help at all. Dr. _____ didn't even tell us there was a state agency that dealt with mental retardation" (Darling, 1979, p. 149).

For many parents, the first source of real help is other parents of similarly disabled children. In parents' groups mothers and fathers receive emotional support as well as practical information about child rearing techniques, resources, and services. As one mother said, "I met other parents of the retarded after we moved here. I felt that made the biggest difference in my life. . . . Down there (where we lived before) . . . I felt that I was just singled out for something, that I was weird. I felt a lot of isolation and bitterness. . . . Meeting other parents you get practical hints — like how someone got their child to chew — that normal parents take for granted" (Darling, 1979, pp. 162–163).

Parents' groups serve, too, as a forum for exchanging "horror stories" about bad experiences with professionals. Favorite stories usually involve the situation in which the parents receive their first information about a child's problem and some professionals' lack of caring or concern for disabled children. When parents hear stories similar to their own they realize that their experiences are shared and their definitions of events are supported. As a result, some parents become more assertive in advocating their rights and their children's rights in interactions with professionals.

During the preschool years, most parental advocacy involves medical professionals. Professionals often claim that parents of disabled children shop around in search of a miracle cure. However, most "shopping" usually involves first, a search for a correct diagnosis, and second, a search for a practitioner who is eager or even willing to have the child as a patient. One family with a severely disabled child describes how they became involved with an alternative treatment program.

> My pediatrician kept after me to put him away (in an institution). (We finally changed pediatricians). Our new pediatrician gushed all over us at first. . . . But then, he never touched Billy. I always had to move him for him. We were never left in the waiting room. It was like I was an embarrassment. . . . It's like when you take your dog to the vet. . . . Not many doctors pick him up and try to communicate with him as a child.
>
> Because nothing was happening, and I was just sitting there with this baby, we got involved with the patterning program. . . . It was the first time that anyone had reacted to him as Billy: "Billy is a person, and we'll help Billy." We were never told he would be cured. They were the first people who reacted to Billy as a person or called him by name. Up to that time he had done nothing. My pediatrician said, "You're just looking for hopes." I said, "No, I'm just looking to *do* something for him. I'm sitting at home doing nothing" (Darling, 1979, pp. 151, 152).

Parents of children with disabilities are probably more likely than other parents to play an active role in their children's medical treatment because of repeated negative experiences with medical professionals. Disabled children are more likely to require frequent hospitalization, and parents are more likely to come into contact with a variety of medical professionals, not all of whom will be sympathetic toward the child. These parents begin to feel as though their child is the "property" of the hospital and the medical professional, and they come to resent their loss of control over their lives and that of their child. As one mother of a spina bifida child said, "We were always going back and forth to _____ Children's Hospital. . . . It was a constantly pulling away. We could never be a family. . . . We got to the point where we hated doctors, we hated _____ Children's Hospital" (Darling, 1979, p. 154).

On the other hand, some professionals do make an effort to include parents as case managers for their children, and such efforts are generally appreciated. As Stotland (1984) wrote,

> The most important aspect of the doctor's presentation was that he involved us as equals in the decision-making process. . . . By involving us in the process and by giving us his professional opinion as an opinion, he returned to us our parental rights of making the important decision that would affect our child's life. We were in control, but we were no longer alone (p. 72).

Parents' expressions of dissatisfaction with medical treatment have been encouraged by the recent growth of the consumer movement in health care. As Reeder (1972) noted, the consumer-provider relationship is not as one-sided as it was in the past, and bargaining and negotiation are now part of the interaction process. Haug and Lavin (1979) found that although most people are willing to challenge a physician's authority today, they have never done so. The strongest impetus to actually challenging a medical practitioner appears to come with the experiencing of medical error (Haug & Lavin, 1981), an experience that is common among parents of disabled children. Pizzo (1983) argued similarly that parent advocacy derives from "acute, painful experiences." (Parent activism is further discussed later in this chapter.)

By the end of the preschool years, most parents have obtained an accurate diagnosis of any early-appearing disability and have found a pediatrician who is willing to treat the child. Many have also found emotional support from family, friends, and especially, from other parents of children with disabilities. The lifestyle of such parents is usually not very different from that of other young parents in American society.

Childhood

By the beginning of the school years, most parents have developed a *realistic acceptance* toward their situation. They remain unhappy about their children's disabilities but they are able to see positive aspects in their children's lives. As one mother said, "I'm not sorry. I think it's opened a whole new world for me — you don't get involved until it strikes home" (Darling, 1979, p. 185). Although they would prefer that their children not be disabled, most parents love them in spite of their disabilities. Some phrases used by one sample of parents (Darling, 1979) to describe their disabled sons and daughters included: "a joy to me and her family," "retarded but can learn," "a binding force in the family as a whole," "a beautiful child," and "a teacher of compassion and love."

Voysey (1975) suggested that the ideology of realistic acceptance is learned from professionals, voluntary associations, and the popular culture. In our society, parents of disabled children are *supposed* to accept their situation. "Success stories" and other images of parents who are coping well are commonly presented in the media, and parents are expected to emulate these models. Most parents do live up to such expectations and learn to make the best of their difficult situation. In attempting to achieve a lifestyle that is as close to normal as possible, these parents often look to professionals to provide needed supports. When such supports are not forthcoming, conflict results.

As already discussed, most parent-professional conflict during the preschool years involves medical professionals. During later childhood the focus of conflict tends to shift to the school. Because our educational system is structured primarily for typical children, it often fails to meet the needs of the exceptional child. Thus, parents once again come to play the role of advocate in attempting to secure an appropriate educational program for their children.

The most common educational problem faced by these parents is the placement of the child in an inappropriate program. Usually such placements are made for the convenience of the school system rather than to meet the needs of the child. As one mother of a spina bifida child explained:

> When Ellen entered kindergarten, she was in a special needs class in the morning and mainstreamed in the afternoon. . . . [In the special needs class], she was with children whose needs were much more demanding than Ellen's. . . . Some were retarded. . . . At the end of the year we had a meeting. The first grade was on the second floor . . . [Ellen was in a wheelchair]. They said we should keep her in the special needs class. I was furious. . . . She had done so well in the mainstreaming

> class. . . . I wanted her in a regular first grade and I suggested moving the class downstairs. . . . They wanted Ellen in the special needs class, because it was easier for *them,* not for any other reason (Darling & Darling, 1982, p. 140).

Sometimes, *no* appropriate placement exists, as revealed in this account by the mother of four multiply handicapped teenagers.

> At Children's Hospital, Tony was in a class with bright, active kids. . . . He just sat in the corner and played in the sandbox. . . . Then he went to the School for the Blind, which is geared for the totally blind child. . . . They mostly concentrated on teaching Braille. Finally, Tony and Jean had to leave the school. They said they were retarded. The teachers were not trained in learning disabilities. . . .
>
> After Tony and Jean were labeled retarded by the School for the Blind, they started in the [city] Public School System, but they had no appropriate program either. . . . After three years, we started fighting. . . . The Board of Education said, "We've got all kinds of retarded programs. We'll just put them in one of those. . . . I visited the programs, and there wasn't one child in a wheelchair. . . . I said, "How are my children going to get around? How are they going to go on these stairs?" . . . They told us we had the only multiply handicapped teenagers in the city. . . . I said, "We have the only *siblings,* but you've got a lot of *misplaced* multiply handicapped children." I knew them all (Darling, 1979, pp. 176–177).

The parents of these children continued to write letters to school system administrators, and a program was finally established. As another parent explained, "You eventually get what you need . . . if you're very persistent, but they always leave you with the feeling that they're doing you a favor . . . to provide your son with an education" (Darling & Darling, 1982, p. 138).

Another common concern involves a lack of coordination among educational services (Orenstein, 1979). Because current legislation mandates that disabled children be mainstreamed in regular classes as much as possible, many children are served by special education teachers or therapists for part of the school day and by regular classroom teachers the rest of the day. Regular teachers who have not been trained to work with the disabled are often not involved with special education programming, and as Scanlon, Arick, and Phelps (1981) noted, most do not attend parent conferences. Some of these teachers resent their exclusion by special education staff. However, parents may come to feel that regular class teachers and other school personnel are not interested in their children's education.

Finally, some parents engage in controversies with school systems over the provision of ancillary services, such as in-school physical therapy or catheterization. In some cases, long court battles have resulted from parents' challenging the school's denial of such services to their children. Catheterization of a spina bifida child, for example, is a procedure that can be performed by a school nurse. When nurses do not perform the procedure, the parent must come to the school every day to do it. This daily requirement is burdensome to parents, especially those who do not have transportation, and it usually generates resentment toward the administrators who refuse to assign the procedure to school personnel. As a result of one parent's persistence, the Supreme Court recently ruled that schools must provide this service ("Related Services and the Supreme Court," 1984).

Sometimes parents are afraid that if they challenge the school system their children will be removed from a mainstream situation and placed in special classes or that the children will be hurt in other ways. As one mother said, "I'm always afraid that if I start making any waves, then they will reflect this on Ellen. I want her to be accepted" (Darling & Darling, 1982, p. 141).

As Seligman (1979) noted, parents may also feel intimidated by teachers for other reasons. They may feel inferior educationally or socially. The teacher may be older than the parent or of a different sex. Most parents are nervous in the conference situation anyway because they are likely to hear negative evaluations of their child. Such fears do not encourage open communication between parents and school personnel.

By the end of the school years, many parents of disabled children do become more assertive as a result of repeated negative experiences with the school system. Just as parents feel the need to challenge professional dominance in the medical realm, they feel pressured to do likewise in the educational realm. Parents are trying to secure services that will permit them to enjoy a normalized lifestyle, one similar to that of families with nondisabled children.

The desire for normalization is the prime motivating force for parents of children with disabilties. For some families normalization is relatively easy to attain because of supportive physicians, cooperative school systems, and other family and community supports. Other families attain normalization only after a series of struggles to obtain needed services. A few families whose children have unusual, continuing needs or who are socially or geographically isolated never attain normalization at all; for them the primary mode of adaptation is continued "crusadership" to create needed services, or resignation to their fate. (See Chapter 4 for a further discussion of these outcomes.) Most commonly, however, families do achieve normalization by the end of the childhood years. As one father described this adaptation, "Retardation is not number one around here. It's just something that Karen has" (Darling, 1979, p. 190).

Adolescence

The bubble of normalization may be burst as adolescence and impending adulthood approach. Typical children become increasingly independent as they grow. They eventually leave home and establish independent lifestyles. For the moderately or severely disabled child such independence is problematic, and parents who have been living "one day at a time" must once again begin to search for solutions as their children's adulthood approaches.

Because concern about the future is a highly salient concern to parents at this time, their interactions with professionals may reflect this. Parents may look to professionals for help in finding appropriate living arrangements, occupational placements, or legal or financial advice for their adult children. When professionals are not able to provide the information and advice that parents seek at this stage in their children's lives, parents may turn to nonprofessional sources for help such as parents' associations.

Parents' worldviews, then, tend to change over the course of their children's life stages. During the prenatal period, most parents hold somewhat negative views of the disabled and somewhat positive views of professionals. In the immediate postpartum period negative views of the disabled generally continue, but professionals may come to be regarded negatively as well. During later infancy and childhood, views of the disabled typically change. As they live with and come to love their own children, parents are able to view disabled individuals in a favorable light and to see some positive aspects of their own life situations. Views of professionals are likely to remain unfavorable, however, as negative interactions with medical, educational, and other professionals continue to occur. Eventually some parents do encounter professionals who are helpful to them, but negative attitudes will continue to prevail as long as large numbers of professionals are uninformed about, uninterested in, or unconcerned abut the needs of children with disabilities and their parents.

THE CLASH OF PERSPECTIVES

Because parents and professionals hold such divergent worldviews, when they meet in various interaction situations each may define the other in a negative way. Although parents and professionals generally do not openly discuss these negative views with one another, the resulting lack of mutual respect is likely to affect the quality of care that the disabled child receives.

The opposing worldviews of parents and professionals that have been described can be summarized by a typology suggested by Parsons (1951). According to Parsons, the role of the professional in our society is characterized by the traits of achievement, universalism, functional specificity, and affective neutrality. When the Parsonian typology is applied to parents of disabled children (or clients or patients in general) their role can be characterized by the traits of ascription, particularism, functional diffuseness, and affectivity. In addition, the professional role is marked by dominance, and the client role is marked by anomie and submission (see Table 5-1). Although these are ideal-typical traits that do not always apply to individual professionals or parents, they describe the normative expectations that accompany the parent and professional *roles* in American society today.

Achievement/Ascription

Whereas the status of professional is *achieved,* the status of parent of a disabled child is *ascribed.* Because professionals *choose* their careers, they are likely to expect the freedom to practice in a manner that is interesting and rewarding to them. As a result, many do not want to be "bothered" with the problems of disabled children. Parents, on the other hand, have little choice; they have given birth to a child with a chronic problem whose care they are expected to assume. Although parenthood is an achieved status, if given a choice, virtually no parents would want their children to be disabled. Most, however, are able to love their child and accept society's expectations about good parenting and doing everything possible to help their child. These parents become frustrated when they interact with professionals who do not share their parental enthusiasm. They may also come to resent the professional who deals with their problems during working hours, whereas they deal with them 24 hours a day.

Universalism/Particularism

The professional is concerned with all cases of a particular type, and the parents are concerned with only one case—their own child. The univer-

TABLE 5-1   Ideal-Typical Role Patterns of Professionals and Parents

Professional	Parent
Achieved	Ascribed
Universalistic	Particularistic
Functionally specific	Functionally diffuse
Affectively neutral	Affective
Dominant	Anomic

salistic orientation of the professional is reflected in the bureaucratic structure of clinical practice and the tendency to treat all clients in a like manner, regardless of each client's unique personal situation. Professionals tend to categorize clients on the basis of clinical theory and past personal and clinical experience. Resulting generalizations may lead them to treat all parents of a given class similarly. Peiper (in Darling & Darling, 1982) noted anecdotally, for example, a case in which a professional gave parents a long lecture about their guilt over having given birth to a disabled child, only to learn that the child who was the subject of their discussion was adopted.

Parents resent universalistic treatment. For them, *this* child is important. Parental reports like the following are typical:

> Whenever there's something wrong, our pediatrician says, "I don't know what I can do for you. That's her condition." . . . He blames all of her [medical] problems on retardation instead of treating them (mother of a severely retarded child).
>
> She had a problem with her knee, and we took her to Children's Hospital. . . . They said, "There's nothing we can do with one of *these* children" (father of a child with Down syndrome).
>
> [Our pediatrician] treated her as an article in a medical journal (mother of a child was a rare congenital syndrome) (Darling, 1979, pp. 151, 152).

Specificity/Diffuseness

As Mercer (1965) noted, clients may be regarded from either a clinical or a social system perspective. In the clinical perspective, the client is defined in terms of his or her problem; in the social system perspective, all of the client's roles—in addition to the role of "client with a problem"— are taken into account. Most professionals employ a clinical perspective, in which the client's specific presenting problem or symptoms become paramount and the other roles played by the client in the community are ignored. Thus the hospital patient becomes "the gall bladder in Room 23," even though he is also a husband, a father, a carpenter, and a churchgoer. One adult with cerebral palsy noted that the message constantly communicated by professionals was, "your weakest point is what is most important to us, we don't care about the rest of you" (Richardson, 1972, p. 533). Similarly, the father of a retarded child with cerebral palsy remarked, "The pediatrician . . . would keep him alive but he wasn't interested in Brian as a *person*" (Darling, 1979, p. 152).

Parents see their children playing a variety of social roles: loving son or daughter, sibling, grandchild, playmate, and student, as well as child with a disability. Their relationship to their child is diffuse, involving all of these roles. Sometimes, when a child's disability does not conflict with the roles played by the child in the family setting, parents do not define the child as disabled at all. A child with a learning disability, for example, may be regarded as perfectly normal at home and in the neighborhood. The parents of such a child may resent a label applied by professional educators that is not relevant to their experience. Professionals sometimes accuse such parents of denying reality; their unidimensional perspective prevents them from realizing that the parents' "reality" may be very different from their own.

Affective Neutrality/Affectivity

Professional training stresses the instrumental nature of the professional role, and the professional is cautioned about becoming too emotionally involved with the client. Overinvolvement is believed to impair the professional's instrumental effectiveness. Consequently, many professionals seek to maintain some emotional distance between themselves and their clients. Stacey (1980) noted, further, that professionals are often not trained in techniques of counseling or supportive communication.

Clients, on the other hand, generally expect professionals to satisfy their socioemotional needs. Freidson (1961) found that patients expected their physicians to be *both* technically competent and able to satisfy emotional needs. Many questioned their physicians' competence in the socioemotional area. Another study (Hickson, Altemeier, & O'Connor, 1983) found that although only 30 percent of the mothers seeking care in private pediatric offices were most concerned about their children's physical health, most parent-physician communication involved only this topic. Psychosocial concerns were not raised because parents believed that pediatricians were not interested in helping them in that area. Pediatricians, on the other hand, assumed that parents were not interested in discussing their psychosocial concerns with them. Many parents interpret professionals' affective neutrality to mean that these professionals do not care about their children. Some parents become involved in unconventional or sometimes even unethical treatment programs because these programs are likely to provide greater emotional satisfaction. Parents who love their children resent teachers, physicians, and other professionals who appear to be indifferent and do not show any appreciation for their children's positive qualities.

Professional Dominance/Anomie

Generally, both professionals and parents have a need to be in control of their situations of mutual interaction. Typically, however, professionals retain control. The ritualized routine of clinical practice supports the professional's dominance. Parents, on the other hand, are likely to feel powerless and resent the professional's control over their lives.

Parents only rarely challenge professional dominance openly, however. As Strong (1979) noted in a study of two hospital outpatient departments, "Many parents disagreed strongly with the doctors' verdict at one time or another. Nevertheless all but a handful made no direct challenge to their authority. Most maintained an outward pose of agreement with what they were told" (p. 87). Stimson and Webb (1975) explained patients' reticence to challenge the physician as follows.

> Our observations and interviews lead us to suggest that the doctor is aided in his ability to exert control over the information he gives and in his way of acting towards patients by their desire to please him, to emerge from the encounter without loss of face (p. 127).

Parents *do* often complain about professionals after they have left the clinical setting. Parents' groups serve an important function by providing a forum for storytelling. As a result of interaction in such groups, many parents change physicians or explore alternative treatment modes against the advice of professionals. As Stimson and Webb (1975) noted, "Whilst the patient's ability to control the outcome of the consultation is limited, he has considerable ability to control what happens after he has left the doctor's presence" (p. 87). Noncompliance with professional advice appears to be related, at least in part, to lack of satisfaction during the parent-professional encounter. Francis, Korsch, and Morris (1968) found in a study of outpatient visits to a children's hospital that the extent to which parents' expectations were not met, lack of warmth in the physician-parent relationship, and failure to receive a diagnostic explanation were key factors in noncompliance. Parents who do not have access to supportive interactions outside of the clinical setting may continue to feel anomie, however. Parents who reside in isolated rural areas or feel inferior socioeconomically are especially likely to remain powerless in the face of professional dominance.

NEW DIRECTIONS IN PROFESSIONAL TRAINING AND PARENTAL ACTIVISM

Are the worldviews of parents and professionals hopelessly in conflict? Until recently little effort was made, either by professionals or by parents, to change attitudes. Within the past few years, however, parents have become actively involved in social movements to bring about change. Even more recently, new professional training curricula are being designed to promote awareness of the needs of disabled children and their families.

Parental Activism

Consumerism in general has been growing in recent years. Various minority groups have also become more vocal in demanding their rights. As part of this larger social movement, parents of disabled children have become more active in asserting their demands for programs and services for their children. This new assertiveness has been aided by legislation such as the Education for All Handicapped Children Act (P.L. 94–142) and by a number of publications that instruct parents in organizing techniques (see, e.g., Biklen, 1974; Dickman, 1985, Markel & Greenbaum, 1979).

So far, most parental challenges have occurred within the realm of education. With the support of recent legislation, parents are confronting school administrators with demands for appropriate educational programs for their children. Challenges in the medical realm are not as common. Most parents are still intimidated by medical authority and are reluctant to confront physicians directly with their concerns. Consumerism in the health care field has been increasing, however, and parents will be more likely to challenge the medical profession directly as support for such challenges grows.

A number of studies have indicated that the professional dominance of physicians may have declined somewhat in recent years. Gallup and Harris polls (reported in Betz and O'Connell, 1983) show that the public's confidence in and respect for physicians have declined since 1950. In 1966, 72 percent of the public expressed confidence in doctors, but only 43 percent expressed such confidence in 1975. Haug and Lavin (1983, p. 16) wrote that "in the dialectic of power relations, the increasing monopolization of medical knowledge and medical practice could only call forth a countervailing force in the form of patient consumerism." Consumerism is fostered further by interaction in self-help groups and stories about successful advocacy efforts printed in the general media and specialized publications, such as *The Exceptional Parent* magazine.

Changing Professional Attitudes

While parents have become more involved in advocacy movements, some professionals have become similarly involved. Although some continue to question the correctness of such involvement and its implied threat to the affective neutrality of the professional role, (see, e.g., Adams, 1973; Kurtz, 1975), more and more professionals are arguing that advocacy is a necessary extension of helping, which is an inherent function of their role (see Council for Exceptional Children, 1981). Parsons (1951) suggested that, in addition to being affectively neutral, achieved, specific, and universalistic, the professional role is also *collectivity-oriented,* that is, the professional has a mission to help the client. When this mission conflicts with other aspects of the role the professional must decide which aspect is most important. Consequently, some professionals are choosing to become involved in advocacy on behalf of their clients.

The advocacy role may even include professionals' teaching parents how to interact with other professionals. Parents may need to learn that they have a right to ask questions, to explore program alternatives, to change physicians, or to challenge their child's school placement. Counselors, psychologists, social workers, and other professionals should inform parents about P.L. 94–142 and other laws that affect their children. Whether or not a professional agrees with a parent's view, he or she should make the parent aware of available alternatives and of advocacy organizations that exist in the community.

Medical school curricula have also been undergoing some changes in recent years. Because the acute infectious diseases of childhood are now largely treatable or preventable, pediatricians and family physicians have been turning their attention to other areas. Although most pediatric curricula do not stress chronic, disabling conditions, a new interest in developmental disability is apparent in a statement issued by the Task Force on Pediatric Education (1978). In addition, curricula on disabled children are being developed for pediatric residents and physician in-service training (Guralnick, Richardson, & Heiser, 1982; Powers & Healy, 1982). New instructional techniques using videotapes, trained parents, and experience with disabled children are also being used to make professionals more aware of the parent worldview (see, e.g., Guralnick, Bennett, Heiser, & Richardson, 1987; Richardson, Guralnick, & Tupper, 1978; Stillman, Sabers, & Redfield, 1977). Additional training components are being included in the field of education as well. At the University of Pittsburgh, for example, students in special education also take courses that familiarize them with the needs of parents and families. Newer assessment instruments and curricula in early intervention programs are also taking the expressed needs of families into account (see, e.g., Bailey et al., 1986).

Is Rapprochement Possible?

Will all these recent efforts bring parents and professionals closer together? In one report (Stacey, 1980), professionals who were made aware of parents' dissatisfaction did not change their behavior at all. However, as Richardson et al. (1978), Wolraich (1979), and others have reported, pediatricians and residents exposed to training programs in developmental disabilities did have more favorable attitudes toward disabled children as a result. Only the future will reveal whether the worldview gap between parents and professionals has been narrowed by recent efforts. Certainly, neither group will ever share the other's experiences completely. As long as human beings are capable of empathy, however, change in the direction of greater mutual understanding is possible.

REFERENCES

Adams, M. (1973). Science, technology, and some dilemmas of advocacy. *Science, 180,* pp. 840–842.

Bailey, D. B., Jr., Simeonsson, R. J., Winton, P. J., Huntington, G. S., Comfort, M., Isbell, P., O'Donnell, K. J., & Helm, J. M. (1986). Family-focused intervention: A functional model for planning, implementing, and evaluating individualized family services in early intervention. *Journal of the Division of Early Childhood, 10,* pp. 156–171.

Bennett, F. C. (1982). The pediatrician and the interdisciplinary process. *Exceptional Children, 48,* pp. 306–314.

Betz, M., & O'Connell, L. (1983). Changing doctor-patient relationships and the rise in concern for accountability. *Social Problems, 31,* pp. 84–95.

Biklen, D. (1974). *Let our children go: An organizing manual for advocates and parents.* Syracuse, NY: Human Policy Press.

Blackard, M. K., & Barsh, E. T. (1982). Parents and professionals' perceptions of the handicapped child's impact on the family. *TASH Journal, 7,* pp. 62–70.

Bloom, S. W., & Summey, P. (1978). Models of the doctor-patient relationship: A history of the social system concept. In E. B. Gallagher (Ed.), *The doctor-patient relationship in the changing health scene* (National Institutes of Health Publication 78-183) Washington, DC: U.S. Government Printing Office.

Council for Exceptional Children. (1981). Editor's note. *Exceptional Children, 198,* pp. 492–493.

Darling, R. B. (1979. *Families against society: A study of reactions to children with birth defects.* Beverly Hills, CA: Sage.

Darling, R. B., & Darling, J. (1982). *Children who are different: Meeting the challenges of birth defects in society.* St. Louis, MO: Mosby.

Davis, F. (1960). Uncertainty in medical prognosis, clinical and functional. *American Journal of Sociology, 66,* pp. 41–47.

Dickman, I. (1985). *One miracle at a time: How to get help for your disabled child—From the experience of other parents.* New York: Simon & Schuster.

Duff, R. S., & Campbell, A. G. M. (1973). Moral and ethical dilemmas in the special-care nursery. *New England Journal of Medicine, 289,* pp. 890–894.

Ford, A. B. (1967). *The doctor's perspective: Physicians view their patients and practice.* Cleveland, OH: The Press of Case Western Reserve University.

Forrer, G. R. (1959). The mother of a defective child. *Psychoanalytic Quarterly, 28,* pp. 59–63.

Francis, V., Korsch, B. M., & Morris, M. J. (1968). Gaps in doctor-patient communication: Patients' response to medical advice. *New England Journal of Medicine, 280,* pp. 535–540.

Freidson, E. (1961). *Patients' views of medical practice.* New York: Russell Sage Foundation.

Freidson, E. (1970). *Professional dominance.* Chicago: Aldine.

Glaser, B. G., & Strauss, A. L. (1965). *Awareness of dying.* Chicago: Aldine.

Gliedman, J., & Roth, W. (1980). *The unexpected minority: Handicapped children in America.* New York: Harcourt Brace Jovanovich.

Goffman, E. (1963). *Stigma: Notes on the management of spoiled identity.* Englewood Cliffs, NJ: Prentice-Hall.

Guralnick, M. J. (1981). Early intervention and pediatrics: Current status and future directions. *Journal of the Division of Early Childhood, 2,* pp. 52–60.

Guralnick, M. J., Bennett, F. C., Heiser, K. E., & Richardson, H. B., Jr. (1987). Training future primary care pediatricians to serve handicapped children and their families. *Topics in Early Childhood Special Education, 6,* pp. 1–11.

Guralnick, M. J., & Richardson, H. B. (Eds.). (1980). *Pediatric education and the needs of exceptional children.* Baltimore: University Park Press.

Guralnick, M. J., Richardson, H. B., Jr., & Heiser, K. E (1982). A curriculum in handicapping conditions for pediatric residents. *Exceptional Children, 48,* pp. 338–346.

Haug, M. R., & Lavin, B. (1979). Public challenge of physician authority. *Medical Care,* pp. 844–858.

Haug, M. R., & Lavin, B. (1981). Practitioner or patient: Who's in charge? *Journal of Health and Social Behavior, 22,* pp. 212–229.

Haug, M. R. & Lavin, B. (1983). *Consumerism in medicine: Challenging physician authority.* Beverly Hills, CA: Sage.

Hickson, G. B., Altemeier, W. A., & O'Connor, S. (1983). Concerns of mothers seeking care in private pediatric offices: Opportunities for expanding services. *Pediatrics, 72,* pp. 619–624.

Kleck, R., Ono, H., & Hastorf, A. H. (1966). The effects of physical deviance upon face-to-face interaction. *Human Relations, 19,* pp. 425–436.

Kurtz, R. A. (1975). Advocacy for the mentally retarded: The development of a new social role. In M. J. Begab & S. A. Richardson (Eds.), *The mentally retarded and society: A social science perspective.* Baltimore, MD: University Park Press, pp. 377–394.

Lorber, J. (1971). Results of treatment of myelomeningocele. *Developmental Medicine and Child Neurology, 13,* pp. 279–303.

Markel, G., & Greenbaum, J. (1979). *Parents are to be seen* and *heard: Assertiveness and educational planning for handicapped children.* San Luis Obispo, CA: Impact.

Mawardi, B. H. (1965). A career study of physicians. *Journal of Medical Education, 40,* pp. 658–666.

Mercer, J. R. (1965). Social system perspective and clinical perspective: Frames of reference for understanding career patterns of persons labeled as mentally retarded. *Social Problems, 13,* pp. 18–34.

Orenstein, A. (1979). *Organizational issues in implementing special education legislation.* Paper presented at the annual meeting of the Society for the Study of Social Problems, Boston.

Parsons, T. (1951). *The social system.* New York: Free Press.

Pizzo, P. (1983). *Parent to parent: Working together for ourselves and our children.* Boston: Beacon Press.

Powell, F. D. (1975). *Theory of coping systems: Changes in supportive health organizations.* Cambridge, MA: Schenkman.

Powers, J. T., & Healey, A. (1982). Inservice training for physicians serving handicapped children. *Exceptional Children, 48,* pp. 332–336.

Powers, J. T., & Rickers, N. (1979). Physician perceptions of in-service training needs: A working paper. Evanston, IL: American Academy of Pediatrics.

Pratt, L. V. (1978). Reshaping the consumer's posture in health care. In E. B. Gallagher (Ed.), *The doctor-patient relationship in the changing health scene.* Washington, DC: U.S. Government Printing Office. (National Institutes of Health Publication 78–183.)

Quint, J. C. (1965). Institutionalized practices of information control. *Psychiatry, 28,* pp. 119–132.

Reeder, L. G. (1972). The patient-client as a consumer: Some observations on the changing professional-client relationship. *Journal of Health and Social Behavior, 13,* pp. 406–412.

Related Services and the Supreme Court: A family's story (1984, October). *The Exceptional Parent,* pp. 36–41.

Richardson, H., B., Guralnick, M. J., & Tupper, D. B. (1978). Training pediatricians for effective involvement with preschool handicapped children and their families. *Mental Retardation, 16,* pp. 3–7.

Richardson, S. A. (1970). Age and sex differences in values toward physical handicaps. *Journal of Health and Social Behavior, 11,* pp. 207–214.

Richardson, S. A. (1972). People with cerebral palsy talk for themselves. *Developmental Medicine and Child Neurology, 14,* pp. 524–535.

Richardson, S. A., Goodman, N., Hastorf, A. H., & Dornbusch, S. M. (1961). Cultural uniformity in reaction to physical disabilities. *American Sociological Review, 26,* pp. 241–247.

Roth, J. A. (1962). The treatment of tuberculosis as a bargaining process. In A. Rose (Ed), *Human behavior and social processes.* Boston: Houghton Mifflin.

Scanlon, C. A., Arick, J., & Phelps, N. (1981). Participation in the development of the IEP: Parents' perspective. *Exceptional Children, 47,* pp. 373–374.

Seligman, M. (1979). *Strategies for helping parents of handicapped children.* New York: Free Press.

Shaw, A., Randolph, J. G., & Manard, B. (1977). Ethical issues in pediatric surgery: A national survey of pediatricians and pediatric surgeons. *Pediatrics, 60,* pp. 588–599.

Slack, W. V. (1977). The patient's right to decide. *Lancet, 30,* p. 240.

Sosnowitz, B. G. (1984). Managing parents on neonatal intensive care units. *Social Problems, 31,* pp. 390–402.

Spina Bifida Association of America. (1982). Mother expresses serious concerns about catheterization program. *Spina Bifida Insights,* p. 9.

Stacey, M. (1980). Charisma, power, and altruism: A discussion of research in a development centre. *Sociology of Health and Illness, 2,* pp. 64–90.

Stillman, P. L., Sabers, D. L., & Redfield, D. L. (1977). Use of trained mothers to teach interviewing skills to first-year medical students: A follow-up study. *Pediatrics, 60,* pp. 165–169.

Stimson, G., & Webb, B. (1975). *Going to see the doctor: The consultation process in general practice.* London: Routledge & Kegan Paul.

Stotland, J. (1984). Relationship of parents to professionals: A challenge to professionals. *Journal of Visual Impairment and Blindness,* pp. 69–74.

Straus, R. (1978). Medical education and the doctor-patient relationship. In E. B. Gallagher (Ed.), *The doctor-patient relationship in the changing health scene.* Washington, DC: U.S. Government Printing Office. (National Institutes of Health Publication 78–18).

Strong, P. M. (1979). *The ceremonial order of the clinic: Parents, doctors, and medical bureaucracies.* London: Routledge & Kegan Paul.

Task Force on Pediatric Education. (1978). *The future of pediatric education.* Evanston, IL: American Academy of Pediatrics.

Todres, I. D., Krane, D., Howell, M. D., & Shannon, D. C. (1977). Pediatricians' attitudes affecting decision-making in defective newborns. *Pediatrics,* pp. 197–201.

U.S. Commission on Civil Rights. (1986). *Protection of handicapped new-*

borns: Hearing held in Washington, DC., June 26–27, 1986, Volume 2. Washington, DC: U.S. Government Printing Office.

Voysey, M. (1975). *A constant burden: The reconstruction of family life.* London: Routledge & Kegan Paul.

Waitzkin, H. (1985). Information giving in medical care. *Journal of Health and Social Behaviors, 26,* pp. 81–101.

Waitzkin, H., & Stoeckle, J. D. (1976). Information control and the micropolitics of health care: Summary of an ongoing research project. *Social Science and Medicine, 10,* pp. 263–276.

Wasow, M., & Wikler, L. (1983). Reflections on professionals' attitudes toward the severely mentally retarded and the chronically mentally ill: Implications for parents. *Family Therapy, 20,* pp. 299–308.

Wolraich, M. L. (1979). Pediatric training in developmental disabilities. *Mental Retardation, 17,* pp. 133–136.

Wolraich, M. L. (1980). Pediatric practitioners' knowledge of developmental disabilities. *Journal of Developmental and Behavioral Pediatrics, 1,* pp. 133–136.

Wolraich, M. L. (1982). Communication between physicians and parents of handicapped children. *Exceptional Children, 48,* pp. 324–329.

Zuk, G. H. (1959). The religious factor and the role of guilt in parental acceptance of the retarded child. *American Journal of Mental Deficiency, 64,* pp. 139–147.

CHAPTER SIX

Fathers of Children With Special Needs

Michael E. Lamb and Donald J. Meyer

Michael E. Lamb, Ph.D. is a research scientist and chief, Section on Social and Emotional Development, Laboratory of Comparative Ethology, National Institute of Child Health and Human Development. He was formerly professor of Psychology, Psychiatry, and Pediatrics at the University of Utah from which he received the Distinguished Research Award in 1986. His research is concerned with social, emotional, and personality development, especially in the context of family relationships. He has written or edited two dozen books, including: The Father's Role: Applied Perspectives, Father Role: Applied Perspectives, Father's Role: Cross-Cultural Perspectives, *and* The Role of the Father in Child Development.

Donald J. Meyer helped begin the SEFAM (Supporting Extended Family Members) Program at the University of Washington, where he developed and implemented programs for fathers, siblings, and grandparents of children with special needs. He is the senior author of curricula on the Fathers Program, Sibshop, and Grandparents Workshop models, as

151

well as the illustrated children's book, Living With a Brother or Sister With Special Needs: A Book for Sibs. *Currently the Early Childhood Education Coordinator at the Children's Hospital and Medical Center in Seattle, Meyer continues to provide training on programs to meet the needs of traditionally underserved family members throughout the United States.*

Until a decade or two ago, students of human development did not think much about paternal influences on child development. An increasing focus on early (infantile) experiences had led to a near-exclusive focus on the formative importance of the mother-infant relationship. In Bowlby's (1951) classic treatise on institutionalization and social deprivation, the father's role as a source of emotional and economic support for mothers was alluded to briefly, but even this limited consideration was rare. Only after publication of Schaffer and Emerson's (1964) research on infant attachment and Rutter's (1972) reconceptualization of the "maternal deprivation" literature did there emerge a realization that in emphasizing the undeniable importance of mothers, theorists lost sight of the broader social context in which children are raised. As a result of this realization, the imbalance has been redressed somewhat in the last several years. Many research projects have been undertaken, and these have helped reshape the traditional conceptualization of the socialization process. Our understanding of socioemotional development in infancy has been revised most dramatically, but other areas of research have also been affected.

Other important changes in perspective have also occurred in the last decade or so. One such fundamental change concerns the way in which the child's role in socialization is portrayed. Formerly, we tended to view children as malleable organisms waiting to be shaped by exogenous socialization processes. We have become increasingly aware, however, that each child has individual characteristics that not only affect the way she or he is influenced by exogenous forces but also help to shape the socializers themselves (Bell & Harper, 1977). Socialization, then, is now viewed as a bidirectional process, whereas it was once viewed as a unidirectional process. Unfortunately, there have been relatively few systematic attempts to explore the ways in which children affect their parents and families (Lerner & Spanier, 1978). Conspicuously lacking are studies designed to explore the differential impact of different types of children — boys versus girls, temperamentally easy versus temperamentally difficult children, chronically-ill versus healthy children, or mentally retarded versus mentally normal children, and so forth—on marital quality and family interaction. Fathers of children with special needs have been conspicuously ignored. As a result, we do not yet know *how much* time fathers spend with children who are developmentally disabled or *how* they spend that time (Bristol & Gallagher, 1986). Traditionally, the focus has been on mothers: In reviewing 24 studies of parents' adaptation to their children's disability, Blacher (1984) found that fathers were rarely assessed.

Although fathers of children with special needs are an emerging focus of research, we still know little about their reactions to filial disability, the types of relationships these fathers have with their children, and the direct and indirect effects that these reactions and relationships have on the family. Consequently, this chapter is of necessity brief and uncomfortably speculative. We begin with a review of studies that have focused on the relationships between fathers and their nonhandicaped children. Thereafter, we review the small but growing body of literature on fathers of children with mental retardation. Finally, we turn attention to evidence concerning family integration and marital satisfaction in families with a child who has a handicap, to suggestions about the effects this may have on children and on parent-child relationships, and finally to implications for practitioners.

PATERNAL INFLUENCES ON CHILDREN

Let us begin by considering evidence suggesting that the father-child relationship deserves more attention than it has traditionally been accorded. The burden of the evidence briefly reviewed here is that most children establish emotionally salient relationships with both of their parents early in infancy and that fathers have a significant impact—which can be either positive or negative—on their children's development. The implication is that fathers have a significant role to play in the lives of disabled children too.

Father-Infant Relationships

Observational studies of infant-mother and infant-father interactions have demonstrated convincingly that infants form attachments to both their parents by the middle of the first year of life, even when their mothers are primary caretakers and their fathers spend relatively little time with them (Cohen & Campos, 1974; Kotelchuck, 1976; Lamb, 1976b, 1977c, 1979; Schaffer & Emerson, 1964). Thus, infants preferentially seek proximity to and contact with their parents, react with distress to separation from either, and are comforted by the presence of either. When they are distressed, infants turn to whichever parent is present for comfort, although distressed 12- and 18-month-old infants turn to their mothers rather than to their fathers when they have the choice (Lamb, 1976a, 1976e). Comparable preferences are not evident in 8- or 24-month-olds, which suggests that these preferences may only prevail during the first part of the second year of life (Lamb, 1976c, 1976d). Presumably, the preference patterns would be different if fathers were the primary caretakers, although the relevant research has yet to be conducted.

Direct Effects   There are two major ways in which mothers and fathers directly influence their children's socioemotional development. First of all, mothers and fathers are the major sources of stimulation and the primary models of socially approved behavior for their young children to emulate. The fact that both parents are attachment figures increases their salience in the eyes of their young children and thus maximizes their impact. Although new parents are initially more responsive to newborns of their own sex (Parke & O'Leary, 1976), it is fathers who remain more likely to accord preferential attention to sons in later infancy (cf., Lamb 1977a), whereas mothers discriminate less between sons and daughters. Probably as a result of their fathers' behavior, boys develop preferences for their fathers in the second year of life (Lamb, 1977b). Furthermore, although there are many ways in which maternal and paternal behavior is similar, there are some characteristic differences between maternal and paternal interactional styles, which ensure that mothers and fathers have distinct and independent influences on their infants' development. Thus, fathers are noted for their playfulness—more particularly their penchant for robust, physically stimulating play—whereas mothers are characteristically associated with caretaking and more conventional, "containing" modes of play (Belsky, 1979; Clarke-Stewart, 1978; Lamb, 1976b, 1977c; Yogman, Dixon, Tronick, Als, & Brazelton, 1977). Infants come to expect their parents to act in these characteristic ways (Lamb, 1981a). They also respond more positively to play bids by their fathers than by their mothers (Clarke-Stewart, 1978; Lamb, 1976b, 1977c), and they initiate playful interaction with their fathers by preference (Lynn & Cross, 1974).

The second way in which fathers may affect socioemotional development depends on the security of the infant-father attachment relationships. The security of attachment relationships is believed to depend on the meshing of the parent's and infant's behavior, usually expressed in terms of the adult's sensitive responsiveness to the infant's signals and needs (Ainsworth, Bell, & Stayton, 1974; Lamb, 1981a, 1981c). Infants establish relationships of different quality with their mothers and fathers, which suggests that the security of attachment characterizes specific relationships (and reflects the responsiveness of specific adults) rather than the infants' interactional style (Grossman & Grossman,1980; Lamb, 1978; Main & Weston, 1981; Sagi, Lamb, Lewkowicz, Shoham, Dvir, & Estes, 1985).

Two groups of researchers have compared the predictive validity of infant-mother and infant-father attachments. Main and Weston (1981) reported that the security of both infant-mother and infant-father attachments was associated with measures of the infant's sociability, but that the security of the relationships with mothers (who were in all cases the primary caretakers) was most important. The most sociable infants were those who were securely attached to both parents, then came those who were securely attached to their mothers only, then those who were securely attached to their fathers only, and finally those who were insecurely attached to both parents. These results suggested that the predictive validity and formative importance of the infant-*father* attachment would increase depending on the father's involvement in child rearing. However, Lamb, Hwang, Frodi (1982) obtained rather different results in their study of Swedish infants, some of whose fathers were unusually involved in child care. Only the security of infant-*father* attachment was related to sociability in this study, and there was no relation between the degree of relative involvement in child care and the relative predictive importance of the attachment relationships. These surprising results raised the possibility that the procedure used to assess security of attachment in the United States is not appropriate in some other cultures. Subsequent research has substantiated these doubts and has further suggested that the Strange Situation procedure is, at best, an imperfect measure on infant-parent attachment, although Strange Situation behavior is often correlated with measures of subsequent behavior (Lamb, Thompson, Gardner, & Charnov, 1985).

Indirect Effects   In addition to the direct effects discussed above, fathers also have significant indirect effects on their children's development (Belsky, 1981; Lewis & Weinraub, 1976; Parke, Power & Gottman, 1979). By this we mean that fathers affect child development — adversely or advantageously — by way of an influence on their wives. When the relationship between the parents are warm, fathers provide the emotional support that facilitates the formation of secure and stimulating infant-mother relationships, and thus they indirectly contribute to healthy socioemotional development. Similarly, in a traditional family, the father's financial support frees the mother of economic concerns and permits her to devote herself to their children's needs. By contrast, when the relationship between the parents is hostile and unsupportive, the quality of the mother-infant relationship is adversely affected. It is interesting to note that hostile marital relationships seem to have more reliably negative effects on child development than does divorce or the permanent absence of one parent (cf. Rutter, 1979).

Cognitive Development   Most of the recent research on father-infant relationships has been descriptive in nature. Consequently, few attempts have been made to determine the extent to which fathers influence the development of their young children. The few outcome-oriented studies that have been undertaken have been concerned with paternal influences on infant cognitive development (e.g., Belsky, 1980; Clarke-Stewart, 1978; Pedersen, Rubenstein, & Yarrow, 1979). These studies have demonstrated positive relationships between paternal involvement and cognitive development, but the interpretation of these relationships remain uncertain. It seems, however, that paternal stimulation can have a beneficial impact on children's cognitive development.

Paternal Influences on Older Children

In comparison with research on infancy, the research on older children is less programmatic and less concerned with defining the processes whereby parents affect their children's development. With few exceptions, this research has been correlational rather than experimental in nature, and longitudinal investigations have been rare. Consequently, few conclusions can be stated with any confidence.

Processes of Influence   Studies have identified both direct and indirect paternal influences on child development. Most directly mediated parental influences on child development involve either of two processes: behavioral conditioning or observational learning. It is obvious that both parents attempt to shape their children's behavior through the discriminating application of punishments and rewards, and these attempts are often successful—at least in the short run. Children also learn by imitating their unwitting parents, and they are most likely to imitate models who are warm, nurturant, and powerful (Bandura, 1977; Mussen, 1976). This of course maximizes the tendency to imitate parents rather than other adults.

Whereas psychologists have written about behavioral shaping and imitation for many years, they have only recently come to appreciate the importance of indirect effects (Belsky, 1981). Indirect effects involve influences of one parent on the other, who then behaves differently toward his or her children. The potential for indirect effects is enormous, and we are only beginning to appreciate the diverse ways in which they may affect child development (cf. Lewis & Feiring, 1981; Parke et al., 1979). Both direct and indirect effects are implicated by the studies discussed in the paragraphs that follow.

Gender Role and Gender Identity   As mentioned earlier, parents (especially fathers) are particular attentive (and thus salient) to children of the same sex from infancy. This may facilitate the acquisition of gender identity, which seems to occur in the first 2 to 3 years of life (Money & Ehrhardt, 1972).

Probably because they are much more concerned about "appropriately" sex-typed behavior than mothers are (Bronfenbrenner, 1961; Goodenough, 1957; Sears, Maccoby, & Levin, 1957; Tasch, 1955), fathers emit reinforcements and punishment for sex-typed behavior more consistently than mothers do (Langlois & Downs, 1980). Boys whose fathers are absent or uninvolved tend to be less masculine than those whose fathers are psychologically and physically present (see Biller, 1974 and 1981, for reviews). On the other hand, it is not the case that masculine fathers have masculine sons (e.g., Mussen & Rutherford, 1963; Payne & Mussen, 1956). Significant correlations between paternal and filial masculinity occur only when the father is also warm. Indeed, nurturance is more reliably related to the masculinity of sons than the fathers' masculinity is (Mussen & Rutherford, 1963; Payne & Mussen, 1956; Sears, et al., 1957). Girls whose fathers are masculine tend to be more feminine (Heilbrun, 1965; Johnson, 1963; Mussen & Rutherford, 1963; Sears, Rau & Alpert, 1965), presumably because these fathers complement and encourage their daughters' femininity. Both boys and girls develop less traditionally sex-stereotyped attitudes about male and female roles when their mothers work outside the home (see Hoffman, 1974, and Lamb, 1982, for reviews) and when their fathers are highly involved in child care (Radin, 1978; Sagi, 1982). Both of these effects are probably attributable to the fact that these parents provide less traditional models for their children to emulate.

Of course, sex role acquisition is affected not only by parental behavior but by other factors as well. From the preschool years through adulthood, significant influences are exerted by peers (Fagot, 1977; Fagot & Patterson, 1969; Lamb, Easterbrooks, & Holden, 1980; Lamb & Roopnarine, 1979; Nash & Feldman, 1981), teachers (Dweck, 1978; Fagot, 1977; Serbin, Tonick, & Sternglanz, 1977), and the media. Most of these socializing agents have a similarly traditionalizing effect, making it difficult to appraise the relative importance of each.

Achievement and Achievement Motivation   As mentioned earlier, appropriate responsiveness to infant signals and needs is believed to foster the development of a sense of personal effectance, which is a basic component of achievement motivation (Lamb, 1981a). Other studies show that parents who provide stimulation that is developmentally appropriate and plentiful have more cognitively competent children (see Stevenson & Lamb, 1981, for a review). High achievement motivation develops in boys whose parent are warm, not controlling, and who encourage independence (Radin, 1976; Rosen & D'Andrade, 1959; Winterbottom, 1958). Girls benefit when they receive less unconditional nurturance than they usually receive (Baruch & Barnett, 1978). In traditional families (i.e., those in which fathers are primary breadwinners and are the instrumental leaders of their families), paternal models are especially important to both boys and girls. Warm encouragement from fathers is important to many highly achieving women, because there are few female role models for them to emulate (Baruch & Barnett, 1978).

Children whose fathers are absent tend to perform more poorly in school than do children from two-parent families (Radin, 1981; Shinn, 1978), but this effect (i.e., paternal absence) is more consistent in lower-class than in middle-class families (Radin, 1981). Perhaps this is because single mothers in lower-class families are subject to more severe economic and socioemotional stress that affect their ability to guide and stimulate their children. Interestingly, Blanchard and Biller (1971) reported that qualitatively similar effects occurred when fathers were nominally present but were uninvolved with their sons. By contrast, children with highly involved, nurturant fathers tend to be more cognitively competent and to manifest the internal locus of control, which is one aspect of higher achievement motivation (Radin, 1978; Sagi, 1982).

Recently, conceptualizations of achievement motivation have been influenced by attributional theory (e.g., Dweck, 1978; Weiner, 1974). According to this theory, individuals can attribute their successes or failures to either controllable or uncontrollable (external) factors and to either effort or ability. Achievement motivation is enhanced when others (a) attribute the child's successes to his or her efforts and failures to the lack of effort and (b) encourage the child to attribute responsibility in this way. By contrast, achievement motivation is squelched when failures are attributed to a lack of ability and success to the easiness of the task. Although most researchers have studied the ways in which teachers affect the development of attributional styles (Dweck, 1978), it is likely that parents are also influential in this regard.

Moral Development   During the 1970s, the ascendence of Kohlberg's cognitive developmental theory of moral development (Kohlberg, 1969) provoked a focus on normative issues and a deemphasis of individual differences. Furthermore, to the extent that environmental influences are explicitly considered, Kohlberg emphasized interactions with peers rather than parents.

A comprehensive review of research on the determinants of moral development two decades ago concluded that parental disciplinary style was indeed influential (Hoffman, 1970). Children develop internalized controls (consciences) most readily when their parents discipline through induction and least when their parents employ a power-assertive strategy. Induction involves encouraging their child to consider the implication of his or her behavior (notably, disobedience) on other people. Although some studies show that boys whose fathers are absent display less moral internalization and are more likely to become delinqent than are boys whose fathers are present, the preponderance of the evidence indicates that mothers have a much greater influence on moral development than fathers do (Hoffman, 1981).

Psychological Adjustment   Most of the research on this topic has been concerned with the antecedents of psychological *mal*adjustment. Many studies show that children whose parents are divorced or whose fathers are absent are more likely to manifest signs of psychological maladjustment (see Biller, 1981, for a review) but the mode of influence is unclear. Most likely, the divorce itself has adverse effects that are exacerbated by the inability of some single parents to supervise their children adequately — perhaps because they are themselves emotionally stressed and lack social supports. Other studies reveal that divorce has an immediate destabilizing influence on parents and children, who gradually return to stability and adjustment over a 2-year period following the breakup (Hetherington, Cox, & Cox, 1978). Large-scale epidemiological studies (e.g., Rutter, 1973, 1979) show that marital hostility and discord are among the most reliable causes of psychological maladjustment.

In one of the few studies concerned with parental influences on psychological adjustment, Baumrind (1971, 1975) reported that socially competent children (those who are friendly, independent, and assertive with peers and compliantly nonintrusive with adults) are likely to have authoritative parents — that is, parents who provide firm and articulately reasoned guidance for their children. Both authoritarian parents (those who fail to provide explanations for their commands) and permissive parents (those who fail to provide adequate guidance) have less socially competent children.

Summary

It is clear that parents have significant influences on their children that are attributable to the way they behave toward their children as well as the way they interact with one another. Direct and indirect parental influences on the development of sociability, sex roles, morality, achievement, cognition, and psychosocial adjustment have been demonstrated, although we can only speculate about processes of influence, given that they have not been explored very thoroughly.

Both mothers and fathers affect their children's development. In cases where the parents' sex role may be important (e.g. the development of sex differences and sex roles), mothers and fathers may affect their children differently, but in the main, they influence their children in similar ways. Single-parent families are at risk, not primarily because they lack an adult of one sex or the other, but because the single adult is socially isolated, without emotional and economic support, and without a partner to help in child rearing. In addition, marital hostility and the divorce process may have adverse effects on the psychological adjustment of the members of the family.

In some areas (e.g., sex role development), fathers appear to exert a disproportionate influence, either because they are especially concerned about the issue or because their relative novelty increases their salience in the eyes of their children. In other respects (e.g., the effects of attachment security), mothers may be more influential. However, in these cases the relative importance of the fathers' influence may increase as their involvement in child rearing increases. Finally, the quality of the marital relationship and other indirectly mediated effects are much more influential than was once believed.

FATHERS OF CHILDREN WITH SPECIAL NEEDS

The few available studies of fathers whose children have disabilities support only the most limited conclusions because the findings are compromised in a variety of ways. First, few researchers have observed fathers whose children have disabilities. Instead, findings are often based on clinical impressions, ratings of parental attitudes, or maternal reports of paternal reactions — emotional and behavioral. Second, many studies are methodologically flawed, particularly with respect to sampling, and researchers often provide few details concerning the procedures used and the range of disabilities represented (Hornby, 1987). Third, most studies have focused on the fathers' reaction to the diagnosis and on their initial adaptation. Much less common are studies examining the impact on fathers of adolescent or adult-age offspring (Meyer, 1986a) even though parents of older children with mental retardation often feel more isolated than do parents of young children with similar capacities (Suelzle & Keenan, 1981). Finally, most researchers have examined the impact of organically caused mental retardation rather than chronic illness, sensory impairments, physical disabilities, or even socioculturally caused mental retardation (Meyer, 1986b). Consequently, this chapter focuses primarily on fathers of children who have mental retardation.

According to Wikler (1981), learning of the diagnosis is often the most disturbing crisis parents face during the lives of their handicapped children. For many fathers, this tragedy is exacerbated by the insensitivity of professionals at the time of diagnosis. Fathers, it appears, experience additional stress when treated as second-class parents at the time of diagnosis. Many of the fathers interviewed by Erickson (1974) reported difficulty in obtaining information from physicians, and others only learned about the disability after their wives had been informed. When a child's disabilities are not evident soon after birth, the father may respond by denying the existence of a disability. According to Kanner (1953), a prolonged period of denial may be especially common among minimally involved fathers, who do not have enough interaction with their children to recognize the evidence of retardation.

Providers agree that mothers and fathers respond differently to the news of their child's disability and in ways that often mirror traditional parental roles. Fathers tend to perceive diagnosis of the disability as an instrumental crisis and are thus especially concerned about the cost of providing for the child; whether the child will be successful; and whether the child will be able to support himself or herself in the future. Mothers, conversely, tend to perceive the diagnosis as an expressive crisis and are thus especially concerned about the emotional strain of caring for the child with special needs and about the child's ability to get along well with others and to be happy (Gumz & Gubrium, 1972). Obviously, parental concerns are by no means exclusive. Gumz and Gubrium also found that many mothers were concerned about the high costs of raising children with special needs, and fathers were also concerned about the day-to-day demands presented by the disability.

Much has been written about the sequences or stages parents pass through while adapting to the reality of their children's handicaps. Blacher (1984) reviewed 24 publications that attempted to describe these stages. Typically, these stages, based largely on clinical impressions, include a period of distintegration, characterized by shock, denial, and emotional disorganization; adjustment, during which the parents may partly accept and partly deny the existence of the handicap; and reintegration, or mature adaptation, during which parents begin to function more effectively and realistically.

Although these descriptions of parental response are not inaccurate, many suggest that parents, following a period of reintegration, assume a life not unlike that of families without children who have disabilities. Wikler (1981) contended that families are subject to chronic, stressful reminders of their children's disability throughout their children's lives. Some stresses are related to hardships associated with mental retardation, such as social stigmatization and the prolonged burden of care. Other stresses are typical parental response to retardation, such as a lack of appropriate information, confusion concerning child care, and periodic grief. Parents may experience periodic grief when there is a discrepancy between what they expect of their children's development and what actually occurs. These discrepancies have a profound impact on some fathers. The parents Wikler interviewed identified the ages at which children typically talk, walk, enter or graduate from school, and leave home as particularly stressful times.

As already indicated, fathers are typically more concerned than are mothers about the adoption of socially approved behavior by their children—especially their sons. Likewise, they are more concerned about the social status and occupational success of their offspring (Lamb, 1981b). Not surprisingly, therefore, fathers are more concerned about the long-term implications of the disability than mothers are. Similarly, fathers are more affected by the visibility of the handicap, presumably because of their greater sensitivity to socially defined norms and evaluations (Tallman, 1965). Price-Bonham and Addison (1978) reported that fathers are more affected by physical aspects of the disability and are more sensitive than mothers are to the ways in which their children might affect the family's community image. They also reported more concern about performance outside the home (Gumz & Gubrium, 1972). Furthermore, because fathers often have higher expectations for sons than for daughters, they are especially disappointed when a son is diagnosed as having mental retardation (Farber, 1959; Grossman, 1972). The behavioral consequences of this disappointment may take a variety of forms, however. Extremes of great involvement, on the one hand, and total withdrawal, on the other, have been observed in fathers of sons with mental retardation (Chigier, 1972; Tallman, 1965). In contrast, these fathers appear more consistently to have limited, routine involvement with retarded daughters (Tallman, 1965), of whom they are more accepting (Grossman, 1972).

For many parents, children are a significant source of fulfillment and self-esteem, but when the child clearly cannot live up to the parents' hopes and expectations, self-esteem suffers (Ryckman & Henderson, 1965). Cummings (1976) noted reduced self-esteem in both the mothers and fathers of children with mental retardation, with fathers being especially concerned about their manifest "inferiority" as fathers. His survey revealed that these fathers were often depressed and preoccupied with their children's special needs, many felt inferior as fathers, and many were dissatisfied with their children and spouses. Cummings suggested that this may be because fathers have fewer opportunities than mothers to do things with and for children who are mentally retarded. They thus have fewer concrete reminders of their own value and competence.

Some have argued that children's handicaps are especially hard for parents to bear when the parents are intellectually talented (i.e., when there is a greater discrepancy between their intellectual skills and those of their children) and when they have high-status occupations (and thus have comparably high expectations for their children) (Holt, 1958a; Michaels & Schuman, 1962; Ryckman & Henderson, 1975). Fathers who view their children as extensions of their egos are apt to become isolated and to withdraw from social interactions (Call, 1958; Illingworth, 1967). This is not necessarily or always the case, however; Farber (1959) found lower-class parents to be more adversely affected by the birth of a child with a disability than were middle- and upper-class parents.

The difficulties experienced by fathers may in turn affect other family members, because the fathers' attitudes may set the pattern for other family members (Peck & Stephens, 1960; Price-Bonham & Addison, 1978). Farber's (1962) report that parents of boys with mental retardation showed lower marital integration than did parents of girls with mental retardation is consistent with this notion (Peck & Stephens, 1960; Brotherson, Turnbull, Summers, & Turnbull, 1986) if we assume that fathers are more deeply affected by sons than by daughters who are retarded and that this in turn affects the couples' marital integration.

The age of children with disabilities may influence the impact of the disabilities on fathers and other family members. Cummings (1976) found that fathers of older children with handicaps (9–13 years) showed slightly lower psychological stress levels than did fathers of younger (4–8 years) children with handicaps. Fathers of older children also rated their depression slightly lower and their enjoyment of their children and their evaluation of their wives slightly higher than did fathers with younger children. These results, however, are inconsistent with the findings reviewed by Gallagher, Beckman, and Cross (1983), which suggests that the children's age and the parents' perceived stress are directly related because of the increasing difficulty of managing older children with increasingly visible disabilities.

Research exploring the extent of paternal involvement in the care of children with disabilities is similarly inconsistent. Tallman (1965) reported that some fathers became very involved in the care of sons who had mental retardation. Shannon's (1978) observations of 29 father-child dyads revealed that the fathers of preschoolers with handicaps did not interact or participate in child-care activities more or less often than did the fathers of non-handicapped preschoolers. These data contrast with other observations that fathers tend to offer little assistance to their wives — the primary providers of care — even when their wives are overwhelmed by the considerable task of raising children with severe handicaps (Andrew, 1968; Holt, 1958b). Although one research team described family roles resembling those of effective families whose children were without handicaps, the authors concluded that "the traditional father roles of physical playmate and model for the male child are largely diminished or not present at all with the moderate to severely handicapped child" (Gallagher, Cross, & Scharfman, 1981, p.13).

Presumably, the differences in paternal involvement reflect the fact that fathers obtain less satisfaction from children with mental retardation than from their nonhandicapped children (Cummings, 1976) and the fact that paternal involvement — unlike maternal involvement — is discretionary. In other words, the paternal role is defined in such a way that fathers can increase or decrease the extent of their involvement depending on their preferences and satisfactions. In contrast, mothers traditionally have been expected to show equivalent commitment to all their children — regardless of personal preferences or the individual characteristics of their children.

When fathers choose to withdraw from children who are mentally retarded, it is not only the children's development that is likely to be affected; the entire family is likely to suffer. Changes in marital satisfaction or integration affect not only the personal fulfillment of the two spouses but also the way each interacts with his or her children, both handicapped and nonhandicapped. Evidence concerning marital satisfaction in families with children who are mentally retarded is discussed in the next section.

MARITAL SATISFACTION

Farber (1959), in one of the most thorough and thoughtful studies on this topic, studied 240 intact families, each of which had one child who was severely retarded as well as at least one other child. Drawing upon sociological formulations concerning the family life cycle, Farber interviewed and questioned both parents. No comparison group was studied, so it was possible only to identify the correlates of marital disruption in the focal families rather than whether these families on the whole differed from comparable families that did not have children who were mentally retarded. Farber reported that boys who were mentally retarded had a greater negative impact on their families than girls did, especially in lower-class families. Presumably, this was because parents have higher expectations for boys than for girls, and so their expectations are most seriously violated when their sons are mentally retarded. The family disruption increased as the children with retardation grew older, probably because their inability to meet age-determined expectations became more notable with age.

Paternal reactions to the diagnosis appear to influence the impact of the disability on the marriage. Tavormina, Ball, Dunn, Luscomb, and Taylor (1977), in an unpublished manuscript cited by Gallagher et al. (1981), suggested that there are four parental styles in adapting to the crisis of having a child with a disability.

1. The father divorces himself from the child, absorbing himself in work or outside activities, leaving the mother entirely responsible for the child.
2. Both parents reject the child, who is often institutionalized as a result.
3. The child becomes the center of the family's universe, and all family members subordinate their needs to accommodate the child who has a disability.
4. Both parents jointly support the child and each other while maintaining their individual identities and an approximation of normal family life.

A major source of strength for many families lies in the quality of personal support. Fathers of preschoolers with moderate to severe handicaps reported that support from their wives and friends was very important, whereas support from their neighbors was less important (Gallagher et al., 1981).

Reed and Reed (1965) reported disproportionately high desertion rates on the part of fathers whose children were mentally retarded, although Fowle (1968) failed to corroborate this finding. Contested, too, are claims regarding the high divorce rates reported for families with children who have disabilities (Tew, Lawrence, Payne & Rawnsley, 1977). Some researchers have reported that, when matched for social class, the divorce rate for families with children who are mentally retarded does not differ significantly from the rate for families with nonhandicapped children only (Davis & McKay, 1973; Schufeit & Wurster, 1976). Furthermore, many parents claim that the disability of their children strengthened their marriages and brought the families closer together (Gath, 1977; Kramm, 1963). Turnbull et al. (in press), however, suggested that a child's disabilities can deliver the final blow to an already-troubled marriage. Even when both parents react adversely to the diagnosis of disability, differences in adaptation can place added stress on a marriage (Price-Bonham & Addison, 1978). Opportunities to effectively support one another may be diminished if, for instance, one parent is grieving and the other is worried about the burden of care presented by the child's special needs.

Severe paternal reactions can have profound second-order effects on other family members, especially mothers. Bristol, Gallagher, and Schopler (1987) reported that fathers of children who were disabled assumed less responsibility for child care than did a comparison group of fathers even when mothers were employed. When their involvement decreases, fathers force mothers to cope alone with the emotionally and physically draining tasks of attending to the children's many needs. Fathers may thus bear a greater responsibility for allowing the handicaps to have adverse effects on their marriages, even though, ironically, fathers report more family and marital discord than do mothers (Schonnell & Watts, 1956). If fathers reacted by becoming more involved, their own satisfaction and the integration of the family might both increase.

IMPLICATIONS FOR INTERVENTION

Because of the way in which much of the research on fathers of children with special needs has been conducted, we know little about the extent to which paternal reactions to the diagnosis of retardation affects the reaction and adjustment of their spouses, or about the effects of their reactions and behavior on the socialization and development of the children concerned. Based on the limited evidence available, we can only speculate about these. As already noted, when fathers reject children with special needs, they create an emotional distance between themselves and their children, reducing the likelihood of positive effects on child development while increasing the likelihood of deleterious ones. Likewise, adverse reactions by fathers can increase the burdens borne by their wives. This can have the effect of straining marriages and affecting the personal satisfaction of mothers. This, in turn, may lead to harmful consequences, not only to children with special needs but to other family members as well. An unhappy, overextended, and isolated mother is likely to be a poorer mother for all her children, disabled or not.

Whether or not the father's reaction exacerbates the family's difficulty in adapting to a child's disability, there is reason to believe that intervention efforts should be directed toward fathers more systematically than they traditionally have been. Meyer (1986b) suggested the following ways in which intervention programs could extend services to fathers of children with special needs.

Staff Attitude Toward Fathers

Programs will not be successful in increasing paternal participation unless staff members believe that fathers are important, expect them to be involved, and treat them as equal parents. This means addressing correspondence to both parents, not just to mothers, with separate mailings to fathers when parents are divorced or separated. It also means adapting brochures, newsletters, and advertisements to appeal to fathers as well as to mothers and providing male staff members in order to facilitate fathers' comfort.

Flexible Scheduling

Evidence of a program's attitude toward fathers will be reflected in its staff's willingness to maintain a flexible schedule in order to accommodate employed fathers and mothers whose work schedules may interfere with participation in weekday parent programs. A survey of 16 U.S. Handicapped Children's Early Education Program demonstration sites revealed that the scheduled time of parent programs correlated with the level of paternal participation. When asked to estimate the number of fathers per 10 mothers in attendance, programs that held day meetings ($N = 4$) reported no paternal attendance; those that held both day *and* evening meetings ($N = 3$) reported an average of 2.6 fathers, whereas programs offering evening meetings ($N = 9$) reported an average of 5.3 fathers (Meyer, 1986b).

Programs Specifically for Fathers

A still small but growing number of groups provide fathers with opportunities for support, education, and involvement with their children who have special needs (Meyer, 1986b, 1986c). One of the longer running such programs is the Seattle-based SEFAM (Support Extended Family Members) Father's Program. Seeking to address the concerns of traditionally underserved family members, SEFAM staff implemented workshops for fathers, siblings, and grandparents of children with special needs. The Fathers Program, a biweekly Saturday morning program, provides fathers with opportunities for peer support, information reflective of their interests, and involvement with their children (Meyer, Vadasy, Fewell, & Schell, 1985). A study of the families participating in the Fathers Program revealed that fathers who participated reported less sadness, fatigue, pessimism, guilt, and stress resulting from their child's incapacitation, as well as more satisfaction, greater feelings of success, fewer total problems and better decision-making abilities than did similar fathers of children with special needs (Vadasy, Fewell, Meyer, & Greenberg, 1985). Generally held on Saturday mornings or on evenings convenient to participants, such programs include three primary components:

1. Information Fathers of children with handicaps need information to answer questions about disabilities and their potential impact. By obtaining information on programs, services, and therapies, fathers can share with their wives the role of expert concerning their children and the implications of their disabilities. This not only helps fathers encourage their children's development but provides support for mothers as well. Most such programs facilitate the sharing of information among participants, augmented by presentations by guest speakers (Meyer et al., 1985).

2. Opportunities for Involvement Gallagher et al. (1981) reported that both mothers and fathers wanted increased paternal involvement. Eighty-three percent of the fathers ($N = 152$) interviewed by Linder and Chitwood (1984) indicated that education was the responsibility of *both* parents and the school. By actively involving fathers, programs can foster increased father-child involvement outside the program and thus contribute to the child's cognitive and social development and foster attachment. Furthermore, when programs involve fathers and children, mothers have opportunities for respite from child-caring burdens.

3. Support Programs that provide fathers with opportunities to discuss their concerns, joys, and interests with other men in similar situations can help decrease the sense of isolation, which may in turn have beneficial effects on mothers (Bristol, 1984). Although most existing programs are for fathers of young children with special needs, there is a growing recognition of the need to support fathers of older children as well. As children with disabilities become adults, fathers may be required to support dependent adults financially and emotionally (Price-Bonham & Addison, 1978). Parents of older children with mental retardation report feeling less supported and more in need of services than fathers and mothers of young children who are mentally retarded (Suezle & Keenan, 1981). This is a problem that needs immediate attention by social service agencies.

The failure to recognize that fathers too are emotionally affected by the birth of children with disabilities not only deprives them of potentially helpful counsel and support, but also conveys the implicit message that they do not matter and that they are not expected to behave or feel differently once this crisis has struck their families. This is unfortunate. The failure to acknowledge fathers' concerns may, in turn, have adverse effects on other family members. Wives of men who were involved in special programs for fathers reported fewer feelings of failure, less stress resulting from their children's handicaps, and more satisfaction with the time that they had to themselves than similar women whose husbands were not involved in programs for fathers (Vadasy et al., 1985).

It is difficult to generalize about fathers whose child has special needs because many factors affect their experiences. These factors include the type of disability, health and behavioral characteristics of the child, as well as the father's education, personal characteristics, financial resources, and interpersonal supports. A father whose passive child has Down syndrome may be affected quite differently from a father whose child is also chronically ill, physically disabled, and has aggressive or autistic behaviors. Similarly, a father whose marriage is sound and whose employment is stable will have a different experience than the father whose marriage is unstable and who is unemployed.

In many ways, fathers of children who have handicaps behave like fathers of children without handicaps (Linder & Chitwood, 1984; Meyer, 1986b). Indeed, Gallagher et al. (1981) cautioned against assuming that fathers whose children have handicaps are under debilitating stress. Some fathers speak of new values and personal growth as a result of successfully adapting to a child's disability: "Before Eric came along I was on what you might call a corporate fast track. That's not so important to me anymore. My family is more important to me now" (Meyer, 1986a).

Despite the varied responses fathers may have to their children's disabilities, families—both traditional and nontraditional—are likely to be strengthened when fathers are emotionally and concretely involved with their families. The potential benefits of paternal involvement may even be greater when children have disabilities, because family members need increased emotional support, understanding, and practical assistance in these circumstances.

REFERENCES

Ainsworth, M. D. S., Bell, S. M., & Stayton, D. J. (1974). Infant-mother attachment and social development: Socialization as a product of reciprocal responsiveness to signals. In M. P. M. Richards (Ed.), *The integration of a child into a social world.* Cambridge, England: Cambridge University Press, pp. 99–136.

Andrew, G. (1968). Determinants of Negro family decisions in management of retardation. *Journal of Marriage and the Family, 30,* pp. 612–617.

Bandura, A. (1977). *Social learning theory.* Englewood Cliffs, NJ: Prentice-Hall.

Baruch, G. K., & Barnett, R. (1978). *The competent woman.* New York: Irvington.

Baumrind, D. (1971). Current patterns of parental authority. *Developmental Psychology Monographs, 1*(Whole No. 2).

Baumrind. D. (1975). *Early socialization and the discipline controversy.* Morriston, NJ: General Learning Press.

Bell, R. Q. & Harper, L. V. (1977). *Child effects on adults*. Hillsdale, NJ: Lawrence Bilbaum Associates.

Belsky, J. (1979). Mother-father-infant interaction: A naturalistic observational study. *Developmental Psychology, 15,* pp. 601–607.

Belsky, J. (1980). A family analysis of parental influence on infant exploratory competence. In F. A. Pedersen (Ed.), *The father-infant relationship: Observational studies in a family context*. New York: Praeger, pp. 87–110.

Belsky, J. (1981). Early human experiences: A family perspective. *Developmental Psychology, 17,* pp. 3–23.

Biller, H. B. (1974). *Paternal deprivation: Family, school, sexuality and society*. Lexington, MA: D. C. Heath.

Biller, H. B. (1976). The father and personality development: Paternal deprivation and sex-role development. In M. E. Lamb (Ed.), *The role of the father in child development*. New York: Wiley, pp. 89–156.

Biller, H. B. (1981). Father absence, divorce, and personality development. In M. E. Lamb (Ed.), *The role of the father in child development* (Rev. ed.). New York: Wiley, pp. 489–552.

Blacher, J. (1984). Sequential stages of parental adjustment to the birth of a child with handicaps: Fact or artifact? *Mental Retardation, 22,* pp. 55–68.

Blanchard, R. W. & Biller, H. B. (1971). Father availability and academic performance among third-grade boys. *Developmental Psychology, 4,* pp. 301–305.

Bowlby, J. (1951). *Maternal care and mental health*. Geneva: World Health Organization.

Bristol, M. M. (October 1984). Families of developmentally disabled children: Health adaptations and the double ABDX model. Paper presented at the Family Systems and Health Pre-Conference Workshop, National Council on Family Relations, San Francisco, CA.

Bristol, M. M., Gallagher, J. J., & Schopler, E. (1987). Home environments: Child disability, parental adaptation and spousal instrumental and expressive support. Paper presented at the Biennial Meeting of the Society for Research in Child Development, Baltimore, MD. April 1987.

Bristol, M. M. & Gallagher, J. J. (1986). Psychological research on fathers of young handicapped children: Evolution, review, and some future direction. In J. J. Gallagher & P. Vietz (Eds.). *Families of handicapped children*. Baltimore: Paul Brookes Publishing, pp. 81–100.

Bronfenbrenner, U. (1961). The changing American child. *Journal of Social Issues, 17,* pp. 6–18.

Call, J. (1958). Psychological problems of the cerebral palsied child, his parents and siblings as revealed by a dynamically oriented small group discussion with parents. *Cerebral Palsy Review, 10,* pp. 3–15.

Carver, N., & Carver, J. (1972). *The family of the retarded child.* Syracuse, NY: Syracuse University Press.

Chigier, E. (1972). *Down's syndrome.* Lexington, MA: D.C. Heath.

Clarke-Stewart, K. A. (1978). And daddy makes three: The father's impact on mother and young child. *Child Development, 49,* pp. 466–478.

Clarke-Stewart, K. A. (1980). The father's contribution to children's cognitive and social development in early childhood. In F. A. Pedersen (Ed.), *The father-infant relationship: Observational studies in a family setting.* New York: Praeger, pp. 111–146.

Collins, G. (June 17, 1979). A new look at life with father. *New York Times Magazine,* pp. 31, 49–52, 65–66.

Cohen, L. J., & Campos, J. J. (1974). Father, mother, and stranger as elicitors of attachment behaviors in infancy. *Developmental Psychology, 10,* pp. 146–154.

Cummings, S. T. (1976). The impact of the child's deficiency on the father: A study of fathers of mentally retarded and of chronically ill children. *American Journal of Orthopsychiatry, 46,* pp. 246–255.

Davis, M., & MacKay, D. (October 27, 1973). Mentally subnormal children and their families. *Lancet.*

Dweck, C. S. (1978). Achievement. In M. E. Lamb (Ed.), *Social and personality development.* New York: Holt, Rinehart & Winston, pp. 114–130.

Erickson, M. (1974). Talking with fathers of young children with Down's syndrome. *Children Today, 3,* pp. 22–25.

Fagot, B. I. (1977). Consequences of moderate cross-gender behavior in preschool children. *Child Development, 48,* pp. 902–907.

Fagot, B., & Patterson, B. R. (1969). An in vivo analysis of reinforcing contingencies for sex-role behavior in the preschool child. *Developmental Psychology, 1,* pp. 563–568.

Farber, B. (1959). Effects of a severely mentally retarded child on family integration. *Monographs of the Society for Research in Child Development, 24,* (Whole No. 71).

Farber, B. (1960). Family organization and crisis: Maintenance of integration in families with a severely mentally retarded child. *Monographs of the Society for Research in Child Development, 25,* (1, Whole No. 75).

Farber, B. (1962). Effects of a severely mentally retarded child on the family. In E. P. Trapp (Ed.), *Readings on the exceptional child.* New York: Appleton Century Crofts, pp. 225–245.

Farber, B., & Jenne, W. C. (1963). Family organization and parent-child communication: Parents and siblings of a retarded child. *Monographs of the Society for Research in Child Development, 28*(Whole No. 91).

Farber, B., Jenne, W. C., & Toiga, R. (1960). Family crisis and the decision to institutionalize the retarded child. *Council of Exceptional Children Research Monographs, A*(No. 1).

Field, T. (1978). Interaction behaviors of primary versus secondary caretaker fathers. *Developmental Psychology, 14,* pp. 183–184.

Fowle, C. M. (1968). The effect of the severely mentally retarded child on his family. *American Journal of Mental Deficiency, 73,* pp. 468–473.

Gallagher, J. J., Beckman, P., & Cross, A. H. (1983). Families of handicapped children: Sources of stress and its amelioration. *Exceptional Children, 50,* pp. 10–19.

Gallagher, J. J., Cross, A. H., & Scharfman, W. (1981). Parental adaptation to a young handicapped child: The father's role. *Journal of the Division for Early Childhood, 3*(1), pp. 3–14.

Gath, A. (1977). The impact of an abnormal child upon the parents. *British Journal of Psychiatry, 130,* pp. 405–410.

Goodenough, E. W. (1957). Interest in persons as an aspect of sex difference in the early years. *Genetic Psychology Monographs, 55,* pp. 287–323.

Gove, F., Arend, R., & Sroufe, L. A. (1979, March). *Continuity of individual adaptation from infancy to kindergarten.* Paper presented at the meeting of the Society for Research in Child Development, San Francisco.

Grossman, F. (1972). *Brothers and sisters of retarded children: An exploratory study.* Syracuse, NY: Syracuse University Press.

Grossman, K., & Grossman, K. (1980, July). *The development of relationship patterns during the first two years of life.* Paper presented at the meeting of the International Congress of Psychology, Leipzig, German Democratic Republic.

Gumz, E. J., & Gubrium, J. F. (1972). Comparative parental perceptions of a mentally retarded child. *American Journal of Mental Deficiency, 77,* pp. 175–180.

Heilbrun, A. B. (1965). An empirical test of the modelling theory of sex-role learning. *Child Development, 36,* pp. 789–799.

Hersh, A. (1970). Changes in family functioning following placement of a retarded child. *Social Work, 15,* pp. 93–102.

Hetherington, E. M., Cox, M., & Cox, R. (1978). The aftermath of divorce. In J. H. Stevens & M. Matthews (Ed.), *Mother/child, father/child relationships.* Washington, DC: National Association for the Education of Young Children, pp. 149–176.

Hoffman, L. W. (1974). Effects of maternal employment on the child: A review of the research. *Developmental Psychology, 10,* pp. 204–208.

Hoffman, M. L. (1970). Moral development. In P. H. Mussen (Ed.), *Carmichael's manual of child psychology* 3rd ed., Vol. 2. New York: Wiley, pp. 261–230.

Hoffman, M. L. (1981). The role of the father in moral internalization. In M. E. Lamb (Ed.), *The role of the father in child development* (Rev. Ed.), New York: Wiley, pp. 359–378.

Holt, K. S. (1957). *The impact of mentally retarded children upon their families.* Unpublished doctoral dissertation, University of Sheffield, England.

Holt, K. S. (1958a). The influence of a retarded child upon family limitation. *Journal of Mental Deficiency Research, 2,* pp. 28–34.

Holt, K. S. (1958b). The home care of severely retarded children. *Pediatrics, 22,* pp. 746–755.

Hornby, G. (1987). *Fathers of handicapped children: A review.* Unpublished manuscript. Peter Adrian Research Center, University of Manchester, England.

Illingworth, R. S. (1967). Counseling the parents of the mentally handicapped child. *Clinical Pediatrics, 6,* pp. 340–348.

Johnson, M. M. (1963). Sex role learning in the nuclear family. *Child Development, 34,* pp. 315–333.

Jordan, T. E. (1962). Research on the handicapped child and the family. *Merrill-Palmer Quarterly, 8,* pp. 243–260.

Kanner, L. (1953). Parents' feelings about retarded children. *American Journal of Mental Deficiency, 57,* pp. 375–383.

Kohlberg, L. (1969). Stage and sequence: The cognitive-developmental approach to socialization. In D. A. Goslin (Ed.), *Handbook of socialization theory and research.* Chicago: Rand McNally, pp. 347–480.

Kotelchuck, M. (1976). The infant's relationship to the father: Experimental evidence. In M. E. Lamb (Ed.), *The role of the father in child development.* New York: Wiley, pp. 329–344.

Kramm, E. R. (1963). *Families of mongoloid children.* Washington, DC: Children's Bureau.

Lamb, M. E. (1976a). Effects of stress and cohort on mother- and father-infant interaction. *Developmental Psychology, 12,* pp. 435–443.

Lamb, M. E. (1976b). Interactions between eight-month-old children and their fathers and mothers. In M. E. Lamb (Ed.), *The role of the father in child development.* New York: Wiley, pp. 307–328.

Lamb, M. E. (1976c). Interactions between two-year-olds and their mothers and fathers. *Psychological Reports, 38,* pp. 447–450.

Lamb, M. E. (1976d). Parent-infant interaction in eight-month-olds. *Child Psychiatry and Human Development, 7,* pp. 56–63.

Lamb, M. E. (1976e). Twelve-month-olds and their parents: Interaction in a laboratory playroom. *Developmental Psychology, 12,* pp. 237–244.

Lamb, M. E. (1977a). The development of mother-infant and father-infant attachments in the second year of life. *Developmental Psychology, 13,* pp. 637–648.

Lamb, M. E. (1977b). The development of parental preferences in the first two years of life. *Sex Roles, 3,* pp. 495–497.

Lamb, M. E. (1977c). Father-infant and mother-infant interaction in the first year of life. *Child Development, 48,* pp. 167–181.

Lamb, M. E. (1978). Qualitative aspects of mother- and father-infant attachments. *Infant Behavior and Development, 1,* pp. 265–275.

Lamb, M. E. (1979). Separation and reunion behaviors as criteria of attachment to mothers and fathers. *Early Human Development, 3/4,* pp. 329–339.

Lamb, M. E. (1981a). The development of social expectations in the first year of life. In M. E. Lamb & L. R. Sherrod (Eds.), *Infant social cognition: Empirical and theoretical considerations.* Hillsdale, NJ: Erlbaum, pp. 155–176.

Lamb, M. E. (1981b). Fathers and child development: An integrative overview. In M. E. Lamb (Ed.), *The role of the father in child development* (Rev. ed.). New York: Wiley, pp. 1–70.

Lamb, M. E. (1981c). Developing trust and perceived effectance in infancy. In L. P. Lipsitt (Ed.), *Advance in infancy research* (Vol. 1) Norwood, NJ: Ablex, pp. 101–127.

Lamb, M. E. (1982). Maternal employment and child development: A review. In M. E. Lamb (Ed.), *Nontraditional families.* Hillsdale, NJ: Earlbaum, pp. 45–70.

Lamb, M. E., Easterbrooks, M. A., & Holden, G. W. (1980). Reinforcement and punishment among preschoolers: Characteristics, effects, and correlates. *Child Development, 51,* pp. 1230–1236.

Lamb, M. E., Frodi, A. M., Hwang, C-P, Frodi, M., & Steinberg, J. (1982a). The effects of gender and caretaking roles on parent-infant interaction. In R. N. Emde & R. J. Harmon (Eds.), *Attachment and affiliative behavior systems.* New York: Plenum Press, pp. 109–118.

Lamb, M. E., Frodi, A. M., Hwang, C-P, Frodi, M., & Steinberg, J. (1982b). Mother- and father-infant interaction involving play and holding in traditional and nontraditional Swedish families. *Developmental Psychology, 18,* pp. 215–221.

Lamb, M. E., & Goldberg, W. A. (1982). The father-child relationship: A synthesis of biological, evolutionary and social perspectives. In L. W. Hoffman, R. Gandelman, & H. W. Schiffman (Eds.), *Perspectives on parental behavior.* Hillsdale, NJ: Erlbaum, pp. 55–73.

Lamb, M. E., Hwang, C-P, Frodi, A. M., & Frodi, M. (1982). Security of mother- and father-infant attachment and its relation to sociability with strangers in traditional and nontraditional Swedish families. *Infant Behavior and Development, 5,* pp. 355–367.

Lamb, M. E., & Roopnarine, J. L. (1979). Peer influences on sex-role development in preschoolers. *Child Development, 50,* pp. 1219–1222.

Lamb, M. E., Thompson, R. A., Gardner, W., & Charnov, E. L. (1985). *Infant-mother attachment.* Hillsdale, NJ: Erlbaum.

Langlois, J. H., & Downs, A. C. (1980). Mothers, fathers, and peers as socialization agents of sex-typed play behaviors in young children. *Child Development, 51,* pp. 1237–1247.

Legeay, C., & Keogh, B. (1966). Impact of mental retardation on family life. *American Journal of Nursing, 66,* pp. 1062–1065.

Lerner, R. M., & Spanier, G. B. (Eds.). (1978). *Child influences on marital and family interaction.* New York: Academic Press.

Lewis, M., & Feiring, C. (1981). Direct and indirect interactions in social relationships. In L. P. Lipsitt (Ed.), *Advances in infancy research* (Vol. 1). Norwood, NJ: Ablex, pp. 131–161.

Lewis, M., & Weinraub, M. (1976). The father's role in the infant's social network. In M. E. Lamb (Ed.), *The role of the father in child development.* New York: Wiley, pp. 157–184.

Linder, T., & Chitwood, D. (1984). The needs of fathers of young handicapped children. *The Journal of the Division for Early Childhood, 7,* pp. 133–139.

Lonsdale, G. (1978). Family life with a handicapped child: The parents speak. *Child: Care, Health and Development, 4,* pp. 99–120.

Love, H. (1973). *The mentally retarded child and his family.* Springfield, IL: Charles C Thomas.

Lynn, D. B., & Cross, A. R. (1974). Parent preference of preschool children. *Journal of Marriage and the Family, 36,* pp. 555–559.

Main, M. (1973). *Exploration, play and cognitive functioning as related to child-mother attachment.* Unpublished doctoral dissertation, Johns Hopkins University.

Main, M. B., & Weston, D. R. (1981). Security of attachment to mother and father: Related to conflict behavior and the readiness to establish new relationships. *Child Development, 52,* pp. 932–940.

Matas, L., Arend, R., & Sroufe, L. A. (1978). Continuity of adaptation in the second year of life. *Child Development, 49,* pp. 547–556.

Meyer, D. J. (1986a). Fathers of children with handicaps: Developmental trends in fathers' experiences over the family life cycle. In R. R. Fewell & P. F. Vadasy (Eds.)., *Families of handicapped children: Needs and supports across the lifespan.* Austin, TX: Pro-Ed, pp. 35–73.

Meyer, D. J. (1986b). Fathers of children with special needs. In M. E. Lamb (Ed.), *The fathers' role: Applied perspectives.* New York: Wiley.

Meyer, D. J. (1986c). Listening in on fathers: Groups at the Down Syndrome Congress share their concerns. *Focus on Fathers, 1,* (2).

Meyer, D. J., Vadasy, P. F., Fewell, R. R., & Schell, G. (1985). *A handbook for the Fathers Program: How to organize a program for fathers and their handicapped children.* Seattle: University of Washington Press.

Meyerowitz, H. D., & Farber, B. (1966). Family background of educable mentally retarded children. In B. Farber (Ed.), *Kinship and family organization.* New York: Wiley.

Michaels, J., & Schuman, H. (1962). Observations on the psychodynamics of retarded children. *American Journal of Mental Deficiency, 66,* pp. 568–573.

Money, J., & Ehrhardt, A. A. (1972). *Man and woman: Boy and girl.* Baltimore, MD: Johns Hopkins Press.

Mussen, P. H. (1976). Early socialization: Learning and identification. In T. M. Newcomb (Ed.), *New directions in psychology III.* New York: Holt, Rinehart & Winston, pp. 51–110.

Mussen, P. H., & Rutherford, E. (1963). Parent-child relations and parental personality in relation to young children's sex-role preferences. *Child Development, 34,* pp. 589–607.

Nash, S. C., & Feldman, S. S. (1981). Sex role and sex-related attributions: Constancy or change across the family life cycle? In M. E. Lamb & A. L. Brown (Eds.), *Advances in developmental psychology* (Vol. 1). Hillsdale, NJ: Erlbaum, pp. 1–35.

Organist, J. E. (1971). *The relationship between parental expectancies and the behavior of mildly-retarded adolescents.* Unpublished doctoral dissertation, University of Wisconsin.

Parke, R. D. (1979). Father-mother-infant interactions. In J. D. Osofsky (Ed.), *Handbook of infant development.* New York: Wiley, pp. 549–590.

Parke, R. D., & O'Leary, S. E. (1976). Father-mother-infant interaction in the newborn period: Some findings, some observations, and some unresolved issues. In K. Riegel & J. Meacham (Eds.), *The developing individual in a changing world. Vol. 2. Social and environmental issues.* The Hague, The Netherlands: Mouton.

Parke, R. D., Power, T. G., & Gottman, J. (1979). Conceptualizing and quantifying influence patterns in the family triad. In M. E. Lamb, S. J. Suomi, & G. R. Stephenson (Eds.), *Social interaction analysis: Methodological issues.* Madison: University of Wisconsin Press.

Parke, R. D., & Sawin, D. E. (1977, March). *The family in early infancy: Social interactional and attitudinal analyses.* Paper presented at the biennial meeting of the Society for Research in Child Development, New Orleans.

Pastor, D. L. (1981). The quality of mother-infant attachment and its relationship to toddlers' initial sociability with peers. *Developmental Psychology, 17,* pp. 326–335.

Payne, D. E. & Mussen, P. H. (1956). Parent-child relations and father identification among adolescent boys. *Journal of Abnormal and Social Psychology, 52,* pp. 358–362.

Peck, J. R., & Stephens, W. B. (1960). A study of the relationship between the attitudes and behavior of parents and that of their mentally defective child. *American Journal of Mental Deficiency, 64,* pp. 839–844.

Pedersen, F. A., Ruenstein, J. L., & Yarrow, L. J. (1979). Infant development in father-absent families. *Journal of Genetic Psychology, 135,* pp. 51–61.

Price-Bonham, S., & Addison, S. (1978). Families and mentally retarded children: Emphasis on the father. *The Family Coordinator, 3,* pp. 221–230.

Radin, N. (1976). The role of the father in cognitive, academic and intellectual development. In M. E. Lamb (Ed.), *The role of the father in child development.* New York: Wiley, pp. 237–276.

Radin, N. (1978, September). *Childrearing fathers in intact families with preschoolers.* Paper presented at the annual meeting of the American Psychological Association, Toronto.

Radin, N. (1981). The role of the father in academic, cognitive and intellectual development. In M. E. Lamb (Ed.), *The role of the father in child development* (Rev. ed.), New York: Wiley, pp. 379–427.

Ramsey, G. B. (1967). Review of group methods with parents of the mentally retarded. *American Journal of Mental Deficiency, 71,* pp. 857–863.

Reed, E. W., & Reed, S. C. (1965). *Mental retardation: A family study.* Philadelphia: Saunders.

Rosen, B. C., & D'Andrade, R. (1959). The psychosocial origins of achievement motivation. *Sociometry, 22,* pp. 185–218.

Rutter, M. (1972). *Maternal deprivation reassessed.* Harmondsworth, England: Penguin.

Rutter, M. (1973). Why are London children so disturbed? *Proceedings of the Royal Society of Medicine, 66,* pp. 1221–1225.

Rutter, M. (1979). Maternal deprivation, 1972–1978: New findings, new concepts, new approaches. *Child Development, 50,* pp. 283–305.

Ryckman, D. B., & Henderson, R. A. (1965). The meaning of a retarded child for his parents: A focus for counselors, *Mental Retardation, 3,* pp. 4–7.

Saenger, G. (1957). *The adjustment of severely retarded adults in the community.* Albany: New York State Interdepartmental Health Research Board.

Saenger, G. (1960). *Factors influencing the institutionalization of mentally retarded individuals in New York City.* Albany: New York State Interdepartmental Health Research Board.

Sagi, A. (1982). Nontraditional fathers in Israel. In M. E. Lamb (Ed.), *Nontraditional families: Parenting and child development.* Hillsdale, NJ: Erlbaum. pp. 205–232.

Sagi, A., Lamb, M. E., Lewkowicz, R. S., Shoham, R., Duir, R., & Ester, D. (1985). Security of infant-mother, father, metaphet attachment among kibbutz-reared children. In I. Bretherton & E. Waters (Ed.), *Growing points of attachment theory and research.* Monograph of the Society for Research in Child Development, *50,* Serial Number 209.

Schaffer, H. R., & Emerson, P. E. (1964). The development of social attachments in infancy. *Monographs of the Society for Research in Child Development, 29,* (Whole No. 94).

Schipper, M. T. (1959). The child with mongolism in the home. *Pediatrics, 24,* p. 132.

Schonnell, F. J., & Watts, B. H. (1956). A first survey of the effects of a subnormal child on the family unit. *American Journal of Mental Deficiency, 61,* pp. 210–219.

Schufiet, L. J., & Wurster, S. R. (1976). Frequency of divorce among parents of handicapped children. *Resources in Education, 11,* pp. 71–78.

Sears, R. R., Maccoby, E. E., & Levin, H. (1957). *Patterns of child rearing.* Evanston, IL: Row Peterson.

Sears, R. R., Rau, L., & Alpert, R. (1965). *Identification and child rearing.* Stanford, CA: Stanford University Press.

Serbin, L. A., Tonick, L. S., & Sternglanz, S. H. (1977). Shaping cooperative cross-sex play. *Child Development, 48,* pp. 924–929.

Shannon, L. B. (1978). *Interactions of fathers with their handicapped preschoolers.* Unpublished doctoral dissertation, University of Kentucky.

Shinn, M. (1978). Father absence and children's cognitive development. *Psychological Bulletin, 85,* pp. 295–324.

Stevenson, M. B., & Lamb, M. E. (1981). The effects of social experience and social style on cognitive competence and performance. In M. E. Lamb & L. R. Sherrod (Eds.), *Infant social cognition* Hillsdale, NJ: Erlbaum, pp. 375–394.

Suelzle, M., & Keenan, V. (1981). Changes in family support networks over the lifecycle of mentally retarded persons. *American Journal of Mental Deficiency, 86,* pp. 267–274.

Tallman, I. (1965). Spousal role differentiation and the socialization of severely retarded children. *Journal of Marriage and the Family, 27,* pp. 37–42.

Tasch, R. J. (1955). Interpersonal perceptions of fathers and mothers. *Journal of Genetic Psychology, 87,* pp. 59–65.

Tavormina, J., Ball, N. J., Dunn, R. C., Luscomb, B., & Taylor, J. R. (1977). *Psychosocial effects of raising a physically handicapped child on parents.* Unpublished manuscript, University of Virginia.

Tew, B. J., Lawrence, K. M., Payne, H., & Rawnsley, K. (1977). Marital stability following the birth of a child with spina bifida. *British Journal of Psychiatry, 131,* pp. 79–82.

Thompson, R. A., & Lamb, M. E. (1981, April). *The relationship between stranger sociability, temperament and social experiences at 12 1/2 and 14 1/2 months of age.* Paper presented at the Midwestern Psychological Association meeting, Detroit.

Turnbull, A. P., Brotherson, M. J., Summers, J. A., & Turnbull, H. R. (1986). Fathers of disabled children. In B. Robinson & R. Barret (Eds.), *Fatherhood.* Austin: Pro-Ed.

Vadasy, P. F., Fewell, R. R., Meyer, D. J., & Greenberg, M. T. (1985). Supporting fathers of handicapped young children: Preliminary findings of program effects. *Analysis and Intervention in Developmental Disabilities, 5,* pp. 151–164.

Vadasy, P. F., Fewell, R. R., Meyer, D. J., Schell, G., & Greenberg, M. T. (1984). Involved parents: Characteristics and resources of fathers and mothers of young handicapped children. *Journal of the Division for Early Childhood, 8,* pp. 13–25.

Wadsworth, H. G., & Wadsworth, T. B. (1971). A problem of involvement with parents of mildly retarded children. *The Family Coordinator, 20,* pp. 141–147.

Weiner, B. (1974). *Achievement motivation and attribution theory.* Morriston, NJ: General Learning Press.

Wikler, L. (1981). Chronic stresses of families of mentally retarded children. *Family Relations, 30,* pp. 281–288.

Winterbottom, M. (1958). The relation of need for achievement in learning experiences to independence and mastery. In J. Atkinson (Ed.), *Motives in fantasy, action, and society.* Princeton, NJ: Van Nostrand.

Yogman, M. (1982). Development of the father-infant relationship. In H. Fitzgerald, B. Lester, & M. W. Yogman (Eds.), *Theory and research in behavioral pediatrics.* New York: Plenum Press.

Yogman, M. J., Dixon, S., Tronick, E., Als, H., & Brazelton, T. B. (1977, March). *The goals and structure of face-to-face interaction between infants and their fathers.* Paper presented at the meeting of the Society for Research in Child Development, New Orleans.

CHAPTER SEVEN

Siblings of Disabled Brothers and Sisters

Milton Seligman

*Milton Seligman, Ph.D., is a professor in the Coun-
seling Psychology Program, Department of Psychology in Education at the University of Pittsburgh. He
has edited or authored books and articles in the area
of group psychotherapy and in the area of childhood
disability and the family.*

*Dr. Seligman teaches courses in individual and
group therapy, clinical supervision, and disability in
the family. He maintains a private practice in Pittsburgh.*

Children who share the anticipation and excitement of a new addition to the family also share the grief and pain that accompanies the birth
of a disabled brother or sister. Recent observations suggest that some siblings may suffer adverse reactions, whereas others do not (Seligman & Darling, 1989; Trevino, 1979).

Research on the effects of a disabled brother or sister on the other
children in the family is beginning to appear in the literature with somewhat
more frequency (Israelite, 1985; Kirkman, 1985; Powell & Ogle, 1985; Simeonsson & Bailey, 1986; Skrtic, Summers, Brotherson, & Turnbull, 1984;
Vadasy, Fewell, Meyer, & Schell, 1984). Professionals and families are recognizing the potential at risk status of some siblings. Also, siblings are becom-

ing more active by forming support groups and by sharing their experiences with the public through various organizations and publications (e.g., Sibling Information Network Newsletter).

The study of the effects of a disabled brother or sister on nondisabled siblings is emerging as a significant area of study and concern. The research literature is beginning to mount as sibling adjustment captures the interest of various professionals. However, we must also heed the voices of parents who inform us of their concerns about their nondisabled children.

The Sibling Bond

Sibling relationships are usually the longest and most enduring of family relationships. The permanency of this relationship makes it possible for two individuals to exert considerable influence over each other through longitudinal interactions. As Powell and Ogle (1985) noted: "Siblings provide a continuing relationship from which there is no annulment (p. 12)." Dunn (1985) further elaborated on the sibling bond:

> Most children grow up with siblings—80 percent in the United States and Europe. The time they spend together in their early years is often far greater than the time they spend with their mothers or fathers. In many cultures children are brought up by their siblings. From the age of one or two they are nursed, fed, disciplined, and played with by a brother or sister only three or four years older than they. It is the beginning of a relationship that lasts a lifetime—longer indeed than that between husband and wife, or between parent and child (p. 4).

Like any intense, long-term relationship, sibling relationships are cyclical. Bank and Kahn (1982) observed that siblings follow a distinct life cycle. They provide a constant source of companionship for one another during the early childhood years. During adolescence, siblings manifest ambivalence about their mutual relationship, yet they still rely on each other as confidants and advisers. In adulthood siblings may interact less often because of marriage and/or geographical distance. Yet, during this period siblings may continue to provide long-distance support and encouragement as they cope with adult life. In addition, as aunts and uncles they provide unique support networks for their siblings' children. And finally, as family members age, as children become increasingly independent, and as spouses pass away, siblings continue to provide a mutual social network. It is not unusual for sibling relationships to become reestablished or to intensify in a manner similar to what occurred during the first stages of life.

According to Bank and Kahn (1982), children are growing up in a mobile and complex world where opportunities for contact, constancy, and permanence have decreased:

> Children are biologically propelled by these biological needs . . . to turn for satisfaction to any accessible person. In a worried, mobile, small family, high-stress, fast-paced, parent-absent America, that person can be a brother or a sister (p. 15).

In the past we have not adequately acknowledged the intense, long-term, and complex nature of sibling relationships. Now that we have begun to focus on this subset of the family we are beginning to comprehend the immense value in understanding sibling relationships and in fostering their positive growth (Kahn & Lewis, 1988).

THE NEED TO BE INFORMED

Siblings of disabled brothers or sisters may have a limited understanding of their disabled brother or sister's condition. In fact, there is a startling lack of information about the handicap, its manifestations, and its consequences (Wasserman, 1983). Ambiguity about a brother's or sister's disability can lead to the development of distorted beliefs that have little basis in fact.

Siblings need to know that they are not responsible for a particular condition. They should be informed about whether the disability is transmittable, as well as if and how they should communicate to family and friends about it. What implications does having a disabled sib hold for the future and how siblings should cope with feelings of anger, hurt, and guilt are issues to be grappled with.

Parents are not always able to share information or provide emotional support for their nondisabled children. The reason for this phenomenon may be a consequence of several factors:

1. the parents' lack of knowledge of their disabled child's condition,
2. the parents' wish to spare their children information that may cause them anxiety,
3. the parents' lack of understanding of their children's needs and wishes to understand their disabled brother's or sister's condition,
4. parental confusion regarding their disabled child's disability based on contradictory information from professionals, and
5. parental denial of their child's condition, its prognosis and consequences.

In regard to providing information, Murphy, Paeschel, Duffy, and Brady (1976) observed in their discussion groups with siblings of Down Syndrome children that the type of information requested appears to be related to age. Children 6 to 9 years of age asked questions about motor development and speech, discussed what their brothers and sisters could and could not do, and were interested in the medical and biological information presented to them. Concerns about the future became evident among the 10- to 12-year-old children, whereas the older adolescents showed concern about their own chances of bearing a handicapped child.

Siblings have become more open about their circumstances, their feelings, and their need to be better informed. They have found that they are not alone and indeed have discovered that disability in the family — and the family's reaction to it — is shared by others. Also, siblings — aided by the newly established Sibling Information Network* — are encouraging a wider dissemination of basic information about disabling conditions so that siblings, parents, and professionals are better informed. Service providers need to understand that siblings (and indeed all family members) will respond with less anxiety when they have accurate information communicated in a compassionate and understanding manner.

Caretaking

The research tends to support the notion that a child's excessive responsibility for a disabled sibling is related to the development of anger, resentment, guilt, and quite possibly, subsequent psychological disturbance.

A disabled child can absorb much of a family's resources. Before they are ready, children may be pressed into parent-like roles they are ill-prepared to assume. As Myers (1978) noted, such youngsters may move too rapidly through developmental stages so necessary for normal growth:

> From the time Roger began going to physicians and consultants, it seemed to me that I carried a five-hundred-pound lead weight around in the front of my brain. Never out of my mind was the idea that my brother was retarded, needed special attention, needed special care, and that I had to provide some of it.

*Sibling Information Network, CUAP, 991 Main Street, East Hartford, Connecticut 06108. The Network also publishes a newsletter in which, in addition to providing information, siblings share their feelings regarding their life with a handicapped brother or sister.

Similarly, the Committee of the National Alliance for the Mentally Ill publishes a newsletter, *The Sibling Bond*. This newsletter reviews relevant publications, provides information, and publishes essays by siblings. Their address: National Sibling Network, 5112 15th Avenue, South, Minneapolis, MN 55417.

> My role in those days was someone who was always around to help care for Roger. My father called me his "good right arm." Roger himself called me "Dad" before he corrected himself and called me *Bobby."*
>
> I never felt I dressed like a kid, never felt comfortable with the clothes I wore, never felt I knew how to act as a boy or a teenager. I was a little man (p. 36).

The enormous burden visited upon nondisabled children as they assume responsibility for their sibling is vividly expressed by Hayden (1974):

> The responsibility I felt for Mindy was tremendous. One year, when my "babysitting" duties involved periodic checking on my sister, Mindy wandered away between checks. After a thorough but fruitless search of the neighborhood, my mother hysterically told me that if anything happened to Mindy, I would be to blame. I felt terrified and guilty. I was seven (p. 27).

A colleague of the author's, in her late 50s, revealed that she has only recently become aware in therapy that her sister with cerebral palsy has had a profound effect on her life. She attributes her early symptoms of debilitating anxiety on the close bond and subsequent agonizing separation of her sister. With her parents and her younger sister now deceased, she has once again been pressed into duty as her sister's overseer and caretaker.

Kirkman's (1985) study of adult siblings showed that resentment and anger regarding caretaking may be directed toward the parents. In her Australian study, Kirkman found that a few of her 151 sibling subjects reacted negatively to their parents because of the parents' failure to provide adequate attention to their disabled brother or sister:

> I feel angered at both my parents for lack of understanding and effort to truly help him. They have neglected their responsibility to their son and have lost my respect in this regard (p. 3).

Children may find their life with a disabled brother or sister incomprehensible when they compare their family to families with normal children.

> The whole situation is profoundly unfair. It is unfair that the family must live with schizophrenia, autism, blindness, or retardation while others do not. It is unfair that some children must function as adjunct parents even before they go to school, while others successfully avoid responsibilities of all sorts well into their second decade. The brothers and sisters of the handicapped child learn to cope with this unfairness, and with their own response to it, the sorrow and the anger (Featherstone, 1980, p. 162).

Family size may bear a relationship to the extent to which a sibling experiences caretaking responsibility. Grossman (1972) reported that the college students she interviewed from two-child families found life with a retarded sibling more stressful than did those with a number of nondisabled siblings. It seems that responsibility is spread out in larger families in which more children are available to help, although more recently, Simeonsson and Bailey (1986) listed residing in a large family as a negative adjustment factor.

The sex of nondisabled brothers and sisters plays a significant part in caretaking. Female siblings tend to be more subject to caretaking behavior than are male siblings and may thus be more prone to psychological maladjustment. However, this observation of the relation of sex and maladjustment has been complicated by recent information that males sometimes fare poorer than do females and that sibling age, age spacing, and sex may interact in complex ways (Simeonsson & Bailey, 1986). In regard to age, children who are younger than their disabled siblings may experience "role tension" when the older disabled child becomes the youngest child socially (Farber, 1960). Nevertheless, when it comes to caretaking, females probably do assume more caretaking roles than do males, but perhaps this does not necessarily lead to problems (McHale & Gamble, 1987). In fact, McHale and Gamble found that an important concern for nondisabled siblings is how "fair" the parents treat them. It may be that the parents' communication of love and concern for all their children buffers the negative effects of caregiving.

Grossman (1972) found that socioeconomic status is related to the amount of responsibility a sibling might assume for a disabled brother or sister. The more financially able a family is, the better prepared the members are to secure necessary help from sources outside the family.* Families that are less financially secure must rely on resources within the family. Financial problems produce additional stress and can detract from general stability when excessive and unrelenting demands are placed on family members. In financially struggling families where financial resources are scarce a disabled child may even be blamed as the source of the financial woes.

The burdening of siblings with the care of chronically physically ill children has been noted (Travis, 1976). Travis observed that signs of mounting resentment among siblings can be seen in their giving hasty or unkind physical care. She noted also that in close-knit families, the care of a disabled child is viewed as a shared responsibility.

---

*It is worth noting here that because family values differ, depending on cultural and ethnic affiliations, there may be considerable resistance to securing outside help, irrespective of the family's financial situation.

Travis pointed out that some chronically ill children enslave their physically normal siblings—"Hand me this, pick up that." Chronically ill children have been observed to be verbally abusive toward their nondisabled siblings, presumably because of envy and confusion. In an informal study by Holt (1958), nondisabled children were reported to have suffered repeatedly from unexpected physical attacks by their disabled brothers or sisters. Disabled children may resent their sibs for having escaped the condition they must confront daily. Strong negative and often unexpressed emotions suggests that counseling may be indicated when sibling relationships are strained (Kahn & Lewis, 1988).

Responsibility for the well-being of a chronically ill child can be taken to great lengths. In instances where the sick child must be guarded from infection—say, in chronic heart disease—Travis reported that mothers warn their children to avoid crowds for fear of bringing home infections. Such responsibility for the welfare of an ill brother or sister places an inordinate burden on nondisabled siblings with possible implications for their subsequent adjustment.

Siblings may be burdened by excessively high aspirations to compensate for parental disappointments and frustrations. The responsibility for high achievement may fall on the shoulders of nondisabled siblings, who may intellectually or psychologically not be able to meet parents expectations.

In instances where a sibling needs lifelong care or supervision, nondisabled brothers and sisters understandably look anxiously to the future. They wonder whether the responsibility that their parents currently assume will later fall to them, and they worry about whether they can cope with the decisions that need to be made in future years and whether a prospective spouse will be able to cope with the situation. A child's sense of obligation for a disabled sib should be a major concern for the professional.

IDENTITY CONCERNS

Featherstone (1980) pointed out that in the wake of a disability, young children may be concerned about "catching" the disability. She noted that anxiety about this is exacerbated when children learn that the disability was caused by an infectious disease like rubella or meningitis. Nondisabled siblings may have anxieties that they will become blind or deaf in the future (Marion, 1981). In addition, as children grow into adolescents they may fear that they might become the parents of a disabled child.

Although nondisabled children will not catch the disability, Marion (1981) and Luterman (1979) pointed out that children have been known to develop somatic complaints in their attempts to gain attention from their parents. Luterman observed that in siblings of hearing-impaired children it is not uncommon for them to develop a pseudo-sensory deficit as an attention-getting behavior. Lechtenberg (1984) noted that siblings of epileptic children have an inordinate fear that they will develop the disorder — a fear disproportionate to the possibility that they will indeed acquire epilepsy or a seizure disorder.

Similarly, Michaelis (1980) noted that as a consequence of a strong identification the children may feel overly responsible for their brother or sister in order to justify psychologically the fact that he or she is not the afflicted one. Moreover, siblings have been known to feel responsible for the disability, particularly when the nondisabled sibling deeply resented the birth of a newborn and the child has fleeting thoughts about a brother's or sister's demise. The notion of overidentifying with a disabled brother or sister may be attributable in part to age, age spacing, and gender similarities between disabled and nondisabled children (Breslau, Weitzman, & Messinger, 1981; Breslau, 1982). Also, relatively undifferentiated siblings may share symptoms with their disabled brother or sister, whereas siblings who have successfully separated tend to act more independent (Bank & Kahn, 1982).

Young children are more likely to be adversely affected by the presence of a disabled sibling of the same sex because of the fear of also being disabled, especially if there is no other sibling in the family with whom to identify (Trevino, 1979). McHale, Simeonsson, and Sloan (1984) observed that young children realize that, at least in some respects, they resemble their disabled siblings. They share the same home, the same parents, and perhaps similar physical characteristics. McHale et al. (1984) stated:

> The question for each of these children therefore becomes: How many of the handicapped sibling's characteristics do I share? That is, these children may come to think of themselves as defective. When children mature, these doubts and questions may result in their developing a fear of giving birth to a handicapped child because of the genetic or biological makeup that is shared with the handicapped sibling (p. 33).

The development of an identity separate from that of a disabled sibling is of considerable importance.

> The issue of being similar to or different from the retarded sibling permeated many of the meetings and seemed to be a source of enormous concern for all of the group members. In fact the experience with this group suggests that the main task of siblings of defective children is to avoid identifying with them (Grossman, 1972, p. 34).

Wasserman (1983) speculated that siblings who are poorly informed about the nature and consequences of their brother's or sister's affliction may be confused regarding their own identity. If adolescents are ignorant about the nature of the disability, identity issues are sure to arise, because this period of development is marked by considerable struggle over self-worth and self-identity. Feigon (1981) consistently observed in her sibling support groups a strong identification with the disabled sibling that resulted in feelings that one is or will be incapacitated.

The type of disablements of chronically ill children may bear a relation to identity problems, although the nature of the relationship is unclear. Tew and Lawrence (1975) concluded from their study that siblings of mildly disabled children were most disturbed, followed by siblings of severely and moderately disabled children. It may be that identity confusion and the ability to differentiate oneself from a disabled sib is a consequence of the perceived "likeness" of the other. In other words, the less abnormal the sibling, the more likely issues of identity may surface. However, the research consistently supports the position that there is no simple linear relation between the severity of a child's disability and sibling adjustment (Lobato, 1983 & Kirkman, 1985). The same conclusion holds when considering the type of impairment involved (Lobato, 1983). In commenting about siblings of seriously emotionally disturbed persons, Bank and Kahn (1982) reported that:

> Every well sibling that we have interviewed has, at one time or another, feared the possibility of becoming like a seriously disturbed brother or sister. Some siblings do not dwell on this fear, while others allow themselves to be haunted and dominated by the possibility that they could wind up in serious trouble or in a mental hospital (p. 253).

Powell and Ogle (1985) noted that siblings may become confused regarding their role in the family. One source of confusion pertains to their role as sibling and as surrogate parent. As noted previously, caretaking responsibility may promote an individual's self-view as a parent surrogate while that person is, in reality, a brother or sister (and child or adolescent).

Children experience confusion when treatment priorities for the disabled sib take precedence over their own needs for attention and affection. Other sources of confusion can arise when parents disagree about child-rearing practices of the disabled child, when they treat the child differently, and/or when parents are not at the same stage of acceptance of the disabled child. Particularly with young children, professionals should help parents understand the nondisabled siblings' need for attention. Parents are often unaware of the needs of their children, especially if there is a disabled child in the family that receives a disproportionate amount of attention. In a recent study Wallinga, Paguio, and Skeen (1987) discovered that parents thought that their healthy children were coping considerably better than the children thought they were. Participation in the study enabled the parents to realize for the first time how much they had neglected their healthy children.

In instances of childhood death, healthy children do not escape the fear of contamination by the disease that killed a brother or sister (Travis, 1976). Binger (1973), in a study of siblings of children dying of leukemia, found that fears that they will die next are not uncommon. Sourkes (1987) reports that the fear of taking ill with cancer runs high among siblings. Healthy children of siblings who have congenital heart disease worry that they, too, may have holes in their hearts or that they are defective in some manner.

Professionals must help siblings express their identity concerns and their worries about becoming ill or disabled. Support groups of similarly-aged youngsters are a useful adjunct to individual counseling. Siblings who may feel different or odd about their experiences and feelings may find comfort in a support group when they learn that others share their feelings. Generally, siblings need reassurance that there is little likelihood of getting the same disease or disability that afflicts their brother or sister and that it is not contagious. Siblings should be encouraged to pursue their own activities and relationships that can counteract the sense of identification implied in sibling relationships.

Careers and Life Goals

Basic life goals of nondisabled siblings may be affected when a disabled child is present in the family. A child's career decision may be shaped by having interacted with and cared for a less-able brother or sister. The continuous act of caring for a disabled youngster, especially in a loving family, may become internalized to the extent that it influences career decisions in the direction of the helping professions. Siblings may internalize helping norms and turn their career endeavors toward the improvement of humanity or at least toward life goals that required dedication and sacrifice (Farber, 1959 & Cleveland and Miller, 1977).

The following comments by a sister of a mentally retarded, cerebral palsied, and epileptic sibling reflects the thinking behind her decision to prepare for a helping profession.

> Having Robin as a member of our family caused me to undergo a great
> deal of introspection which led me to insights into certain aspects of my

character that needed to be changed. My contact with him, coupled with some sound advice from my parents, also unquestionably influenced my decision to pursue a career in special education. I had originally intended to enter the field of chemistry, and indeed I completed a bachelor's degree in that area. However, something about my choice bothered me. I enjoyed the lab work and the excitement of scientific discovery, but something was missing. It wasn't until my father, during the course of one of our "What are you going to do with your life?" discussions, pinpointed the problem when he quoted the following statement made by the philosopher Kierkegaard: "The door to happiness opens outward." What this meant to me was that one could find true happiness through serving others. The choice of a career then became obvious to me. What better way was there to serve others than to enter the field of special education where I could help people like my brother lead more fulfilling lives? (Helsel, 1978, p. 112).

Illes (1979) reported that her subjects exhibited compassion, tolerance, and empathy—characteristics valued in the helping professions. Furthermore, Skrtic et al., (1984) speculated that a sibling's identification with a disabled brother or sister and a desire to understand his or her problems may provide the impetus to choose a career in education or the human services. However, some siblings who believe they have already made a significant contribution to a difficult life circumstance may seek fulfillment in careers that are less interpersonally intense.

There is not enough research on siblings, their life goals, and specific careers to draw firm conclusions about the relationship between living with a disabled brother or sister and choosing a particular career path. There is only enough information for some armchair speculation about the influence a disabled child may have on a sibling's career choice and life goals.

EMOTIONAL REACTIONS

A friend of mine who is in her late 60s mentioned once that she still harbors angry and resentful feelings about her youth because of the attention her diabetic sister received from her parents. In our conversation, the friend expressed surprise about her feelings that on the one hand felt very distant in time yet continued to evoke strong negative reactions.

Siblings of disabled children may experience anger more often and perhaps more intensely than siblings of nondisabled brothers and sisters. Whether siblings harbor or openly express their feelings of anger and resentment depends on the extent to which a sibling feels responsible for the disability, the extent to which the disabled child restricts the sibling's social life or is considered a source of stigma, the extent to which the disabled child requires excessive time and attention from the parents, etc.

Featherstone (1980) noted that anger may arise in relation to numerous conditions in a home with a disabled child:

> Children feel angry: at parents, at the disabled child, at the wider world, at God or fate, perhaps at all four. Some blame their mother and father for the disability itself (just as they blame them for any new baby). A handicap creates unusual needs; many children envy their brother or sister this special attention. And older children may rage secretly about the sometimes colossal sums of money spent on diagnosis and therapy-resources that might otherwise finance family comforts and college tuition (p. 143).

Reactions from others regarding a disabled brother or sister may lead to open expressions of hostility, as illustrated in the following comments from a college student:

> I heard some guy talking in the back about Mark and how stupid he was, and you could make him do anything and he is so gullible, and all this kind of stuff. I walked back to the kid and slugged him in the face . . . I always felt that I had to protect him from someone, from teasing, from fights, and any other kids trying to put things over on kids who are at a disadvantage to them. If you love somebody you cannot help but get emotionally involved in that (Klein, 1972, pp. 12, 13).

Nondisabled siblings may be placed in a difficult bind. Parental demands that a child should care for and protect a disabled sibling clash with those of the child's playmates who may encourage shunning. Then there are ambivalent feelings — anger, guilt, love, protectiveness — to contend with. The nondisabled sibling may feel resentment toward the parents for demanding that he or she love and take care of a disabled brother or sister; the result may be tension-filled situations.

> Wherever I went, Mindy went too . . . I was often excluded from neighborhood games because of my sidekick. And then there was the unwritten family rule that I must leave with Mindy whenever my playmates made fun of her. They often did mock her, of course, and we would leave — except for one time which to this day gives my conscience no rest, when I joined in. I lost many playmates by having to side with Mindy. I felt neglected by my family and shunned by my peers. I was a very lonely little girl (Hayden, 1974, p. 27).

Feeling ignored and unappreciated for one's achievements leaves life-long scars on normal siblings. Hayden continues:

> Mindy's achievements always met with animated enthusiasm from our parents. In contrast it seemed, mother and daddy's response to my accomplishments was on the pat-on-the-back level. I was expected to perform well in every circumstance. I wanted my parents to be enthusiastic about my accomplishments, too. I didn't want to have to beg for praise. I didn't want to be taken for granted. I wanted to be noticed (p. 27).

There are many reasons for siblings to experience anger — and the guilt that often follows. However, in the literature dealing with counseling families there is a paucity of information on helping siblings understand, tolerate, or accept and express the anger they so often feel.

Parents and professionals must understand the sources of a sibling's anger. In addition, siblings should be enabled to understand the universality of angry feelings and how such feelings are related to guilt. Siblings need to know that their feelings are normal and that their expression is healthy.

In regard to anger, Bank and Kahn (1982) addressed the issue of this emotion in relation to siblings of emotionally disturbed children:

> Aggressiveness is one natural way through which siblings communicate. But when one sibling is defective, or is seen as defective and needs special treatment by parents, the well child must learn to inhibit, to refrain from aggressive taunts and actions. To establish himself as "well," he must give up and suppress these vital angry parts of himself, or submerge or hide them, lest he further injure his vulnerable sibling. Further, the well sibling learns not to rock the parents' boat, not to roil already troubled waters. Inhibition of anger also means that other forms of spontaneity — such as kidding, humor, and "messing around" — get squelched. The relationship between disturbed and rigidly avoidant siblings is serious and drab and lacks playfulness (pp. 259-60).

The presence of a disabled child in the family may inhibit communication. The lack of communication within a family over a child's disabling condition contributes to the isolation siblings experience. They may sense that certain topics are taboo and that negative feelings should remain hidden; they are thereby forced into a peculiar kind of loneliness — a sense of detachment from those one typically feels closest to. Family secrets or implicit rules forbidding the discussion of a problem force siblings to pretend that circumstances are other than they seem. For some parents discussing their disabled child with their other children is as threatening as discussing sex.

Siblings may not ask questions of their parents because of their wish to protect the parents. Children fear that the parents may lack the capacity to tolerate the disability and that their questions may precipitate family tensions or a rejection of themselves. Such a pattern of diminished communication spreads to other aspects of family life, producing a generalized web of silence.

Some parents "teach" their children that aggression toward a disabled sibling is bad, disloyal, and rebellious. As a result angry feelings are kept hidden or only discharged in the parents' absence.

> Rather than invigorating the relationship with the give-and-take of insults and punches, easily dished out and quickly forgotten, the well sibling must be wary of hostile impulses toward a sick brother or sister, or risk being charged with kicking the crippled or hurting the handicapped. The well sibling, being presumed to have many riches and advantages is expected to show restraint, charity, kindness, and loyalty. Being a true-blue Boy Scout is, of course, impossible; and well siblings may vent their dammed-up anger in sneaky and violent ways (Bank & Kahn, 1982, pp. 260–61).

Communication

Powell and Ogle (1985) believe that communicating with children about their disabled brother or sister is difficult, yet not impossible. They offer the following suggestions to help parent-child communication:

1. Active (not passive) listening
2. Take the time
3. Secure needed knowledge
4. Be sincere and honest
5. Respond in a comprehensive fashion
6. Adopt an open attitude
7. Provide balanced information
8. Be aware of nonverbal communication
9. Follow up earlier communication

Siblings may resent that the disabled child plays when they themselves must work so hard (Michaelis, 1980). Communicating the educational methods used with the disabled child and the skills that are being taught will help make it possible for the sibling to be supportive rather than critical and resentful. They may even volunteer to help educate their disabled brother or sister.

Wentworth (1974) reported that above all else, children want their parents to be honest with them. Siblings need to know what caused the handicap, how severe the disability is, and what the prognosis is. Parents should answer inquiries as truthfully as possible according to each sibling's age and level of comprehension.

Siblings can become isolated from family members when they are fearful or anxious about discussing their disabled brother or sister because the subject is not acceptable conversation. McKeever (1983) observed that siblings may fear loss of contact with their parents and disapproval of significant adults and therefore keep thoughts and feelings to themselves.

Peer reactions may isolate siblings from their social group. Siblings who feel rejected by their peers and are ignored by their parents are youngsters at risk. Add the caretaking role siblings may assume and the making of emotional problems may be set in motion. To help these children professionals need to be sensitive to communication problems within the family. They must also be aware of sibling reactions that may require some type of intervention. Siblings who have disturbing thoughts and repress their feelings may act out behaviorally, manifest problems in sleeping and eating routines, have nightmares, or begin to show decreased interest in peer relations and school. These are indications that a child is not coping well and requires parental attention and, in some cases, professional help.

PARENTAL ATTITUDES

Because children's views are often extensions of their parents' views, their ability to accept the disability and cope with the hardship is largely influenced by parental attitudes (Trevino, 1979). Parental attitudes of authoritarianism and overindulgence, augmented by such feelings as anxiety, depression, guilt, and uncontrolled hostility, help color the views, feelings, and behaviors of their children. Some parents react so negatively to a disabled child that their other children will, accordingly, be adversely affected (Lobato, 1983), whereas other parents unconsciously structure the roles nondisabled siblings assume vis á vis their disabled brothers and sisters (Bank & Kahn, 1982). For example, a sibling may learn that to be appreciated and loved one must assume a caretaking role within the family. Such behavior will garner the desired reaction from parents and also solidify an individual's position within the family.

Parental responses and adaptation is highly individualistic and is a consequence of numerous factors. Seligman and Darling (1989) cite studies that demonstrate *both* negative and positive reactions. Religious and cultural factors help shape parental attitudes, but these factors unfortunately have been largely ignored in the literature. Seligman and Darling (1989) point out that culturally acquired attitudes about others can influence the quality of friendships and professional relationships the family establishes.

Some preliminary research tends to support the view that Catholic parents may perceive the birth of a disabled child as a gift, a blessing that God would bestow only on the most deserving (Zuk, 1959). Such positive sentiments surely influence sibling attitudes.

PSYCHOLOGICAL EFFECTS ON SIBLINGS

The presence of a disabled sibling changes the experiences of each child in the family. A family with a disabled child offers the other children unusual opportunities for growth but also provides fertile ground for the development of problems. A number of potential areas of difficulty have been noted. How these factors interact to culminate in adjustment problems is difficult to determine.

The potential for adjustment problems tends to be viewed differently. Poznanski (1969), Trevino (1979), and San Martino and Newman (1974) appear to be the most pessimistic about the effects that a disabled brother or sister has on sibling adjustment. Poznanski reported that psychiatrists treat more siblings of disabled children than disabled children themselves. For San Martino and Newman, guilt provides the foundation for subsequent difficulties siblings are likely to experience. From their interviews of 239 families, Breslau, Weitzman, and Messinger (1981) found conflicting results regarding sibling adjustment. They did discern a marked trend toward aggressive behavior and confused thinking by siblings.

Bank and Kahn (1982) observed that a sibling's adjustment can be affected by his or her age and developmental stage. This is because siblings' ability to comprehend their brother's or sister's illness and what it means for the family changes over time. Another factor, chronicity, determines whether the sibling must cope with a time-limited condition or with a more lasting and perhaps more devastating situation. Bank and Kahn also noted that the rate of onset, especially with a mentally ill sibling, can be the source of some confusion for the sibling. And finally, the stigmatizing aspects of an ill sibling's condition can cause considerable consternation. In a public situation, a well-behaved mildly retarded youngster will most likely go unnoticed, whereas a drooling, bent figure in a wheelchair will draw considerable attention.

Featherstone (1980)—from personal experience and in recounting the experiences of others—and Grossman (1972) and Kibert (1987)—from their research on brothers and sisters in college—take a cautious view of the effects on nondisabled children. They believe disability in the family may have differential outcomes: little impact, negative impact, or positive outcome on subsequent adjustment and coping. Farber's (1959, 1960) research tend to support the same conclusion, which is further reinforced by Klein (1972) and Schreiber and Feeley (1965). Grakliker, Fishler, and Koch (1962) did not find any adverse effects reported by the siblings interviewed in their study. A recent study reported that siblings of ill children had comparable self-concept scores to children with nondisabled brothers and sisters (Tritt and Essess, 1988). However, the mothers of the children with ill siblings observed a significantly greater amount of behavioral problems (withdrawal and shyness) than the mothers of the matched control group.

From an empirical point of view, the question of whether siblings are affected, not affected, helped, or harmed by the presence of a disabled brother or sister is unanswerable. Available data have not yet established the prevalence of magnitude of emotional problems among siblings residing with a disabled brother or sister compared with the problems found in "normal" families. The factors that interact and subsequently lead to psychological difficulties are many and they may be combined in complex ways. Although some contributors to the professional literature are pessimistic about the effects that a disabled child has on family members, others are more optimistic, especially parents and siblings who have written about their experiences.

For example, Illes (1979) reported that siblings of cancer victims are compassionate, tolerant, empathic to parents, and appreciative of their own health. Such positive sentiments underscore both the capacity of children to function under stress and the important contributions they make to their families. Glendinning's (1983) British study, in which she interviewed in-depth 17 parents (mostly mothers) of severely handicapped children, revealed that siblings apparently face life optimistically.

Drotar (quoted in Wallinga et al., 1987) argued that a child's chronic disability brings family members together. A common adversity tends to mobilize positive efforts on behalf of the disabled child, which is actually beneficial to the family. Simeonsson and Bailey (1986) noted that siblings who have been actively involved in the management of their disabled family member tend to be well adjusted.

In their research Grossman (1972) and Kibert (1986) reported that a number of college students who discussed their relationship with their retarded brother or sister appeared to have benefited from growing up with their disabled siblings. "The ones who benefited appeared to us to be more tolerant, more compassionate, more knowing about prejudice" (Grossman, p. 84). In support of Grossman's findings, Miller (1974) found a number of siblings who had experienced involvement in the growth and development of a retarded sibling and exhibited a sense of pride that they had been a part of it.

This review suggests that our knowledge of siblings is still in its infancy, yet one is not without some guidance. In general, we should heed the admonition that sibling adjustment is dependent on a unique configuration of numerous variables and that a simple cause and effect explanation is misleading. The impact of a disabled child may be "for better or for worse" and depends on various mediating factors. In general, though, it is essential that parents and professionals consider more seriously the feelings and experiences of siblings. Much needless suffering can be avoided if these children are taken into account as professionals try to better understand family response to childhood disability.

REFERENCES

Bank, S. P., & Kahn, M. D. (1982). *The sibling bond.* New York: Basic Books.

Binger, C. M. (1973). Childhood leukemia: Emotional impact on siblings. In J. Anthony & C. Koupernik (Eds.), *The child in his family.* New York: Wiley.

Breslau, N. (1982). Siblings of siblings of disabled children: Birth order and age-spacing effects. *Journal of Abnormal Child Psychology, 10,* pp. 85–96.

Breslau, N., Weitzman, M., & Messinger, K. (1981). Psychologic functioning of disabled children. *Pediatrics, 67,* pp. 344–353.

Cleveland, D. W., & Miller, N. (1977). Attitudes and life commitments of older siblings of mentally retarded adults. *Mental Retardation, 15,* pp. 38–41.

Dunn, J. (1985). *Sisters and brothers.* Cambridge, MA: Harvard University Press.

Farber, B. (1959). Effect of a severely retarded child on family integration. *Monographs of the Society for Research in Child Development, 24*(Whole No. 71).

Farber, B. (1960). Family organization and crisis: Maintenance of integration in families with a severely mentally retarded child. *Monographs of the Society for Research in Child Development, 25*(Whole No. 75).

Featherstone, H. (1980). *A difference in the family.* New York: Basic Books.

Feigon, J. (1981). A sibling group program. *Sibling Information Network Newsletter, 1,* pp. 2–3.

Glendinning, C. (1983). *Unshared care.* London: Routledge & Kegan Paul.

Grakliker, B. V., Fishler, K., & Koch, R. (1962). Teenage reactions to a mentally retarded sibling. *American Journal of Mental Deficiency, 66,* pp. 838–843.

Grossman, F. K. (1972). *Brothers and sisters of retarded children.* Syracuse, NY: Syracuse University Press.

Hayden, V. (1974). The other children. *The Exceptional Parent, 4,* pp. 26–29.

Helsel, E. (1978). The Helsels' story of Robin. In A. P. Turnbull & H. R. Turnbull (Eds.), *Parents speak out.* Columbus, OH: Merrill.

Holt, K. S. (1958). The home care of severely retarded children. *Pediatrics, 22,* pp. 746–755.

Illes, J. (1979). Children with cancer: Healthy siblings' perceptions during the illness experience. *Cancer Nursing, 2,* pp. 371–377.

Israelite, N. (1985). Sibling reaction to a hearing impaired child in the family. *Journal of Rehabilitation of the Deaf, 18*(3), pp. 1–5.

Kahn, M. D., & Lewis, K. G. (1988). *Siblings in therapy: Life span and clinical issues.* New York: Norton.

Kibert, R. (1987). *College-aged siblings' perceptions of their retarded brothers and sisters.* Unpublished doctoral dissertation, University of Pittsburgh.

Kirkman, M. (1985). The perceived impact of a sibling with a disability on family relationships: A survey of adult siblings in Victoria, Australia. *Sibling Information Network Newsletter, 4,* pp. 2–5.

Klein, S. D. (1972). Brother to sister: Sister to brother. *The Exceptional Parent, 2,* pp. 10–15.

Lechtenberg, R. (1984). *Epilepsy and the family.* Cambridge, MA: Harvard University Press.

Lobato, D. (1983). Siblings of handicapped children: A review. *Journal of Autism and Developmental Disorders, 13,* pp. 347–364.

Luterman, D. (1979). *Counseling parents of hearing-impaired children.* Boston: Little, Brown.

Marion, R. L. (1981). *Educators, parents, and exceptional children.* Rockville, MD: Aspen Systems.

McHale, S. M., Simeonsson, R. J., & Gamble, W. C. (1987). Sibling relationships and adjustment of children with disabled brothers and sisters. *Journal of Children in Contemporary Society, 19,* pp. 131–158.

McHale, S. M., Simeonsson, R. J., & Sloan, J. L. (1984). Children with handicapped brothers and sisters. In E. Schopler & G. B. Mesibov (Eds.), *The effects of autism on the family.* New York: Plenum Press.

McKeever, P. (1983). Siblings of chronically ill children. *American Journal of Orthopsychiatry, 53, 2,* pp. 209–218.

Michaelis, C. T. (1980). *Home and school partnerships in exceptional children.* Rockville, MD: Aspen Systems.

Miller, S. (1974). An exploratory study of sibling relationships in families with retarded children. Unpublished doctoral dissertation, Columbia University, New York.

Murphy, A., Paeschel, S., Duffy, T., & Brady, E. (1976). Meeting with brothers and sisters of children Down's syndrome. *Children Today, 5,* pp. 20-23.

Myers, R. (1978). *Like normal people.* New York: McGraw-Hill.

Powell, T., Ogle, P. (1985). *Brothers and sisters — exceptional families.* Baltimore, MD: Paul H. Brookes.

Poznanski, E. (1969). Psychiatric difficulties in siblings of handicapped children. *Pediatrics, 8,* pp. 232-234.

San Martino, M., & Newman, M. B. (1974). Siblings of retarded children: A population at risk. *Child Psychiatry and Human Development, 4,* pp. 168-177.

Schreiber, M., & Feeley, M. (1965). A guided group experience. *Children, 12,* pp. 221-225.

Seligman, M. (Ed.) (1983). *The family with a handicapped child.* Orlando, FL: Grune & Stratton.

Seligman, M., & Darling, R. B. (1989). *Ordinary families, special children: A systems approach to childhood disability.* New York: Guilford Press.

Simeonsson, R. J., & Bailey, D. B. (1986). Sibling of handicapped children. In J. J. Gallagher & P. M. Vietze, *Families of handicapped persons.* Baltimore, MD: Paul H. Brookes.

Skrtic, T., Summers, J., Brotherson, M. J., & Turnbull, A. (1984). Severely handicapped children and their brothers and sisters. In J. Blacker (Ed.), *Severely handicapped young children and their families.* Orlando, FL: Academic Press.

Sourkes, B. M. (1987). Siblings of the child with a life threatening illness. *Journal of Children in Contemporary Society, 19,* pp. 159-184.

Tew, B., & Lawrence, K. (1975). Mothers, brothers and sisters of patients with spina bifida. *Developmental Medical Child Neurology, 15*(Supp. 29), pp. 69-76.

Travis, C. (1976). *Chronic illness in children: Its impact on child and family.* Stanford, CA: Stanford University Press.

Trevino, F. (1979). Siblings of handicapped children: Identifying those at risk. *Social Casework, 60,* pp. 488-493.

Tritt, S. G. and Esses, L.M. (1988). Psychosocial adaptation of siblings of children with chronic medical illness. *American Journal of Orthopsychiatry, 58,* pp. 211-220.

Vadasy, P. F., Fewell, R. R., Meyer, D. J., & Schell, G. (1984). Siblings of handicapped children: A developmental perspective on family interactions. *Family Relations, 33,* pp. 155-167.

Wallinga, C., Paguio, L., & Skeen, P. (1987). When a brother or sister is ill. *Psychology Today,* pp. 42, 43.

Wasserman, R. (1983). Identifying the counseling needs of the siblings of mentally retarded children. *Personnel and Guidance Journal, 62,* pp. 622–627.

Wentworth, E. H. (1974). *Listen to your heart: A message to parents of handicapped children.* Boston: Houghton Mifflin.

Zuk, G. H. (1959). The religious factors the role of guilt in parental acceptance of the retarded child. *American Journal of Mental Deficiency, 64,* pp. 139–147.

CHAPTER EIGHT

Parenting Moderately Handicapped Persons

Rebecca R. Fewell

Rebecca R. Fewell, Ph.D., is the Karen Gore Professor of Special Education at Tulane University. Previously, she was director of the Model Preschool Programs at the University of Washington. She has been a teacher of handicapped children and has trained teachers of young handicapped children.

Dr. Fewell is the author of numerous journal articles and book chapters. She served as the coeditor of the following books: Educating Handicapped Infants: Issues in Development and Intervention, Families of Handicapped Children: Needs and Supports across the Life-Span, Living with a Brother or Sister with Special Needs, and Learning through Play, *and has co-authored two tests, the* Developmental Activities Screening Inventory *and the* Peabody Developmental Motor Scales. *She is an editor of the journal,* Topics in Early Childhood Special Education.

Any means of dividing children with special needs into mild, moderate, and severe categories is arbitrary and disputable, especially at the confluence of categories. It is not likely that mildly and severely handicapped individuals will be confused with each other, but moderately handicapped children who range from the upper limit of mild to the lower limit of severe are most open to ambiguity in definition. Having made this admonition, I will begin our discussion by defining the moderately handicapped individual.

One meaning of *moderate,* according to Webster's dictionary (1977 edition), is "keeping within reasonable bounds." The definition of moderately handicapped children used in this chapter extrapolates from Webster: They are those children whose disabilities obviously are sufficiently substantial to require special services, yet their restrictions are such that substantial areas of normal functioning exist. The moderately handicapped child is markedly deficient in one area (at least), whereas he or she is perhaps normally functioning in others. By contrast, the severely handicapped child's disability is not "within reasonable bounds"; it pervades most if not all areas of functioning. The mildly handicapped child differs from the moderate in the degree of disability. Here the handicap is less obvious and has less impact on the child's life.

The severely handicapped child is one who is generally perceived by others to be abnormal. The mildly handicapped child, despite the existence of a problem, is generally perceived to be normal. The moderately handicapped child occupies a more ambiguous position and may be defined at some times as normal and at others as abnormal. This overlap and its implications for parents and professionals is a consistent theme in this chapter.

It should be noted that these designations are functional rather than categorical. That is, an individual seen as severe at one time may, after developing mastery, be (by this definition) moderate at a later time. The nature of the handicap may be marked in some respects yet be "within reasonable bounds" in its effect on the individual's life.

The major sections of this chapter elaborate on the theme of ambiguity that pertains to this intermediate level of disability. First, the psychosocial aspects of parenting the moderately handicapped child are reviewed. Parents must cope with the social evaluation of disability made by our culture, as well as with the marginality of their child vis-à-vis society.

Second, the service needs of these children and their families are discussed. Ambiguity can result in individuals falling between the cracks with regard to receiving available services. Moderately handicapped children may be too normal for services aimed at more severely handicapped children, yet nevertheless be in need of such services.

The concluding section of the chapter describes ways professionals may assess family needs and determine strategies that will work to meet identified needs. An emphasis is placed on identifying and working with the existing strengths of the family unit.

PSYCHOSOCIAL ASPECTS OF PARENTING MODERATELY HANDICAPPED CHILDREN

Parents cannot be properly understood in isolation from their sociocultural context. Bronfenbrenner (1976), Brim (1975), Gallimore, Weisner, Kaufman, and Bernheimer (1989), Fewell (1986a) and Sameroff, Seifer, and Zax, (1982) have helped raise awareness of the many ecological variables that affect parents. These factors are no less potent for the families of moderately handicapped children. These parents are normal individuals subject to the same forces and changes in modern life that influence all families. As parents of children with special needs, they must adjust to other factors as well. The first of these is the nature of the disability itself. Equally important, however, is the attitude of the community toward the disabled child (Carey, 1982; Mallory, 1986). As Roskies (1972) noted, the child's role within the family is inseparable from his or her status in the community.

A disability, whether mental or physical, is of itself not a psychological event. Its impact on a family or individual is determined by its meaning within an ecological context (Fewell, 1986a; Grossman, 1972; Jablow, 1982; MacGregor, Abel, Bryt, Lauer, & Weissman, 1953; Myerson, 1963; Wright, 1960). Disabilities are evaluated according to cultural attitudes and the cause (putative or real) of the disability. Myerson (1963) noted that "disability is not an objective thing in a person, but a social value judgment" (p. 11).

Cultures vary in their attitudes toward persons with disabilities. Edgerton (1970, 1981) described a wide range of evaluations of persons who are retarded in traditional societies. They ranged from complete intolerance leading to neglect or outright killing to the granting of the status of "saint." Maisel (1960) provided similar examples of cultural variety in response to persons who are physically disabled. The Palaung of the Malay peninsula, for example, considered a person especially fortunate to have been born with a cleft palate.

The perceived cause of a facial deformity was found to strongly influence its meaning, both to the disfigured and to others (MacGregor et al., 1953). Congenital deformities were evaluated negatively, whereas war-inflicted injuries were evaluated more highly. The authors concluded that "what the deformity symbolizes for the patient and others around him seems to have in many instances more significance than the specific defect itself" (MacGregor et al., 1953, p. 75).

Haffter (1968) provided an excellent example of the way in which a culture's evaluation of a disability as well as perception of its cause affected parents of handicapped children. In Europe during the Middle Ages, children with birth defects were called changelings. They were believed to be the offspring of a woman's union with the devil. A woman suspected of practicing witchcraft would be asked if she had given birth to a changeling, and an admission could result in her being burned at the stake. Not surprisingly, families with disabled children were fearful, secretive, and unaccepting of the child (Haffter, 1968). The parents' behavior was not pathologic; it was a realistic response to social pressure.

In America in the 1980s it is society's attitude and assumptions about her that Georgie Miller (1981) finds offensive:

> I detest the thought of anyone saying, "she's blind." It makes me madder than anything because I am not blind. I'm visually impaired . . . a lot of people automatically start treating me like a piece of china, and I detest that. I am a person, and I don't need to be handled like I am going to break. I've always felt that way (p. 152).

If we study families with a member who has a disability in isolation from their social context, we miss the meaning of their behavior. Our judgments are likely to be unfair to parents and we are likely to wind up "blaming the victim" (Ryan, 1971). We would also overlook the manner in which ecological forces influence a family's ability to cope and adapt to their child with special needs (Crnic, Friedrich, & Greenberg, 1983).

A society's negative evaluation of a child places severe strain on the child's parents. Parental aspirations for the child and the realization of cherished goals can be thwarted by social obstacles as well as by the disability itself. In addition, parents are forced into conflicting roles as providers who desire the best for their children and as members of a society that views the child as socially unworthy. Finally, when the child's handicap is a moderate one, the parent faces the added uncertainty of not knowing in a given situation whether the child will be accepted or rejected. The uncertainty engendered by this marginality is especially stressful.

Parental Aspirations

There is a great variability in human parenting behavior across cultures. Nevertheless, human parents everywhere have some common goals for their children (Fewell, 1986a). One of these is the achievement of a culturally valued role within the community (Levine, 1980). The realization of this parental aspiration depends not only on the child but also on the community's assessment of the child. When a society rejects a child it deprives the parent of the possibility of achieving this aspiration. Moreover, parents whose children are devalued by their culture are devalued themselves as parents. If a prime role of parenting is the transmission of culture, those whose children are rejected by the culture are left with a role stripped of its purpose. Such parents must raise their children in what Roskies (1972) described as a "social void."

The American mainstream culture places high values on normal appearance and behavior. Persons (including those who are the disabled) who deviate from the norm are stigmatized (Goffman, 1963). Goffman described the stigmatized person as one who "is reduced in our mind from a whole and usual person to a tainted and discounted one" (pp. 2–3). The stigmatized person is, by this definition, seen as less than fully human. The stigma of disability is linked with shame and inferiority (Wright, 1960). The handicapped role expected of disabled people is characterized by incompetence, helplessness, and deviance. The role precludes other more normal social roles, such as friend, lover, co-worker, or autonomous adult (Gliedman & Roth, 1980). Sarason and Doris (1979) wrote: "In our society the retarded child has always been a second-class human being for whom one should have pity, and toward whom one should be humane, but for whom society has no use" (p. 77). This statement is also true for children with other disabilities (Gliedman & Roth, 1980).

The magnitude of their disabilities exclude severely handicapped persons from assuming normal social roles. But the separation of the moderately handicapped persons from society has a different cause. The stigma applied to them is a response to their difference from the norm, not to the differing characteristics themselves. Ethnic groups have been stigmatized for different dress, language, or skin color. Midgets and dwarfs are stigmatized although they do not have impairments in mental or physical functioning (Sagarin, 1969). A facial deformity is a handicap leading to inferior status, but not because of any impairment in physical functioning (MacGregor et al., 1953).

The effect of the moderate disability on functioning is, according to our definition, limited. Moderately handicapped individuals are not of themselves socially deviant. They are penalized, however, by virtue of the "handicapped" label. They are identified with severely handicapped persons, although they could as easily be identified with the nondisabled. Their social isolation is no less palpable for being undeserved, and it strongly affects their parents.

Roskies's (1972) study of thalidomide-deformed babies and their mothers found social factors deeply enmeshed in parents' reactions to the disabled babies. "Even at the moment of the mother's initial awareness of the fact that she had borne a deformed baby, her attitudes towards this crisis were based not only on her own feelings, or on the physical diagnosis of the child, but also on the social prognosis" (p. 169). Moreover, the importance of social factors on the mothers' reactions to their children increased as time went on. Their optimism was directly related to the degree of social normalization the child had achieved in the eyes of the community. The mothers strove to believe that "to engage in the maternity of thalidomide children was not a socially futile act" (Roskies, 1972, p. 180).

A measure of social futility is inescapable when societal attitudes deny parents the opportunity to raise a child who will assume a culturally valued role. The denial of this aspiration when the child's disability is of an intermediate rather than severe nature may be the result either of the child's features or of social discrimination. The difficulty in distinguishing between the two factors is one characteristic of the particular quandary faced by the parents of moderately handicapped children.

The Parent in the Community: The Conflict of Roles

The role of the parent of a disabled child is in conflict with the role of the parent as a member of the community (Roskies, 1972). Parents are expected to be selflessly devoted to their child while remaining members of a society that devalues that child. The conflict presents a psychological dilemma to parents and manifests itself in relations with community members and professionals.

As "normal" members of the community, parents share cultural definitions of normality and abnormality with other community members. As parents they have a need to love and accept their child. Many parents describe themselves as "blessed" or "better human beings" from experiences in parenting their special needs child. Frey, Greenberg, and Fewell (1989) found the parents who believed in themselves and had positive perceptions of their situations coped better and experienced less stress than did parents who felt sorry for themselves and their child. Yet, parents must choose between viewing their child through the eyes of the community to which they belong or through their own eyes which may be in conflict with community perceptions (Roskies, 1972).

If parents see their child as abnormal and deserving of stigma, they jeopardize their ability to identify with and love the child. A child seen this way will suffer rejection and isolation within the family. The parents maintain their continuity with the community and its values at the cost of their ability to parent their child. Because parents are expected to love and accept their child even when society will not, parents who reject their child may be expected to experience conflict and guilt.

Those parents who reject society's evaluation of the handicapped child also suffer. They find themselves in opposition to their culture's definition of normality. By identifying with the child they will be forced to redefine their values and their relationship to the community. They may become part of subculture formed around the needs and value of children like theirs (Darling, 1979).

The conflict of roles is keenly experienced in encounters in the community. Strangers stare, make comments, or offer advice when they see children who appear different. The comments usually reflect stereotypical negative judgments about disability and often assume that the parents share the same perspective. Darling (1979) reported that a mother was told by a stranger that she would be better off if her child had died. Featherstone (1980) described a woman who began to avoid going out with her child because she could not longer bear hearing people tell her to "put her child away" (p. 9).

Gloria, a parent of a deaf daughter, in the videotape "Today is not Forever" (Knox & Chrisman, 1979), tells of a party guest in her home who comments to her concerning the noise level: "You are so lucky your child can sleep through all this." The pain Gloria felt at that moment remained real for a long time.

The conflict is reexperienced as the parent attempts to obtain professional services for the child. Many professionals share society's evaluation of these children (Finkelstein, 1980). Darling (1979) found that one-half of a group of pediatricians whom she had interviewed had substantially negative attitudes toward disabled children. She elaborates further on parent-professional relationships in Chapter 5.

In addition to expressing negative attitudes about the child, community members and professionals may treat the parents as if they too are discounted. The "courtesy stigma" (Goffman, 1963) is extended to those closely associated with the disabled. In this way parents experience a loss of status in the community by virtue of parenting a handicapped child.

The family may be seen as a "handicapped family" whose lives revolve around their child's disability. Featherstone (1980) related the story of one family whose child was being helped by volunteers. Several of the volunteers became angry when they discovered the parents were planning to redecorate their home. Redecorating was seen as inappropriate by the volunteers who expected the parents to spend all their time working to enhance the development of the child with special needs.

Professionals may view the parents as patients who are in need of treatment (Seligman, 1979; Turnbull & Turnbull, 1978). The parents of one child were threatened with the loss of services if they terminated unneeded and irrelevant psychiatric counseling (Akerley, 1978).

Parents who speak out against condescending treatment by professionals may have their objection trivialized and treated as a manifestation of an underlying pathologic condition (Gliedman & Roth, 1980). They may be labeled "guilty," "conflicted," or "angry."

The conflicted situation of parents vis-à-vis society is unresolvable. A resolution would require either that their child become nondisabled or that society change its evaluation of such children. Family members pay a cost for society's attitude toward the disabled child. The parent unable to find a babysitter because the child is handicapped, or the family whose siblings are teased by other children, may find their ties to the community weakened because of their child. The interests of the child and the interests of the parents are thus placed in partial conflict (Riskies, 1972). This fact may be partly responsible for the higher than average risk of child abuse faced by handicapped children.

Marginality of Moderately Handicapped Individuals

The marginally handicapped individual is one who claims partial membership in two worlds but is not completely accepted in either (Stonequist, 1937). Moderately handicapped individuals are marginal, both in the nondisabled world and in the world of the severely handicapped persons. This in-between status creates ambiguity for them and their parents. Uncertainty is experienced in response to overlapping situations in which the role of disabled persons is unclear (Barker, 1948; MacGregor et al., 1953; Myerson, 1963; Roskies, 1972; Wright, 1960). Myerson (1963), in reference to the physically disabled, said that "the disabled person lives in two psychological worlds. Like everyone else he lives in the world of the non-disabled majority. He also lives in the special psychological world that his disability creates for him" (p. 42). The moderately handicapped person cannot be sure whether he or she will be treated according to normal or handicapped expectations in any given situation. Wright (1960) provided the sample of blind people wishing to find work: They are uncertain as to whether society will accept them for their normal abilities or reject them because they are fit only for a sheltered workshop that accommodates their blindness.

The reaction of the nondisabled to the severely handicapped is more predictable than is their reaction to the more moderately, less obviously handicapped person. In their study of people with facial deformities, MacGregor et al. (1953) found that severely deformed individuals evoked consistent (and negative) responses in others. By contrast, more moderately deformed persons are never quite certain of what kind of reaction they might get. Thus, they alternate between feelings of relief and tension and adjustment to their situation is made more difficult" (p. 87).

David Raymond (1982) described painful memories of his elementary school experiences in coping with his dyslexia.

> Sometimes my teachers would try to be encouraging. When I couldn't read the words on the board they'd say, "Come on, David, you know that word." Only I didn't. And it was embarrassing. I just felt dumb, and dumb was how the kids treated me. They'd make fun of me every chance they got, asking me to spell "cat" or something like that . . . about the worst thing I had to do in fifth and sixth grade was go to a special education class in another school in our town. A bus picked me up and I didn't like that at all. The bus also picked up emotionally disturbed kids, and retarded kids. It was like going to a school for the retarded. I always worried that someone I knew would see me on that bus. It was a relief to go to the regular junior high school (p. 22).

The parents of the moderately handicapped child live with the same uncertainty. They will never be completely sure if their child will be seen as alien or acceptable by the community. The more moderate the handicap, the more difficult it becomes to predict the response of others to the disabled child.

The construct of marginality predicts that moderately handicapped people will have more adjustment problems than more severely handicapped individuals; some studies have substantiated this theory. Sanua (1966) examined the attitudes of adolescents with cerebral palsy in eight countries. Those with fewer physical defects were more prejudiced toward moderately disabled individuals than toward the more severely handicapped. MacGregor et al. (1953) reported that the more severely facially deformed persons in their sample were less conflicted than were those who were mildly deformed. The less-disfigured group experienced anxiety in response to the uncertainty of others' responses to them.

Marginality was a focus in a study of 127 blind and partially sighted adolescents and 140 deaf and hard-of-hearing adolescents (Bowen & Bobrove, 1966). The totally disabled were found to be better adjusted than were the more moderately disabled; the partially sighted and hard-of-hearing group scored higher on a scale of perceived pity and lower on perceived acceptance. The total disability group made higher adjustment scores than did the more marginal group on 20 or 28 comparisons. The authors concluded that marginality, although an issue for all disabled people, is especially salient to those with intermediate handicapping conditions.

Ambiguity fosters anxiety in parents as well. A mother in a parents' discussion group stated that she was glad to know her child was completely blind rather than visually impaired. She was relieved to be free of the uncertainty of what the future held for her child's visual acuity. She preferred irreversible blindness to a less clearly defined situation.

In Grossman's (1972) study of college students who had handicapped siblings, the positive adjustment of some brothers was directly related to the severity of the physical handicap of the retarded sibling. "This result seemed closely tied to the entire family's greater clarity about, and comfort with, a visible defect in their child, in contrast to their discomfort and uncertainty with retarded children who showed no visible evidence of defects" (p. 178).

Uncertainty is the bane of the parents' thoughts about the future. For moderately handicapped children the future may be especially ambiguous. Parents may perceive it as holding both a promise and a threat (Roskies, 1972). The promise lies in the hope that the child will be accepted in the world of the "normal" people. The threat hangs on the fear that rejection and social isolation will result from the disability. Zigler (1984) pointed to social competence as the ultimate criterion for determining whether a mainstreaming experience has been successful. Although indicators of social competence in youngsters are available throughout their early years, the natural goals that parents yearn for in their offspring are social competence and independence. Finding out whether these goals are achieved takes many years.

Resolution of the disabled child's marginality in relation to the worlds of the "normal" and "abnormal" is beyond parental control. Ultimately, the social context, through the attitudes and opportunities it presents to the disabled person, will define his or her status as a member of the community or as an outsider.

Our culture is one in which disability breeds social isolation and inferior status (Finkelstein, 1980; Gliedman & Roth, 1980). This important social feature can make "acceptance" of a disability difficult for parents. In this case the locus of the problem is not only in the family but in the community as well.

The adjustment of parents to a moderately handicapped child has been analyzed from a psychosocial perspective. This perspective gives meaning to parental behavior that cannot be wholly understood by studying the family in isolation. As noted earlier, a disability has no psychological value of its own; it assumes its meaning within the society in which it occurs. The status of the child in the family is invariably linked to his or her status in the community.

Negative evaluation and rejection of disabled children have a strong impact on their parents. Moderately handicapped children, because of the in-between nature of their disability, are especially affected by social definitions of normality and deviance. They and their parents can be caught between two worlds. Parents may be denied their parental aspirations, experience a conflict between their lives as parents and as members of the community, and be caught in the ambiguity created by their child's marginality.

Parents may have good reason to resist accepting the social judgment conveyed by the word *handicapped*. The term is indiscriminately applied to persons who are not similar to persons considered to be normal (Keniston, 1980). Keniston noted that the child with cerebral palsy and the blind child (to give an example) are each more similar to normal children than they are to each other. What they have in common, according to Keniston, are the attitudes of society: They share a stigma and a social destiny. Parents' difficulty with that destiny is inevitable and normal, and not a sign of pathologic functioning.

The psychosocial influences on parents are, however, not the entire picture. The psychology of family members, their belief systems, the existence of support networks, their personal appraisal of their own situation, the availability (or lack) of needed services, the family's financial status, and the temperament and disability of the child are all significant factors in family adjustment. These factors appear to have special salience for the family when a member has a moderate handicap.

We move now from the "macro" level to the "micro," and discuss the impact of handicaps on parenting.

THE IMPACT OF THE HANDICAP ON PARENTING

This book has continuously stressed the factors that shape responses of handicapped children and their families to personal and societal demands. Each person's individual history, experiences, talents, goals, and contributions to each situation, along with society's expectations and exploitations through its policies and practices account for the circumstances parents of handicapped children face. These are multilevel, complex contributions that involve "systems within systems, some interlocking, some overlapping, some encased one within another—all interacting with and affecting the others . . . these systems are not supergistic. They interact in complex ways and are often at serious odds with one another" (Zigler, 1984, pp. 22–23).

There are similarities in the experiences that all parents of children with special needs face. They encounter the dilemmas of finding appropriate services, of marshaling resources, of explaining their child's needs as well as their own needs to a society that tells them in subtle ways that their child is unworthy. Parents enumerate common experiences with service professionals as well: They tell of being forced to interact continually with professionals who do not realize how it feels to be a parent or who view parents as unable to understand what the problems are and yet, nevertheless, expect parents to be understanding and cooperative, passive, and appreciative.

Although most experiences of domestic life are shared by all families, there are certain experiences that are felt more strongly by parents whose children have one impairment as opposed to another. For a more thorough understanding of the impact of the various individual handicaps on the child and the family, the reader will find information in the literature on these handicaps. In the following section we draw on examples across four different areas of impairment in an effort to illustrate, in an abbreviated manner, the impact that various moderate impairments has on children and especially on the parents of these children.

Parenting Visually Impaired Children

For most people without personal knowledge of the blind, the condition of blindness conjures up memories of street vendors selling pencils, of beggars strumming guitars for coins in cups, of persons being led on the arms of others or swinging white canes from side to side, of guide dogs leading their masters across busy intersections. Perhaps even more striking are recollections of religious writings that describe the blind as possessed by demons, worthy of scorn, to be left to die in the wilderness. In contrast, positive images of the blind—of the talented Tom Sullivan, musician, songwriter, and frequent television guest star, for example, or of talented musicians such as Stevie Wonder, Ronnie Millsap, and Diana Schurr, may be buried in our consciousness. These images of productive people, as well as images of blind persons reading bus schedules with the help of sophisticated mechanical devices, or of a successful, though blind, district attorney prosecuting criminal cases, might also come to mind. More than likely, however, these positive images are not the ones that parents will conjure up when they receive the initial information that their child is visually impaired. At first, grief and self-recrimination are dominating emotions, and parents may feel estrangement from their own child.

Blindness can be caused by many things. Genetic conditions, infections, and diseases are common etiologies. Parents of blind children, like those of other handicapped children, search for the cause of their child's blindness. A genetic cause can result in parents blaming themselves and feeling guilty. Adventitious blindness presents a very different set of conditions. In families where children are born with sight, normal parent-child relationships develop. For the normally sighted infant-parent dyad, the attachment that develops is mediated through vision. Smiling on recognition, discriminating looks, using call sounds and responses, visual memory, scanning, tracking, and mutual gazing are all signifiers of attachment that are basically visual in the forming of human relationships. If blindness occurs after 18 months of age, early bonding experiences are likely to provide the secure basis for continued emotional growth as well as a basis for many cognitive discoveries that build on schemas acquired during the attachment phase. If blindness comes later, parents must face the task of dealing not only with their own personal adjustment but the child's adjustment as well. Explaining why it happened, what it means, and how it will affect the child now and in the future culminates in stressful interaction, the success of which depends on the many contributory factors described earlier in this chapter.

The severity of the visual loss is a most important factor in any case of blindness. The presence of some sight, despite the fact that it is minimal, makes a difference in parental reactions. It is the opinion of Lairy and Harrison-Covello (1973) that parents of children with some remaining vision can ignore the blindness for a longer period of time or can "valorize" the remaining sight. This reaction may be quite similar to the frequent reactions of partially sighted children to their own visual competency. They attempt to use it to the best advantage. It is not at all unusual for these children to pretend to see things in the same way as do sighted children, because they are unaware of what others are seeing when they look at images. A teacher may ask a boy if he sees a street sign and he may see the diamond-shaped sign and respond in the affirmative, yet the child may never realize that a message is written on the sign. Likewise, parents may not realize the extent of their child's impairment and may treat their child as one whose vision resembles that of nonvision impaired persons.

Whether or not a visual impairment is stressful or not is situation dependent. If one is listening to a concert and sharing reactions to the performance with a friend, then a visual impairment is not a source of stress. However, if in leaving the concert persons are impatient and do not allow the visually impaired individual the space needed to exit effectively and efficiently, then the situation is likely to produce stress. In this case it is the environment and the behavior of others that are often the sources of stress. It is the social stigma of blindness and visual impairment that one tries to avoid at all cost.

The strain of trying to "pass" as a normally sighted person is a frequent and expected reaction of moderately visually impaired persons. Criddle (1953) described this experience quite insightfully: "That I could keep a girl from knowing about my eyes through the intimacies of courtship, even a rapid one, seems improbable. That I did seems a little fantastic even to me now that I realize how little I could see at that time. This concealment became habitual. I would refrain from exposing my eye condition as unconsciously as I would refrain from touching a fire; for it was often just as painful" (p. 76).

Parents of visually impaired children must rely on professional judgment to ascertain how seriously the visual loss affects the child's ability to see. Can he or she see print, large print, or will he or she need to read braille or use a machine such as the Optacon that converts print to tactile letters? Answers to these questions have serious implications for where and how the child will be educated. Can a student who needs training in braille be accommodated in the local public school, or will it be best to send that child to a residential school for the blind? Because vision services are needed by very few students, the parents of these children are more likely to face the decision of whether an alternative to the neighborhood school is a more appropriate educational environment. For these parents, this decision may force them to confront their child's differences or needs whereas parents of children for whom more educational options exist, may not have to acknowledge their child's disability as openly.

Parenting Hearing Impaired Children

As we stated earlier, society is not always kind to its members who are different. Schlesinger and Meadow (1972) reported that people are more uncomfortable around deaf persons than those with other disabilities, and they experience a "shock-withdrawal-paralysis" reaction on their first exposure to such people.

Many of the parents of deaf children have experienced deafness in their family or are deaf themselves. They are aware before having a child of the possibilities that their child may be deaf. For these parents, there are different reactions, and life experiences that are major problems for hearing parents of deaf children are not problems for deaf parents of deaf children. For example, deaf children of deaf parents consistently have higher language scores than do deaf children of hearing parents, are better adjusted (Brill, 1960, 1969), and receive manual language training earlier. These children thus benefit from an earlier exposure to receptive and expressive language. Moreover, deaf parents demonstrate greater acceptance of deafness and experience greater ease in childrearing (Schlesinger & Meadow, 1972).

Knowledge that their child is deaf comes to many parents as they notice subtle signs, such as the child not responding to loud noises or to his or her own name or failing to show increasing use of babbling sounds or initial words. Once a suspicion is confirmed, parents experience the disappointment, hurt, guilt, shame, blame, and variable feelings so many other parents of handicapped children share.

With deafness, technology can help if the child's loss is of the kind that will respond to amplification. This makes a tremendous difference in that parents can actively help their child. Parents can get help in securing aids and helping their child learn to use them. In so doing, they have the satisfaction of knowing they are doing something that can make a difference.

With hearing aids come many other problems that are stressful to parents. Aids are expensive; they operate on batteries that must be checked daily and replaced frequently; earmolds do not always fit and they must be cleaned and also replaced; service for the aid is seldom near at hand. Another set of aid problems center around psychological adjustment to the aid, learning to accept it and use it. Just getting the child to tolerate wearing it is a major accomplishment. Many parents have described the frustrations of the early months and years of their child adjusting to this foreign object, the crying, the aids thrown down toilets or hidden, earmolds chewed, and cords discarded. Parents have the major responsibility of helping their child cope with the aid and learn to use it. The realization that the important language, listening, and speaking skills are not immediately forthcoming can be disappointing and cause doubt, depression, and more frustration in both the child and the parents.

Learning to accept the aids as a part of the child is another very difficult experience, and on that was poignantly stated by Norma in the penetrating videotape, "Today is Not Forever": "We put the (hearing aids) on (Tracy) and my first reaction was those ugly hearing aids on my pretty little girl. And I just couldn't stand it and I cried" (Knox & Chrisman, 1979).

Grandparents and other extended family members have their own problems learning to deal with their deaf family member. Relatives find the deafness hard to believe and can be adamant in their expectation that sudden miracles will occur or in their tenacious hold on misinformation. For those one step removed from parenting, the importance of learning and using signs is less well understood. Grandparents, for instance, have other grandchildren with whom they can communicate. One mother's description of this sadness in relation to her daughter says it well, "My sisters still won't learn to sign . . . A hug just isn't enough" (Ferris, 1980, p. 68).

Siblings of deaf children, like those of all handicapped children, are also affected. For some the handicap is viewed as a burden, whereas for others, as a blessing. Some parents express their concerns about female siblings mothering the deaf child; others describe the hearing sibling's loneliness when the deaf child leaves each Monday to return to the school for the deaf. If the sibling is also deaf, the bond between them can be unusually strong, as they indeed have a language to share—one that is not frequently understood by other neighborhood children.

Parents of deaf children, like those of some blind children, may have to make a difficult decision about whether to educate their child in a residential school or a public school. Parents describe this as an agonizing decision and one that they may reverse later. Among the issues raised in making such a decision are the following: Where is the better education, the better resources, and can the family tolerate weekly, monthly, or longer separations? If the child goes to a residential school, will he or she reside in the world of the deaf — for life? If the child stays at home, will mainstreaming work, can a special class be formed, or will a resource room be available? The advantages and disadvantages of the child's social life in the deaf community and in the hearing community are another major consideration. One variable that continues to be conspicuous in terms of the child's success or failure is the classroom teacher — that individual's sensitivity to the child, his or her needs and capacities.

Many parents of deaf children can look to a future that holds promise of college, employment, and family life. There are many examples of successful deaf persons. This knowledge can be the basis for dreams and long-term goals. Knowing about the success of other hearing impaired persons and that a productive future is possible for their child is indeed crucial in helping parents through the early years. A parent's views of what the future holds for his or her child can be an important influence in the life of the parent and the parent's perception of the child. For children who have additional or more severe impairments, the future may not be as optimistic, and longer years of dependency are likely.

Parenting Children with Physical Impairments

Parents become aware of a child's physical impairments during the early years, when rapid growth change and the achievement of familiar motor milestones occur. As with other conditions, the earlier the impairment is manifest the more severe the damage is likely to be. Children with moderate physical impairment achieve motor milestones significantly later than normal children do, and the motor patterns are less efficient and frequently abnormal. Dodge (1976) examined the impact of a cerebral palsy child on the family and described the results of these multiple stresses as "stir crazy syndrome." Chronically ill children present a set of practical care problems, for example, problems with sleeping, washing, dressing, feeding, and toileting. The extra demands on parental time often result in physical exhaustion as well as psychological and interpersonal strain.

Parents of physically impaired children express their initial concerns through attention to the child's physical needs. This usually means frequent hospitalizations, special shoes, braces, and other adaptive equipment. In addition, physical therapy during the early years is almost always recommended. Parents are encouraged to seek early educational programs for their children, because the possibility of developmental delays in other domains is greatly increased when physical impairments are known already to exist. Such programs advocate the use of sensory-motor integration procedures in providing physical therapy (Ayres, 1972); others focus on the effects of impaired movement on perceptual development (Abercrombie, 1968; Rosenbloom, 1975), cognition (Campbell, 1974) or motor facilitation as a general aspect of learning (Bobath, 1971). The lack of well-designed studies of intervention effects comparing theoretical and educational models (Guralnick & Bennett, 1987) and therapeutic models (Ottenbacher et al., 1986) make the task for parents of program selection even more difficult and in some cases, stressful.

In some cases parents of physically impaired children are faced with decisions as to which program is best for their child, but more likely they are restricted in their choices by what is available. If choices are to be made, several factors will be taken into consideration: the recommendation of their physician, transportation, related services, program philosophy, and cost.

The heavy emphasis on therapy and early intervention for the child with moderate handicaps gives parents hope that their hard work and sacrifices will culminate in positive results and that the future will be a happy and productive one for their child. This period of intensive effort provides parents the opportunity to learn more about their child's problems. In public and in parent groups they see other children and their parents with similar problems, some more severe, others perhaps less so, and they learn from these other parents things no professional could ever teach them. They begin to learn what to expect when their child is older—the emotional, social, and mobility problems, the academic problems that might be associated with physical impairment, and the continued attention to the child's physical needs. Through this experience they may come to see their child withstand pain and learn skills and tasks that for others are easily mastered and taken for granted but that for them are very difficult to master.

A major concern for parents of moderately physically impaired children is the child's educational placement. Many children are quite able to participate in the academic program of their nonhandicapped peers. They may, however, need more time to complete assignments, their speech or writing may be difficult to interpret, and they may not be as socially adept. Given an understanding teacher who knows when and how to make appropriate demands, however, many students can make a remarkable adjustment to the requirements of the regular classroom.

Although a parent's primary concern may be for their child to gain the knowledge he or she needs to do well in school, the parent will be likewise concerned about the child's social integration. One of the most important human traits is the ability to form friendships. Having friends who select a friend based on character rather than on physical condition is the social integration that parents hope will happen. If, from an early stage, a handicapped child is placed in settings in which he or she must make friends on personal strengths—as do most children who are nonhandicapped—then the child will learn the process of building relationships, and this valued lesson will go far in helping him or her overcome the isolation that can result in a more restricted lifestyle. Changing schools and leaving familiar support systems is especially difficult for families of children with special needs. Using their scale, Family Inventory of Life Events and Changes, McCubbin et al. (1981) found that the two most frequent events experienced by families of cerebral palsy children were child related, namely, "child changing to a new school" and "becoming seriously ill" (p. 36). It is interesting to note, however, that the school change was far less stressful for these families than was the strain of increased expenses for such basic needs as food and clothing. Moreover, the increase in the cost of special education for their child was also a frequent source of strain.

The presence of a physical handicap is usually obvious to casual observers (less so in cases of deafness, emotional handicaps, mental retardation, and other impairments). This has both positive and negative effects; observers might assume that other differences in the person are caused by or related to the physical impairment, and thus there may be less curiosity on their part, whereas on the other hand they make numerous assumptions about the person that are not true. Especially helpful to our understanding of the impact of disabilities are the first-hand experiences shared by those who experience the disabilities. Two books that provide these insights are Orlansky and Howard's (1981) *Voices: Interviews with Handicapped People,* in which handicapped persons tell their own stories, and Baum's (1982) *The Human Side of Exceptionality.*

Parenting Children with Mild Handicaps

Parents of children with mild handicaps (learning disorders, mild mental retardation, mild behavior disorders, etc.) are slow to recognize the problem and to seek the help that the child needs because these handicaps can be easily overlooked or ignored. The child's behavior may be accepted as normal, even if it perhaps is affected by slow development; such behavior will no doubt change as the child catches up in the next few years.

Little help is available from professionals during the early years. Infants and preschool-age children come to the attention of physicians and other health-related persons as impairments become obvious. Milder handicaps are identified when children are observed over an extended period of time and under conditions that place demands on them. Structured school experiences are needed to answer the question, "Is Johnny immature?" Entrance into organized learning environments means having to cope with the demands of working and playing in groups, responding to new stimuli, organizing, retaining, retrieving, and producing information, adapting to a preferred learning style, motivating oneself and others, and regulating one's activity level. These factors interact to increase the impact on the child. In some children this impact is manifested in performance on academic tasks, in others it is more apparent in regard to social relationships.

Parents may suspect that something is different about their child, but the subtle cues appear singly and can always be explained as "immaturity," "takes after Daddy," "just ornery," "lazy," while the best course of action seems to be to "wait and see."

Teachers are usually the first persons to consistently observe the child over time and to see the many facets of child behavior that collectively suggest a learning problem. To determine whether suspicions are indeed on target, the teacher may have a conference with the parents and request their permission to have the child tested. This seldom presents a problem for parents because the school is an appropriate setting for both identifying and dealing with learning problems.

Parental reactions to the news that their child does have a learning disability are quite varied. For some it is relief, for others it is amazement, shock, disbelief, or anger. Osman (1979) reported that parents of children in her clinic go through emotional stages similar to those experienced after a severe loss or death of a family member or someone close — perhaps the loss of the "superchild." Parents invariably seek answers to questions, some of which are quite predictable: Why this child? What were the early signs we should have seen? Whose fault is it? Is it because I have failed as a mother or father? What can be done about it? How long will it last? What differences will it make in his or her education? Although answers can be given based on the performances of thousands of children who have previously been identified, it does not necessarily follow that the same outcomes can be predicted for every child.

Wadsworth and Wadsworth (1971) examined parental involvement in education programs with parents of mildly retarded children and found two interesting differences in responses to questionnaires. Parents whose children had higher IQs were significantly less likely to respond to the questionnaire, and middle-class parents were significantly less likely to respond to the questionnaire than were the higher occupation-status parents. The experimenters concluded that the parents with children who had IQs in the borderline area were less reluctant to accept a mental retardation diagnosis, and middle-class parents as opposed to higher class parents were less accepting of their retarded children. The authors suggested that the higher status parents were more disposed to respond to the questionnaire and less threatened by the fact of having an intellectually limited child.

In the preceding sections we have discussed impairments considered to be moderate and some of the particular stresses each has on the family. In most cases, the presence of a child with a moderate impairment creates the following concerns: the dilemma of where one's educational needs might best be met; the stress of heavy involvement in physiotherapy; the stress of acknowledging the existence of the handicap or simply covering it up. In each case, the family members' own contributions to the situation are so critical that they too must be carefully considered.

ECOLOGY OF IMPACT ON THE FAMILY

During the process of diagnosing a problem and planning intervention strategies, it is important to understand the dynamics of the family, to appraise how a family copes with the handicap, and to identify family strengths that can be used to deal effectively with future events. The perspective implied is transactional, in that what happens to one family member affects other family members or persons directly related to the person most centrally involved. Extending this perspective further, there is a mutual interdependence between persons, their behaviors, and their environments. Insights into individual family members' past experiences in relating to crises, coping with personal stress, accepting role responsibilities, rearing children, using support networks, making decisions, resolving conflicts, and setting and achieving goals are crucial for understanding the ways in which individuals and the family unit cope with the problem now confronting them. Sarason (1975) described the reactions of copers and noncopers. Copers organize the anxiety-provoking situation so that they and others survive. A second level of copers completes the tasks assigned to them by others even though they are considerably self-preoccupied. On the other hand, noncopers wallow in their self-preoccupation, doing nothing for themselves or for others. The study by Frey, Greenberg, and Fewell (1989), referred to earlier suggests the personal appraisal of one's life situation is highly related to one's coping skills.

How the family operates as a unit and the ways in which family members relate to one another will have a major impact on the outcome of intervention for the young handicapped child. Belsky (1981) proposed that the family system be viewed not just in terms of parent-child relationships but also in regard to how the marital relationship (see Crnic, Greenberg, Ragozin, Robinson, & Basham, 1983; Fewell, 1986a; Friedrich, 1979) and other relationships within the family affect the child. Relationships between family members cannot be studied in isolation but must be viewed as they influence and subsequently shape the behavior of all family members. Gabel, McDowell, and Cerreto (1983) and Sonnek (1986) extended the analysis of the second order effects (described by Belsky) to grandparent-parent relationships and other relationships within the context of the extended family of young handicapped children. As noted in Chapter 1, the way in which the family system reacts to the disabling condition of a family member affects every other member of the family. Osman (1979) referred to learning disability, for example, as "a family affair." Any impairment or disabling condition may or may not become a "handicap," depending on the family's interpretation of the child's state.

The importance of involving family members in intervention is well known. Bronfenbrenner (1974) concluded after reviewing intervention programs with and without parent participation that "the evidence indicates that the family is the most effective and economical system for fostering and sustaining the development of the child. The evidence indicates further that the involvement of the child's family as an active participant is critical to the success of any intervention program" (p. 55).

Research with developmentally delayed children (Christophersen & Sykes, 1979), behaviorally disordered children (Bristol, 1984; Christophersen, Barnard, Barnard, Gleeson, & Sykes, 1981; Schopler & Mesibov, 1984; Strain, 1981), deaf children (Simmons-Martin, 1981), blind children, deaf-blind children (Vadasy & Fewell, 1986), and physically impaired children supports Bronfenbrenner's contention. Nevertheless, after reviewing parent education programs during the 1970s, Clarke-Stewart (1981) described the contemporary uncertainties:

> Parent child-rearing techniques are still embedded in an abiding and persistent sociocultural context, and there is no evidence that they are easily shaped by expert opinion or educational literature. Although direct educational programs for parents have been successful in changing some of the more superficial kinds of parent behavior, such as caretaking, talking, and teaching, they have been less successful in modifying other more subtle and perhaps more critical aspects, such as responding, caring, and playing (p. 57).

PERIODS OF FAMILY STRESS DUE TO THE IMPAIRMENT

In previous sections we discussed the impact of various impairments on family members. Each type of handicap presents problems for the affected family member and related problems for the entire family. The importance of all relationships within the family system to the outcome of the handicapped child has also been discussed. Equally important is the impact of society's reaction to "difference" in everything that happens to the child and to the family. In this section we discuss impact-reduction strategies on two levels: strategies that focus directly on reducing the impact of the handicap (hearing aids, drugs, prosthetic devices, speech therapy, basic care, home instruction, etc.) and strategies that more directly reduce negative impact through changes in a variety of interacting factors (family interactions, economic relief, social policy, litigation, and legislation). Although realizing that these two levels are not entirely separable, we dichotomize for purposes of relating more specifically to the impact and the strategies.

Impact During the Screening and Referral Phase

When physicians, parents, grandparents, teachers, or other observers of children see behaviors that are different than expected they ask questions: Is something wrong with my child? Can Sally see? Shouldn't Lydia be sitting up by now? Have you asked the doctor why Sarah breathes with those noises? Why can't Bill learn to read? These questions are attempts to determine whether a problem exists. Generally, parents of mildly and moderately handicapped children have a longer and lonelier discovery period. Doubts, fears, questions, attempts to link current observations to pregnancy events, guilt feelings, and so forth can date from before the birth and continue for several years, even when parents are assured by authorities that their child is normal. Parents have seen, heard, or read too much to dismiss the possibility that the child may be handicapped in some way (Barsch, 1968). According to Barsch, "the data suggest that the parent is aware of a deviancy from one to four years before someone establishes a diagnostic label to characterize the parental concern" (p. 95). When there is a problem, knowledge comes slowly, bit by bit, until the parent acts to seek an answer. With many moderately handicapped children, parents are unaware, or do not have suspicions confirmed, until the child manifests a learning or adjustment problem in school. Parents sometimes dismiss these problems with such remarks as "He is just like his Uncle Harry" or "That's the way little girls are." These behaviors are easy to overlook if major milestones such as walking and toilet training are accomplished at the appropriate age.

Once problems are recognized by parents, steps must be taken to determine their validity. A variety of professionals in both public and private sectors are available to provide screening services. Answers to assessment questions that confirm the existence of the problem lead to its eventual identification. A process involving several successive steps is usually followed when parents or professional act to answer these questions. Parental reaction during this phase can be characterized by the desire to move on to the diagnostic phase, which will help them identify the problem and perhaps the cause.

Impact During the Identification and Diagnosis Phase

After referral and screening and if a problem is confirmed, identification and diagnosis are likely to follow, according to a model that medical professionals have used to determine causes for purposes of prescribing treatment. For many impairments, this procedure results in immediate intervention that terminates symptoms or else identifies a very precise plan for intervention. For example, the symptoms of a seizure disorder may be virtually eliminated through identification of the type of seizure followed by chemotherapy designed to control the behavior. Although the problem is not likely to be eliminated, it can be controlled, and the stress upon both the child and the family is greatly reduced.

The age of the child is an important factor in assessing the impact that the initial diagnosis has on the family. When parents of handicapped children rated the importance of categories of concern, there was an important relationship between the age of the child and the impact of initial diagnosis (Bray, Coleman, & Bracken, 1981). When the child's handicap was diagnosed before age 2, 44% of the parents reported the initial diagnosis to be the most critical event or stress they had faced as parents; when diagnosis occurred at age 6, the importance of the initial diagnosis dropped to 26%, and when it occurred after age 6, initial diagnosis was viewed as primary by only 16% of the parents. This suggests that the lower the child's age at the time of diagnosis, the more likely the problem will require additional services; it points directly to the need for early intervention. Parents will want to pursue all channels in getting the early education, medical, and psychological services their child requires.

With the moderately impaired, who in many cases are more difficult to accurately assess, educational and emotional problems are not easily identified nor are treatment avenues as obvious. Testing is not as reliable and treatments not as sure. Opinions regarding diagnosis and treatment sometimes differ widely from one professional to another. These factors cause families to seek a favorable diagnosis from many sources, which prolongs initiation of a treatment plan and thrusts the family into a state of stress. In many cases, several intervention strategies must be tried and results monitored before an appropriate plan for minimizing the impact of the problem can be determined.

Impact of Daily Parenting Responsibilities

Parents of children with learning disabilities, for example, experience stress daily as they face the disability while the child is doing homework. Because the task is painful, the child may delay it or become frustrated and angry. The parent may get upset and place demands on the child that the child is unable to meet; the confrontation may result in a tearful shouting match that accomplishes nothing more than creating a wider gap between parent and child.

The homework problem is another situation resulting in guilt for the child. David Raymond (1982), who has severe dyslexia, described his experience.

> Homework is a real problem . . . When I get home my mother reads to me. Sometimes she reads an assignment into a tape recorder and then I go into my room and listen to it. If we have a novel or something like that to read, she reads it out loud to me. Then I sit down with her and we do the assignment. She'll write, while I talk my answers to her. Lately, I've taken to dictating into a tape recorder, and then someone—father, a private tutor, or my mother—types up what I've dictated. Whatever homework I do takes someone else's time, too. That makes me feel bad (p. 23).

When diet management is an important aspect of a child's medical regimen (e.g., in diabetes, kidney disease, or Prader Willi syndrome), parents can find daily responsibilities extremely frustrating. They may feel guilty about withholding certain foods and so yield to the demands of a youngster who may become defiant and mistrustful if a parent even tries to learn what foods the child has eaten during the parent's absence. The same kind of situation may exist when children are beginning to accept responsibility for their own medication.

Parents of moderately handicapped children may feel caught in a time bind: They have been told that each day in the life of a young child is very important and that they should be involved each day in the child's educational program. The inability to take an active, daily role can cause guilt and may be a source of stress between staff members who encourage parental involvement and the parent who must respond to other family priorities. On the other hand, parents of the severely impaired child may have realized how much of a difference their involvement really makes, whereas the parents of the mildly handicapped child may think that current involvement, which staff members consider so crucial for the child, can be easily postponed to some future time. Parents who do become involved in daily activities such as classroom participation may view the experience positively, as a real contribution to the child's development, or negatively, as a drain on their energy and time. Harris and McHale (1989) investigated family life problems of mothers and reported two common themes: "Both the way in which caregiving responsibilities were distributed (with mothers assuming primary or sole caregiver status) and the ambiguity associated with child-related problems . . . were important factors in the stress experienced in a number of the domains of family life" (p. 237). Parents' reactions are subject to so many perceptions and experiences.

Parents who can realize the kind of facilitative role their child needs at any given point in time have a major advantage over those who cannot. For example, observations of just how the child can best learn new material, along with the use of prompting, modeling, ignoring, and positive reinforcement, can provide a critical plan that the child may adopt for self-direction long after the parents' support has ended. The means by which parents facilitate learning remains critical throughout the child's life. Zigler (1984) cautioned parents that learning is not a program that can be forced into a child. Learning is a natural condition, and it is the quality and sensitivity of the social interactions between the child and his or her adult caregivers that holds the key to the child's future.

STRATEGIES FOR HELPING PARENTS

The family that is sufficiently open about a child's problem to discuss it with the child and to help siblings and members of the extended family respond in a positive and understanding manner can contribute much to the child's adjustment. The ability of parents to respond in a supportive manner is sometimes difficult. Nevertheless, certain factors have clearly emerged as likely to produce positive results.

Family organization is critical. Many mildly handicapped children have difficulty making small decisions, handling emotional extremes, or coping with changes, chaos, and turmoil. It is not uncommon for disorganization to occur more frequently in families of learning disabled children than in other families (Osman, 1979). If the family can define and implement a structure for its daily life together, then routine will follow: The children will know what to expect, have fewer decisions to make, and be less vulnerable to environmental changes as they gain better control over their environment. As organizing features become routine in the home as well as in the school environment, the process of learning and coping also becomes easier.

Clearly, an underlying theme in parent-child relationships is consistency. Emotionally healthy children are reared in families that have very different styles of relating. A family's belief system about children and child-rearing techniques contributes significantly to parental teaching and managerial strategies. These belief systems, or values, vary significantly from family to family. They are formulated from the parents' experiences as members of previous family units, by their cultural, social, and educational environments. The consistency with which parental reactions can be predicted by children is a major factor in child adjustment.

Parents of a moderately handicapped child can eliminate much confusion for their child (who does not always make decisions easily) by being consistent in their responses. This strategy is based on the premise that both parents are in agreement about responding to a variety of circumstances. The child will learn what to expect if similar situations evoke similar responses. This consistency is particularly useful to the handicapped child for whom understanding parental cues may not be easy.

For parents it is a matter of knowing how and when to help, when to reward or withhold reward, and when to respond in other ways. There are no sure formulas to follow. Each child presents a different set of problems; the attitudes and experiences that the family members bring to the situation will also determine how the child responds. Nevertheless, the stories of parents (e.g., Featherstone, 1980; Knox, 1981; Moeller, 1986; Murphy, 1981; Roberts, 1986; Schiff, 1980; Seligman, 1979; Turnbull & Turnbull, 1978) consistently convey the sometimes unarticulated but deeply felt empathy that parents express toward other parents who have had the same or similar experiences. Helping parents get in touch with other parents who share similar concerns is an important professional activity. Parent-to-parent programs are especially helpful.

Some strategies for professionals to use in their work with parents have been clearly and simply stated by Gorham, Des Jardins, Page, Pettis, and Scheiber (1975) and by Peters and Noel (1982). Strategies from these two sources are summarized as follows.

1. Involve parents as team members every step of the way.
2. Make a realistic management plan part of the assessment outcome.
3. Inform yourself about community resources.
4. Avoid professional jargon in your reports and communications.
5. Give copies of the reports to parents.
6. Be sure the parents understand that the diagnosis is subject to change.
7. Help the parents to think of life with this child in the same terms as life with their other children.

8. Be sure the parents understand their child's abilities and assets as well as disabilities.

9. Warn the parents about service deficiencies.

10. Explain to the parents that although some professionals may dwell on negatives, parents should think about the positives.

11. Be frank and open.

12. Be a positive professional.

13. Listen.

14. Refrain from making quick judgments.

15. Encourage.

16. Recognize parents' other supports.

In a similar way, there are strategies parents can use to strengthen themselves and their relationships with professionals who serve their handicapped child. Fewell (1986b) and Peters and Noel (1982) noted these strategies.

1. Reach out to other parents.

2. Be informed.

3. Be assertive

4. Support your child, yourself, and your other family members.

5. Know your child's present and future needs.

6. Take charge of your problems.

7. Acknowledge and support deserving professionals.

8. Know the sources of positive support for yourself. Use and value these.

There are instances in which incentives have been used to encourage families' involvement in the care of their handicapped members. In the state of North Dakota, families who keep their severely handicapped family members at home rather than place them in institutions receive monthly compensation. The family reports on how it disperses the funds. In the Extending Family Resources Project (EFR) at the Children's Clinic and Preschool in Seattle, Washington, 16 family support units, who worked as a team and consisted of parents, aunts, uncles, or other relatives, friends, or neighbors, signed a unit performance contract to provide care and training for the person in need. For example, an uncle may agree to take the child to community parks for 2 hours a week and to work on developing motor skills as one portion of the performance contract. In return, the family unit was given up to $200.00 per month to spend to fulfill its contract. These funds were usually spent in three areas — training, equipment, and respite. Evaluation data on this project enabled the staff to support a number of conclusions that have implications for the design of other programs to support families under stress. Some of the findings were as follows.

- The EFR concept provides for individualized family programs that share a common framework, but account for circumstances that are variable among families, such as income, size, and relatives present or absent.
- The EFR project demonstrated that family support systems can and should have a variety of participants.
- The EFR project showed that parents, relatives, friends, and volunteers can be trained to work with a handicapped child as an extended family group.
- The EFR project demonstrated that appropriately trained extended family members can provide a range of support services to families of handicapped children.
- The EFR project provided a model for reducing family stress related to a child's handicapping condition.
- The EFR project was an effective demonstration of how a child's family-based program can be designed to complement the child's school or center-based program.
- The EFR service model demonstrated that the goal of implementing a family support network can usually be completed in a 6- to 10-month period.
- The stipend money was important for removing barriers for families, but its significance was found in combination with other elements of the EFR project.
- The role of the project's family clinicians was crucial to the families' successful completion of the program.

Certainly careful monitoring of other incentive programs will provide more information on the effectiveness of such procedures for helping families in their caretaking roles.

In this chapter we discussed the psychosocial aspects of parenting a moderately handicapped child, the impact of handicaps on the child and family, and strategies to consider while working with families of handicapped children. We have focused on the difficulties unique to families of the moderately handicapped, where expectations are more uncertain than certain. We have provided examples of why each handicap must be considered separately in order to understand the community's reaction to it. Finally, we have described selective strategies that are effective with all parents. These guidelines have validity for all professional relationships with parents regardless of whether the child is handicapped.

REFERENCES

Abercrombie, M. L. (1968). Some notes on spatial disability: Movement, intelligence quotient and attentiveness. *Developmental Medicine and Child Neurology, 10,* pp. 206–213.

Akerley, M. S. (1978). False gods and angry prophets. In A. P. Turnbull & H. R. Turnbull (Eds.), *Parents speak out.* Columbus, OH: Merrill, pp. 33–37.

Ayres, A. J. (1972). *Sensory integration and learning disorders.* Los Angeles, CA: Western Psychiatric Services.

Barker, R. G. (1948). The social psychology of physical disability. *Journal of Social Issues, 4*(4), pp. 28–38.

Barsch, R. H. (1968). *The parent of the handicapped child: The study of childrearing practices.* Springfield, IL: Charles C Thomas.

Baum, D. D. (1982). *The human side of exceptionality.* Baltimore, MD: University Park Press.

Belsky, J. (1981). Early human experience: A family perspective. *Developmental Psychology, 17,* pp. 3–23.

Bobath, B. (1971). Motor developmental, its effect on general development, and application to the treatment of cerebral palsy. *Physiotherapy, 53,* pp. 26–33.

Bray, N. M., Coleman, J. M., & Bracken, M. B. (1981). Critical events in parenting handicapped children. *Journal of the Division for Early Childhood, 3,* pp. 26–33.

Brill, R. G. (1960). A study in adjustment of three groups of deaf children. *Exceptional Children, 26,* pp. 464–466.

Brill, R. G. (1969). The superior IQs of deaf children of deaf parents. *The California Palms, 15,* pp. 1–4.

Brim, O. (1975). Macro-structural influences on child development and the need for childhood social indicators. *American Journal of Orthopsychiatry, 45,* pp. 516–524.

Bristol, M. M. (1984). Family resources and successful adaptation to autistic children. In E. Schopler & G. Mesibov (Eds.), *The effects of autism on the family.* New York: Plenum Press, pp. 289–310.

Bronfenbrenner, U. (1974). Development research, public policy and the ecology of childhood. *Child Development, 45,* pp. 1–5.

Bronfenbrenner, U. (1976). The experimental ecology of education. *Educational Research, 5,* pp. 5–15.

Campbell, S. K. (1974). Facilitation of cognitive and motor development in infants with central nervous system dysfunction. *Physical Therapy, 54,* pp. 345–353.

Carey, G. E. (1982). Community care — care by whom? Mentally handicapped children living at home. *Public Health, 96,* pp. 269–278.

Christophersen, E. R., Barnard, S. R., Barnard, J. D., Gleeson, S., & Sykes, B. W. (1981). Home-based treatment of behavior-disoriented and developmentally delayed children. In M. Begab, H. C. Haywood, & H. L. Garber (Eds.), *Psychosocial influences in retarded performance: Vol. 2. Strategies for improving competence.* Baltimore, MD: University Park Press, pp. 257–272.

Clarke-Stewart, K. A. (1981). Parent education in the 1970s. *Educational Evaluation and Policy Analysis, 3*(6), pp. 47–58.

Cowen, E. L., & Bobrove, P. H. (1966). Marginality of disability and adjustment. *Perceptual and Motor Skills, 23,* pp. 869–870.

Criddle, R. (1953). *Love is not blind.* New York: Norton.

Crnic, K. A., Friedrich, W., & Greenberg, M. (1983). Adaptation of families with mentally retarded children: A model of stress, coping and family ecology. *American Journal of Mental Deficiency, 88,* pp. 125–138.

Crnic, K. A., Greenberg, M. T., Ragozin, A. S, Robinson, N. M., & Basham, R. B. (1983). Effects of stress and social support on mothers and premature and full-term infants. *Child Development, 54,* pp. 201–217.

Darling, R. B. (1979). *Families against society.* Beverly Hills, CA: Sage.

Dodge, P. (1976). Neurological disorders of school aged children. *Journal of School Health, 46,* pp. 338–343.

Edgerton, R. B. (1970). Mental retardation in non-Western societies: Towards a cross-cultural perspective on incompetence. In H. C. Haywood (Ed.), *Sociocultural aspects of mental retardation.* New York: Appleton-Century-Crofts, pp. 523–559.

Edgerton, R. B. (1981). Another look at culture and mental retardation. In M. J. Begab, H. C. Haywood, & H. L. Garber (Eds.), (1981) *Psychosocial influences in retarded performance* (Vol. 1). Baltimore, MD: University Park Press, pp. 309–323.

Featherstone, H. (1980). *A difference in the family.* New York: Basic Books.

Ferris, C. (1980). *A hug just isn't enough.* Washington, DC: Gallaudet College Press.

Fewell, R. R. (1986a). A handicapped child in the family. In R. R. Fewell &

P. F. Vadasy (Eds.), *Families of handicapped children*. Austin, TX: Pro-Ed, pp. 3–43.

Fewell, R. R. (1986b, March 14–15). *Parents and professionals: Strengthening the partnership to improve planning and coordination*. Paper presented at the Helen Keller Technical Assistance Conference for Parents and Professionals, Kansas City, Missouri.

Finkelstein, V. (1980). *Attitudes and disabled people: Issues for discussion*. (Monograph No. 5). New York: World Rehabilitation Fund.

Frey, K. S., Greenberg, M. T., & Fewell, R. R. (1989). Stress and coping among parents of handicapped children: A multidimensional approach. *American Journal of Mental Retardation, 94*(3), pp. 240–249.

Friedrich, W. N. (1979). Predictions of the coping behavior of mothers of handicapped children. *Journal of Consulting and Clinical Psychology, 47*, pp. 1140–1141.

Gabel, H., McDowell, J., & Cerreto, M. C. (1983). Family adaptation to the handicapped infant. In S. G. Garwood & R. R. Fewell (Eds.), *Educating handicapped infants: Issues in development and intervention*. Rockville, MD: Aspen, pp. 455–493.

Gallimore, R., Weisner, T. S., Kaufman, S. I., & Bernheimer, L. P. (1989). The social construction of ecocultural niches: Family accommodations of developmentally delayed children. *American Journal on Mental Retardation, 94*(3), pp. 216–230.

Gliedman, J., & Roth, W. (1980). *The unexpected minority: Handicapped children in America*. New York: Harcourt Brace Jovanovich.

Goffman, E. (1963). *Stigma: Notes on the management of spoiled identity*. New York: Aranson.

Gorham, K. A., Des Jardins, C., Page, R., Pettis, E., & Scheiber, B. (1975). Effects on parents. In N. Hobbs (Ed.), *Issues in the classification of children* (Vol 2, pp. 154–188). San Francisco, CA: Jossey-Bass.

Grossman, F. K. (1972). *Brother and sisters of retarded children: An exploratory study*. Syracuse, NY: Syracuse University Press.

Guralnick, M. J. & Bennett, F. C. (1987). *The effectiveness of early intervention for at-risk and handicapped children*. Orlando, FL: Academic Press.

Haffter, C. (1968). The changeling: History and psychodynamics of attitudes to handicapped children in European folklore. *Journal of History of the Behavioral Sciences, 4*(1), pp. 55–61.

Hanson, M. J. (1985). An analysis of the effects of early intervention services for infants and toddlers with moderate and severe handicaps. *Topics in Early Childhood Special Education, 5*(2), pp. 36–51.

Harris, V. S. & McHale, S. M. (1989). Family life problems, daily caregiving activities, and the psychological well being of mothers of mentally retarded children. *American Journal on Mental Retardation, 94*(3), pp. 231–239.

Jablow, M. M. (1982). *Cara: Growing with a retarded child.* Philadelphia, PA: Temple University Press.

Keniston, K. (1980). Preface. In J. Gliedman & W. Roth. *The unexpected minority: Handicapped children in America.* New York: Harcourt Brace Jovanovich.

Knox, L. (1981). *Parents are people too.* Englewood Cliffs, NJ: Prentice-Hall.

Knox, L. & Chrisman, C., Producers (1979). *Today is not forever* [Videotape]. Nashville, TN: Intersect.

Lairy, G. C., & Harrison-Covello, A. (1973). The blind child and his parents: Congenital visual defect and the repercussion of family attitudes on the early development of the child. *American Foundation for the Blind Research Bulletin,* No. 25.

MacGregor, F. C., Abel, T. M., Byrt, A., Lauer, E., & Weissman, M. S. (1953). *Facial deformities and plastic surgery.* Springfield, IL: Thomas.

Maisel, E. (1960). Meet a body. Manuscript (1953) cited in B. A. Wright, *Physical disability: A psychological approach.* New York: Harper & Row.

Mallory, B. L. (1986). Interactions between community agencies and families over the life cycle. In R. R. Fewell & P. F. Vadasy (Eds.), *Families of handicapped children,* Austin, TX: Pro-Ed, pp. 317–356.

McCubbin, H. I., Nevin, R. S., Larsen, A., Comeau, J., Patterson, J., Cauble, A. E., & Striker, K. (1981). *Families coping with cerebral palsy.* St. Paul: Family Social Science, University of Minnesota at St. Paul.

Miller, G. (1981). Georgie Miller. In M. D. Orlansky & W. L. Heward (Eds.), *Voices: Interviews with handicapped people.* Columbus, OH: Merrill, pp. 151–155.

Moeller, C. M. (1986). The effect of professionals on the family of a handicapped child. In R. R. Fewell & P. F. Vadasy (Eds.), *Families of handicapped children.* Austin, TX: Pro-Ed, pp. 149–166.

Moore, J. A., Hamerlynck, L. A., Barsh, E. T., Spieker, S., & Jones, R. (1982). *Extending family resources.* Seattle, WA: Children's Clinic and Preschool Spastic Aid Council.

Murphy, A. T. (1981). *Special children, special parents.* Englewood Cliffs, NJ: Prentice-Hall.

Myerson, L. (1963). Somatopsychology of physical disability. In W. Cruikshank (Ed.), *Psychology of exceptional children and youth.* Englewood Cliffs, NJ: Prentice-Hall, pp. 1–52.

Orlansky, M. D., & Heward, W. L. (1981). *Voices: Interviews with handicapped people.* Columbus, OH: Merrill.

Osman, B. B. (1979). *Learning disabilities: A family affair.* New York: Warner Books.

Ottenbacher, K. J., Biocca, Z., DeCremer, G., Gevelinger, M., Jedlovec, K. B., & Johnson, M. B. (1986). Quantitative analysis of the effectiveness of pediatric therapy. *Physical therapy, 66,* pp. 1095–1101.

Peters, M., & Noel, M. M. (1982). Parent perspectives about professional and parent cooperation. In M. Peters (Ed.), *Building an alliance for children: Parents and professionals.* Seattle: Program Development Assistance System, University of Washington, pp. 49–76.

Raymond, D. (1982). On being seventeen, bright—and unable to read. In D. D. Baum (Ed.), *The human side of exceptionality.* Baltimore, MD: University Park Press, pp. 21–23.

Roberts, M. (1986). Three mothers: Life-span experiences. In R. R. Fewell & P. F. Vadasy (Eds.), *Families of handicapped children.* Austin, TX: Pro-Ed, pp. 193–220.

Roskies, E. (1972). *Abnormality and normality: The mothering of thalidomide children.* Ithaca, NY: Cornell University Press.

Ryan, W. (1971). *Blaming the victim.* New York: Vintage.

Sagarin, E. (1969). *Odd man in.* Chicago: Quadruple Books.

Sameroff, A., Seifer, R., & Zax, M. (1982). Early development of children at risk for emotional disorder. *Monographs of the Society for Research in Child Development, 47,* (7, Serial No. 199).

Sanua, V. D. (1966). *A cross cultural study of cerebral palsy.* New York: Yeshiva University.

Sarason, I. (1975). Anxiety and self-preoccupation. In I. Sarason & C. Spielberger (Eds.), *Stress and anxiety.* New York: Wiley.

Sarason, S. B., & Doris, J. (1979). *Educational handicap, public policy, and social history: A broadened perspective on mental retardation.* New York: Free Press.

Schiff, H. S. (1980). *The bereaved parent.* New York: Penguin.

Schlesinger, H. S., & Meadow, K. P. (1972). *Sound and sign: Childhood deafness and mental health.* Berkeley: University of California Press.

Schopler, E., & Mesibov, G. B. (1984). *The effects of autism on the family.* New York: Plenum Press.

Seligman, M. (1979). *Strategies for helping parents of exceptional children.* New York: Free Press.

Simmons-Martin, A. (1981). Efficacy report: Early education project. *Journal of the Division of Early Childhood, 4,* pp. 5–10.

Sonnek, I. M. (1986). Grandparents and the extended family of handicapped children. in R. R. Fewell & P. F. Vadasy, *Families of handicapped children* (pp. 99–120). Austin, TX: Pro-Ed.

Stonequist, E. V. (1937). *The marginal man: A study in personality and culture conflict.* New York: Scribners.

Strain, P. S. (1981). Conceptual and methodological issues in efficacy research with behaviorally disordered children. *Journal of the Division of Early Childhood, 4,* pp. 111–124.

Turnbull, A. P. & Turnbull, R. R. (1978). *Parents speak out: Views from the other side of the two-way mirror.* Columbus, OH: Merrill.

Vadasy, P. F. & Fewell, R. R. (1986). Mothers of deaf-blind children. In R. R. Fewell & P. F. Vadasy, *Families of handicapped children.* Austin, TX: Pro-Ed, pp. 121–148.

Wadsworth, H. G., & Wadsworth, J. B. (1971). A problem of involvement with parents of mildly retarded children. *The Family Coordinator, 20,* pp. 141–147.

Wright, B. A. (1960). *Physical disability: A psychological approach.* New York: Harper & Row.

Zigler, E. (1984). Handicapped children and their families. In E. Schopler & G. Mesibor (Eds.), *The effects of autism on the family.* New York: Plenum Press, pp. 21–39.

CHAPTER NINE

Collaboration with Families of Persons with Severe Disabilities

Steven R. Lyon and Grace A. Lyon

Steven R. Lyon, Ph.D., is associate professor and coordinator of the Program in Severe Disabilities, Department of Instruction and Learning, School of Education, University of Pittsburgh. Lyon has published numerous articles, chapters, research reports, and curriculum monographs related to the education, employment, and community integration of persons with severe disabilities. Currently, Lyon's research is focused on school to work transition of youth with severe disabilities.

Grace A. Lyon is research associate in the Program in Severe Disabilities, Department of Instruction and Learning, School of Education, at the University of Pittsburgh. Currently, Lyon coordinates a graduate-level personnel preparation program for teachers of secondary students with severe disabilities. Prior professional experiences include the following: classroom teaching, teacher training, and administration of community residential facilities. She has published in the areas of preschool education and transdisciplinary programming.

One of the most difficult tasks our society has undertaken in recent years has been to assume a larger responsibility for the provision of comprehensive social services to persons with severe disabilities. As a result of pervasive legislation, litigation, and subsequent "community reintegration" (Blatt, Bogdan, Biklen, & Taylor, 1977), many parents are choosing to keep their severely disabled children at home in the community. The reintegration of severely handicapped people into mainstream American society has created the need for new and greatly expanded services and for effective ways of understanding and working with families of persons with severe disabilities.

Formerly, most persons with severe disabilities were incarcerated within large residential institutions where conditions were often inhumane and services extremely limited (Blatt & Kaplan, 1974). The largest portion of persons in these large residential institutions were those with the most challenging disabilities whose needs were the most extensive (Hewitt & Forness, 1977). Typically, persons with severe disabilities have been regarded by society as the least capable, the most dependent, requiring the most effort to habilitate (Sontag, Smith, & Sailor, 1977).

In the past, the predominant approach to habilitation, education, and treatment of persons with severe disabilities was custodial maintenance. That is, because these children's prognoses for educational and social learning and independence was considered so poor, many pediatricians routinely recommended institutionalization to parents at birth (Caldwell & Guze, 1960). Parents and families of these children often faced a difficult dilemma: Concede to institutional placement and in all likelihood relinquish the chance for a reasonably normal life for their child, or keep the child at home in the community where few (if any) services for the child and family would be available. That issue was undoubtedly traumatizing to many parents and families. Indeed, historically, only limited assistance, support, and understanding have been available to persons with severe disabilities, their parents, and families.

Recently, social, educational, and legal events have changed trends in service delivery. Parents and professionals have joined together to affirm the entitlement of basic rights and services for persons with severe disabilities. As a result, institutional reform, deinstitutionalization, right to treatment, nondiscrimination, and mandated educational services have taken place (Gilhool & Stuttman, 1978). Parents have played critical roles in garnering improved services for themselves and their children (Katz, 1961).

As services evolved and expanded in the mid-1960s, initial efforts were made to understand and collaborate with the parents and families of these children. Although methods and approaches to working with families have varied widely over the years (Lillie, 1976), early services focused primarily on providing parent counseling or parent training. Parents were commonly viewed by professionals as being in need of counseling to help them accept their child (Ballard, 1978) or in need of training to better enable them to manage their child at home (O'Dell, 1974). Research on families with children with severe disabilities was also somewhat narrowly focused. Studies attempted to clarify the psychological stress and adjustment of parents and to assess the allegedly negative impact of a severe disability on the family unit (Jacobson & Humphrey, 1979).

Although these early efforts to understand and work with families were useful in many respects, they also, we believe, contributed to a rather circumscribed and even condescending attitude that many professionals held toward family members. In many cases professionals have made assumptions about the needs of parents and families of children with severe disabilities without obtaining solid empirical evidence or even bothering to confirm or refute these assumptions by listening to parents themselves (Roos, 1977).

During the past 10 to 15 years, services and attitudes toward persons with severe disabilities and their families have changed dramatically. Institutions have been reformed and depopulated; (Hill, Bruininks, Lakin, Hauber, & McGuire, 1985); important legislation has been implemented (Section 504 of the Rehabilitation Act, and the Education of All Handicapped Children Act of 1975); community-based services have been established in many parts of the nation; (Heal, Hanley, & Novak Amado, 1988), and many valuable technological advancements in the education and services for persons with severe disabilities have taken place (Horner, Meyer, & Fredericks, 1986). These advances have been accompanied by a broader understanding and a more cooperative approach to collaborating with parents and families.

Currently, the services for persons with severe disabilities is in a period of adjustment; sweeping social changes have occurred, and interpretations of and direct administrative regulations for services are being implemented and monitored. Although many severely handicapped persons remain within institutions, trends toward deinstitutionalization and the establishment of services within the community are continuing. Because of these trends, a wide variety of social service agencies (e.g., those in school systems, health clinics, rehabilitation and vocational training centers) are extending their services to include persons with severe disabilities who now reside in the community, either in their natural homes or in other community living arrangements. Many new community-based programs are being developed to attempt to meet the needs of persons with severe disabilities.

Most professionals involved in providing services to persons with severe disabilities agree that working effectively with parents and families is a vital aspect of service provision. There are at least three important reasons why professionals need to collaborate with families. First, an adequate understanding of the home and family is necessary for designing and delivering services that are vitally important for the individual and the family. Second, if services provided to the individual are to be effective, then parents and families need to be involved in and supportive of the specific programs or treatments. Educational, vocational, or health-related services must be delivered in a manner consistent and congruent with the ongoing structure, routines, and ecology of the family. Third, professionals should understand that families as unique and distinct units have important needs of their own that extend beyond the immediate needs of their disabled family member (Dornberg, 1978). Providing direct treatment to persons with severe disabilities without addressing the needs of the other family members may have negative effects on the family itself. Professionals should remember that the goals of treatment or intervention should not be exclusive of the goals and needs of the family. Individual members of these families (parents and siblings) have specific needs apart from those addressed by the program established for the family member with a disability. It is essential that an approach to understanding and working with these families maintains a balanced perspective. Indeed, as demonstrated in Chapter 2 on family systems theory, a childhood disability impacts both the nuclear and extended family.

As social service agencies and professionals begin to realize the importance of meeting the needs of families, more productive networks of parent-professional alliances are being created. Although much progress in this area has been achieved in recent years, parents and professionals alike realize that much more remains to be accomplished. Many more high-quality, community-based services and support systems are needed (Schalock, 1985). Creative efforts must be directed toward the development and establishment of services that result in meaningful family involvement and participation in service programs (Matson, 1977). Attempts must also be made to develop coordinated and longitudinal services so that the lifelong needs of these persons and their families can be met. Professionals in a wide variety of education, health, and human service fields must become knowledgeable and skillful in working with persons with severe disabilities and in understanding and working with their families (Shell, 1981).

This chapter aims to provide information that will help professionals better understand the problems and needs of people with severe disabilities and to prepare professionals to communicate and collaborate cooperatively with their families.

Three major areas are emphasized here: the nature and implications of severe disabilities, a discussion of the unique needs of families of persons with severe disabilities, and suggestions for working with these families. If persons with severe disabilities are to assume their rightful place in society, then professionals will need to address the pervasive and complex problems of these persons and their families.

NATURE AND IMPLICATIONS OF SEVERE DISABILITIES

In order for professionals to be able to relate with ease and effectively serve these persons and their families, a general understanding of the nature and implications of severe disabilities is important. There are several general facts about severe disabilities that must be understood.

First, the term *severely disabled,* as used here, refers to a heterogeneous population of *persons* whose abilities and needs vary greatly. Second, many diagnostic and classification systems have produced labels and definitions for different types of disabilities. Although these labels are justifiable when used to determine eligibility for services, they have often been stigmatizing. Third, these persons constitute an extremely small proportion of the general population. Fourth, functionally, it is probably at least as important to understand the nature of services required by persons with severe disabilities as it is to understand the nature and manifestations of their disabilities. The remainder of this section therefore addresses the nature of severe disabilities, the resulting service needs, and a description of the existing service-delivery system.

Historically, a variety of different classification and definition schemes have been used to describe persons with severe disabilities (Seltzer, 1983). Generally, our society's agencies and institutions and the services they provide have often been organized around the placement of these persons into certain homogenous disability categories. Once a person is diagnosed as belonging to a certain specific group of persons with similar disabling characteristics, then eligibility is established and services are provided accordingly. Unfortunately, the services provided were (and still are) more often a function of the perceived needs of people with similar disabilities than of the actual needs of the individual.

As suggested earlier, the nature of severe disabilities ranges widely in terms of cause, type, extent, and impact. Severe disabilities may result from genetic or chromosomal abnormalities, prenatal, perinatal, or postnatal injury or toxification, maternal and/or childhood disease, environmental influence or trauma, as well as other unknown causes (Bleck & Nagel, 1975). Disabilities may be physical (e.g., cerebral palsy), sensory (e.g., blindness and hearing impairment), intellectual (e.g., mental retardation), or psychological (e.g., autism or schizophrenia), and many persons experience multiple, severe disabilities (e.g., deaf-blindness or dual-diagnosis). For each of these types of handicapping and disabling conditions, the extensiveness may range from mild to severe as determined functionally by its impact upon a person's abilities and performance. Importantly, the impacts of these various conditions also vary widely from person to person. (Just as persons with similar abilities respond differently to the same situations, so too do persons with similar disabilities.) In the past, professionals often failed to recognize or acknowledge human differences, and people were referred to as their disabilities (e.g., "the retarded") rather than as people. Expectations for individual people were often shaped by expectations associated with the disabilities rather than determined by an individual's abilities.

Traditional disability-based homogenous classification systems, however, are beginning to give way to more functional approaches to understanding the nature and implications of severe disabilities. Because the old systems have generally been highly stigmatizing and have nurtured lowered expectations (and in many cases have not been accurate predictors of individuals' abilities and learning potential), more emphasis is now being placed on gaining an understanding of the functional abilities of people with severe disabilities. There is also an interest in understanding the types of services and treatment that are needed for the maximal habilitation of severely disabled persons. Sontag, Smith, and Sailor (1977) called for a new approach, one that rejects the idea that people can be neatly classified in homogenous groups based upon a specific type or combination of disabilities. Sontag, Burke, and York (1973) noted that the exact nature of a disability or the degree of mental retardation is less important than understanding the type of services needed to develop functional skills that lead to independence. An approach that stresses assessment of functional abilities and the identification of services to promote maximal functional development and adaptation has recently been established as a meaningful way of understanding and working with severely disabled persons. Even though there is widespread support for such an approach, many state and local service agencies are only now beginning to adapt their regulations accordingly. Only a few states currently use the term *severely handicapped,* whereas many others continue to use such categories as trainable, profoundly retarded, or multiply handicapped, or deaf-blind (Justin & Brown, 1977).

Although the population of persons with severe disabilities is heterogeneous and is difficult to divide into classifications, there are a number of unique challenges persons in this population experience, and their parents and families in turn also experience. Education and human services professionals and agencies are also challenged by the circumstances as well. The prevalence of intellectual disabilities is a frequent circumstance of people with severe disabilities. Implications are that many of these persons are substantially delayed cognitively, display different or less functional cognitive styles, do not readily acquire conceptual skills, and are extremely limited in the acquisition and use of language (Baumiester & Brookes, 1981). Many of the skills and abilities that nonhandicapped persons learn are not acquired at all. This requires highly specialized, intensive, and systematic educational instruction and long-term support systems.

Another circumstance common among persons with severe disabilities is the presence of physical limitations and problems. Chief among these is cerebral palsy, a nonprogressive disorder resulting from damage to the central nervous system and manifested by partial or total paralysis of various parts of the body (Bobath & Bobath, 1975). Cerebral palsy and other related developmental disabilities may severely restrict physical development as well as the learning or ability to perform very basic movements such as walking, using the hands, and speaking or eating. Although effective forms of intervention now exist to minimize the long-term deleterious effects of these central nervous system disorders, the presence of such physical problems is extremely restrictive to these persons and also places a great burden on the family, which, in many instances, must provide extensive amounts of assistance and care.

A third general type of severe disability is sensory impairment. Many persons labeled typically as "multiply handicapped" or "deaf-blind" experience various degrees of visual and/or auditory impairment (Lehr, 1982). It is also common for sensory impairments to be accompanied by various degrees of intellectual and physical disabilities as well as chronic medical or health problems. There is little doubt that the presence of multiple severe disabilities is devastating to the health and well-being of those affected and their families, if only in terms of the level of effort required to overcome the loss of these important vehicles for the quality of life. Yet, even with these individuals, experience has proven that with proper services and with support and assistance to families, many positive benefits can accrue. Children with severe and multiple disabilities are at present attending public schools in increasing numbers, living at home with their natural families, and learning many important skills critical to greater independence.

People with severe disabilities also often experience extreme difficulty in developing typical and functional social behaviors and relationships. Social performance differences may be associated with intellectual disabilities (Guess & Horner, 1976, Mulligan, 1982) or may be a function of such chronic and severe emotional disorders as childhood autism (see Rutter, 1978). Many children diagnosed as "autistic" possess an extremely limited social repertoire and may also demonstrate socially nonfunctional behaviors such as echolalic speech, self-stimulation, and even self-destruction. These types of social behaviors are extremely difficult to treat successfully and often require extensive effort and commitment on the part of parents and family members to remedy or even tolerate (Browning, 1980; Koegel, Egel, & Dunlap, 1980).

NEEDS OF PERSONS WITH SEVERE DISABILITIES

The implications of these circumstances and difficulties pose great challenges for professionals and family members as children and youth with severe disabilities are often extremely difficult to care for (Tizard & Grad, 1961) and to teach (Liberty, Haring, & Martin, 1981), and seldom generalize skills that are learned (Stokes & Baer, 1977). Additionally, many of these children may never attain total independence and will require extensive assistance all their lives.

Not surprisingly, the needs of these persons are as heterogeneous as the challenges and circumstances they must overcome. As their needs vary, so do those of their families. Some of these needs stem directly from the problems already discussed: Medical problems may require treatment from pediatricians or neurologists; sensory disabilities will require treatment from ophthalmologists and audiologists; physical disabilities may require extensive therapeutic intervention from orthopedists; physical therapists, and occupational therapists; cognitive language deficits will require the expertise of specially trained speech and language therapists and special education teachers; and as these children grow older, vocational trainers, counselors, and engineers will be needed to attempt to aid in the preparation for meaningful work. The pervasiveness and relentlessness of the needs of persons with severe disabilities seem staggering. However, if one considers that the goals for these individuals are maximal development, health, happiness, and inclusion within the mainstream of our society, it becomes clear that they do not differ substantially from those for nondisabled people. It is the realization of these universal human needs that some may find difficult. Our experience has been that just as parents share in the desire for the attainment of these goals for their children, they also often share in the agony of attempting to secure the needed services.

Beyond the more obvious types of services just described, there are some overriding concerns that must also be addressed that transcend day-to-day matters and relate more to the longitudinal needs of individuals with severe disabilities. To begin with, these persons and their families often need adequate and sometimes highly specialized health care over a long period of time. As noted by Upshur in Chapter 4 of this volume and by Gordon

(1977), parents speak of the difficulty they experience in securing adequate health care for their child. Indeed, depending on the particular physical problems of their child, they may need the services of several different specialists. Although professionals have been rather judgmental in terming parents' efforts as symptomatic of denial (see, e.g., "Search for the cure," Rosen, 1955), often parents do need to contact several different agencies and professionals before the proper services can be identified and secured for their child. Additionally, because many persons with severe disabilities experience rather brittle medical existences (e.g., congenital heart defects, uncontrolled seizure disorders, acute hydrocephalus), emergency medical treatment may be needed to respond to a variety of life-threatening crises. Now that increasing numbers of these persons are residing in the community (rather than in institutions), a wide spectrum of routine maintenance and emergency health care services must be accessible to them.

Specialized family assistance and support services are also needed. As noted earlier, many more severely disabled persons now reside with their families, and these families often need various types of assistance (e.g., in-home professional consultation, respite care services) in order to adequately manage their disabled children and to ensure that a family's resources and energies are not depleted and that the family can be as normal as possible.

Bersani (1987) provided a general description of family assistance and support, the major purposes of which are to provide direct support to families caring for their (developmentally disabled) child at home and to reduce out-of-home placements. Currently, family assistance may include a wide array of services and may be funded by different methods including direct payment, reimbursement, and direct cash subsidies. According to Bersani, although the family assistance concept is relatively new, it appears effective in meeting the two previously mentioned goals. Currently, however, states and municipalities vary widely in what they offer families.

We believe that direct family assistance and support is a critically important service delivery option for families with severely disabled family members. Clearly, if the goal is effective collaboration to attain treatment and service goals mutually beneficial to both the individual with severe disabilities and the individual's family, then services need to be focused directly on the family and the home. Providing services and/or treatment away from the home and family may serve only to further isolate the "problems" from their natural context.

For other persons with severe disabilities, residential placement in alternative community living arrangements (CLAs) may be more appropriate and even necessary. That is, some families may be unable to provide the needed specialized care at home, some older parents may themselves be unable physically to handle their children who have grown to adolescence or adulthood, whereas still others may prefer that their child be placed in a CLA for other reasons. Decisions regarding selection of and placement in an alternative residential arrangement can be extremely difficult and are affected by many factors unique to individual families. Persons with severe disabilities and their families need to know of a variety of options for community living, and they need professionals and agencies who will work with them to find the most appropriate placement (O'Conner, 1976).

Central to the successful maintenance of these people in the community is the need for appropriate educational services. Now that appropriate public education has been mandated by federal legislation, most public school districts serve students with severe disabilities. Even so, parents have had to struggle long and hard for the inclusion of their children in such programs (Turnbull & Turnbull, 1978). Even though Public Law 94–142 outlines guidelines for these programs, many parents find themselves assuming adversarial positions toward school personnel in order to exercise their legal right to due process of law to bring about appropriate services for their children. In many respects the problems public school districts face are the same as those faced by other social agencies: lack of adequate facilities, inadequately trained and inexperienced staff, and insufficient funds to pay for services (Semmel & Morrissey, 1981). Additionally, educating these students is a relatively new challenge in the field of education, and although great strides have been made (Sontag, Certo, & Button, 1979), much remains to be learned about how best to teach these children (Burton & Hirshoren, 1979). At a time when available resources from the public and private sectors continue to decrease, it is becoming increasingly difficult to continue to develop and implement new and effective methods and programs for educating persons with severe disabilities (Sontag et al., 1979). Under these conditions parents and professionals will need to work closely together if strides in the education and treatment are to be made.

Encompassing each of these types of basic service delivery needs is the overall need for continuity, coordination, and consistency of services. As noted from the preceding discussion, the needs of persons with severe disabilities differ in some respects from persons with mild handicaps (see Chapter 8 by Fewell): The needs of people with severe disabilities are pervasive and may extend across all major aspects of their lives and across all age periods of their lives. At any given time a person with severe disabilities may be receiving services from four to six different agencies and may be in contact with 15 to 20 different professionals. With all of these different agencies and highly specialized professionals assuming their individual roles, the attainment of continuity, coordination, and consistency of services can become a problem of considerable magnitude. It is the families, then, who are primarily responsible for creating order out of what may seem to be chaos.

Indeed, lack of coordination of services is one of the most frequently heard complaints of parents (see Upshur, Chapter 4). For this reason professionals who serve these individuals and their families must be knowledgeable about the different agencies and services available in the local community. If professionals are knowledgeable about these services and willing to work cooperatively with families, then the ultimate goals of habilitation for these children can be better realized: maximization of independence, an improved quality of life, and the preparation for adulthood. From the earliest point at which a severe disability is identified and the child is placed in an early intervention program, to the point at which that child reaches adulthood and exits school, service agencies need to converge around common and reasonable goals for the child and find consistent and effective ways of working with the child's family.

Advocacy can be a critical need of the child's family. For the most part, persons with severe disabilities are either unable or ineffective in advocating for themselves. As a result, parents, professionals, and agencies must provide this important function if the rights, opportunities, and privileges of these persons are to be protected. Agencies and professionals can play an important role in this area either by assuming advocacy functions or by assisting or supporting parents, who bear the brunt of the burden.

A further overriding concern is the need for services and support to the parents and families. Many parents as well as professionals have described the numerous needs of parents and families of children with severe disabilities as falling into three major categories: (a) psychological and emotional support and understanding; (b) information, education, and training; and (c) effective services for their children (Dean, 1975; Turnbull & Turnbull, 1978). Professionals must be mindful that families are, ultimately, the most important advocates, caretakers, and teachers of their children. If the families of these children are not adequately supported, or are disrupted, then very important family functions may also be disrupted. For professionals to adequately support and work with parents and families, they must have an understanding of the impact and implications of a severe disability upon the family. This understanding will enable professionals to better address the unique needs that these families face.

IMPACTS ON FAMILIES

Attempts to assess the impact of children with severe disabilities on their families and to determine appropriate courses of action are extremely difficult. Because children and families vary so widely on their specific characteristics and because any number of different psychological, social, and practical day-to-day factors affect each family differently, attempts to develop a characteristic profile of families of severely disabled children are fruitless. Just as different families react and adjust uniquely to different crises, families react idiosyncratically to their severely disabled child. The research in this area supports this contention — namely, that it is difficult and even erroneous to assume that all families of persons with severe disabilities are similarly affected, possess similar characteristics, or are in need of similiar services. Just as persons with severe disabilities vary widely in their characteristics and needs, so too do families.

With the above considerations in mind, it is likewise important to understand that some family members experience feelings, burdens, and stresses that families of nondisabled or less disabled children will not experience. In this section we described those experiences unique to families of persons with severe disabilities and discuss the implications for various family members, as well as for families as a whole. Three areas of impacts on families are discussed: psychological or emotional, financial, and practical and logistical implications on the overall functioning of the family.

One frequently discussed area pertaining to the families of severely handicapped children has been the psychological or emotional impact upon the family. Literature in this area has been concerned primarily with psychological or emotional reactions and has generally attempted to describe the deleterious and stressful effects of the presence of a disabled child on the family. The major areas examined include the impact on the parents, impact on the siblings, and effect on the family unit.

Many authors have described the psychological and emotional impact that a disabled child has on parents and their reaction and subsequent adaptation. An early account of parental reactions to the birth of a disabled child came from Kanner (1953) who, on the basis of clinical observations of parents, suggested that three types of parental reactions are common: acceptance, disguise, or denial. Rosen (1955) stated that parental reactions to a handicapped child occur in a fairly predictable order and generally include the following stages of psychological adaptation: awareness of a problem, recognition of the problem, search for a cause, search for a cure, and acceptance of the problem. Rosen's discussion and interpretation of the mother's understanding and adaptation to a child with mental retardation are widely cited by authors in this field (Baum, 1962). Roos (1963), the parent of a disabled child, also suggests that many parents experience difficult emotional trauma over having a handicapped child: loss of self-esteem, shame, ambivalence, depression, self-sacrifice, and defensiveness. Menolascino and Egger (1978) describe parental reactions as a series of crises to be resolved: the crises of shock and novelty, the personal values crisis, and the crisis confronted when the daily burden of care manifests itself.

Research in this area has generally followed the lines of the above constructs of parental reaction and adjustment to the presence of a disabled child. Several early studies attempted to assess associated differences in the psychological reactions of parents of institutionalized versus noninstitutionalized children (Jacobson & Humphrey, 1979). Caldwell and Guze (1960) surveyed parents of both groups and did not find significant differences in adjustment between mothers of institutionalized and noninstitutionalized children. Fowle (1968), however, noted that fathers of noninstitutionalized children tended to experience more role tension than did fathers of institutionalized children, and generally more tension than did mothers. Graliker, Fishler & Koch (1962) attempted to identify parent and family factors related to the decision to institutionalize a child. The authors did not find a relation between institutionalization and social class, religion, education, or age; however, parents of first-born severely disabled children were more apt to institutionalize their children. Farber (1959, 1960) conducted a series of studies to compare the effects of institutionalization with home care on families of children with mental retardation. Although these studies were not related specifically to effects on parents, he did find that the overall "family integration" of parents and families who kept their child at home tended to be negatively affected.

Other authors have addressed the difficulties parents face when they are initially informed or counseled about the fact that their newborn is severely disabled. The communication of this event is often traumatic for professionals (see Chapter 5 by Darling) as well as for parents. Ballard (1978) also noted the difficulty of initial counseling and suggested that professionals responsible for informing and advising parents also need assistance and support. Parents have reported that the specific manner in which physicians handle these situations, as well as how knowledgeable the physician is of the infant's condition, influences initial reactions of parents (Zwerling, 1954). Undoubtedly, the manner in which parents are initially informed or receive counseling contributes to their psychological reactions to what may be shocking news. One of the most difficult situations faced by both parents and professionals is the decision of whether to provide medical treatment to a severely injured neonate. Duff (1981) suggested that this event may be extremely difficult for all involved and that the resolution of this question is an important social as well as personal issue.

Relatively few studies have examined directly whether parents of children with severe disabilities actually do progress through a series of predictable stages of reaction. Dunlap and Hollinsworth (1977) reviewed survey studies of parents of severely handicapped children that revealed no serious consequences of adjustment in parents or family members. These reports contradict two clinical case study reports by Taichert (1975) and Menolascino and Pearson (1974). These authors confirm after observational reports that the parents of these children do experience severe negative emotional reactions and tend to follow a fairly predictable sequence of experiences. Drotvar, Baskiewicz, Irvin, Kennel and Klaus (1975) interviewed 20 parents of congenitally malformed infants and also found support for the existence of a series of stages of emotional reactions. In one of the few experimental studies in this area, Bitter (1963) attempted to improve what were considered undesirable attitudes and expectations of parents toward their Down Syndrome children. Although the results were inconclusive, the author suggested that counseling may fulfill an important role for those parents who experience difficulty in developing healthy and appropriate attitudes toward their child. Matheny and Vernick (1969) were able to positively change the attitudes of parents toward their disabled children through a direct approach consisting of providing information and education about their child's disability and its implications. These authors noted that counseling strategies may, in fact, be less successful than more direct educational approaches with some parents. Gath (1977), who extensively studied the effects of Down's syndrome children on their families and parents, found these parents tended to evidence more depression, tension, hostility, and lack of warmth than did a control group of parents of "normal" children.

Although still others have suggested that the presence of a child with severe disabilities has negative psychological effects on the parents (Dornberg, 1978), the data in this area are clearly equivocal. Zucman, (1982) noted that the literature does not lead to the conclusion that the presence of a severely disabled child necessarily results in negative or harmful effects on parents. Rather, a more reasonable interpretation, is that there are a variety of factors that contribute to parental reaction, and it is difficult if not impossible to predict what type of reactions to expect from parents. It is, however, important for professionals to realize that some parents may react strongly, be affected negatively, and in fact need professional counseling to help them adjust or adapt to the birth of a child with a severe disability.

A related area of interest is the impact on other children in the family (see also Chapter 7, "Siblings of Disabled Brothers and Sisters," by Seligman). Many of these studies have consisted of either directly interviewing the siblings or of administrating various types of psychological test batteries. Early work in this area was pioneered by Farber (1960) who studied families of institutionalized and noninstitutionalized children to assess differences in family integration between the two groups. In a frequently cited study, Farber (1959) reported that for families who kept their child with mental retardation at home, siblings — particularly older females — were negatively affected psychologically. Farber's work was an important precursor to later studies in this area, and in particular, his concept of "family integration" as it related to families of persons with disabilities was a milestone. Although Farber did report data supporting the negative effects of disabled children on their siblings, his account was carefully restricted. Unfortunately, it appears that other authors have overstated Farber's results and have failed to carefully interpret the findings.

Several others have also suggested that the siblings of these children are negatively affected. Hormuth (1953), in reporting on three case studies, stated that often siblings of disabled children may be prejudiced and that older siblings may be more apt to be than younger siblings. In a study discussed earlier, Fowle (1968) also reported negative impact on normal siblings, particularly in the form of increased role tension among families who kept their child with mental retardation at home.

In a series of studies, Gath (1973, 1974) attempted to identify the amount and the nature of these negative effects on siblings. Her studies were similar, methodologically, to those discussed earlier and involved either direct interview or the administration of psychological tests or both to identify the presence of psychiatric disorders. In each study, responses of siblings of children with Down Syndrome were compared to those of nondisabled or minimally disabled children. Gath reported that older sisters revealed higher levels of psychiatric disorders, siblings from low socioeconomic status families were negatively influenced, as were boys from large low socioeconomic status families. It should be noted that each of these studies employed rather small samples and that in an earlier study (Gath, 1972) no significant negative impact on siblings was noted.

Still other authors have suggested that siblings of children with severe disabilities are negatively affected in numerous ways. Grossman (1977) stated that the siblings of these children may experience a variety of negative emotional reactions, including fear, death wishes, apprehension, and a lack of understanding. Hunter, Schucman, and Friedlander (1975) found that many siblings may exhibit anger over having a sibling with a disability. It has been recommended that because many different emotional reactions of siblings may be observed, parents must be open and candid about the situation with their children (Wentworth, 1974). Furthermore, attempts should be made to provide these siblings with opportunities to communicate openly with others so that they can adequately deal with their feelings (Chinn, Drew, & Logan, 1979; Chinn, Winn, & Walters, 1978).

Based on the literature just discussed, although there is limited evidence that some siblings experience negative impacts owing to the presence of a severely disabled child in the family (Dornberg, 1978), the research data in this area are far from conclusive. In fact, several authors argue that no assumptions or generalizations should be made about siblings. Caldwell and Guze (1960) for example, found no evidence of such negative impact when they studied mothers and siblings of retarded children kept at home. Chinn and his colleagues (1978) suggested that although these siblings may sometimes need assistance from parents or professionals, it is extremely difficult to predict the type of response a sibling will make to having a disabled child in the family. Zucman (1982) also stated that the responses or reactions of normal siblings may be influenced by a variety of different factors that are difficult to isolate. Wolfensberger (1968), in a review of studies investigating the impact of disabled children on their siblings, also concluded that the research does not support the notion that all siblings are negatively affected or that they are affected in similar ways.

Lobato and Barerra (1988) conducted research on the impact that disabled and nondisabled siblings have on each other and the impact that professional services and practices have on sibling relationships. These authors suggested that some professional practices aimed at addressing the needs of the disabled siblings may fail to address the needs of the nondisabled siblings. Lobato and Barerra suggested that services provided to these families should attempt to integrate the nondisabled children into the family-professional services experience. Similar to the literature on the impact of a severely disabled child, studies of the impact on siblings also lead to few conclusions.

Families of severely disabled children have also been discussed in terms of the overall psychological and emotional impact they experience. The literature in this area is also not conclusive, with some authors reporting relatively little negative impact of severely disabled children on their families, whereas others suggest that the impact is predominantly negative. Many accounts have been reported describing the extremely emotionally and physically exhausting effects of a severely disabled child on the family (Christ-Sullivan, 1976; Gordon, 1977; Tizard & Grad, 1961). In one of the few attempts at describing these families, Odle, Greer, and Anderson (1976) provided a brief review and discussion of the potentially negative effects that these children had on their families. These authors suggested that all family members may be affected and that other factors outside of the family may also influence the nature of the impact.

Several studies investigating the psychological impact on parents and siblings, which were discussed earlier, also report results of negative impact of a severely disabled child on family functioning (Farber, 1960; Caldwell & Guze, 1960; Hormuth, 1953). These authors reported negative emotionality, role tension, and increased divisiveness within these families. In studying a group of families of children with Down Syndrome, Gath (1977) reported that these families evidenced more negative emotions than did a group of families of otherwise disabled children, but that the families of other handicapped children also reported that they felt more drawn together emotionally as a result of the event. Farber (1976) suggested that many of these families progress through a series of adaptation stages to the birth of a disabled child (similar to those described by Rosen) and that this adaptation is helpful in integrating the family unit. Fost (1981) stated that an important and effective approach to counseling these families is to facilitate family members' adaptation and adjustment to these types of emotional stages.

The evidence in support of negative psychological impact of a child with a severe disability upon the family is contradictory. Fowle's (1968) study revealed relatively few differences between families who institutionalized their child and those who kept their child with mental retardation at home. Dunlap and Hollinsworth (1977) also reported no serious negative psychological or emotional effects on families, but they did report that these families were greatly in need of financial assistance and adequate educational programs for their disabled children. In a survey study, Dunlap and Hollinsworth (1977) interviewed 400 families of children with disabilities and found their adjustment was good and generally found no serious consequences. The authors did report, however, that families of children with multiple disabilities and seizure disorders were more burdened with financial concerns and had more time constraints that circumscribed their social life than did the other families. In a more recent study, Blackard and Barsch (1982) surveyed both parents and professionals to compare their appraisals of the impact that a severely disabled child has on the family. The results indicated that special education personnel tended to overestimate the negative impact of the disability on the family as compared to parents' appraisals. These authors reported that the difficulties these families experienced were centered more around practical matters (e.g., obtaining respite care) than around concerns regarding psychological reactions.

Several authors have summarized the literature in this area and concur that there is little empirical support that families are negatively effected or badly disrupted by the presence of severe disability in the family. On the basis of their review, Jacobson and Humphrey (1979) drew three conclusions about the effects that a child with a severe disability has on the family: The negative effects have been overstated, the positive aspects have been ignored, and many other family variables have been neglected from study. The authors further state that there are differing family responses to be ultimately identified and a much deeper understanding and study of these families is needed. Carr (1974) and Wolfensberger (1968) also reviewed the research in this area and found many studies so limited by methodological problems that there was a general lack of support for the conclusion that families are negatively influenced.

It appears that much more research in this area is needed before it can be assumed that children with severe disabilities do, in fact, generally influence their families in negative ways. Based on a review of the articles just mentioned, several problems or limitations of the literature seem apparent. First, many of the published studies are flawed methodologically (e.g., the studies are of small or biased samples; they lack valid and reliable measures). In addition, few of these studies identified their populations in specific and concrete terms. Because the population referred to here as severely disabled is so heterogeneous in nature, with many different types of concerns and needs, it is difficult to generalize reported results to any specific family or even to any specific subgroup of families. Although studies with more precisely defined populations and more direct and reliable measures might lead to more conclusive results, the appropriateness and importance of this type of research seems questionable. Rather than continue to view these families as functioning pathologically, we might better and more productively focus on those practical matters that are of great concern to the families themselves.

Two such areas frequently have been reported by the parents themselves: financial difficulties, and the burden on the practical and logistical day-to-day operations of the family. Several survey studies cited earlier stressed that many parents reported difficulty with financial matters stemming from the need to obtain numerous services for their children (Dunlap & Hollinsworth, 1977; Gath, 1973). Christ-Sullivan (1976) also stated that when many different services are needed, expenses can be great, which sorely burdens the financial solvency of the family.

As already discussed, although strides have been made in providing health and educational services to these children and their families, there are many other needed services that are not commonly available at public expense. Parents experience difficulty in locating dentists, doctors, opthamologists, and even babysitters who are either willing or able to work effectively with their children. For the parents of very seriously challenged and multiple disabled children this problem is even more severe. Abramson, Gravnik, Abramson, and Summers (1977) surveyed a large percentage of the parents of children with disabilities in the state of Connecticut and found that many were dissatisfied with the services they were receiving. Blackard and Barsch (1982) reported that most problems were related to difficulties in locating and paying for needed services.

In addition to these difficulties, parents also incur extra expenses in attempting to meet the needs of their children, many of whom need wheelchairs, adaptive equipment, hearing aides, communication augmentation devices, orthopedic shoes, and many other types of equipment. Because many of these items are very expensive and because government assistance may only partially reimburse for expenses, parents end up paying for the bulk of the items. Financial burdens are even more devastating to low-income families, who have even fewer resources available to them. One of the most important, expensive, and difficult to secure services is respite care (short-term care and management of the child by trained personnel, usually in the home). This type of short-term care is very important for parents of children with challenging behaviors, particularly if there are other younger children in the home. In many respects these financial pressures may be much more difficult for families to deal with than some of the more subtle psychological or emotional problems they may experience.

A related area of the impact on the family is the stress involved in the simple, day-to-day logistics of maintaining the family functions. Helsel (1978) offered a frank and direct account of typical logistical problems families encounter. Meeting the needs of the disabled child, caring for the other, nondisabled siblings, maintaining satisfying marital relationships, and fulfilling professional commitments, as well as meeting the more mundane concerns of daily living can sometimes be overwhelming for families of children who need to be fed, dressed, toileted, and so on several times a day, each day, for years. Gorham (1975) believes that many professionals are often either ignorant or insensitive to the realities of daily living faced by these families. In many respects the manner in which professionals have attempted to understand families of severely handicapped children has been influenced by a rather problem-oriented preoccupation with the family's mental health, to the virtual exclusion of the ongoing and daily practical, financial, and logistical priorities.

Furthermore, although much has been written about the various problems and characteristics of these families, little has been done in terms of viewing these families as systems. Adopting a family systems approach to understanding families of these children might make a more meaningful understanding possible and also allow for the development of more effective means of meeting their needs. Several authors have called for a family systems approach to understanding and working with families of handicapped children (Berkowitz & Graziano, 1972; Chinn et al., 1978; Turnbull & Turnbull, 1978; Zucman, 1982).

Benson and Turnbull's (1986) description, in particular, lends itself readily to a deeper understanding of families in general and families of handicapped children in particular. Three aspects of the family system are described: structure, functions, and life cycle. From a family systems approach the structure consists of several subsystems between the spouses, parents, siblings, and other extrafamilial persons (e.g., extended family members, friends, neighbors). Within each subsystem, then, different families are expected to vary on several different factors, such as culture, ideology, or role parameters. Family functions are described as including those areas in which every family member receives assistance and support from the total family: financial, physical, rest and recuperation, socialization, self-definition, affect, guidance, vocational, and educational. Finally, Benson and Turnbull (1986) also described the life cycle of a family in terms of developmental stages: transitions, changes and catalysts, and sociohistorical context.

Powers, Thorwath, and Bruey (1988) provided a similar description of a family systems approach. They underscore the uniqueness of families and suggest that a continuum of services is needed in order for the service system to respond adequately to the wide ranging needs of families. Powers and Bruey state that the goals of therapy provided to families should be to facilitate a healthy response to diagnosis; to facilitate functional forms of organization within the family systems; to facilitate the development and maintenance of social networks; to facilitate service access and coordination; and to facilitate the development of advocacy skills.

We concur with Seligman in Chapter 2 that this type of ecological approach to understanding families offers the possibility for more meaningful understanding of families in general and for understanding differences among families as well. Undoubtedly, the characteristics and needs of families with severely disabled children will vary considerably with differences in the various aspects of the family system. This model accommodates the view that families with children with severe disabilities are complex entities with unique ways of responding to significant events in their lives.

EFFECTIVE COLLABORATION WITH FAMILIES

To work effectively with persons with severe disabilities and their families, it is important that professionals develop a basic understanding of the common needs of these families as well as the ability to identify specific needs that are unique to individual families. As the preceding discussion indicates, a variety of factors may affect the types of collaboration or assistance needed or requested by families.

The literature contains two types of reports about parental needs that are worthy of consideration: individual reports of parents themselves (Gorham, 1975; Greer, 1975) and large-scale surveys of groups of parents (Justice, O'Conner, & Warren, 1971; Kenowitz et al., 1977). Over the years these two sources of information have yielded rather consistent information about the needs of parents and families of disabled children: support, information, and adequate services are most frequently noted by parents themselves. This section provides suggestions for understanding and meeting these needs, particularly as they pertain to families of persons with severe disabilities.

One of the most important areas of need often reported by parents is for professionals and others to attempt to better understand their problems and provide emotional support in a nonjudgmental manner (Schlesinger & Meadow, 1976). Professionals should understand that the responsibility of parenting is often very demanding and may drain the resources of the family. Positive feedback and encouragement can be extremely helpful to family members who feel at times exhausted, overwhelmed, or even uncertain about the care and treatment they are providing to their child. Persons working with these families can be supportive and understanding without having necessarily to assume roles as counselors. When and if family members do need counseling to ease adjustment problems, then this should be left to well-trained professionals.

Informational assistance is also a commonly reported need of families (Dean, 1975). One of the most common types of assistance parents need is accurate information. As suggested earlier, the presence of a child with a severe disability in the family often means that parents need to obtain, understand, and use all kinds of information. The type of information needed by these parents could include the nature of their child's disability, characteristic patterns of normal development, methods of parenting and management, agencies providing training and consultation, the availability of health or related services, the selection of an educational program, legal protection and advocacy services, parent self-help and support groups, respite care, and the long-term expectations or implications for the child. Again, these informational needs will vary from family to family and also from one time to another. Some families need assistance in obtaining information, some with interpreting or understanding the information, and some with using the information to make decisions. Still other parents may have more information available to them than most agencies and will not need assistance, although some may need clarification regarding confusing and contradictory opinions. In providing parents with information, care should be taken to avoid the use of technical, professional jargon or of communicating in a condescending manner.

One of the most important needs of families of children with severe disabilities is to obtain the necessary services for their child within the community (Justice et al., 1971; Kenowitz et al., 1977). One of the areas in which parents often experience great difficulty is in obtaining appropriate and effective educational programs. Public educational programs for children with severe disabilities are often highly centralized in large, segregated centers far from the child's homes. These types of programs may require them to spend large amounts of time riding buses each day, which may restrict the child's recognition and acceptance within the local community and may, furthermore, fail to offer opportunities for the learning of important socialization skills (Brown et al., 1977). Many parents are calling for more decentralized services located closer to families' homes, to be provided by local school districts in order to alleviate many of these problems.

A related need is for meaningful involvement and participation in educational and other services provided to the child. Although federal and state legislation now mandates the protection of certain specific rights of parents' participation (e.g., prior written informed consent, access to records, due process procedures), there are accounts of circumstances in which these basic rights have been violated or ignored. It has also been noted that professionals or agencies do not make meaningful attempts to involve parents beyond what is minimally required by law (Matson, 1977). Professionals should attempt to work toward overcoming obstacles between themselves and parents (Roos, 1977) and should attempt to establish close working relationships (Perske, n.d.) so that the family and the child can benefit to the greatest extent possible (see Chapter 5 by Darling).

One important form of involvement with professionals and agencies that parents and families may need is training. Children with severe disabilities may need extensive supervision, care, and possibly even highly specialized treatment on a frequent basis. Parents (and even siblings) may need specific training from professionals in many different areas related to the care of their child, such as feeding, handling, positioning, managing challenging behaviors, and toilet training. Over the years, a variety of different approaches and programs have been used to provide parents with training (Berkowitz & Graziano, 1972; O'Dell, 1974). In fact, it could be argued that training parents has been the predominant approach of many professionals. Professionals (particularly in the field of education) have often been quick to assume that they know the best treatment for the child, that parents lack the necessary skills to provide treatment, and that certain designated training approaches should be provided solely by the professional so that "correct" techniques can be used.

There are several problems with this approach to understanding and working with these families. First, although it is often true that parents may need and request specific training to better care for their child, it should not be assumed that all parents want or even need training in any or all areas involving the caring and management of their child. Second, the implicit assumption that family members are essentially without skills in caring for their severely handicapped child is often blatantly false. Many times parents possess extensive amounts of expertise in caring for their child, and may, in fact, be able to train professionals in the most effective techniques. Vincent, Dodd, and Henner (1978) called for professionals to recognize that parenting is a specialized discipline and that parents bring valuable assets of their own to the care of their child. Therefore, it may be useful to consider the parents and the professional as a collaborative team. Third, the preoccupation with training has probably inhibited many parents from selecting other forms of participation and involvement in their child's life. There are many other needs and preferences that families have that cannot be satisfied only by parent training. Fourth (and perhaps most important), in limiting the scope of interaction with families to parent training programs, professionals may fail to understand the family as a system, with its own unique structure, functions, and life cycle. This failure can, and often does, result in families feeling or even actually being compelled to comply with professionals' expectations for home treatment, which may be intrusive to the family itself. Approaches to providing training should be carefully considered by professionals so that the preferences and styles of families are respected.

As noted earlier, an additional need of many families is for direct home care and assistance, often referred to as respite care. This short-term care may be helpful in some families — where both parents work, where several other children are in the home, and when and if the family simply wishes or needs to obtain relief from intensive and exhausting 24-hour care routines. This type of assistance may also be critical for single parent families in which no other family members are available to help out. For these families, in-home assistance may make the difference between maintaining the child at home and placing him or her in a residential placement. Traditionally, our service delivery systems have been highly centralized, and families in need of services are expected to go to the center, the clinic, the school, or the hospital, for assistance. We believe that professionals working with these families should make every effort to extend their services into the homes, where the very important needs of these children and their families exist and must be dealt with on a long-term basis.

PLANNING FOR THE FUTURE

Finally, families of children with severe disabilities also need support and assistance in the transitions their child must progress through as they grow older and move into different educational and service programs (McDonnell, Wilcox, & Boles, 1986). The most commonly discussed transitions are those from kindergarten to elementary school, from elementary to middle school, from middle to secondary school and, ultimately the transition from school to adult life. Although many families experience minor difficulties and need to adjust to these transitions, they are, for the most part, considered normal and expected reasons for change. For many families with children who are severely disabled, however, periods of transition may be extremely traumatizing. At the very least, it is important that education and social service professionals collaborate closely with families so that they and their severely disabled members can negotiate these periods of change without experiencing extreme difficulty or disruption to the individual or the family. Parents and professionals need to plan carefully to determine the needed courses of action and to determine specific roles and responsibilities (Everson & Moon, 1987).

Although each of the above transitions may pose serious challenges to families, the transition from school is particularly imposing because it means the end of service from the school district (which, in many cases, ceases after an individual reaches the age of 21 years) and the beginning of an entirely new search for adult services and programs. This transition is further complicated by the fact that community programs and opportunities for severely disabled adults may not even be available in some communities. The three ingredients needed for successful school-to-work and adult life transition are planning, collaboration, and advocacy. Planning should begin by the time the child is 14 years old and should continue through the age of 21. Individual transition plans are used to target needed activities, delegate responsibilities, and set a timetable for action. Collaboration between parents and school professionals is also a necessary element of transition. Parents and professionals should begin collaboration early on and continue to develop positive and productive interaction during the child's school experience. School professionals can be particularly helpful in meaningfully involving them in the educational program of their child, helping parents clarify long-term goals for their child, and informing parents about services available beyond the school years and connecting parents with postschool service providers. A third element of transition, advocacy, is an important role for both parents and professionals. Parents naturally have the long-term role of searching out the best possible vocational, residential, and social situations for their child. Some parents may need assistance in setting expectations for their child and in balancing what may sometimes seem to be widely different concerns (e.g., health and safety vs. quality of opportunity for normalization). Teachers, and other human services professionals, may also advocate for the securing of what they consider the best possible outcomes. However, they should also consider the perspective of the family members while doing so. Working together, parents and professionals can minimize the stress of school transition and maximize the opportunities for both the severely disabled youth and the family.

TRANSDISCIPLINARY TEAM ORIENTATION

In each of the areas of collaboration outlined above, it is important that parents and professionals work effectively together if the needs of the family and of the severely disabled individual are to be addressed. Although many different models of collaboration have been proposed, the transdisciplinary approach appears to offer the best opportunity for effective teamwork among parents of children with severe disabilities and the many different professionals who will be involved. Lyon and Lyon (1980) described the transdisciplinary approach as a joint team approach in which staff development is accomplished through the process of role release. Role release is conceptualized as consisting of various levels including general information, informational skills, and performance competencies. What occurs is that as the child's needs are identified (through group process), the various team members — including parents — participate actively in a give-and-take to determine goals and action steps. This is followed by the free exchange of information and instruction (role release) such that all team members' competencies and roles are broadened, and thus the service delivery capabilities are enhanced and the child and family benefit.

The transdisciplinary model is particularly effective for the development of collaboration between professionals and parents. First, under the transdisciplinary model, parents are equal members of the team with valued expertise to offer the other team members (Lyon & Lyon, 1982). Second, parents play important roles in their own right as advisers and consultants to other professionals. Third, the transdisciplinary team model is fully compatible with the family systems approach, which recognizes the complexity and integrity of the family and its component parts. This approach to collaboration with parents transcends the more traditional, limited view of parents and families as the recipients of professional expertise and allows for meaningful collaboration to effectively support families.

CONCLUSION

Education and human service professionals and other personnel must realize several important principles when attempting to collaborate with these families. First and foremost is the fact that these children and their families' characteristics, needs, and preferences differ widely; therefore, what may be important or appropriate for one family may not be for another. Second, families are complex units with varying and unique interactional styles. Professionals should not ignore the importance of the differences in family styles, for they are as important in their own right as how family interactions may affect an individual child. Third, the focus of intervention with these families should not be narrowly defined. Parents, in particular, should be respected for their efforts as well as their expertise. Fourth, parent/family collaboration may be broadened and enhanced by extending options for assistance, involvement, and participation. Finally, service agencies and professionals should be more family oriented than individually oriented and should direct more of their efforts toward positively affecting the social system of the family.

Effective collaboration with families of persons with severe disabilities may require professionals to do many things, ranging from providing simple encouragement and support to assisting in providing and interpreting information, training parents in caring for their child, providing crisis intervention and assisting in special problems to help parents clarify goals and needs for themselves, their severely disabled child, and their family.

Several important areas must be addressed if we as a community of professionals, parents, and families are to fully attain our goals. More naturalistic research needs to be conducted, focusing on the identification, analysis, and development of more effective service delivery models and strategies for helping these children and their families. Training must be provided to the many different professionals who are expected to work effectively with these children and their families. More community-based services, such as respite care and in-home assistance, must be made available to assist these families. Finally, professionals must adopt an ecologically valid approach toward these families as well as to their own particular roles: The child and the family must be viewed within the context of one another.

REFERENCES

Abramson, P. R., Gravnick, M. T., Abramson, L. M., & Summers, D. (1977). Early diagnosis and intervention of retardation: A survey of parental reactions concerning the quality of services rendered. *Mental Retardation, 15,* pp. 28–31.

Ballard, R. (1978). Help for coping with the unthinkable. *Developmental Medicine and Child Neurology, 20,* pp. 517–521.

Baum, M. H. (1962). Some dynamic factors affecting family adjustment to the handicapped child. *Exceptional Children, 28,* pp. 387–392.

Baumiester, A., & Brookes, P. (1981). Cognitive deficits in mental retardation. In J. Kauffman (Ed.), *Handbook for special education.* Englewood Cliffs, NJ: Prentice-Hall, pp. 87–107.

Benson, H., & Turnbull, A. P. (1986). Approaching families from an individualized perspective. In R. H. Horner, L. H. Meyer, and H. D. Bud Fredericks (Eds.), *Education of learners with severe handicaps: Exemplary service strategies.* Baltimore, MD: Paul H. Brookes, pp. 127–160.

Berkowitz, B. P., & Graziano, A. (1972). Training parents as behavior therapists: A review. *Behavior Research and Therapy, 10,* pp. 297–317.

Bersani, H. (1987, January). Center provides timely answers to family support questions. *TASH Newsletter,* pp., 4–5.

Bitter, J. A. (1963). Attitude change by parents of TMR children as a result of group discussion. *Exceptional Children, 30,* pp. 173–177.

Blackard, M. K., & Barsch, E. T. (1982). Parents' and professionals' perceptions of the handicapped child's impact on the family. *Journal of the Association for the Severely Handicapped, 7,* pp. 62–69.

Blatt, B., Bogdan, R., Biklen, D., & Taylor, S. (1977). From institution to community: A conversion model. In E. Sontag (Ed.), *Educational programming for the severely and profoundly handicapped.* Reston, VA: Council for Exceptional Children, Division on Mental Retardation, pp. 40–52.

Blatt, B., & Kaplan, F. (1974). *Christmas in purgatory: A photographic essay on mental retardation.* Syracuse, NY: Human Policy Press.

Bleck, E. E., & Nagel, D. A. (Eds.). (1975). *Physically handicapped children: A medical atlas for teachers.* New York: Grune & Stratton.

Bobath, B., & Bobath, K. (1975). *Motor development in the different types of cerebral palsy.* London: William Heineman Medical Books.

Brown, L., Wilcox, B., Sontag, E., Vincent, B., Dodd, N., & Gruenwald, L. (1977). Toward the realization of the least restrictive environments for severely handicapped students. *AAESPH Review, 2,* pp. 195–201.

Browning, R. M. (1980). *Teaching the severely handicapped child.* Boston: Allyn & Bacon.

Burton, T. A., & Hirshoren, A. (1979). Some further thoughts and clarifications on the education of severely and profoundly retarded children. *Exceptional Children, 45,* pp. 618–625.

Caldwell, B., & Guze, A. (1960). A study of the adjustment of parents and siblings of institutionalized and noninstitutionalized retarded children. *American Journal of Mental Deficiency, 64,* pp. 845–861.

Carr, J. (1974). *Young children with Down's syndrome: Their development, upbringing and effect on their families.* London: Butterworths.

Chinn, P., Drew, C., & Logan, D. (1979). *Mental retardation.* St. Louis, MO: Mosby.

Chinn, P. C., Winn, J., & Walters, R. H. (1978). *Two way talking with parents of special children.* St. Louis, MO: Mosby.

Christ-Sullivan, R. (1976). The role of the parent. In A. Thomas (Ed.), *Hey don't forget about me: Education's investment in the severely and profoundly and multiply handicapped.* Reston, VA: Council for Exceptional Children, pp. 36–45.

Dean, D. (1975). Closer look: A parent information service. *Exceptional Children, 41,* 527–530.

Dornberg, N. L. (1978). Some negative effects on family integration of health and educational services for young handicapped children. *American Journal of Orthopsychiatry, 39,* pp. 107–110.

Drotvar, D., Baskiewicz, B., Irvin, N., Kennel, J., & Klaus, M. (1975). The adaptation of parents to the birth of an infant with a congenital malformation: A hypothetical model. *Pediatrics, 56,* pp. 710–717.

Duff, R. (1981). Counseling families and deciding care of severely defective children: A way of coping with medical Vietnam. *Pediatrics, 67,* pp. 315–320.

Dunlap, W. R., & Hollinsworth, J. S. (1977). How does a handicapped child affect the family? Implications for practitioners. *Family Coordinator, 26,* pp. 286–293.

Everson, J. M., & Moon, S. M., (1987). Transition services for young adults with severe disabilities: Defining professional and parental roles and responsibilities. *Journal of the Association for Persons With Severe Handicaps, 12,* pp. 87–95.

Farber, B. (1959). Effects of a severely mentally retarded child on family integration. *Monographs of the Society for Research in Child Development, 24,* (2, Serial No. 71).

Farber, B. (1960). Organization and crisis: Maintenance of integration in families with a severely retarded child. *Monographs of the Society for Research in Child Development, 25,* (Serial No. 1).

Farber, B. (1976). Family process. In W. Cruickshank (Ed.), *Cerebral palsy: A developmental disability* (3rd rev. ed.) New York: Syracuse University Press, pp. 459–475.

Fost, N. (1981). Counseling families who have a child with a severe congenital anomaly. *Pediatrics, 67,* pp. 321–324.

Fowle, C. M. (1968). The effect of the severely mentally retarded child on his family. *American Journal of Mental Deficiency, 73,* pp. 468–473.

Gath, A. (1972). The mental health of siblings of congenitally abnormal children. *Journal of Child Psychology and Psychiatry, 13,* pp. 211–218.

Gath, A. (1973). The school age siblings of Mongol children. *British Journal of Psychiatry, 123,* pp. 161–167.

Gath, A. (1974). Sibling reactions to mental handicap: A comparison of mothers and sisters of Mongol children. *Journal of Child Psychology and Psychiatry, 15,* pp. 187–198.

Gath, A. (1977). The impact of an abnormal child upon the parents. *British Journal of Psychiatry, 130,* pp. 405–410.

Gilhool, T., & Stuttman, E. (1978). *Integration of severely handicapped students: Toward criteria for implementing and enforcing the integration imperative of P. L. 94-142 and Section 504.* Paper presented at the Bureau of Education for the Handicapped Conference on the Concept of the Least Restrictive Environment, Washington, DC.

Gordon, R. (1977). Special needs of multi-handicapped children under six and their families. In E. Sontag (Ed.), *Educational programming for the severely and profoundly handicapped.* Reston, VA: Council for Exceptional Children, Division on Mental Retardation, pp. 61–71.

Gorham, K. A. (1975). A last generation of parents. *Exceptional Children, 41,* pp. 521–525.

Graliker, B., Fishler, K., & Koch, R. (1962). Teenage reactions to a mentally retarded sibling. *American Journal of Mental Deficiency, 66,* pp. 838–843.

Greer, B. G. (1975). On being the parent of a handicapped child. *Exceptional Children, 41,* p. 519.

Grossman, H. (1977). *A manual on terminology and classification in mental retardation.* Washington, DC: American Association on Mental Deficiency.

Guess, D., & Mulligan, M. (1982). The severely and profoundly handicapped. In E. Meyer (Ed.), *Exceptional children and youth: An introduction* (2nd Edition). Denver, CO: Love.

Heal, L. W., Hanley, J. I., & Novak Amado, A. R. (Eds.). (1988). *Integration of developmentally disabled individuals into the community.* Baltimore, MD: Paul H. Brookes.

Helsel, E. (1978). The Helsel's story of Robin. In A. P. Turnbull & H. R. Turnbull (Eds.), *Parents speak out: View from the other side of the two-way mirror.* Columbus, OH: Merrill.

Hewitt, F. M. & Forness, S. R. (1977). *Education of exceptional learners* (2nd ed.). Boston: Allyn & Bacon.

Hill, B. K., Bruininks, R. H., Lakin, C. K., Hauber, F. A., & McGuire, S. P. (1985). Stability of residential facilities for people who are mentally retarded: 1977–1982. *Mental Retardation, 23,* pp. 108–114.

Hormuth, R P. (1953). Home problems and family care of the mongoloid child. *Quarterly Review of Pediatrics, 8,* pp. 274–280.

Horner, R. H., Meyer, L. H., & Fredericks, H. D. Bud. (Eds.). (1986). *Education of learners with severe handicaps: Exemplary service strategies.* Baltimore, MD: Paul H. Brookes.

Hunter, M. H., Schucman, F., & Friedlander, G. (1975). *The retarded child from birth to five: A multidisciplinary program for the child and family.* New York: John Day.

Jacobson, R. B., & Humphrey, R. A. (1979, December). Families in crisis: Research and theory in child mental retardation, *Social Casework: The Journal of Contemporary Social Work,* Vol. 60, pp. 597–601.

Justice, R. S., O'Conner, C., & Warren, N. (1971). Problems reported by parents of mentally retarded children — Who helps? *American Journal of Mental Deficiency, 75,* pp. 685–691.

Justin, J., & Brown, G. (1977). Definitions of severely handicapped: A survey of state departments of education. *AAESPH Review, 2*(1), pp. 8–14.

Kanner, L. (1953). Parent's feelings about retarded children. *American Journal of Mental Deficiency, 57,* pp. 375–389.

Katz, A. H. (1961). *Parents of the handicapped.* Springfield, IL: Charles C Thomas.

Kenowitz, L. A., Gallagher, J. & Edgar, E. (1977). Generic services for the severely handicapped and their families: What's available? In E. Sontag (Ed.). *Educational programming for the severely and profoundly handicapped.* Reston, VA: Council for Exceptional Children, Division on Mental Retardation, pp. 17–30.

Koegel, R. L., Egel, A. L., & Dunlap, G. (1980). Learning characteristics of autistic children. In W. Sailor, B. Wilcox, & L. Brown (Eds.), *Methods of instruction for severely handicapped students.* Baltimore, MD: Paul H. Brookes, pp. 259–302.

Lehr, D. (1982). Severe multiple handicaps. In E. Meyer (Ed.), *Exceptional children in today's schools: An alternative resource book.* Denver, CO: Love, pp. 453–484.

Liberty, K. A., Haring, N. G., & Martin, M. M. (1981). Teaching new skills to the severely handicapped. *Journal of the Association for the Severely Handicapped, 6*(1), pp. 5–13.

Lillie, D. (1976). An overview to parent programs. In D. Lillie & P. L. Trohanis (Eds.), *Teaching parents to teach.* New York: Walker, pp. 3–15.

Lobato, D., & Barerra, R. D. (1988). Impact of siblings on children with handicaps. In M. Powers (Ed.), *Expanding systems of service delivery for persons with developmental disabilities.* Baltimore, MD: Paul H. Brookes, pp. 43–52.

Lyon, S. R., & Lyon, G. A. (1980). Team functioning and staff development: A role release approach to providing integrated services to severely handicapped students. *Journal of the Association for the Severely Handicapped, 5,* pp. 250–263.

Lyon, S. R., & Lyon, G. A. (1982). Transdisciplinary programming. In E. Meyen (Ed.), *Exceptional children and youth in today's schools: A resource book.* Denver: Love, pp. 555–582.

Matheny, A. P., & Vernick, J. (1969). Parents of the mentally retarded child: Emotionally overwhelmed or informationally deprived? *Journal of Pediatrics, 74,* pp. 953–959.

Matson, B. D. (1977). Involving parents in special education: Did you really reach them? *Education and Training of the Mentally Retarded, 12,* pp. 358–360.

McDonnell, J. J., Wilcox, B., Boles, S. M., & Bellamy, G. T. (1985). Transition issues facing youth with severe disabilities: Parent's perspective.

Journal of the Association for the Severely Handicapped, 1(1), pp. 53–60.

McDonnell, J. J., Wilcox, B., & Boles, S. M. (1986). Do we know enough to plan for transition? A national survey of state agencies responsible for services to persons with severe handicaps. *Journal of the Association for the Severely Handicapped, 11,* pp. 53–60.

Menolascino, F. J., & Egger, M. (1978). *Medical dimensions of mental retardation.* Lincoln: University of Nebraska Press.

Menolascino, F. J., & Pearson, P. H. (1974). *Beyond the limits in services for the severely and profoundly retarded: A crisis model for helping them cope more effectively.* New York: Special Child Publications.

O'Connor, G. (1976). *Home is a good place: A national perspective of community residential facilities for developmentally disabled persons* (Monograph of the American Association on Mental Deficiency, No. 2). Washington, DC: American Association on Mental Deficiency.

O'Dell, S. (1974). Training parents in behavior modification: A review. *Psychological Bulletin, 81,* pp. 418–433.

Odel, S. J., Greer, J. G., & Anderson, R. M. (1976). The family of the severely retarded individual. In R. M. Anderson & J. G. Greer (Eds.), *Educating the severely and profoundly retarded.* Baltimore, MD: University Park Press, pp. 251–262.

Perske, R. *Parent-teacher relationships that go beyond the ordinary.* Unpublished manuscript.

Powers, M. D., & Thorwath Bruey, C. (1988). Treating the family system. In M. Powers (Ed.), *Expanding systems of service delivery for persons with developmental disabilities.* Baltimore, MD: Paul H. Brookes, pp. 17–42.

Roos, P. (1963). Psychological counseling with parents of retarded children. *Mental Retardation, 1,* pp. 345–350.

Roos, P. (1977). A parent's view of what public education should accomplish. In E. Sontag (Ed.), *Educational programming for the severely and profoundly handicapped.* Reston, VA: Council for Exceptional Children, Division on Mental Retardation, pp. 72–83.

Rosen, L. (1955). Selected aspects in the development of the mother's understanding of her mentally retarded child. *American Journal of Mental Deficiency, 59,* pp. 522–528.

Rutter, M. (1978). Diagnosis and definition of childhood autism. *Journal of Autism and Childhood Schizophrenia, 8,* pp. 139–161.

Schalock, R. L. (1985). Comprehensive community services: A plea for interagency collaboration. In R. H. Bruininks & K. C. Lakin (Eds.), *Living and learning in the least restrictive environment.* Baltimore, MD: Paul H. Brookes, pp. 37–63.

Schlesinger, H. S., & Meadow, K. P. (1976). Emotional support for parents.

In D. Lillie & L. Trohanis (Eds.), *Teaching parents to teach.* New York: Walker, pp. 35–47.

Seltzer, G. B. (1983). Systems of classification. In J. L. Matson & T. A. Mulick (Eds.), *Handbook of mental retardation.* New York: Pergamon Press, pp. 143–156.

Semmel, D. S., & Morrissey, P. A. (1981). Serving the unserved and underserved: Can the mandate be extended in an era of limitations? *Exceptional Education Quarterly, 2*(2), pp. 17–26.

Shell, P. M. (1981). Straining the system: Serving low-incidence handicapped children in an urban school district. *Exceptional Education Quarterly, 2*(2), pp. 1–10.

Sontag, E., Burke, P. J., & York, R. (1973). Considerations for serving handicapped in public schools. *Education and Training of the Mentally Retarded, 8,* pp. 20–26.

Sontag, E., Certo, N., & Button, J. (1979). On a distinction between the education of the severely and profoundly handicapped and a doctrine of limitations. *Exceptional Children, 45,* pp. 604–616.

Sontag, E., Smith, J., & Sailor, W. (1977). The severely and profoundly handicapped: Who are they? Where are we? *Journal of Special Education, 11*(1), pp. 5–11.

Stokes, T., & Baer, D. (1977). An implicit technology of generalization. *Journal of Applied Behavior Analysis, 10,* pp. 341–367.

Taichert, L. (1975). Parental denial as a factor in the management of the severely retarded child. *Clinical Pediatrics, 14,* pp. 666–668.

Tizard, J., & Grad, J. C. (1961). *The mentally handicapped and their families.* London: Maudsley Monograph, No. 7.

Turnbull, A. P., & Turnbull, H. R. (Eds.). (1978). *Parents Speak Out: Views from the other side of the two-way mirror.* Columbus, OH: Merrill.

Vincent, L. J., Dodd, N., & Henner, P. J. (1978). Planning and implementing a program of parent involvement. In N. G. Haring & D. D. Bricker (Eds.), *Teaching the severely handicapped* (Vol. 3), Columbus, OH: Special Press.

Wentworth, E. H. (1974). *Listen to your heart: A message to parents of handicapped children.* Boston: Houghton Mifflin.

Wittman, J. (1987, July). In-home support for children with multihandicaps. *TASH Newsletter,* p. 2.

Wolfensberger, W. (1968). Counseling the parents of the retarded. In A. Baumeister (Ed.), *Mental retardation: Appraisal, Education and Rehabilitation.* Chicago: Aldine Publishing Co., pp. 329–400.

Zucman, E. (1982). *Childhood disability in the family.* World Rehabilitation Fund — International Exchange of Information in Rehabilitation, Monograph No. 14, New York.

Zwerling, I. (1954). Initial counseling of parents with mentally retarded children. *Journal of Pediatrics, 44,* pp. 467–479.

CHAPTER TEN

The Family with an Autistic Child

Sandra L. Harris, Mary Jane Gill,
and Michael Alessandri

Sandra L. Harris, Ph.D., is professor of Psychology and Clinical Psychology at Rutgers—The State University of New Jersey. She is chairperson of the Department of Clinical Psychology, Graduate School of Applied and Professional Psychology at Rutgers, and director of the Douglass Developmental Disabilities Center, a university-based program for the treatment of children with autism. She has written many articles and book chapters, and several books on the diagnosis and treatment of autism and on the special needs of the family with an autistic child. She has served on a variety of editorial boards and was an associate editor of Behavior Therapy.

Mary Jane Gill, Ph.D., Eden II Institute, Staten Island, New York. Her research interests are in the area of stress and coping in families with handicapped children and she is the co-author of several chapters in that area. Gill is currently studying the roles of social support and individual characteristics in maternal adaptation to stress.

Michael Alessandri is a Phi Beta Kappa graduate

of the University of Rochester with a B.A. in psychology. He is currently a clinical psychology doctoral student at Rutgers — The State University of New Jersey and a classroom supervisor at the Douglass Developmental Disabilities Center of Rutgers. Alessandri's main interests are in developmental disabilities, particularly the biological determinants of autism.

Case Report: Dan's Family

Frank and Karla J. were in their late 20s when they married. Feeling the press of time, they elected to have their first child a little more than a year later. Although they would have preferred to wait a bit longer, they intended to have several children and feared they should not wait too long to begin. Following a normal, healthy pregnancy and labor they were both delighted with the arrival of their son Dan. Counting his fingers and toes, they exclaimed with joy and relief about his perfection.

Frank, a college professor, took a leave of absence for the first 6 months of Dan's life while Karla worked full time. After that Karla cut her activities as a social worker to 25 hours a week and Frank adjusted his teaching schedule so that he was home with his son when Karla was at the office. Although Frank and Karla had moments of feeling constrained and limited by their son's demands, they also felt considerable pleasure in watching his early development. Life felt hectic but gratifying.

As time progressed, this initial pleasure was displaced by a sense of nagging concern that neither parent was able to articulate fully. Dan seemed to need so little from them. Was it possible for a baby to be too good? Were they failing to stimulate him enough? He seemed content to lie in his crib, gazing at the patterned animals on the wall or staring at his fingers. If they picked him up he grew restless and cranky, seeming to be much happier when left alone.

By the time Dan was 18 months old, his parents' concerns had crystallized. Their son was not talking, seemed quite indifferent to them, and had developed a disconcerting behavior of rocking his body to the exclusion of other activities. His play seemed simple and repetitive in contrast to that of children in the neighborhood, and he avoided other youngsters who approached him. Dan threw tantrums when his parents intruded on his activities, clearly wishing to be left to his own devices.

Karla and Frank sought the advice of their pediatrician. Was Dan not speaking because he was deaf? Could he be mentally retarded? Had they been too busy with their own careers to pay enough attention to him? He looked so normal—what could possibly be wrong with such a sturdy, agile little boy?

It took nearly 6 months and an extensive workup at the local community mental health center before Karla and Frank had the painful answer to their questions. Dan was not deaf, mentally retarded, or suffering from parental neglect. He had infantile autism.

The diagnosis was a stunning blow to Frank and Karla, both of whom reacted in their own way. Karla found the diagnosis hard to accept, and suggested to Frank that they seek other doctors and more evaluations. She was sure Dan's problem could not be autism and found herself impatient with Frank's depression and tears. Gradually, over the course of several months, Karla and Frank began to assimilate the reality of their son's disability and mobilize themselves to respond to his needs. They found a good preschool special education class to provide Dan with the intensive education he needed, and they enrolled in a behavioral parent training workshop to learn how to cope with Dan's behavior problems. In addition, Frank and Karla joined a parent support group in which they could explore their own emotional reactions to their son's diagnosis and its meaning in their lives.

In spite of their effective responses to Dan's disability, a number of issues remained for Frank and Karla. For example, they had wanted to have several children and now worried whether they were likely to produce another child with autism. They also feared what effect Dan's behavior would have on his siblings. In addition, they felt so burdened by Dan's needs that they wondered how they could have more children and still retain the personal time they needed for their own careers and for their marriage. The special school, parent training, and support group helped, but they could not resolve all of the issues raised for their family by their son's disability.

Case Report: Lorna's Family

Lorna J. is 19 years old. Diagnosed as autistic at the age of 36 months, she did not receive placement in a special class until she was 5 years old and was not in an appropriate program for children with autism until she was 7; until that date she had been in a class for severely and profoundly mentally retarded children where her autistic behaviors made her unusual, even among very impaired youngsters.

In spite of her slow educational beginnings Lorna made good progress in school. Although she rarely initiates conversation, she is able to express her needs in simple phrases. Her self-help skills are quite good. Thanks to the efforts of her parents and teachers, she cares for herself fully at the toilet; takes a shower and dresses with minimal supervision; helps set the table, clears the dishes, and loads them in the dishwasher. The profound indifference that characterized Lorna's childhood has given way to a modicum of interpersonal awareness and attachment to her parents, sister, and brother.

Raising Lorna was a challenge to the entire family. Once they recovered from the initial jolt of the diagnosis, her parents found they were largely alone in meeting their daughter's needs. There were few special preschool programs in the community and those that did exist would not accept a child as impaired as Lorna. Her first 2 years of school brought little relief because the classroom in which she was placed was so clearly inappropriate. These early years took a toll on the entire family, demanding considerable reorganization of their home and familiar patterns of interaction.

Life grew a bit easier when Lorna was finally placed in an appropriate class. In this environment she showed that she was capable of learning when a behaviorally based curriculum was in effect. Her parents mastered the management techniques from Lorna's teacher and applied the same principles in helping their daughter learn to care for herself at home. It was the first time they felt truly effective in their role of parents for their little girl.

In spite of these years of progress, a new crisis looms on the threshold for Lorna's family. Her older brother and sister have left home for college and she is the only child at home. Her parents, although deeply committed to their daughter's needs, are also beginning to long for more time to themselves, including opportunities to travel and be together. In general, they are longing to enjoy the good health and resources of their "postparenting" years. Furthermore, they are not convinced that Lorna's remaining at home until they die or are incapacitated is in her best interests. The transition to a group home might be more difficult for her in 20 years when they are gone than now when they can help her make the adjustment.

Her sister was upset about the notion of Lorna moving out of the family home and declared stoutly that she would always care for her sister. Lorna's parents responded that Lorna needed to be free to develop as independent a life as possible. They said they hoped her sister would always oversee her welfare, but it was not in either young woman's best interest that Lorna remain dependent on her sister.

In spite of their firm conviction that the change is best for the entire family, it is a time of turmoil and stress for everyone. Not since the time of their daughter's diagnosis have her parents felt this acutely stressed by their daughter's needs and those of the family.

Case Commentary

We have opened our chapter with two clinical vignettes to share with the reader some of the day-to-day realities that impinge on the families whom we serve. Although personal details of these families were altered to protect their identities, the compelling realities of their lives are unobscured.

Our cases describe two families at different points in the life cycle: Dan is a preschooler and Lorna an adolescent. The specific needs and demands imposed on their families differ as a product of the child's developmental phase and the development of the family as a unit. Nonetheless, it is evident that both families are encountering extraordinary stress created by their child's autism. Understanding these families requires an appreciation of infantile autism and its effects on a child's development; it also requires a sensitivity to the family as a functioning unit with its own history of coping and adaptation.

To know only the symptoms of autism and their treatment, or only the developmental experiences of the family members, would be incomplete – it is through an understanding of the interaction of the child's special needs and the resources and responses of the family as a functioning unit that it becomes possible to assess fully the family and their collective and individual developmental status. Such an understanding is essential if we are to offer effective support or clinical intervention, or be able to address ourselves to meaningful research questions about the family of a child with a severe developmental disorder.

INTRODUCTION

Two basic sets of information are useful in understanding the material to follow in the remainder of this chapter. One set includes the basic diagnostic criteria for autism and the other focuses on the concept of the family life cycle.

Diagnosis of Autism

Infantile autism is a pervasive developmental disorder that begins in the earliest stages of life and typically lasts a lifetime. Autism was first identified by the American child psychiatrist, Leo Kanner (1943), whose initial characterization remains in many respects consistent with current definitions. Perhaps the most important changes in our understanding of autism over the years include the current view that it is biologically rather than emotionally based, and the knowledge that in the majority of cases it is associated with intellectual functioning in the mentally retarded range. Furthermore, the definitions of autism have grown more liberal over time and now encompass a more diverse group of youngsters than Kanner would have included within his diagnosis.

According to the American Psychiatric Association's *Diagnostic and Statistical Manual (DSM-III;* APA, 1980), the criteria for the diagnosis of autism include (a) onset before 30 months of age, (b) a pervasive lack of response to others, (c) gross deficits in the development of language and peculiar patterns of speech in those youngsters who do talk, and (d) bizarre responses to the environment such as self-stimulation and resistance to change. These symptoms must occur in the absence of signs of thought disorder, including hallucinations and delusions, which would suggest a diagnosis of schizophrenia rather than autism.

Another current definition of autism used in the United States was developed by the National Society for Adults and Children with Autism (NSAC; Schopler, 1978). Schopler, Reichler, and Renner (1986) pointed out that the NSAC definition had a goal of shaping social policy along with facilitation of diagnosis. It appears to encompass a larger group of children than the *DSM-III* system and thus may be useful for identifying children who would benefit from the same kind of educational structure as children who fit more traditional criteria for autism.

Regardless of which set of criteria one uses to diagnose the child with autism, it is clear that this pervasive disorder has a dramatic impact on every aspect of the child's life and that of his or her family. A child who cannot speak, whose emotional attachment is limited, and whose behavior is marked by often unmanageable episodes of tantrums, self-injury, self-stimulation, and/or behavioral rigidity will have an inevitable impact on the life of the family. In order to appreciate these effects, it is helpful to consider the child's needs at various developmental points and how these effect the family's movement through its own developmental cycle.

The Family Life Cycle

The concept of the family life cycle is useful for describing the normative, but potentially stressful, transitions through which families move as their children grow up (Carter & McGoldrick, 1980; McCubbin & Figley, 1983). Although for the most part described in terms that reflect the children's maturation, these events are also an integral aspect of adult development and refer to the reciprocal influences of family members.

Examples of major milestones in the family life cycle include the couple's initial marriage and definition of themselves as a unit, the birth of the first child, the children's gradual separation as they start school and enter into a wider world, adolescence, the launching of young adult children, postparenting, and the eventual death of a spouse and one's self. Each of those events demands a response from the family because each involves major shifts in roles and responsibilities. Furthermore, we often respond to different transitions at the same time. For example, a child may be in the midst of adolescence at the same time that grandparents are facing issues of aging and loss. The parents in the middle of these two generations must cope with both sources of change simultaneously.

For the family of the child with autism each of the developmental transitions of the life cycle may be intensified because of the special demands of the child's disability (Wikler, 1986b). As we saw in the case of Dan and his family at the beginning of this chapter, his parents not only had to adapt to the stress inherent in being the parent of a small child but to Dan's diagnosis, unusual behaviors, and lack of emotional response as well. Similarly, Karla's family must cope with the separation process for her two young adult siblings at the same time that they must create the possibility of a similar transition for a child who might otherwise remain dependent on them during the remainder of their lives.

We now examine the impact that the autistic child's special needs has on the family at various phases of the family life cycle. The interaction between the developmental activities of the family as a whole and the child as an individual are considered in terms of the time of diagnosis, early childhood, middle childhood, adolescence, and adulthood. Following that overview, we focus on adaptive and maladaptive responses families make when confronted by their own developmental needs in addition to the special requirements of their child.

INFANCY — THE CRISIS OF DIAGNOSIS

Learning that their child is disabled is one of the most stressful events confronting the family of the child with a serious developmental disorder (Featherstone, 1980; Wikler, 1981; Wikler, Wasow, & Hatfield, 1981). For the parent of the child with Down Syndrome or other disabilities evident from birth, there is an immediate encounter with the reality of the child's disorder; these parents must begin immediately to surrender their dreams about their child's future.

The normal appearance and early development of the child with autism make this process of discovery somewhat different (Waterman, 1982).

As we indicated in the case of Dan at the beginning of this chapter, the parents of an autistic child will typically experience the birth and early months as normal. They are allowed to retain their joyful visions of their child's future. It is only as the child gets older, and does not develop the expected degree of emotional attachment of language and begins to show disconcerting patterns of behavioral rigidity, that the family is confronted by the disability. Furthermore, such confrontation is uneven because distressing symptoms may coexist with seemingly normal responses. These parents experience an ambiguous situation with a prolonged period of conflicting expectations before they receive a definitive diagnosis.

The interval of experiencing the child as normal, and all of the consequent reinforcing cognitions and affect that accompany such an experience, may make the acceptance of the diagnosis even more difficult for these families than for families who are faced with their child's disability from birth (Harris, 1984a). Dan's mother manifested her resistance to changing her vision of Dan by wishing to "shop" for expert opinions about her son's difficulties. Although seeking a second opinion in the case of an ambiguous diagnosis is probably an appropriate response—both in terms of ensuring the accuracy of the information and allowing parents to assimilate slowly the facts about their child's condition—prolonged searching from one expert to another may reflect the difficulty in surrendering one's early dreams for the current reality.

The family brings to the diagnostic crisis all of the resources and all of the limitations that have characterized them in the past. To the extent that they have solved previous transitional demands and established family cohesiveness, adaptability, social supports, and personal capabilities, they will be able to draw on these resources to cope with the present crisis. However, effective coping with the diagnosis does not hinge on the family's personal resources alone. Other factors, such as the data they are given to help them interpret their experience, the facilities available to them in the community, and the way in which the informing clinician helps them deal with the initial news, all contribute to how the family copes (e.g., Abramson, Gravink, Abramson, & Sommers, 1977; Gath, 1978; Shea, 1984).

Although it is realistic to expect that most families will come to terms with their autistic child's diagnosis and will mobilize themselves to provide appropriate resources for their youngster, it is also important to be sensitive to the concept of *chronic sorrow*. Olshansky (1962) described this mourning experience of the parent of the developmentally disabled child as one in which there is never full recovery. Rather, there will be periodic episodes of acute sorrow often triggered by major developmental milestones (Wikler, 1981, 1986b) that reawaken painful feelings of loss.

EARLY CHILDHOOD—MANAGEMENT

Once a family has come to preliminary terms with their child's diagnosis, there are a variety of adaptive responses that will enable them to function effectively as as unit while still meeting the needs of their child.

The child with autism typically requires vast amounts of parental time and energy. This drain on family resources can affect the marital relationship (e.g., DeMyer, 1979) and the individual functioning of family members (e.g., Holroyd, Brown, Wikler, & Simmons, 1975; Holroyd & McArthur, 1976). Perhaps because of the greater difficulties in child management, such stress may be greater for the family with an autistic child than for families of the mentally retarded (e.g., Holroyd & McArthur, 1976). These findings are compatible with Beckman's (1983) observations that handicapped infants who pose more caregiving problems, are less socially responsive, have more difficult temperaments, or display more repetitive behavior create greater maternal stress than do other handicapped infants. Without considerable planning, external support, and effective communication, such needs may overwhelm the functioning of the family as a system, creating a dysfunctional marriage, distressed siblings, and/or individual symptoms of discomfort.

Parent Training

One of the most valuable coping tools for the family of a child with autism is training in the behavioral principles of child management. The self-stimulatory, noncompliant, self-destructive, or aggressive behaviors of the child must be brought under control, and parents must learn how to teach their child myriad adaptive skills such as dressing, bathing, and eating that will be essential to the child's development and integration in the community. A child who continually throws tantrums, bites himself or herself, or pinches and pulls hair can make family life intolerable.

Fortunately, there is an extensive body of research on training parents of children with autism to be effective child managers and language teachers (e.g., Harris, 1983; Howlin, 1981; Koegel, Schreibman, Britten, Burke, & O'Neill, 1982). Well-trained parents can cope with the majority of behavior problems and instructional needs of their child within the home, although ongoing consultation and support is probably essential to maintain these efforts over time (Handleman & Harris, 1986).

Training parents to effectively manage their child's needs is not aimed at the welfare of the child alone, but also is important for creating a sense of parental efficacy, reducing the frequency of aversive parent-child interactions, and creating more free time for family members to enjoy one another (Harris, 1984a; Koegel et al., 1982). Other important forms of support for the family of the young child with autism may include parent discussion groups, sibling groups, and respite care. An appropriate educational placement, however, is probably the single most critical requirement.

Even when a family has access to a full range of community services to meet their child's needs, it is important for the clinician to be sensitive to the additional emotional stress that the family faces as the child enters school and begin what is for other children the normal process of separation from the family.

Although the child's beginning school is doubtless experienced as a significant relief for parents who have had to bear the burden of care alone, there may also be a reintensification of their sense of grief as they once again confront how their child differs from other youngsters. Their child may be picked up in a van to be taken to a special class in a distant community while other youngsters walk a few blocks to the community school. Their child will not come home with stories of new experiences and new friends in kindergarten. In fact, their child may still not speak. Thus, the symbolic event of beginning school, although a transitional event for all families, becomes more painful for the family of the child with autism because it is one more reminder of their child's differences.

MIDDLE CHILDHOOD – THE WIDENING GAP

As their autistic child grows older, parents are faced with the ever-widening gap between their youngster and his or her age peers. When other children of middle childhood are developing ties in the community, finding best friends, showing initiative in exploring their world, and developing an increasing sensitivity to other people's feelings, the child with autism continues to need a great deal of custodial care. Parents who had willingly committed themselves to the tasks of changing diapers, dressing and undressing an infant, may find they have a 10-year-old who is not fully toilet trained, or who resists having to change clothes, or who remains dependent at the dinner table – all of which are sources of increasing burden.

Furthermore, the continued needs of the child with autism have important implications for parents in their own developmental tasks. For example, a woman who planned to take a few years off to devote to full-time childcare may find it difficult to envision being able to return to work because of the autistic child's needs. Similarly, a mother or father may have to pass up an important job opportunity because it would mean moving to another community that does not have adequate resources for autistic children. Such disappointments may stymie personal growth and affect the entire family emotionally and financially.

Siblings may also show the effects of prolonged demand on the resources of the family. Little research has been done on the personal functioning of siblings of children with autism as opposed to siblings of children with other developmental disorders (Lobato, 1983). One recent study found that children with autistic and mentally retarded siblings did not differ from one another on self-report measures (McHale, Sloan, & Simeonsson, 1986). There were nonetheless some siblings for whom the relationships were quite problematic, which suggests that although these youngsters as a group adapt to stress, there are some children who suffer considerable distress. There are some newly emerging data that suggest that siblings of children with autism, especially more impaired children, may themselves be at risk for some symptoms of cognitive dysfunction (e.g., Baird & August, 1985).

There is also research suggesting that siblings of autistic children may fill an effective child management role – they may apply the same basic behavioral principles that are used by parents and teachers (e.g., Colletti & Harris, 1977; Schreibman, O'Neill, & Koegel, 1983). When done with careful respect for the sibling's developmental status and sibling relationship, such involvement may provide the siblings with a vehicle for relating to their brother or sister and may relieve the parents of some small portion of childcare. This freed parental time may then be devoted to the sibling and serve to improve that child's experiences in the family.

ADOLESCENCE – THE END OF ILLUSION

Adolescence, a crucial developmental phenomenon in western culture, is a time of challenge and growth for most families (Ackerman, 1980). During this period the normally developing child grows increasingly autonomous – a normative and inherently stressful transition requiring considerable readjustment in family roles. Families who effectively complete this demanding transition can move on to greater personal independence while still retaining close ties among their members.

In contrast to the family of the normally developing youngster, the family of the autistic adolescent witnesses their child growing older, bigger, and physically mature, but unable to strive for individual autonomy. Thus, the child with autism, although able to acquire useful new skills in an appropriate educational setting, remains grossly different from his or her normal peers (Mesibov, 1983), and continues to require extensive supervision in basic self-care (Harris, 1984b).

Regardless of how forthright professionals are in describing the course of the disorder and the extent to which parents intellectually understand the nature of autism, some parents nonetheless struggle to retain the hope that their child will be restored to normalcy. Although some young children benefit from intensive early intervention (e.g., Lovaas, 1987), for most children the future remains one of continued disability. Thus for most families, this dream of normalcy is difficult to sustain in adolescence (Harris, 1984b); realization of the permanence of the child's disability and the meaning of that for their own lives can be a significant stressor for the family.

As the families of adolescents with autism struggle to reconcile their child's continuing basic needs and their own developmental goals, they may require a great deal of formal and informal support. It is profoundly painful to accept on an emotional as well as intellectual level the fact that their adolescent child will not learn to drive a car, date, or make plans for an independent future. Rather, their adolescent will continue to require substantial caretaking. The needs of the child and the caretaking responsibilities of the parents begin to assume an endless quality (Harris, 1984b) — a reality that demands careful planning as well as emotional acceptance by parents and siblings alike.

Research suggests that during the autistic child's adolescence the parenting role grows more stressful than it was earlier. Parental stress, especially for mothers, has been found to be greater with older as compared to younger autistic children (Bristol, 1984; Holroyd et al., 1975). To make matters worse, although parents of older developmentally disabled children may be in greater need of services than are parents of younger children, they are actually offered less support (Suelzle & Keenan, 1981).

DeMyer (1979) found that although the specific kinds of problems confronted may change, the sheer demands on families do not diminish as the autistic child grows older. Rather, parents of autistic adolescents report numerous problems dealing with psychosexual development, puberty, locating appropriate educational facilities and professional services, fears of perpetual caretaking, financial worries, and distress over the reactions of other people to their autistic youth.

As the autistic child grows up, there is increased risk of isolation for the family because of reduced community acceptance of the older child (Bristol, 1984). This may lead families to essentially remove themselves from community life. Rather than subject themselves to public scrutiny, some families rarely go out for dinner, movies, or on a family vacation (Akerley, 1984). Such avoidance serves to create stagnation in their lives and to intensify the rigidity of existing routines (Harris & Powers, 1984). The resulting lifestyle limits the growth of individual family members (Ackerman, 1980) and the family unit and may induce negative emotions (e.g., resentment, anger, depression) among family members.

Parents of autistic adolescents begin to question whether they will ever be able to escape the demands of the child's disability. They are unable to anticipate the freedom that normally accompanies the end of a child's adolescence. Instead, they see a lifelong, unabating responsibility awaiting them.

ADULTHOOD — SEPARATION AND DEATH

The transition from adolescence into adulthood is exceptionally stressful for parents of autistic individuals. In fact, parents note their developmentally disabled child's twenty-first birthday as second only to diagnosis in degree of stress (Wikler et al., 1981). Issues and concerns that were beginning to take form in adolescence are intensified and become even more salient in adulthood. The issue of separation becomes particularly prominent as parents begin to face their own mortality (Harris, 1984b). The realization that they will not live forever forces parents to deal with very pragmatic concerns: who will care for the child after they die, where will the child live, and how will the child's basic needs be met (Appolloni, 1984; Kotsopoulos & Matathia, 1980). Parents need to prepare carefully for their child's future to ensure that he or she will receive adequate care. This includes locating an appropriate residence (e.g., group home, supervised apartment, home of a sibling) and planning for the child's financial future.

As we saw in the case of Lorna J. at the beginning of this chapter, the decision to place a family member in any out-of-home residence is inherently painful. Although parents desire freedom and recognize that the move is in the best interests of their young person, most parents, like Lorna's, find it extremely stressful to separate from their child. For many families this may be an understandable concern about protecting their most vulnerable member; for others, the reluctance may be tinged by a discomfort about disrupting an adaptive family system. The dependence of the autistic child may have served to stabilize a distant marriage or avoid confronting the issues of the post parenting years (Harris, 1984b).

In spite of their commitment to their adult child with autism, aging parents may lack the physical resources to provide essential care to a person who may be larger and stronger than themselves. The behavior management skills they learned over the years may become increasingly difficult to implement. In addition, their other children will have left home to lead their own lives and will no longer be available to lend a hand as they once may have done. Such changes may press parents to consider alternative means of caretaking. This can initially include an adaptation of behavior management skills to fit parental capabilities; more important, however, it should include the search for alternative placements that are designed to provide the necessary services and care that the parents are no longer able or willing to provide.

In preparation of this eventual separation, parents and educators need to make accurate assessments of the autistic person's independence and functional abilities. The focus should be on enhancing self-help skills (i.e., toileting, eating, dressing, personal hygiene), reducing persistent behavior management problems, and increasing vocational skills (Adams & Sheslow, 1983; Stokes, 1977). All are important to ensure an optimum level of independence (Levy, 1983).

Parents also need to consider estate planning (Appolloni, 1984; Mesibov, 1983). Consultation with an attorney and an accountant who are familiar with the special problems of the developmentally disabled and the various legal options available for the handicapped person's protection is vital (Frolik, 1983). A will drawn up in accord with the laws of one's state helps to ensure that the estate will be disbursed in the best interests of all the family.

COPING RESPONSES – ADAPTIVE AND MALADAPTIVE

As our preceding review of the family life cycle suggests, the family of an autistic child must cope with two sets of demands – those inherent in family living and those created by the child's handicap (Harris, Boyle, Fong, Gill, & Stanger, 1987). Although this dual demand is present for all parents of handicapped children, the parents of autistic children appear particularly vulnerable to severe effects of long-term stress. For example, the families of autistic children report more stress than do families of retarded children, children with other psychiatric problems (Holroyd & McArthur, 1976), or children with chronic illnesses (e.g., Cummings, Bayley, & Rie, 1966). Furthermore, families of autistic children experience more embarrassment and disappointment about their child's handicap than do families of retarded children (Holroyd & McArthur, 1976). These observations are congruent with the finding that the amount of care a handicapped child demands, as well as the child's characteristics, influence the amount of stress experienced by parents (Bristol, 1984; Gallagher, Beckman, & Cross, 1983).

Impact on Mothers and Fathers

The measurable effects of stress are not evenly distributed within the family; mothers of autistic children report more distress than do fathers (Bristol, 1984; Holroyd, 1974). These women describe themselves as unable to pursue personal goals, as having little free time (Holroyd, 1974), and as suffering ambivalence and grief over the amount of time devoted to their autistic child at the expense of the rest of the family (DeMyer, 1979).

The presence of depressive symptoms among mothers of handicapped children is particularly striking (e.g., Cummings et al., 1966; Waisbren, 1980). One study of mothers of autistic and dysphasic children suggested that almost one third of these mothers reported depression associated with the stress of living with their handicapped child (Cox, Rutter, Newman, & Bartak, 1975). Such depressive symptoms do not, however, appear to be linked to the incidence of major depressive disorders (Breslau & Davis, 1986). Rather, mothers of handicapped children appear to experience a number of dysphoric periods, usually associated with significant events in the child's life.

Coping with an Autistic Child

We know that the ambiguity, severity, and duration of a stressor, and the degree to which it places one in a state of noncongruence with community norms, all serve to make coping more difficult (Bristol, 1984). The family with an autistic child encounters precisely this difficult set of circumstances: Having an autistic child is a severe stressor of long duration that sets the family apart from other families in the community. Furthermore, the learning potential and eventual placement of the child are often difficult to assess, creating a situation with a high degree of ambiguity.

Given this high degree of risk for stress effects, it is important to explore how families cope. The existing literature on coping identifies at least two major modes of dealing with stress: instrumental and palliative strategies (Cohen & Lazarus, 1979). Instrumental strategies such as parent education and information programs focus on implementing change directly in persons or the environment. Palliative coping strategies, such as finding alternative modes of satisfaction or being committed to a supporting set of values, are attempts to tolerate and minimize stress through internal mechanisms.

Both instrumental and palliative coping strategies can aid the adaptation of families with autistic children. For example, parent training and information programs are successful in teaching action-oriented instrumental coping strategies (Bristol & Schopler, 1983). Similarly, families using palliative coping strategies, including holding philosophically comforting views of life and searching for satisfaction in other areas of life, cope more easily with the stresses of an autistic child than do families not using these strategies (Bristol & Schopler, 1983).

Gallagher, Cross, and Scharfman (1981) found that parents who successfully adapted to the needs of a handicapped child often took comfort in a set of values congruent with the sacrifices and stress they were experiencing. Families who report finding a "broader meaning" for interpreting a child's condition function better than do families who have not found alternative explanations for their difficulties (Venters, 1982). Bristol (1987) stressed the important role that one's personal definition of a stressor can play in adaptation to crisis.

Several other variables have been associated with successful adaptation to the stresses of living with an autistic child. These include family characteristics such as degree of cohesion, degree of expressiveness, and the presence of active recreation in the family (Bristol, 1984). Families high in commitment to and support for one another more easily accept and cope with the autistic child than do other families (Bristol, 1984). Cohesion and harmony within the family are also conducive to the development of support among members (Mink, 1986; Mink, Nihira, & Myers, 1983). In the individual domain, a high level of self-esteem also appears to serve as a buffer against the effects of stress (Gallagher et al., 1981).

Social Support

It would be valuable in planning intervention programs to know which families of children with autism are at greatest risk for dysfunction. One variable in making that determination may be the presence of social support. Cobb (1976) defined social support as information that leads an individual to believe he or she is cared for, loved, esteemed, valued, and part of a network of mutual communication and obligation. Cobb emphasized the meeting of relational needs, rather than the exchange of goods and services, as the primary feature of supportive relationships.

Social support has a buffering effect in families (Johnson & Sarason, 1978) and has been postulated as a major coping resource for families of handicapped children (Bronfenbrenner, 1979; Byrne & Cunningham, 1985; McCubbin, 1979). Cohen and Wills (1985) emphasized that the perception of the availability of social support may be more critical then the receipt of functional social support.

Social support can be divided into formal and informal. Formal support focuses on resources made available by the professional community, whereas informal support emphasizes the availability of resources from one's family, friends, and neighbors.

Informal Support

Perhaps the most critical element of informal social support in intact families is the degree of marital satisfaction experienced by the mother. Several studies suggest that marital satisfaction or support from the husband to the wife are important predictors of maternal coping with handicapped children (Belsky, 1984; Friedrich, 1979; Friedrich, Wilturner, & Cohen, 1985).

Furthermore, mothers who report adequate support from their spouses also describe happier marriages and fewer symptoms of depression than do those women who view themselves as less supported (Bristol & Schopler, 1983). McKinney and Peterson (1987) found that spouse support was a more powerful predictor of maternal stress than was either diagnosis or type of early intervention.

A series of studies by Bristol (1984) with mothers of autistic children revealed that mothers experiencing the least stress were receiving the greatest support, particularly from their spouses and relatives. The elements of such support include encouragement, assistance, feedback (Gallagher et al., 1981), and pragmatic help in the completion of tasks important in daily life (Wolfensberger, 1967).

Those parents of developmentally disabled children who report lack of sufficient support also describe being poorly understood by others. The development of intimacy and relationship satisfaction is clearly related to feelings of being understood (Harris, Handleman, & Palmer, 1985), the validation of one's self-concept (Schullo & Alperson, 1984), and reciprocal emotional support (Hays, 1985). Yet, it is precisely these elements of relationships that the parents, particularly the mothers, of autistic children report as lacking in relationships with significant others (DeMyer, 1979; Harris et al., 1985; Holroyd, 1974).

The size of informal support networks is another important factor in determining the contribution of these networks to the amelioration of stress. In general, large social networks are associated with more successful coping and adaptation (Hirsch, 1979, 1980; Wilcox, 1981). Families of handicapped children often have smaller informal networks and therefore report more social isolation than do other families (Kazak, 1987; Kazak & Wilcox, 1984; McAndrews, 1976, McAlister, Butler, & Lei, 1973). It may be that the excessive demands placed on the family limit the time and energy that can be devoted to the creation and nurturance of intimacy (Kazak, 1987).

The density of social networks, or the extent to which members of the network know and interact with one another, is also an important factor (Mitchell & Trickett, 1980). Lower density networks are generally associated with reduced stress and more successful adaptation (Hirsch, 1979, 1980; Wilcox, 1981). Families with handicapped children tend to have high density networks, which predisposes them to stress effects (Kazak & Wilcox, 1984).

Formal Support

In addition to a loving family and friends, support from professionals is also important in aiding adaptation to stress. Bristol (1984) found that families of autistic children experiencing minimal amounts of stress received more formal support than did parents reporting high degrees of stress. Formal support services can aid the development of coping strategies and are critical in the mediation of periodic crises (Farran, Metzger, & Sparling, 1986). Professional involvement with the families of autistic children has emphasized the implementation of techniques for relieving parental burdens and bringing about change (Bristol, 1984). In particular, parent training programs have reduced stress by helping parents teach their children functional skills and appropriate behavior (Bristol, 1984; Harris, 1982, 1984). In addition, some programs have introduced parents of handicapped children to others in similar situations. Many parents have reported that these interventions made them more able to accept responsibility and to assess realistically the future of their child (Meadow & Meadow, 1971).

Some formal service programs have also recognized the necessity of helping the family adapt to the child's handicapping condition by establishing a network of support (Bristol, 1985; Harris, 1982, 1983; Harris et al., 1985). Families with autistic children treated with a family systems focus have a significantly lower rate of institutionalizing their autistic children than do other families (Schopler, Mesibov, & Baker, 1982). In addition, therapist sensitivity to family context and structural issues seems to facilitate helping the family cope and helping the child learn (Bristol, 1985; Harris, 1983).

Support and Individual Characteristics

Although social support has been consistently demonstrated to be related to coping ability and psychological well-being, it may not be the causal factor in determining the ability to cope or remain emotionally healthy (Cohen & Wills, 1985). Rather, social support may be correlated with individual or personality variables that are responsible for these observed effects. Social competence, for example, may enable some people to develop strong support networks.

There is some support for this hypothesis in that significant differences in the social skills of persons high and low in social support have been found (Sarason, Sarason, Hacker, & Basham, 1985). In addition, people who describe themselves as low in social support have been evaluated less favorably and as having fewer social skills than were those who report strong social support networks (Sarason et al., 1985). Thus, individuals who receive less social support may be less socially competent to begin with and possess less social skill than individuals high in social support.

Several models of coping and adaptation that incorporate individual variables and the ecological variable of social support have been proposed (e.g., Farran, Metzger, & Sparling, 1986; McCubbin & Patterson, 1983). One model of coping identifies potential personal variables as important in predicting coping ability (Hill, 1949, 1958; McCubbin & Patterson, 1983). This ABCX model of the effect of a stressor (A) emphasizes the role of crisis meeting resources (B) and the definition of the event (C) as important factors in the response of a family to a stressor and the development of a crisis (X). Crisis-meeting resources include formal supports, informal supports, and individual characteristics. The definition of the event refers to the subjective meaning given to the stressor (Wikler, 1986b). Family members may, for example, view the presence of a handicapped child as a challenge that will enable the family to grow. In these families, members become active agents of adaptation.

Hardiness

A recent line of research examining the role of individual factors in moderating the effects of stress has concentrated on the personality attribute known as *hardiness* (Ganellen & Blaney, 1984; Kobasa, 1979). Individuals with hardy personalities are those who remain healthy after experiencing high degrees of stress because of a constellation of characteristics that differentiate them from those who are vulnerable to physical illness and other negative side effects of stress (Ganellen & Blaney, 1984). These characteristics include control, commitment, and challenge. Ganellen and Blaney hypothesized that hardiness serves to reduce effects of life stress both directly, by its adaptive coping style, and indirectly, by the tendency of the individual to seek supportive social contacts. In turn, this social support helps to maintain the adaptive personality style.

Hardiness is especially intriguing as a potential moderator of stress in the parents of autistic children. The dimensions of hardiness—control, challenge, and commitment—have all been proposed as important factors in the reaction to the presence of a handicapped family member and in adaptation to this event. The commitment dimension of hardiness assesses variables similar to palliative coping strategies. The challenge dimension of hardiness is quite similar to the definition of the stressor that has been posited as a crucial factor in the ABCX model of family adaptation. Finally, the control dimension assesses a person's perception of efficacy in coping, which has been shown to be important in the adaptation of these families.

The roles of hardiness and social support in the experience of stress-related symptoms among the mothers of autistic children was recently investigated (Gill, 1987). The perception of available support and hardy attitudes were both correlated with positive coping. Hardiness, however, was a significantly more powerful predictor than was social support of somatic and depressive symptoms in these women. The personal characteristics comprising hardiness, therefore, were shown to be powerful predictors of adaptation to the stress of living with an autistic child.

SUMMARY

We have traced the course of the family life cycle for the family of a child with autism. The chapter has highlighted the interactive effects of the child's disability and the normative transitional events that confront every family. The demands on the family of the child with autism vary with the child's developmental status: Coming to terms with the diagnosis of autism of a preschool child requires different responses than does learning to manage his or her disruptive behaviors or facilitating the autistic young person's movement out of the home in late adolescence or adulthood.

A review of the responsibilities of parenting the child with autism makes clear that it is not simply the lifelong task we suggested earlier. Rather, as one parent said to us recently, "the responsibility extends even beyond the grave." Such demands place extraordinary stress on a family.

Although the specific responses demanded from the family vary according to the child's behavior and the developmental status of the family as a unit, it is important to note that formal and informal social support serve to promote adaptive parenting responses. The personal variable of hardiness may be especially facilitative in coping across the life cycle and offers one possible target for professional intervention in the dysfunctional family. The existing data suggest that when family members are characterized by a high degree of hardiness they may be better able to create an effective network of social support than less hardy individuals.

REFERENCES

Abramson, P. R., Gravink, M. J., Abramson, L. M., & Sommers, D. (1977). Early diagnosis and intervention of retardation: A survey of parental reactions concerning the quality of services rendered. *Mental Retardation, 15,* pp. 28–31.

Ackerman, N. J. (1980). The family with adolescents. In E. A. Carter & M. McGoldrick (Eds.), *The family life cycle: A framework for family therapy.* New York: Gardner Press, pp. 147–169.

Adams, W. V., & Sheslow, D. V. (1983). A developmental perspective of adolescence. In E. Schopler & G. B. Mesibov (Eds.), *Autism in adolescents and adults.* New York: Plenum, pp. 11–36.

Akerley, M. S. (1984). Developmental changes in families. In E. Schopler & G. B. Mesibov (Eds.). *The effects of autism on the family.* New York: Plenum, pp. 85–98.

American Psychiatric Association. (1980). *Diagnostic and statistical manual of mental disorders, III.* Washington, DC: Author.

Appolloni, T. (1984). Who'll help my disabled child when I'm gone? *Academic Therapy, 20,* pp. 109–114.

Baird, T. D., & August, G. J. (1985). Familial heterogeneity in infantile autism. *Journal of Autism and Developmental Disorders, 15,* pp. 315–321.

Beckman, P. J. (1983). Influence of selected child characteristics on stress in families of handicapped infants. *American Journal of Mental Deficiency, 88,* pp. 150–156.

Belsky, J. (1984). The determinants of parenting: A process model. *Child Development, 55,* pp. 83–96.

Breslau, N., & Davis, G. C. (1986). Chronic stress and major depression. *Archives of General Psychiatry, 43,* pp. 309–314.

Bristol, M. M. (1984). Family resources and successful adaptation to autistic children. In E. Schopler & G. B. Mesibov (Eds.), *The effects of autism on the family,* New York: Plenum, pp. 289–310.

Bristol, M. M. (1985). Designing programs for young developmentally disabled children: A family systems approach to autism. *RASE, 6,* pp. 46–53.

Bristol, M. M. (1987). The home care of developmentally disabled children: Empirical support for a model of successful family coping with stress. In S. Landesman-Dwyer & P. Vietze, & M. J. Begab (Eds.), *Living environments and mental retardation.* Washington, DC: Monographs of the American Association of Mental Deficiency, pp. 401–423.

Bristol, M. M., & Schopler, E. (1983). Stress and coping in families of autistic adolescents. In E. Schopler & G. B. Mesibov (Eds.), *Autism in adolescents and adults.* New York: Plenum, pp. 251–278.

Bronfenbrenner, U. (1979). *The ecology of human development.* Cambridge, MA: Harvard University Press.

Byrne, E. A., & Cunningham, C. C. (1985). The effects of mentally retarded children on families: A conceptual review. *Journal of Child Psychology and Psychiatry, 26,* pp. 847–864.

Carter, E. A., & McGoldrick, M. (1980). *The family life cycle. A framework for family therapy.* New York: Gardner Press.

Cobb, S. (1976). Social support as a moderator of life stress. *Psychosomatic Medicine, 38,* pp. 300–314.

Cohen, F., & Lazarus, R. (1979). Coping with the stress of illness. In G. C. Stone, F. Cohen, & N. Adler, (Eds.), *Health psychology: A handbook.* San Francisco: Jossey-Bass.

Cohen, S., & Wills, T. A. (1985). Stress, social support, and the buffering hypothesis. *Psychological Bulletin, 98,* pp. 310–357.

Colletti, G., & Harris, S. L. (1977). Behavior modification in the home: Siblings as behavior modifiers, parents as observers. *Journal of Abnormal Child Psychology, 1,* pp. 21–30.

Cox, A., Rutter, M., Newman, S., & Bartak, L. (1975). A comparative study of infantile autism and specific developmental receptive language disorder: II. Parental characteristics. *British Journal of Psychiatry, 126,* pp. 146–159.

Cummings, S. T., Bayley, H. C., & Rie, H. E. (1966). Effects of the child's deficiency on the mother: A study of mothers of mentally retarded, chronically ill, and neurotic children. *American Journal of Orthopsychiatry, 36,* pp. 595–608.

DeMyer, M. K. (1979). *Parents and children in autism.* New York: Wiley.

Farran, D. C., Metzger, J., & Sparling, J. (1986). Immediate and continuing adaptations in parents of handicapped children: A model and an illustration. In J. J. Gallagher & P. M. Vietze (Eds.), *Families of handicapped persons.* Baltimore: Brooks, pp. 143–156.

Featherstone, H. (1980). *A difference in the family.* New York: Basic Books.

Friedrich, W. N. (1979). Predictors of the coping behavior of mothers of handicapped children. *Journal of Consulting and Clinical Psychology, 47,* pp. 1140–1141.

Friedrich, W. N., Wilturner, L. T., & Cohen, D. S. (1985). Coping resources and parenting retarded children. *American Journal of Mental Deficiency, 90,* pp. 130–139.

Frolik, L. A. (1983). Legal needs. In E. Schopler & G. B. Mesibov (Eds.), *Autism in adolescents and adults.* New York: Plenum, pp. 319–334.

Gallagher, J. J., Beckman, P., & Cross, A. H. (1983). Families of handicapped children: Sources of stress and its amelioration. *Exceptional Children, 50,* pp. 10–19.

Gallagher, J. J., Cross, A., & Scharfman, W. (1981). Parental adaptation to a young handicapped child: The father's role. *Journal of the Division of Early Childhood, 1,* pp. 3–14.

Ganellen, R. J., & Blaney, P. H. (1984). Hardiness and social support as moderators of life stress. *Journal of Personality and Social Psychology, 47,* pp. 156–163.

Gath, A. (1978). *Down's syndrome and the family — The early years.* London: Academic Press.

Gill, M. J. (1987). The effects of social support and hardiness as buffers against stress in mothers of autistic children. Unpublished master's thesis, Rutgers, The State University of New Jersey, Piscataway NJ.

Handleman, J. S., & Harris, S. L. (1986). *Educating the developmentally disabled. Meeting the needs of children and families.* San Diego, CA: College Hill Press.

Harris, S. L. (1982). A family systems approach to behavioral training with parents of autistic children. *Child and Family Behavior Therapy, 4,* pp. 21–35.

Harris, S. L. (1983). *Families of the developmentally disabled: A guide to behavioral intervention.* Elmsford, NY: Pergamon Press.

Harris, S. L. (1984a). The family and the autistic child: A behavioral perspective. *Family Practice, 33,* pp. 127–134.

Harris, S. L. (1984b). The family of the autistic child: A behavioral-systems view. *Clinical Psychology Review, 4,* pp. 227–239.

Harris, S. L., Boyle, T. D., Fong, P., Gill, M. J., & Stanger, C. (in press). Families of developmentally disabled children. In M. L. Wolraich (Ed.). *Advances in developmental and behavioral pediatrics, Vol. VIII.* Greenwich, CT: JAI Press.

Harris, S. L., Handleman, J. S., & Palmer, C. (1985). Parents and grandparents view the autistic child. *Journal of Autism and Developmental Disorders, 15,* pp. 127–137.

Harris, S. L., & Powers, M. D. (1984). Behavior therapists look at the impact of an autistic child on the family system. In E. Schopler & G. B. Mesibov (Eds.). *The effects of autism on the family.* New York: Plenum, pp. 207–224.

Hays, R. B. (1985). A longitudinal study of friendship development. *Journal of Personality and Social Psychology, 48,* pp. 909–924.

Hill, R. (1949). *Families under stress.* New York: Harper & Row.

Hill, R. (1958). Generic features of families under stress. *Social Case Work, 49,* pp. 139–150.

Hirsch, B. (1979). Psychological dimensions of social networks: A multidimensional analysis. *American Journal of Community Psychology, 7,* pp. 263–277.

Hirsch, B. (1980). Natural support systems and coping with major life change. *American Journal of Community Psychology, 8,* pp. 159–172.

Holroyd, J. (1974). The questionnaire on resources and stress: An instrument to measure family response to a handicapped member. *Journal of Community Psychology, 2,* pp. 92–94.

Holroyd, J., Brown, N., Wikler, L., & Simmons, J. (1975). Stress in the families of institutionalized and non-institutionalized autistic children. *Journal of Community Psychology 3,* pp. 26–31.

Holroyd, J., & McArthur, D. (1976). Mental retardation and stress on the parents: A contrast between Down's syndrome and childhood autism. *American Journal of Mental Deficiency, 80,* pp. 431–436.

Howlin, P. A. (1981). The effectiveness of operant language training with autistic children. *Journal of Autism and Developmental Disorders, 11,* pp. 89–105.

Johnson, J. H., & Sarason, I. G. (1978). Life stress, depression, and anxiety: Internal-external control as a moderator variable. *Journal of Psychosomatic Research, 22,* pp. 205–208.

Kanner, L. (1943). Autistic disturbances of affective content. *Nervous Child, 2,* pp. 217–240.

Kazak, A. (1987). Families with disabled children: Stress and social networks in three samples. *Journal of Abnormal Child Psychology, 25,* pp. 137–146.

Kazak, A., & Wilcox, B. (1984). The structure and function of social networks in families with handicapped children. *American Journal of Community Psychology, 12,* pp. 645–661.

Kobasa, S. C. (1979). Stressful life events, personality, and health: An inquiry into hardiness. *Journal of Personality and Social Psychology, 37,* pp. 1–11.

Koegel, R. L., Schreibman, L., Britten, K. R., Burke, J. C., & O'Neill, R. E. (1982). A comparison of parent training to direct child treatment. In R. L. Koegel, A. Rincover, & A. L. Egel (Eds.). *Educating and understanding autistic children.* San Diego, CA: College Hill, pp. 260–279.

Kotsopoulos, S., & Matathia, P. (1980). Worries of parents regarding the future of their mentally retarded adolescent children. *International Journal of Social Psychiatry, 26,* pp. 53–57.

Levy, S. M. (1983). School doesn't last forever; Then what? Some alternatives. In E. Schopler & G. B. Mesibov (Eds.), *Autism in adolescents and adults.* New York: Plenum, pp. 133–148.

Lobato, D. (1983). Siblings of handicapped children: A review. *Journal of Autism and Developmental Disorders, 13,* pp. 347–364.

Lovaas, O. I. (1987). Behavioral treatment and normal educational and intellectual functioning in young autistic children. *Journal of Consulting and Clinical Psychology, 55,* pp. 3–9.

McAlister, R., Butler, E., & Lei, R. (1973). Patterns of social interaction among families of behaviorally retarded children. *Journal of Marriage and the Family, 35,* pp. 93–100.

McAndrews, I. (1976). Children with a handicap and their families. *Child: Care, Health, and Development, 2,* pp. 213–237.

McCubbin, H. (1979). Integrating coping behavior in family stress theory. *Journal of Marriage and the Family, 41,* pp. 237–244.

McCubbin, H. I., & Figley, C. R. (Eds.) (1983). *Stress and the family. Vol. 1. Coping with normative transitions.* New York: Brunner/Mazel.

McCubbin, H., & Patterson, J. (1983). Family stress adaptation: A double

ABCX model of family behavior. In H. I. McCubbin, M. Sussman, & J. Patterson (Eds.), *Social stress and the family: Advances and developments in family stress theory and research*. New York: Haworth Press, pp. 7–73.

McHale, S. M., Sloan, J., & Simmeonsson, R. J. (1986). Sibling relationships of children with autistic, mentally retarded and nonhandicapped brothers and sisters. *Journal of Autism and Developmental Disorders, 16,* pp. 399–413.

McKinney, B., & Peterson, R. A. (1987). Predictors of stress in parents of developmentally disabled children. *Journal of Pediatric Psychology, 12,* pp. 133–150.

Meadow, K., & Meadow, L. (1971). Changing the perceptions for parents of handicapped children. *Exceptional Children, 38,* pp. 21–27.

Mesibov, G. B. (1983). Current perspectives and issues in autism and adolescence. In E. Schopler & G. B. Mesibov (Eds.), *Autism in adolescents and adults*. New York: Plenum, pp. 37–53.

Mink, I. T. (1986). Classification of families with mentally retarded children. In J. J. Gallagher & P. M. Vietze (Eds.), *Families of handicapped persons*. Baltimore: Brooks, pp., 25–44.

Mink, I. T., Nihira, K., & Myers, C. E. (1983). Taxonomy of family life styles: I. Homes with TMR children. *American Journal of Mental Deficiency, 87,* pp. 484–497.

Mitchell, R., & Trickett, Ed. (1980). Social networks as mediators of social support: An analysis of the effects and determinants of social networks. *Community Mental Health Journal, 16,* pp. 27–44.

Olshansky, S. (1962). Chronic sorrow: A response to having a mentally defective child. *Social Casework, 43,* pp. 190–193.

Sarason, B. R., Sarason, I. G., Hacker, A., & Basham, R. B. (1985). Concomitants of social support: Social skills, physical attractiveness, and gender. *Journal of Personality and Social Psychology, 49,* pp. 469–480.

Schopler, E. (1978). Discussion. (National society for autistic children definition of the syndrome of autism). *Journal of Autism and Childhood Schizophrenia, 8,* pp. 167–169.

Schopler, E., Mezibov, G. B., & Baker, A. (1982). Evaluation of treatment for autistic children and their parents. *Journal of the American Academy of Child Psychiatry, 22,* pp. 262–267.

Schopler, E., Reichler, R. J., & Renner, B. R. (1986) *The childhood autism rating scale*. New York: Irvington.

Schreibman, L., O'Neill, R. E., & Koegel, R. L. (1983). Behavioral training for siblings of autistic children. *Journal of Applied Behavior Analysis, 16,* pp. 129–138.

Schullo, S. A., & Alperson, B. L. (1984). Interpersonal phenomenology as a function of sexual orientation, sex, sentiment, and trait categories in long-term dyadic relationships. *Journal of Personality and Social Psychology, 47,* pp. 983–1002.

Shea, V. (1984). Explaining mental retardation and autism to parents. In E. Schopler & G. B. Mesibov (Eds.). *The effects of autism on the family.* New York: Plenum, pp. 265–288.

Stokes, K. S. (1977). Planning for the future of a severely handicapped child. *Journal of Autism and Childhood Schizophrenia, 7,* pp. 287–302.

Suezle, M., & Keenan, V. (1981). Changes in family support networks over the life cycle of mentally retarded persons. *American Journal of Mental Deficiency, 86,* pp. 267–274.

Venters, M. (1982). Familial coping with chronic and severe illness: The case of cystic fibrosis. In H. I. McCubbin (Ed.). *Family stress, coping, and social support.* Springfield IL: C. C. Thomas, pp. 200–239.

Waisbren, S. E. (1980). Parents' reactions after the birth of a developmentally disabled child. *American Journal of Mental Deficiency, 84,* pp. 345–351.

Waterman, J. (1982). Assessment of the family system. In G. Ulrey & S. J. Rogers (Eds.). *Psychological assessment of handicapped infants and young children,* New York: Thieme-Stratton, pp. 172–178.

Wikler, L. (1981). Chronic stress of families of mentally retarded children. *Family Relations, 30,* pp. 281–288.

Wikler, L. M. (1986a). Family stress theory and research on families of children with mental retardation. In J. J. Vietze, (Ed.). *Families of handicapped persons.* Baltimore: Brooks, pp. 167–196.

Wikler, L. M. (1986b). Periodic stresses of families of older mentally retarded children: An exploratory study. *American Journal of Mental Deficiency, 90,* pp. 703–706.

Wikler, L., Wasow, M., & Hatfield, E. (1981). Chronic sorrow revisited: Parent vs. professional depiction of the adjustment of parents of mentally retarded children. *American Journal of Orthopsychiatry, 51,* pp. 63–70.

Wilcox, B. (1981). The role of social support in adjustment to marital disruption: A social network analysis. In B. Gottlieb (Ed.). *Social networks and social support in community mental health.* Beverly Hills: Sage, pp. 97–115.

Wolfensberger, W. (1967). Counseling parents of the retarded. In A. Baumeister (Ed.), *Mental retardation: Appraisal, education, rehabilitation.* Chicago: Aldine, pp. 329–400.

CHAPTER ELEVEN

Pediatric Chronic Illness
Cystic Fibrosis and
Parental Adjustment

Ginny Poole Brinthaupt

*Ginny Poole Brinthaupt, Ph.D., lives in Murfrees-
boro, Tennesee. Her research and clinical interests include health psychology and pediatric chronic illness.
She has presented at national psychology and child
health conferences as well as the most recent international congress on cystic fibrosis.*

Pediatric chronic illness represents a special category of physical disability because it defines children as physiologically, structurally, and/or
psychologically different from their healthy peers (cf., Dunham & Dunham,
1978; Lavigne & Burns, 1981). A distinguishing feature of pediatric chronic
illness is that family members (particularly the parents) play a vital role in
the care and treatment of the ill child (Sargent & Liebman, 1985). In contrast to the case of acute illness, the role of the family is of paramount importance in influencing adjustment to the disease. As noted by Shapiro
(1983), "It is by now clear that an undeniable relationship exists between
family and illness, and that a specific illness both affects and is affected by
the family context" (p. 913). In fact, families seem to experience illness as a
unit. Because a number of stresses — intellectual, emotional, social, and
behavioral — emerge over the course of the disease progression, families frequently require the attention of the mental health professional.

Perhaps one of the most eloquent and moving accounts of life with a chronically ill child appears in Frank DeFord's (1983) book, *Alex: The life of a child*. This book is a father's bittersweet tribute to his daughter who died of cystic fibrosis at eight years of age. In it, he shares the private experience of both himself and his family from the birth of Alexandra until her death. While DeFord provided an intimate glimpse into the poignant issues, emotions, and challenges felt by many families in which a child has a chronic illness, a major benefit of this book was that he increased public awareness about the particular disorder of cystic fibrosis. It has only been in recent years, with increased educational promotions and funding efforts by the Cystic Fibrosis Foundation, that most people, when asked, are at least aware that cystic fibrosis is a genetic disorder most often seen in children. Beyond that, they are hard pressed to provide an accurate description of what the disease entails. This is surprising since cystic fibrosis is the most frequently occurring, lethal, and hereditary disorder among Caucasians.

The goal of this chapter is to review the many issues and challenges shared by parents who have children with pediatric chronic illnesses. As a specialized case of this type of disability, the medical and psychosocial implications of cystic fibrosis will be discussed in depth. An understanding of parental response to cystic fibrosis is critical because of its tremendous effect on the adaptation of both the ill and healthy children involved (cf., Canam, 1986; Cowen et al., 1985; Levison, et al., 1987; Patterson, J. M., 1985; Stewart, 1984). The chapter concludes with a number of recommendations and recurring themes which should be of assistance to professionals working with families affected by cystic fibrosis.

PEDIATRIC CHRONIC ILLNESS: AN INTRODUCTION

With a typical prevalence rate of less than one birth in one thousand, it may not be surprising that chronically ill children and their families are not the target of significant public policy or attention (Perrin, 1985). Upon further examination, however, the cumulative impact of this rate is by no means inconsequential. For example, Gortmaker and Sappenfield (1984) estimate that, taken together, approximately one million children are affected by the more severe chronic illnesses, while another ten million are affected by less severe forms. Extrapolating from the one million severe cases alone, one can speculate that there may be another three million family members who are influenced by the emotional-psychological sequelae of having a loved one with a chronic illness. These stresses include not only the burden of unending health care costs and possible economic ruin, but also the specter of a precarious and unpredictable future which may portend the untimely loss of a child or sib (Perrin, 1985).

Hobbs, Perrin, and Ireys (1985) observe that the national response to children with chronic illnesses has "lagged grievously" in meeting their needs. Pless and Perrin (1985) present three reasons why this status quo should be changed. First, this population comprises an enormous consumer group with respect to total dollars spent on health care. A conservative estimate is that the 1-2 percent of children with severe chronic illnesses are responsible for 30 to 40 percent of the child health dollar in the U.S. (Butler, et al., 1985; Perrin & MacLean, 1988). Second, this population presents unique needs unlikely to be adequately serviced via current or proposed programs designed for healthy children, children with mild chronic or acute illnesses, or children with stable handicapping conditions. Third and finally, because of numerous biomedical advances, children with chronic illnesses who in the recent past may have succumbed to an early death are now surviving to adulthood, often with an increased probability of handicap and/or complexity of treatment (Leventhal & Sabbeth, 1986; Sargent & Liebman, 1985). Indeed, Drotar (1981) has observed that these advances have evolved without concomitant development of the psychosocial resources and support necessary to ensure an equally enhanced quality of life (cf., Stein & Jessop, 1982).

Chronicity and Severity Defined

Research, treatment strategies, and psychosocial services for families of chronically ill children have evolved from two primary orientations. In the first, diseases are studied individually. This specialized approach has resulted in a technological sophistication largely responsible for increases in life expectancy and more efficacious treatment of chronically ill children (Pless & Perrin, 1985). A second approach has been to study the psychosocial implications of certain disease characteristics shared by a range of disorders. These features are helpful for classifying illness and may influence choice of treatment strategies (Pless & Perrin, 1985). Examples of disease characteristics typically investigated include the age of the child at the onset of the disorder, the degree to which the disease course is predictable, the degree to which the condition is visible, and the extent to which the child's mobility is affected (Eiser, 1985; Lavigne & Burns, 1981). For example, the child's age at the onset or diagnosis of the disorder appears to have qualitatively different consequences for his or her adjustment to the condition (Maddison & Raphael, 1971). In general, disorders that are acquired tend to be accompanied by more acute psychological response and adjustment difficulties than congenital disorders, that are more frequently associated with diffuse personality problems (Freeman, 1968; Perrin & Gerrity, 1984). (An important exception, however, may occur in disorders involving major sensory deficits, where adaptation appears less problematic when the condition is acquired rather than congenital, (Perrin & MacLean, 1988).

"Age of onset," disease "chronicity" and "severity" are terms used to circumscribe the impact of particular illnesses. Therefore, in order to understand parental response to the more severe pediatric chronic illnesses, it is important to arrive at some consensus as to the definition of these commonly used terms.

Disease Chronicity   In its most literal sense, a pediatric chronic illness may be defined as a disorder with a protracted course accompanied either by (1) a progressive, possibly fatal end or (2) a relatively normal lifespan with considerable variability in physiological and/or psychological functioning (Mattsson, 1972; Sargent & Liebman, 1985). As a means of contrast, the features of chronic illness become more readily apparent when juxtaposed against those of the "common" diseases of childhood. For example, typical childhood diseases have a self-limiting course of a few hours, days, or perhaps weeks (Hobbs et al., 1985). Even among the more serious and acute of these illnesses (such as pneumonia), proper medical care typically yields convalescence within a month or so. By comparison, most chronic illnesses have a duration of at least several years following onset. In addition, the course of the illness may be quite variable with some disorders showing improvement, some showing deterioration, and some remaining relatively stable (Perrin, 1985). Accounting for these physiological variations, Perrin (1985) has defined pediatric chronic illness as "a condition that interferes with daily functioning for more than three months in a year, causes hospitalization of more than one month in a year, or (at the time of diagnosis) is likely to do either of these" (p. 2). Irrespective of its particular manifestations, chronic disease "defines the child as physiologically different and in need of special and often specialized attention" (Sargent & Liebman, 1985, p. 294).

One distinguishing feature not alluded to by this definition is the fact that most pediatric chronic illnesses are considered treatable but not curable (Johnson, 1985). Indeed, the disease is often "managed" for an extended period of time, typically until the patient's death. Furthermore, in contrast to the care of acute illness, the role of the family—particularly the parents—in the monitoring and treatment of chronic illness becomes paramount (Masters, Cerreto, & Mendlowitz, 1983; Stein & Jessop, 1984). Except for periodic exacerbations of the condition which require medical intervention and supervision, responsibility for the management of the illness ultimately lies with the patient and family (Johnson, 1985; Masters et al., 1983). Obviously, parents must assume full responsibility for the care of the young child; however, as the child ages and the illness progresses, parents and child must continually evaluate, shift, and adapt to new roles and obligations regarding disease management. In this regard, for example, adolescence is clearly a critical time of balancing demands for treatment compliance with the child's need for independence.

Disease Severity Within the rubric of chronic illness, judgments of disease severity are considerably more problematic than those of chronicity. For example, the presenting symptoms of chronically ill children (for example, the blood sugar levels of diabetics) are often a function of compliance to treatment rather than an unbiased indication of physiological severity (Hobbs et al., 1985). In addition, the psychosocial sequelae of a given disease may not be positively correlated with more objective indices of disease severity (e.g., McAnarney, Pless, Satterwhite, & Friedman, 1974). For example, some studies indicate that mildly affected children, especially those relatively normal in appearance, tend to be more maladjusted than those with more severe disease manifestations (Eiser, 1985; Jessop & Stein, 1985; see Chapter 8 by Fewell). Given these considerations, Perrin (1985; Hobbs et al., 1985) proposes five criteria to supplement physiological estimates of severity. While the temporal criteria for Perrin's definition of disease chronicity may be typified by a number of chronic illnesses (including mild manifestations of some disorders), the conjunction of this definition with disease severity attenuates the range of possible disorders considerably. These criteria of severity are:

1. Management of the illness is acquired at a large financial cost to the family. Perrin specifies that in order for diseases to be considered severe according to this criterion, out-of-pocket medical expenses must exceed 10 percent of the family income after taxes.
2. The child's physical development is significantly curtailed. That is, the child's height and weight are considerably below the norm for his or her age group.
3. The child's ability to engage in age-appropriate activities is significantly restricted.
4. The disease significantly contributes to behavioral and psychological maladaptation in the child.
5. Familial disruption (e.g., sibling acting out, marital strain) is rendered more probable by the presence of the disease.

For purposes of this chapter, use of the phrase "chronic illness" refers to those *severe* pediatric chronic illnesses which "interfere in an important and continuing way with the child's physical growth and abilities or with the functioning of the child or family" (Hobbs et al., 1985, p. 35). Diseases prototypic of severe pediatric chronic illness include cystic fibrosis, hemophilia, spina bifida, and muscular dystrophy (Perrin, 1985).

While the two approaches to chronic illness noted above (such as studying diseases individually versus studying the effects of particular disease characteristics) provide valuable information to guide the work of healthcare professionals, there is a recent interest in examining the generic issues shared by these diseases (Perrin & McLean, 1988; Stein & Jessop, 1982). Pless and Perrin (1985) note, for example:

> . . . that there are a limited number of difficulties frequently experienced by many, if not most, families who have a child with a chronic disorder. . . . the difficulties vary only slightly from disorder to disorder or from family to family. If anything, the nature of the family, more than the nature of the disorder, is likely to determine the frequency with which certain problems are experienced (p. 50).

The following section describes the psychosocial stresses frequently encountered by most parents of children with severe chronic illnesses.

Psychosocial Stresses Associated with Pediatric Chronic Illness

The global stresses commonly experienced by parents encountering pediatric chronic illness may be categorized into several types, including intellectual, instrumental, emotional, interpersonal, and existential (cf. Chesler & Barbarin, 1987). These stresses are important for the manner in which they impact upon parents' ability to effectively meet three goals (Johnson, 1985). First, parents are responsible for the supervision and management of their child's illness. Second, they must facilitate the child's healthy psychosocial development while working within the constraints of the illness. Third, they must attempt to achieve these first two tasks with as little disruption as possible to routine family functioning.

Intellectual Stress During the course of almost any physical disorder, there is a point at which parents gradually realize that something is wrong with their child. The pronounced stresses associated with pediatric chronic illness consequently begin during the process of determining an accurate diagnosis of their child's condition. It is not uncommon, particularly in the case of disorders such as cystic fibrosis, for this to be a frustrating process characterized by visits to a number of specialists and subspecialists. A series of misdiagnoses are not unusual before arriving at a correct diagnosis. However, once the diagnosis is in fact confirmed, parents often experience a compelling need for knowledge (Hobbs et al., 1985). Particularly during the early stages of the disease process, their quest for information regarding etiology and possible cures allows for a semblance of control in a very threatening situation. Parents may research both the popular press and medical literature; however, their vulnerability may prompt "doctor shopping" behavior as well as a susceptibility to "quack" treatments (Lavigne & Burns, 1981).

While parents may intuitively seek certain types of information once their child is diagnosed with a chronic illness, various intellectual stresses are imposed upon them at this time. In general, parents are required to integrate vast amounts of data about (1) disease physiology; (2) rationale for, proper administration, and timing of treatments; (3) symptoms of decline; (4) potential complications; and, (5) side effects of treatment. The importance of these demands is apparent. For example, Chesler and Barbarin, in writing about parents of children with cancer, note that "the stress of wondering if they are handling treatments and side effects properly is escalated by the stakes involved—the child's comfort and even life may hang in the balance" (1987, p. 42). In addition, the overriding task of learning the skills necessary to effectively operate within a medical subculture is an intellectual stress not to be underestimated for its difficulty as well as importance.

Instrumental Stress   In addition to the cognitive aspects of dealing with a child's chronic illness, there are also behavioral or instrumental, stresses encountered. These involve the tasks necessary to incorporate the child's routine treatment and medical care into the family lifestyle while simultaneously attempting to maintain as much equilibrium as possible (Eiser, 1985; Lavigne & Burns, 1981; Sargent & Liebman, 1985).

Chesler and Barbarin (1987) have noted that parents function as the "frontline" caregivers of their child and are therefore required to become as proficient as professionals in the routine medical management of the disease. More generally, however, they must be vigilant in ensuring that family members are neglected as little as possible as a result of the illness—neither ill child, siblings, nor spouse. In order to meet these goals, the various instrumental challenges facing parents include pragmatic tasks such as:

1. financial management necessary to cover the expense of treatment;
2. determining how, if in any way, the division of labor and family roles must change in order to assure adequate care for the child;
3. accomplishing household chores despite the time and energy demands in caring for the ill child;

4. learning to recognize the possible deleterious impact of the illness on all family members;
5. knowing when and how to seek assistance in order to negotiate negative reactions to the illness; and,
6. determining how to foster a sense of normalcy despite the bio-psychosocial demands of the illness.

In addition, decisions must be made regarding location of residence and whether or not the family is within reasonable proximity to a treatment facility. Continued access to specialized medical care must be a priority for families of chronically ill children.

Financial demands in pediatric chronic illness. One instrumental stress, noteworthy because of its excessive demands often imposed on families, is that of exorbitant costs associated with care of the child (Johnson, 1985; Leventhal & Sabbeth, 1986; Perrin, 1985). High-cost pediatric chronic illness typically encompasses both direct medical care and routine home-care or self-care expenses (Perrin & Ireys, 1984). Direct medical care involves the gamut of possible inpatient and outpatient services, supplies, and diagnostic procedures. Less easily categorized expenses are those necessary for maintaining the daily, long-term care of the child (including such things as special diets and dietary supplements, transportation costs, long-distance telephone calls to medical personnel, costs associated with time lost from school or work, costs associated with special schooling or tutoring services, and structural and environmental modifications within the home). Although the number and types of direct medical and home-care costs tends to vary between diseases as well as within, nearly all families of chronically ill children must contend with both of these expenses (Pless & Perrin, 1985). However, because third-party payment sources are largely skewed toward reimbursement of medical and surgical services rendered, the full range of childcare costs is rarely covered *in toto*. Remaining debts must therefore be absorbed by the parents or treatment providers (Hobbs et al., 1985). For example, Lansky et al. (1979) have observed that noninsured expenses in the care of pediatric cancer (e.g., travel expenses, food, loss of pay) often amount to 25 percent of parents' weekly income.

It is not difficult to imagine that the stress of endless medical bills, the emotional and physical strain involved in the care of an ill child, and the reluctance of daycare or afterschool facilities to assume responsibility for an ill child may collectively undermine a family's hopes for a stable financial future (Hobbs et al., 1985). Consequently, one parent, usually the mother, often relinquishes a career in order to remain at home to care for the child. Such a decision negates a second income which could help defray noninsured expenses. Likewise, one parent, often the father, may be dissuaded from pursuing more lucrative or personally challenging career options if, for example, such a choice would remove the family from reasonable proximity to a treatment facility (McKeever, 1981).

The financial demand of major medical and home health expenses may also prohibit the use of services and opportunities which could lessen the strain of child care. For example, services that provide emotional relief (such as baby sitting or respite care) or ease the burden of routine care (such as home health support or special transportaton services) may be totally out of reach for some families (Hobbs et al., 1985). Likewise, limited funds may make potentially integrative and restorative family activities (e.g., routine recreational activities or a vacation) seem inaccessible.

Emotional Stress   A third type of stress inevitably experienced by parents of chronically ill children is emotional stress (Piersma, 1985). This stress encompasses both psychogenic factors and reactive sequelae (such as worry, fear, lack of sleep, and loss of energy) which result from the demands of caregiving (Chesler & Barbarin, 1987).

A major factor influencing the range of parental emotional adjustment to a child's chronic illness is uncertainty regarding disease prognosis and the clinical significance of periodic exacerbations (Jessop & Stein, 1985; Perrin & MacLean, 1988; Sargent & Liebman, 1985). A primary reason for the importance of uncertainty is its relation to parents' sense of perceived control. As noted by Wright (1960), uncertainty affects an individual's perceived

> inability to structure his situation in a stable way because at any moment events could shift dangerously beyond his control. . . . Whenever a situation occurs in which the consequences of behavior are seemingly unpredictable or uncontrollable, and in which benefits and harms occur in an apparently inconsistent, fortuitous, or arbitrary manner, insecurity of the deepest sort may be expected (p. 101).

This sentiment is well expressed by a parent of a child with cancer:

> For us, the unknown is much more difficult to deal with. When unknown factors are in our lives, that becomes very stressful. When we can confront these difficulties and resolve them—we work much better. When we see a problem coming, face the problem, and get it over with, resolve it, we can go on living. I don't think any of us deals well with going on for long periods of time with unknown factors (Chesler & Barbarin, 1987, p. 48).

Perrin and MacLean (1988) observe that the rarity of certain child-hood chronic illnesses appears to exacerbate a family's sense of isolation. For example, unless a family is involved in a specialized treatment center for the care of a particular disorder, it is unlikely they will encounter another family with the same condition. This is especially true for less well-known diseases which occur with extremely low frequency. Consequently, "this feel-ing of isolation tends to diminish the sense of control that many families feel they have over the health and welfare of themselves and their children" (p. 20). Perhaps one of the most poignant and heartwrenching experiences parents must endure is that of watching a child suffer and, in many cases, being totally helpless to alleviate that suffering. Certain illnesses, such as cystic fibrosis, are inevitably fatal: Only the timing of death remains un-known. In other illnesses, such as cancer, both the child's prognosis and ex-pected lifespan are more ambiguous, in large part due to advances in medical technology. This ambiguity often heightens parents' emotional dis-tress. Whereas pediatric cancer was once synonymous with acute fatal ill-ness, for example, it is now considered a chronic, life-threatening disease. Consequently, parents have had to shift from adapting to the imminence of death to uncertainty about survival (VanDongen-Melman & Sanders-Woudstra, 1986).

In general, knowledge about an outcome can lead to an increased sense of control and thereby influence parental emotional response to a child's chronic illness (cf. Shapiro, 1983). Expectations of whether or not a child will have a normal lifespan is obviously crucial knowledge in this re-spect (Perrin & MacLean, 1988). For many pediatric chronic illnesses, a heightened vigilance for signs of relapse or disease exacerbation is a com-mon response by parents and can prove both physically and emotionally taxing (Chesler & Barbarin, 1987; Sargent & Liebman, 1985).

In addition to issues of control and uncertainty which determine par-ents' emotional response to chronic illness, grief reactions are common and likewise have an impact. Solnit and Stark (1961) have described a grief proc-ess in parents which follows the birth of a child with a congenital anomaly. They speculate that parental mourning occurs in response to the perceived loss of a healthy child. Until parents work through the grief that accompa-nies disappointment, attachment with the child may be impaired. A pri-mary emotional challenge of parents is that they relinquish certain preconceptions and expectations for the child and learn to accept him or her with whatever disorder is involved (Leventhal & Sabbeth, 1986). While their grief over the loss of an idealized, healthy child generally subsides over time, it has been suggested that feelings of chronic sorrow nonetheless re-main (cf. Olshansky, 1962; Travis, 1976). As noted by Lavigne and Burns (1981): "Unlike the child who dies in childbirth or later, the parent of a living child with . . . a chronic physical disorder faces a daily reminder of their loss[:] a living reminder who requires care and attention" (p. 337). It should be noted, however, that the grieving process is a fairly continuous one, with periodic exacerbations during particularly stressful episodes (such as the child's hospitalization) or during developmental transition periods when the child's difference becomes accentuated (Sargent & Liebman, 1985; Stein & Jessop, 1984).

In general, it is reasonable that parents' ability to work through grief and the numerous other emotions which result from uncertainty in chronic illness will influence their ability to resolve crises throughout the disease process (Leventhal & Sabbeth, 1986).

Interpersonal Stress The crisis of pediatric chronic illness sets the stage for interpersonal stresses involving relations with family, friends, medical personnel, and the community at large. For example, while anecdotal reports have long suggested that a child's chronic illness has a predominantly negative impact on parents' marriage (Sabbeth, 1984), these findings are inconclusive (Masters et al., 1983).

Recent reviews (Kalnins, 1983; Sabbeth & Leventhal, 1984) indicate that divorce rates among parents of chronically ill children are virtually equivalent to those in families with healthy children. However, few studies have attempted to ascertain if there are covert differences in marital intactness which could be related to particular disease stressors or characteristics (Kalnins, 1985; Masters et al., 1983). For example, Begleiter, Burry, and Harris (1976) suggest that risk of genetic recurrence of a disease may function as a moderator of family intactness. They postulate that high-recurrence risk diseases serve as a threat to marital stability. In support of this position, they observe that the incidence of divorce in families in which a child has a nonhereditary illness (e.g., leukemia) or a low-recurrence illness (e.g., spina bifida) is lower than the national average; conversely, the divorce rate in families with a high-recurrence risk illness (e.g., cystic fibrosis) is comparable to the national average. Certainly, while the presence of chronic illness in a child does not preordain a family to dissolution, stressors resulting from the disease are inevitable.

In their review of marital adjustment to chronic illness, Sabbeth and Leventhal (1984) did not find persuasive evidence of divorce rate differences between parents of ill and healthy children, whereas there did appear to be a consistent pattern of marital distress in families of the ill: "We are convinced by the research, albeit imperfect, that parents of chronically ill children experience more marital distress—they express more dissatisfaction, and they argue and disagree more—than other parents; yet, the data do not suggest that these parents tend to become divorced" (p. 767). They caution, however, that little is known about the relationship between marital distress and divorce; furthermore, additional inquiry is needed to clarify the role of marital distress in families of the chronically ill—whether, for example, it is necessarily maladaptive or whether it may at times serve an adaptive function.

Not only must parents contend with interpersonal stresses generated within the marital dyad, but their relationship to their healthy children must be dealt with as well. That healthy brothers and sisters react in profound yet varied ways to chronic illness in a sibling is undeniable (Harder & Bowditch, 1982; see Chapter 7 by Seligman). While a range of behavioral and psychological sequelae are reported to occur, a complex matrix of family and demographic factors have been found to influence the nature and direction of this response. Given the systemic nature of family adjustment to chronic illness, sibling reactions inevitably affects parental functioning and vice versa (cf. Shapiro, 1983). Raising the healthy siblings of a chronically ill child inevitably presents a range of interpersonal challenges for parents (Sabbeth, 1984; Chesler & Barbarin, 1987).

In addition to the stresses generated within the immediate family system, parents must redefine their relationship with the extended family (Seligman & Darling, 1989) and with the large social community through the context of their child's chronic illness. Depending upon the extent to which parents "go public" with their child's diagnosis, they must negotiate a number of potential issues and interactions with the community. These include feelings about burdening others with the medical realities of the disease and its consequent implications for changes in lifestyle, as well as a concern for others' reactions. Parents must determine appropriate standards for the behavior of their ill children when they are with their healthy peers.

Existential Stress   The fifth type of personal stress that accompanies the birth and care of a child with a chronic illness is existential stress. Clearly, pediatric chronic illness, particularly those forms that are life-threatening (such as cancer) or fatal (such as cystic fibrosis), is an affront to an assumed developmental order for the family lifecycle (Spinetta, Swarner, & Sheposh, 1981; Sourkes, 1982). As noted by Stein and Jessop (1984), "childhood is supposed to be a time of well being, or, at worst, a period of self-limited, transitory illness, not a time of threats to viability or function" (p. 194). Inevitably, parents must wrestle with the issue of "why me?" or "why my family?" (cf. Kushner, 1981). Consequently, they must utilize or create an explanatory meaning framework to deal with issues of uncertainty regarding the future for their child. Preconceived notions about God, fate, a "just world" and their implications for personal existence, are often challenged as well (Chesler & Barbarin, 1987).

In studying parental coping with a child's cystic fibrosis, Venters (1981) found that families able to attribute meaning to the child's illness did so from either a religious or medical-scientific life philosophy. "Thus, these previously established approaches to life could be viewed as crisis-meeting resources which for these families reduced the stress of events surrounding their child's illness. Both philosophies provided a predictable explanation of the occurrence of events . . ." (p. 294).

In addition, Venters noted that parental optimism was a personal resource for dealing with existential stress, enabling the family to act with confidence in the present and feel hope for the future. In fact, an ability to endow the child's illness with meaning and a sense of optimism were characteristics of the more highly functioning families in her sample (see also Blotcky, Raczynski, Gurwitch, & Smith, 1984).

While some parents are able to explain their child's illness within the rubric of a particular life philosophy, others respond by altering or abandoning their prior religious-spiritual commitments. Whatever their reaction, it is apparent that existential stresses present a formidable challenge for parents of chronically ill children.

REVIEW OF THE CYSTIC FIBROSIS MEDICAL LITERATURE

Introduction

In order to understand the profound impact of cystic fibrosis (CF) on parental functioning, information regarding the disease process is essential. Perhaps more than other pediatric chronic illnesses, CF is an extremely complex and involved disorder, quite variable in its manifestations. Consequently, knowledge of the disease pathophysiology, symptomatology and treatment leads to a better appreciation of its psychosocial implications for parents.

Description

Cystic fibrosis is a genetic disorder characterized by pervasive dysfunction of the exocrine glands (glands in which secretions are passed through ducts). Perhaps the most serious manifestation of this disease is an increased thickness and stickiness of mucous secretions (e.g., in the lungs and pancreas). While there are varying degrees of organ system involvement in CF, fully manifested cases present with the prototypic triad of chronic pulmonary disease (due to pronounced mucous drainage in air passages), pancreatic enzyme deficiency (due to obstruction of pancreatic ducts), and inordinately high sweat electrolytes (Frank, Park, & Stafford, 1983; Matthews & Drotar, 1984; Taussig, 1984). Cystic fibrosis is an extremely complex, heterogeneous disorder which may present at different ages as primarily a pulmonary, hepatic, pancreatic, elecrtolytic, or reproductive condition (Matthews & Drotar, 1984).

Genetics and Epidemiology of Cystic Fibrosis

Cystic fibrosis is generally recognized as having an autosomal (or, non sex chromosome) recessive mode of transmission. In order for an individual to be born with CF via this means of inheritance, one CF gene must be received from *each* heterozygote parents. Consequently, out of four offspring from parents who are carriers (i.e., having 1 CF gene and 1 normal gene), the probability is that one of the children will receive the CF gene from both parents (and thus have CF), two children will inherit only one CF gene (and thus be carriers), and one will inherit only normal genes and thus be disease-free and not a carrier.

Because of the complexity of the disease and its variability of presentation, estimates regarding the incidence of CF are somewhat imprecise. What is certain, however, is that CF is the most frequently occurring genetic disorder of Caucasians both in the United States and in many European countries. While the frequency of occurrence of the disease is somewhat debatable, most researchers report an incidence of approximately one birth out of every 1600–2000 among North American Caucasians (Littlewood, 1980; Orenstein & Wachnowsky, 1985; Wood, Boat, & Doershuk, 1976). Oddly, the frequency of CF for both Caucasians and non-Caucasians residing outside of North America and Great Britain appears lower. In fact there is evidence of both geographic and ethnic variability in the disease. For example, the incidence of CF has found to range from 1 out of 8000 births among native Swedes (di Sant'Agnese & Davis, 1976) to 1 out of 17,000 among North American blacks (Stern et al, 1976). Cystic fibrosis is virtually non-existant among Orientals (Wright & Morton, 1968).

With regard to North American and European Caucasians, it is generally agreed that 1 out of 20 are *carriers* of the CF gene (Orenstein & Wachnowsky, 1985). This estimate may be extrapolated to include an estimated 12 million individuals in the United States alone (cf. *Whitaker's Almanack,* 1989). Given the fact that there is currently no reliable test for either carrier or antenatal detection of CF, the carrier state is highly undesirable (Lewiston, 1985).

Diagnosis

Significance   In light of its prognostic and genetic implications, the diagnosis of cystic fibrosis is one of the most serious to be offered by a physician (Littlewood, 1980; Rosenstein & Langbaum, 1984). Unfortunately, while the typical patient presents indicative symptoms during the first few weeks or months of life, misdiagnosis and delays are not uncommon (Rosenstein & Langbaum, 1984). This finding is troublesome for a number of reasons, not the least of which is evidence indicating that early diagnosis in conjunction with intensive treatment may prolong survival.

Not only does timely diagnosis take on urgent significance given the potentially life-threatening complications which may arise in untreated patients, but it is also crucial for informed reproductive decisions by parents (Rosenstein & Langbaum, 1984). As noted previously, however, CF may be quite variable in presentation. While most children are diagnosed in the first few years of life, some are diagnosed in later childhood and adolescence, and some, in mildly affected cases, in adulthood. Moreover, it is not uncommon for a patent with symptoms highly suggestive of CF to have gone undetected. In fact, there have been reported cases in which the diagnosis was determined only at postmortem examination.

Medical Criteria   A cardinal feature for the diagnosis of CF, and one of the most consistent laboratory findings in relation to the disease, is a substantially elevated concentration of chloride, sodium, and, to a lesser extent, potassium, in the patient's sweat. This sweat abnormality is evident at birth and persists throughout life.

The most reliable and frequently used procedure to test for sweat electrolyte abnormalities involves the analysis of a substantial amount of sweat induced by electrical stimulation (Gibson and Cooke, 1959). A positive sweat test occurs in approximately 98 percent of patients with CF (Kuzemko & Heeley, 1983; Matthews & Drotar, 1984) and is thus considered "the most important procedure for the diagnosis of cystic fibrosis" (Kuzemko & Heeley, 1983, p. 16). Matthews and Drotar (1984) maintain that the diagnosis of CF requires a positive clinical finding on two of four criteria:

> (1) an elevated sweat chloride level; (2) chronic respiratory disease; (3) pancreatic enzyme deficiency; or, (4) positive family history (cf. Littlewood, 1980).

In general, the diagnosis of CF is based upon indicative clinical features in conjunction with a positive sweat test; however, there are rare cases of CF in which patients have presented primarily with chronic respiratory disease, minimal pancreatic involvement, and normal sweat electrolyte levels.

Pathophysiology, Symptomatology, and Treatment

Pulmonary Involvement   Pulmonary dysfunction is the most significant clinical manifestation of CF, responsible for over 90 percent of patient deaths. This dysfunction is evidently an acquired one, since the lungs of children born with CF appear structurally normal at birth. However, many patients develop respiratory symptoms in the first year of life, most probably precipitated by an inflammatory response to infection. If not controlled, chronic mucous hypersecretion results, and a vicious cycle of infection, mucous overproduction, and lung damage ensues. If this cycle is not interrupted by treatment, life-threatening complications involving both the cardiovascular and respiratory systems will likely occur.

The prevention and treatment of infection and its sequelae is of paramount importance to the longevity of the patient with CF. While there is always a small number of individuals who rapidly decline toward respiratory failure despite aggressive treatment, 80 percent or more of those who follow prescribed treatment regiments should survive to at least 20 years of age and enjoy a good quality of life (Grand et al, 1983). In fact, the median survival age is somewhat greater than 25 years (National Cystic Fibrosis Foundation, 1987).

Symptomatology. One of the earliest signs of respiratory involvement in CF is a persistent dry cough (Kuzemko & Heeley, 1983). As the disease progresses, the patient's respiratory rate increases, breathing becomes more labored and coughing episodes become characterized by gagging, choking, and/or bouts of vomiting. As lung involvement becomes more pronounced with consequent adjustment in rib structure, the patient develops a hyperinflated (or, barrel-shaped) chest. Not uncommon respiratory-related features are finger and toe clubbing,[1] nasal polyps (or, growths), reduced exercise tolerance, and cyanosis.[2] Moreover, pulmonary complications can lead to secondary features such as retarded maturation, evidenced by smaller than average height and weight, and delayed secondary sexual characteristics (Rosenstein & Langbaum, 1984).

Overview to Treatment. Two treatment strategies are employed to delay the progression of pulmonary lesion (Orenstein & Wachnowsky, 1985). These procedures are designed to relieve airway obstruction (via the loosening and removal of bronchial secretions) as well as to control infection (generally via the use of antibiotics).

---

[1]Clubbing refers to growth at the end of the nail, resulting in a decrease in the angle between the skin and the base of the nail where it is embedded. This condition results in the fingers and/or toes appearing rounded or bulbous at the ends. Clubbing is thought to be a consequence of substances involved in pulmonary infection (Harris & Super, 1987).

[2]Cyanosis is the bluish discoloration of the skin—for example, in the lips—due to low levels of oxygen in the blood.

Therapy of Obstruction. Segmental postural drainage and chest physiotherapy are techniques designed to employ gravity for dislodging mucous buildup from various areas of the lung so it can descend to the large central bronchi and trachea for expectoration (Orenstein & Wachnowsky, 1985). This procedure involves placing the patient in several different positions (up to 12) in which the upper or lower body is typically elevated. A physiotherapist (or, most often, the parent) assists the patient by using percussion (hand cupping), vibration procedures (vibratory shaking of the rib cage using both hands), or compression of the chest wall in order to release mucous secretions. Ten to fifteen minutes may be necessary to adequately drain each area. Each treatment session (which focuses on 2–3 lung areas) may last 20–45 minutes. Most individuals will need one to four treatments per day, and sometimes up to six during periods of disease exacerbation.

For individuals who do not have pronounced respiratory pathology, a regular exercise conditioning program is highly recommended in addition to physiotherapy treatments. Trials of such programs (including aerobic activities such as running and swimming) demonstrate physiological gains and improved fitness levels, exercise tolerance, and pulmonary functioning. For example, not only has swimming been found to promote greater respiratory functioning in patients with CF, but it may parallel chest physiotherapy for effective mucous clearance (Zach, Purrer, & Oberwaldner, 1981). Exercise is of importance not only because of improvement in an individual's physiological status, but its normalization effect and contribution to well-being are paramount to an enhanced quality of life. For example, one can only imagine the enhanced pride and self-esteem among three teenagers with CF who recently completed the New York City Marathon (Kvalvik-Stanghelle, 1984).

An adjunctive treatment to the physiotherapies includes various types of nebulization therapy. These aerosol treatments involve direct inhalation of substances designed to loosen mucous secretions or deliver medications such as antibiotics. While short-term benefits have been reported, controlled studies provide mixed results regarding their efficacy. Moreover, these procedures are often complicated, with drug effectiveness varying as a function of factors such as the respiratory status of the patient, type of substance or medication employed, and drug interactions.

Therapy of Infection.   As noted previously, nearly all patients with CF are vulnerable to respiratory invasion and infection by a number of bacteria. Once these bacteria become established, their presence may be reduced but often not entirely eradicated. A comprehensive treatment regimen of physiotherapy, exercise, inhalation therapy, nutrition therapy, and antibiotics probably contributes in an integrative fashion to contain respiratory infections. However, there is nearly unanimous agreement that antibiotic therapy has been of exceptional importance in contributing to an increased lifespan and improved prognosis of patients with CF.

Pancreatic Involvement　One of the primary diagnostic features of CF is a pancreatic enzyme deficiency, caused by obstruction of the pancreatic ducts and acini. This complication occurs in 85–95 percent of all patients with CF (di Sant'Agnese & Davis, 1979) and leads to a loss of fat, bile, nitrogen, protein, certain trace minerals, and other essential vitamins and nutrients (di Sant'Agnese & Hubbard, 1984b). While carbohydrates appear adequately absorbed, it is not uncommon for patients to excrete up to 70 percent of their ingested fat (Forstner et al., 1980). In addition to a pronounced loss of energy, this fat malabsorption leads to a deficiency of liposoluble vitamins (such as A, D, E and K) and essential fatty acids (Chase, Long, & Lavin, 1979; Zentler-Munro, 1983). Less frequent complications due to pancreatic involvement in CF are acute pancreatitis, pancreatic calcifications, glucose intolerance, and diabetes melitus.

Symptomatology.　Steatorrhea, or the frequent passage of odorous, greasy, and bulky stools, is the cardinal feature of pancreatic exocrine insufficiency. In order for steatorrhea to occur, over 90 percent of pancreatic exocrine function must be lost (DiMagno, Malageleda, Go, & Moertel, 1977). Because of its offensive nature, particularly with respect to its accompanying smell, steatorrhea may be socially embarrassing and potentially incapacitating (Zentler-Munro, 1983). Other presenting features associated with steatorrhea are abdominal distension and cramping.

Treatment　Historically, pancreatic exocrine insufficiency has been treated with a high protein, high caloric diet with moderate to low fat restrictions. However, with recent findings of inadequate caloric consumption among patients with CF, restrictions on fat have been revised. This has been necessary since a normal or near-normal fat intake is required to achieve high caloric levels (di Sant'Agnese & Hubbard, 1984b). Consequently, a newly diagnosed patient with CF exhibiting pancreatic exocrine deficiency will typically be encouraged to consume a normal diet with supplemental snacks. Primary indicators of adequate dietary intake are the continued growth of a child and maintenance of an acceptable weight in an adult (di Sant'Agnese & Hubbard, 1984b).

For all patients presenting with pancreatic exocrine deficiency, supplements of pancreatic extracts and liposoluable vitamins are required as part of the nutritional treatment regime. Medium chain triglycerides, essential fatty acid supplements, and iron may be required in some cases. Moreover, for patients who sweat excessively in the summer or who are otherwise physically active, oral salt supplements may be recommended unless contraindicated by cardiac complications.

Gastrointestinal Involvement   Due to the abnormalities of mucousal secretions in CF (i.e., its typically viscous, tenacious, stringy nature), all patients are subject to obstructions in the intestinal tract. Among newborns, the best known of these is meconium ileus, which presents itself in approximately 5–10 percent of CF births (di Sant' Agnese & Hubbard, 1984a; Rosenstein, Langbaum, & Metz, 1982). This condition involves the obstruction of the lumen (or, inner cavity) of the small intestine by grayish, rubbery, putty-like meconium (matter first discharged from the intestines of the newborn). In approximately half of the cases of meconium ileus, complications occur (Dinwiddie, 1983; Mabogunje, Wang, & Mahour, 1982).

Intestinal obstruction may appear at any age in patients with CF. When this presents later in life, it represents one of the most serious diagnostic and therapeutic challenges secondary to pulmonary care (di Sant'Agnese & Davis, 1979; di Sant'Agnese & Hubbard, 1984a). Although there have been some exceptions, it appears highly circumscribed to patients with steatorrhea and/or malabsorption. Consequently, undigested protein and fat seem to serve an etiologic or contributory function in this disorder.

It should be noted that while the conditions discussed above are among the most well-known of gastrointestinal complications of CF, many others occur as well., These range from the gastroesophageal reflux to other obstructive conditions, rectal prolapse, and duodenal ulcers (di Sant'Agnese & Hubbard, 1984a; Zentler-Munro, 1983).

Symptomatology.   Meconium ileus is the failure of a newborn to pass meconium following birth. This is often accompanied by bile-stained vomiting and abdominal distension which, in severe cases, may be present before birth (Dinwiddie, 1983). Similarly, vomiting and distension are symptoms in older patients, in addition to constipation, possible abdominal pain, and anorexia. Intestinal obstruction may be precipitated by the patient's consumption of an unusually large or fatty meal, by dehydration due to increased respiratory activity, or by the accidental omission of pancreatic extracts.

Treatment.   The preferred treatment for gastrointestinal obstructive complications appears to be the contrast enema. However, such treatments must be administered judiciously and continually monitored (i.e., by x-ray) due to risks involved in the procedure (cf. di Sant'Agnese & Hubbard,

1984a). Conservative measures such as improved control of steatorrhea and dietary changes to prevent constipation are recommended as well. In general, noninvasive procedures are the treatment of choice for intestinal obstructions since high mortality due to surgical or respiratory complications is a frequently reported (Zentler-Munro, 1983) though not a universal phenomenon (di Sant'Agnese & Hubbard, 1984a). This is a particular concern among infants, where the postoperative mortality rate is approximately 50 percent for patients with complicated meconium ileus (di Sant'Agnese & Hubbard, 1984a; Santulli, 1980). The postoperative period is an extremely tenuous one for all patients, necessitating comprehensive care such as possible artificial ventilation, nutritional support, and microbiological monitoring and treatment (Dinwiddie, 1983).

Reproductive Involvement   Reproductive difficulties are common in patients with CF. While the reproductive tract is anatomically intact and normal in women, a desiccated cervical mucous functions as a mechanical barrier to sperm and accounts for difficulties in conception (Brugman & Taussig, 1984). Other gynecologic conditions which may impede conception are present as well. A number of women with mild pulmonary involvement have been able to successfully complete viable pregnancies with minimal risk to the infant; however, those with moderate to severe involvement are extremely at risk for both fetal and infant mortality and morbidity (Cohen, di Sant'Agnese, & Friedlander, 1980). Not surprisingly, there appears to be a high positive correlation between postpartum maternal deaths (within six months after delivery) and pregravid pulmonary status (Brugman & Taussig, 1984).

Unlike women, anatomical abnormalities of the reproductive tract are the norm for men. Maldevelopment of the epididymis and seminal vesicles in addition to blockage of the vas deferens leads to aspermia in over 95 percent of men with CF (Davis, 1984; Matthews & Drotar, 1984). However, there have been rare cases of men who have had a normal sperm count and thus able to father children (Taussig, Lobeck, di Sant'Agnese, Ackerman, & Kattwinkel, 1972).

Miscellaneous Involvement   As noted earlier, cystic fibrosis affects nearly all organ systems in either a primary or secondary fashion (Taussig, 1984). It is clear that the systems most markedly vulnerable to the disease process are the respiratory, gastrointestinal, reproductive, and sweat glands. Abnormalities due to secondary causes (resulting from disease complications such as malabsorption and infection) are occasionally found in the skeletal, visual, auditory, skin, and neurological systems. In addition, the kidneys, adrenal, and thyroid glands are periodically involved (Schwartz & Milner, 1984).

PSYCHOSOCIAL ISSUES IN CYSTIC FIBROSIS: PARENTAL ADJUSTMENT

Introduction

The following discussion reviews issues in the home care and management of CF that influence parental response to the disease. First, the medical and psychosocial significance of CF as a disease entity is noted. Second, demands that impact upon parental adjustment are reviewed within the context of three developmental crises in the progression of CF. It should be noted that this developmental framework for understanding the psychosocial impact of CF is intended strictly as a heuristic to examine the challenges and tasks parents encounter throughout the evolution of the disease. The disease crises and substages to be reviewed are not intended as exclusively distinct or self-contained. There is certainly overlap, and some issues remain salient throughout the course of the disease even though they may come to the fore primarily at one time, such as knowledge of the child's impending death. Third and finally, at the end of this section there will be a brief discussion of parental gender differences in terms of role adaptation and emotional response to CF.

Significance

A number of researchers have emphasized the significance of CF due to its high incidence and clinically formidable morbidity. In fact, Lewiston (1985) has described the illness as one of "the most serious, most common, and least understood genetic diseases affecting children" (p. 196). Moreover, because of its inexorable course of progressive deterioration and death, he has characterized CF as "the most cruel genetic disease known" (p. 197).

Given the nature of the disorder and its treatment requirements, there is nearly universal agreement that CF imposes serious challenge for the coping skills and adjustment of the family as a whole, and parents in particular. Profound demands are placed on the family unit; indeed, the psychosocial implications are potentially devastating (Hymovich & Baker, 1985; McCubbin, 1984; Schroder et al., 1988). As noted by Travis (1976), "the child's life depends on nothing less than the family's ability to put him first as long as he lives" (p. 275). Moreover, because of the relationship between treatment compliance and certain aspects of the progression of the disease, parents often feel an inordinate sense of responsibility for the health status of the ill child. This is particularly evident when the child's health deteriorates, with parents frequently assuming guilt for their child's demise. Consequently, care for a child with CF is often an exacting experience for parents.

Three Developmental Crises of Cystic Fibrosis

Bronheim (1978) has suggested that families in which a child has CF encounter three crises — diagnosis, adolescence, and death — which follow the developmental progression of the disease. These crises entail a number of psychological issues and behavioral demands that must be adequately resolved for the successful coping of subsequent stages.

Diagnosis   The first disease crisis revolves around *diagnosis and the initiation of treatment* (Bronheim, 1978). Three rather temporally distinct stages occur within this diagnostic period (cf., McCollum and Gibson, 1970). The *prediagnostic stage,* For example, spans the time between parents' first suspicion that something is awry with their child's health and the determination of a correct diagnosis. As noted previously, inordinate delays and misdiagnoses are not uncommon. Consequently, parents not only incur considerable expense during their repeated attempts to obtain an accurate diagnosis, but their relationship to the ill child may be jeopardized in the process. Not surprisingly, this prediagnostic stage is often characterized by anger, frustration, and increasing mistrust of the medical profession.

Once the diagnosis has been confirmed, parents enter into what has been termed the *confrontational stage* (McCollum & Gibson, 1970). Their reactions are comparable to those of other parents receiving life-threatening or lethal diagnoses for their children (e.g., shock, denial, depression, anxiety). Perhaps one of the primary emotional responses to diagnosis is an acute, anticipatory mourning. During the confrontational stage, parents are presented with the knowledge of their child's impending death. There is some evidence that parents' reactions are more problematic the older the child at the time of diagnosis and the more protracted the pre-diagnostic phase (Burton, 1975).

Bronheim (1978) has noted that parents must integrate a rather mixed valence of messages embedded in the diagnosis of CF: That is, they must reconcile the sentence of a fatal illness in their child with the knowledge that the predictable evolution of the disease may be significantly delayed by complying with a prescribed course of treatment. For some parents, this treatment is an action which affords them a semblance of control. Others, however, do not have that luxury. John Turner, for example, wrote the following prior to his son's death from CF in a neonatal intensive care unit (after already having lost one child recently to the disease): "The last, and, in some ways, the worst of emotion [*sic*] is the utter helplessness at our inability to control circumstances, treatment, and, of course, the eventual outcome" (Turner, 1984, p. 24). Clearly, the issue of control is a fundamental one for parents. The uncertainty associated with CF is a critical feature, psychologically, for parents' adjustment to the disease.

Other problematic reactions may follow the child's diagnosis. For example, parents may feel guilt or a sense of having "hurt" the child, particularly because "damage" derives from a genetic origin (Bronheim, 1978; Mattsson, 1972; Patterson, 1973). Especially in cases where every child born to a couple has CF, it is not unusual for parents to develop a "bad seed" complex, thus generating negative self-perceptions and a sense of inadequacy which intensify an already stressful situation (Sabinga, Friedman, & Huang, 1973). As noted previously, there is some indication that high-recurrence risk genetic disorders may contribute to marital strain or dissolution (cf. Begleiter et al., 1976). In Bywater's (1981) sample of parents of children with CF, for example, four of the five divorced couples attributed the genetic basis of the illness to their breakup. Three of four couples who were unhappily married likewise blamed the disease genetics for their marital difficulties.

The fundamental task for diagnosis and treatment issues becomes most pronounced during the final phase of the diagnostic crisis period. This *long-term adaptational stage* encompasses the post-confrontational period when the family must engage in the lifelong practice of home care (McCollum & Gibson, 1970). The challenge parents face is to responsibly carry out home treatment with a minimum of adverse psychological consequences or disruption to routine family functioning. A corollary to this task is that parents must learn to treat the ill child in as impartial a manner as possible, not yielding to special privilege or exceptional treatment. Such restraint may run counter to their desire to "make up" for having passed on to the child a genetically-based disease, or to overprotect the ill child. Efforts to promote normalcy and neutrality ultimately contribute to the child's ability to grow as a responsible and self-sufficient individual.

Perhaps the most difficult, haunting aspect of CF for parents in the long-term adaptational phase is the prospect of unrelenting care with no guarantee of concomitant long-term survival of their child (Denning & Gluckson, 1984). Not to mention the emotional issues involved, the behavioral (or instrumental) challenge of carrying out day-to-day care is, in itself, "time-consuming, disruptive, and exhausting" (Denning & Gluckson, 1984, p. 462).

> What problems do the parents face? Primarily they are the active managers of the child's treatment program, giving 24-hour care in terms of daily physiotherapy, modifying the diet, ensuring administration of drugs, nebulisers, and the use of a mist tent at night if necessary. Measured in time and energy, the cost is enormous (Stewart, 1984, p. 26).

Problems in the long-term adaptational phase arise when parents are unable to carry out the treatment protocol in a balanced, healthy manner.

Unresolved feelings of denial, anger and/or resentment at the disruption of family life caused by the child's treatment may covertly be expressed via noncompliance or nonreinforcement of the treatment regimen, displacement of anger toward other family members or doctors, or excessive but detached care (e.g., reaction formation) (Bronheim, 1978).

There are several family types considered at risk with respect to successful resolution of the challenges of the long-term adaptational phase. One case occurs when the family has already experienced the death (or deaths) of other siblings due to CF. Consequently, a defensive desire to abandon the child may prompt the family to withdraw from the ill child and invest energies primarily into those who will survive (Bronheim, 1978). Or, more overtly, the previous death of a sib may have been characterized by deterioration despite tireless, faithful adherence to the treatment protocol. In this case, treatment compliance for the remaining ill child may be markedly reduced or ill-enforced by parents. An irregular or haphazard approach to treatment may be justified by parents because of its seeming futility, not to mention the accompanying discomfort and restriction placed upon the child (Denning & Gluckson, 1984).

Lifestyle decisions made during the long-term adaptational phase. There are numerous practical, tangible impositions in dealing with CF which invariably alter the lifestyles of family members. For example, most couples either do not have the opportunity or choose not to pursue dual, fulltime careers. In caring for a child with CF, there needs to be a fulltime income as well as flexible, available supervision and support. Couples must, therefore, determine the preferred allocation of "breadwinning" and "caregiving" responsibilities for each partner. Traditionally, it is the mother who opts to provide medical care for the child while the father bears financial responsibilities (cf. Travis, 1976; or, see the demographic data of Hymovich & Baker, 1985; McCubbin, 1984; Stullenbarger et al., 1987).

The financial expense associated with CF may indeed be staggering. Circa 1980, the Cystic Fibrosis Foundation estimated that disease-related expenses cost a family approximately $10,000 to $12,000 per annum; expenses were considerably higher for those individuals requiring several hospitalizations per year (Lewiston, 1985). Not surprisingly, family savings are frequently limited. Consequently, parents and children often forego luxuries which might otherwise have been affordable.

In addition, there are a number of other considerations which may influence the lifestyles of families in which a child has CF. For example, choice of geographical residence is of utmost importance. Parents must consider proximity and ease of access to a local or regional Cystic Fibrosis

Clinic. Consequently, they may accept lower level career positions in order to reside in a locale close to medical facilities. Furthermore, the demands required in adequately caring for a child with CF may, at times, discourage family participation in leisure and social activities. For example, vacations require extra planning to ensure the availability of medical services if needed and electricity to run equipment (Travis, 1976). Certain medical precautions must be taken for air travel by patients with CF, and it is occasionally prohibitive. Given these and other logistic considerations, vacations may appear to entail too much effort and thus not occur as often desired.

Finally, parents may opt to hire part-time or full-time help to assist with housework responsibilities and/or with postural drainage treatments. Arriving at a satisfactory arrangement may be difficult, however. For example, some parents are extremely solicitous about who they will allow to care for their chronically ill children. Likewise, there are sitters who will refuse to take on the added responsibility, or feel insecure regarding their ability to care for the child or handle a medical emergency. In general, services of a homemaker or health care aide are preferable to outside day care as a means of relieving the mother's load (Travis, 1976).

Adolescence The second major disease crisis which must be dealt with by parents and patient is that of *adolescence* (Bronheim, 1978; McCracken, 1984). Adolescence is an extremely difficult period for those with CF because the manfestations of the disease often make resolution of developmental tasks more difficult. For example, while the ill youth must grapple with the psychosocial issues of independence, identity, and intimacy, the disease often engenders increased dependence (Matthews & Drotar, 1984). As with the previous disease crisis, the task of adolescence, for both child and parents, is to balance strivings for independence with responsible treatment compliance in as minimally disruptive a fashion as possible. If diagnostic and treatment maintenance issues have been adequately confronted and reconciled, then the youth has likely taken on increased responsibility for self-care. Consequently, he or she will have established a foundation to better encounter the challenging issues of independence during adolescence (McCracken, 1984).

As with any chronic illness, the struggles of the child with CF inevitably impact other family members (Johnson, 1985; Levison et al., 1985). For the adolescent patient, one aspect of CF which may seem most painfully pronounced is the physical stigmata of the disease. As an indication of this concern, the human figure drawings of adolescent patients often reflect dissatisfaction with their perceived body image (Boyle et al., 1976; Denning & Gluckson, 1984; Williams & Rosenberg, 1981). In many cases, the ill youth must contend with a thin physique, delayed sexual development, finger and toe clubbing, a barrel-shaped chest, or protuberant abdomen. Moreover, he or she may be embarrassed in the presence of peers because of a cough, uncontrollable flatus, the need to take enzyme supplements with meals and snacks, and the need for expectoration. There may be attempts to avoid using public restrooms because of the offensive nature of stools. In addition, the probable sterility of males and the delayed sexual development of both sexes likely reinforce feelings of inadequacy and/or anxiety in the adolescent which are contraposed against a press toward intimacy and thought regarding future marriage or children (Bronheim, 1978; Norman & Hodson, 1983).

The adolescent's identity is shaped not only by desires regarding a future family, but also by career aspirations. Health professionals encourage individuals with CF to achieve their highest ambitions (Hodson, 1980; Norman & Hodson, 1983); however, these need to be tempered within the constraints of the disease. Likewise, the work sites of patients with CF must be such that there is minimal exposure to infectious agents or irritants that could induce respiratory decline (such as exposure to dust, fumes, severe weather conditions). In general, however, an increasing number of patients are attending college graduate school, and succeeding in their academic endeavors (Norman & Hodson, 1983).

Although certain limitations (such as family and career goals) are usually confronted during adolescence, it is when faced with the death of peers attending the same CF clinic that the existential notion of personal mortality is most keenly felt (cf. Klass, 1988). Particularly when the youth exhibits rather marked deterioration despite faithful adherence to the treatment program, a number of goals must be realistically reappraised. Not surprisingly, patients become increasingly vulnerable to depression, hopelessness, and anger which will, in turn, impact the family unit. Feeling an oppositional impulse against limitation or authority and a desire to engage in activities prohibited by their illness, these youths may engage in "passive suicide" or "death by rebellion" (Hilman, 1973; Meyerowitz & Kaplan, 1973; Sabinga et al., 1973). For example, the patient may refuse to carry out the treatment protocol, eat unwisely, and generally ignore the restrictions necessary to maintain health. This behavior is alarming to the parents and CF team because it can easily prove fatal, especially since it is often precipitated by a decline in health status (Bronheim, 1978). As noted by Denning and Gluckson (1984): "There is probably no other period in the life of a child with CF that so accurately assesses the success or failure of the treatment team's efforts [than adolescence]" (p. 472).

Adequate resolution by parents of the diagnostic crisis will play a crucial role in the resolution of adolescence. For example, if parents have not reconciled their private issues regarding diagnosis (which may manifest, for example, as a failure to fully comply with treatment or openly discuss the implications of the disease), then the youth may feel betrayed and angry, or, conversely, maladaptively supported in dangerous denial of the illness (Bronheim, 1978). Similarly, unresolved guilt and resentment regarding the diagnosis may assume the form of parents' volatile anger and intolerance toward acts of passive suicide. Even when such feelings have essentially been resolved, the family may still be stymied by such helplessness at passive suicide that external help must be sought. In general, the family's ability to reconcile issues stimulated by adolescence will predicate their ability to work through the death of the patient. If the patient does indeed die via passive suicide, the family's guilt and anger must be addressed if adequate mourning is to occur (Bronheim, 1978).

Death

The last disease crisis encountered by families with CF is the *final deterioration and death* of the patient (Bronheim, 1978). While the family's reactions to death are comparable to those of other disease states, CF has unique features as well. Predominant among these is an uncertainty regarding life expectancy, thus making anticipatory mourning problematic at best. Moreover, it is not unusual for a family to encounter multiple episodes of the impending death of the patient, only to have him or her remit (the so-called "Lazarus syndrome," Lloyd-Still & Lloyd-Still, 1983). With each of these episodes the family must confront fears and anxieties regarding the impending loss, and engage in a process of anticipatory grief and emotional divestment (Bronheim, 1978). When the patient recovers, anger, guilt, and confusion may be experienced by both the patient and the family. Each brush with death brings with it the pain of grief as well as potential for relief and release: Remission may consequently be laden with guilt. This roller coaster of emotions is particularly problematic for parents who have not confronted their death wishes and resentments against the child (Bronheim, 1978).

Parents' resolution of issues from the previous disease crises will circumscribe their ability to accept various determinants of their child's death. For example, if parents have been unable to come to terms with their initial guilt regarding the child's genetic condition, they may assume a self-imposed "guilt of the omnipotent" (Bronheim, 1978, p. 336). That is, if they are unable to accept that certain aspects of the disease process are indeed uncontrollable, then they may forever believe they were in some way negligent — that something could have been done to prevent a fatal outcome. Likewise, if they did not arrive at an acceptance of the risks of adolescence while allowing the child some lenience in striving for independence, then they may punish themselves for acts of omission. Or, conversely, they may perceive acts of omission on their child's behalf and thus angrily blame him or her for dying. These issues are especially acute in cases of passive suicide, where intense anger and guilt often obstruct the grieving process.

In the only published attempt to assess the impact of a child's death from CF, Kerner, Harvey, and Lewiston (1979) provided a retrospective, anecdotal review of 16 families from Children's Hospital at Stanford University. The average time of the interview was 2.5 years following the child's death (range: 6 months to 4.75 years). In seven families, either one or both parents admitted to troublesome psychiatric sequelae following the death of their child. These involved either psychiatric consultation to deal with grief, or complaints of sleep disturbance, excessive irritability, or melancholia. The same number of families exhibited "incomplete mourning" as evidenced by maintaining the child's room as a shrine or visiting the child's grave at least weekly for more than six months. The authors suggest that the nature of CF may create a paradox of grief whereby parents usually engage in anticipatory mourning given the realities of the disease, but appear less able to psychologically "surrender the child" (p. 225) once death does occur. Given this finding, provision of psychosocial follow-up care of families appears to be a prudent, integral aspect of CF professional services. Counseling may be necessary to ensure a more adaptive grieving process.

Gender Differences in Parental Response to Cystic Fibrosis

As noted earlier, the need for both extensive supervision of the child with CF and a steady income often results in parents assuming traditional, stereotypic roles: Mothers tend to be the primary caregivers, while fathers are the financial providers. Anecdotally, this pattern manifests in more extreme form as an overprotective mother and withdrawn father (Belmonte & St. Germaine, 1973; Boyle et al., 1976; Falkman, 1977). Either by choice or as a result of feeling excluded, fathers have been typified as both uninvolved in the ill child's physical care as well as aloof and reluctant to discuss their feelings (Burton, 1975; Falkman, 1977; Kulczycki et al., 1973).

Studies investigating parental coping with CF generally reflect this dynamic. For example, Gibson (1986) found that mothers invested significantly more effort toward maintaining family integration and strengthening themselves than did fathers. Similarly, mothers made greater efforts to comprehend the medical situation when the child was diagnosed at a younger age. In general, mothers appear to be more medically sophisticated about CF than fathers (Nolan et al., 1986). However, there is evidence that income and the child's age are positively related to fathers' involvement in health care and consultation with CF staff (McCubbin, 1984). In this same study, fathers with higher levels of income were also more involved in maintaining family integration.

Perhaps because of the physical and emotional demands in monitoring the child, mothers have been found to feel significantly more "worn out" than fathers, whereas fathers appeared more concerned about their child's comfort or happiness (Hymovich & Baker, 1985). Again, because of the potential for overinvolvement with the ill child by the mother and reduced involvement by the fathers, communication problems are frequently reported (Phillips et al., 1985). While there is some indication that outside employment tends to counteract feelings of isolation in the mother, as well as foster balance and support (Boyle et al., 1976; DeWet & Cywes, 1984), this is not always the case (Bywater, 1981).

The impact on fathers of caring for a chronically ill child has not been well documented (Kazak, 1987; see Chapter 6 by Lamb & Meyer, this volume). This is particularly true in the case of CF (DeWet & Cywes, 1984). Nevertheless, research to date suggests that the stresses experienced by mothers are greater than that for fathers, at least as outwardly expressed (Bywater, 1981). As would be expected, however, there is evidence that families are more integrated and highly functioning when both parents are involved in the care of the child with CF (Dushenko, 1981).

DISCUSSION AND RECOMMENDATIONS

Pediatric chronic illness, as a specialized case of physical disability, has profound emotional and psychosocial implications for the adjustment of the ill child and his or her family. Family response to the disease impacts upon medical care, treatment compliance, and, ultimately, patient outcome (Jessop & Stein, 1985; Patterson 1985). Familiarity with issues involved in pediatric chronic illness is important to medical personnel and mental health professionals for several reasons. Primary among these is the fact that a number of biomedical advances, which have dramatically altered the morbidity and mortality of individuals affected by these conditions, allow children with a wide range of chronic illnesses to survive into adolescence and adulthood (Stein & Jessop, 1982). While these advances have prolonged lifespan, they often involve complex treatment that increases risk for serious psychosocial and behavioral difficulties. Consequently, an increasing number of professionals will have contact with families as they attempt to adjust to the demands of chronic illness. Clearly, knowledge of the stresses in pediatric chronic illness, and the normative ways of dealing with these, is an asset in clinical practice (Sargent & Liebman, 1985). Likewise, an understanding of developmental crises in the disease progression, an awareness of adaptive versus maladaptive response, and an identification of families at risk facilitates effective intervention. At the outset, it is imperative that the mental health professional keep abreast of developments in both medical and psychosocial research in order to best fashion direct service efforts.

This chapter has reviewed the major issues affecting parental adjustment to pediatric chronic illness in general, and cystic fibrosis in particular. As noted, there are a number of psychosocial stresses associated with pediatric chronic illness that cross diagnostic bounds. These include intellectual, instrumental, emotional, interpersonal, and existential stresses. They are important for the manner in which they influence parents' ability to effectively incorporate care of the child into the family lifestyle. Cystic fibrosis is a pediatric chronic illness which presents rather unique psychosocial problems for patients and families (Denning & Gluckson, 1984). One framework for understanding these challenges, and for planning intervention strategies, is within the context of developmental crises associated with disease progression.

When a child is diagnosed with CF, it is almost imperative that the child and family be followed by one of the specialized cystic fibrosis centers established in conjunction with the Cystic Fibrosis Foundation (Bronheim, 1978). Such involvement insures both comprehensive medical as well as psychosocial care for families. For parents, the diagnosis of CF in their child, and the implications of an abbreviated lifespan are accompanied by emotional upheaval. Because parents' affective response to diagnosis may impede their retention of accurate information about the disease and/or selectively bias what information is in fact retained, physicians often recommend an initial hospitalization. This practice serves several functions. First it allows for the disease to be brought under control and the patient's response to different therapeutic modalities to be carefully monitored. Second, parents (and the child, if old enough) are able to slowly integrate knowledge about the disease and practice, with the CF professional team, the components of the treatment regimen they must employ at home. This process helps alleviate fears about the disease as well as establish an effective prophylactic medical home care program (Matthews & Drotar, 1984). Finally, an indoctrination period allows for a positive rapport and good working relationship to develop between the patient/parent and professional CF team (Denning & Gluckson, 1984), which is an essential ingredient for slowing the progression of the disease (Matthews & Drotar, 1984).

At the time of diagnosis, support groups for parents are sometimes recommended so parents may meet others encountering the same issues and difficulties, and share coping strategies and tips for incorporating treatment into routine daily functioning. However, there are some individuals for whom such groups may be counterprodutive (e.g., parents undergoing other major life stressors, cf. Bywater, 1984). Moreover, while groups may be beneficial in providing a sense of universality and support, many families need individualized attention to address idiosyncratic response to the disease (Bronheim, 1978). For example, short-term individual sessions that have an educational or psychotherapeutic focus may be offered. Or, particularly as the disease progresses, family therapy is often the treatment of choice for addressing communication difficulties or dysfunctional patterns of interaction. It is crucial, however, that marital sessions are available to parents so they may address their unique needs, emotional response to the illness and child care, and difficulties in coping (Bronheim, 1978). In general, support for the parents during the diagnostic stage should be available on both an informal as well as formal basis.

As the child with CF reaches adolescence, a number of practitioners recommend that he or she be seen at the Clinic for routine medical checkup without the parents present. Following the history and examination, and after the child's questions have been addressed, parents are invited into the office for further discussion and recommendations by the physician or team (Denning & Gluckson, 1984). It is essential that enough time is afforded parents so they do not feel left out in this process. The goal of this procedure is to transfer responsibility of care from the parents to the patient and thereby offset some of the difficulties which arise around issues of dependence and independence during adolescence.

Similarly, support groups appear to be a particularly effective intervention modality with adolescent patients (Lippincott, Wery, & Stone, 1988). These groups serve several functions. Not only are developmental issues in the context of school, peer relations, and career planning discussed, but difficulties and suggestions regarding medical care are reviewed as well. There is evidence that these peer adolescent groups do in fact facilitate treatment compliance, promote an openness to optional treatments, and solidify relationships and improve communication with the treatment team (cf. Lippincott et al., 1988).

In the last stage of the disease progression, such as the patient's final deterioration and death, psychosocial support must be available to the child and the family on both a formal and informal basis. It is imperative that the child's physician and CF team social worker and/or psychologist be available for consistent, frequent contact with the family during this difficult time. Not surprisingly, the collective features of the relationship between the family and CF team will manifest themselves during the patient's death (Barbero, 1973). Beyond the medical staff's attempt to make the child as comfortable as possible, the primary goals at this time are to provide compassionate, supportive care for all involved (see Barbero, 1973, for a detailed review of pertinent issues). After the patient's death, a time should be scheduled for followup of the parents (and/or siblings). As noted earlier in this review (cf. Kerner et al., 1979), difficulties in mourning often occur following the death of a child with CF. Moreover, after some time has passed from the child's death, parents often experience a number of emotional "aftershocks" and self-doubts regarding their care for the child. These need to be addressed for adequate resolution of their grief. Likewise, siblings are also at risk and need evaluation and support at this time (Bronheim, 1978).

In addition to the "developmental" issues that arise during the progression of the disease, there are a number of themes that are pertinent at any time during a family's care for a child with CF. For example, fathers' involvement in family life, care of the ill child, participation in general childrearing, and support of their wives appears crucial to the successful psychosocial adaptation of the family (cf. Allen, Townley, & Phelan, 1974; McCubbin et al., 1983; McCubbin, 1984). As previously noted, since mothers often assume the majority of responsibility for home treatment of the child, a coalition may develop with fathers functioning primarily on the periphery of the family unit. Health professionals should be aware of this pattern, and assess the way in which it may manifest in individual families. The roles of all family members need to be assessed, with possible recommendations for change. In addition, it is important for mothers to cultivate interests (whether for work or recreation) outside of the home. This not only allows her some time for personal revitalization, but also discourages an overly dependent relationship with the child (e.g., Boyle et al., 1976).

In general, a family-centered perspective is essential for professionals working with pediatric chronic illness. The ill child, healthy siblings, and parents all have needs and issues that must be monitored and addressed individually as well as in the family context. There should be a focus on quality of life, a balanced approach to treatment and caregiving, and participation, by all family members, in personally restorative activities. An overriding goal for the health professional is to facilitate in families the ability to successfully manage the disease while promoting the growth and development of all involved (cf. Sargent & Liebman, 1985). With regard to any direct service contact being considered, however, it is imperative that the family be involved in the decision-making process with the physician and mental health consultant (Matthews & Drotar, 1984). For some families, both denial and resistance to psychosocial support and/or intervention may be quite strong, and therefore, should be handled sensitively and collaboratively with the family.

One way to provide a forum that may be less threatening for some parents (and thereby promote a greater willingness for professional dialogue) is with the "panel discussion group" (Miller, 1988). Panel participants include representative parents, patients, siblings, physicians, and other medical personnel. The audience is likewise comprised of both lay and professional persons. Issues discussed may include such things as difficulties which arise in compliance and carrying out the treatment regimen, coping with hospitalizations, parenting issues, response by siblings to an ill brother or sister, and patient-parent-staff relationships. Miller suggests that these panel discussions facilitate greater dialogue among professional staff and families; provides a rather structured format for the exploration of emotional as well as intellectual issues; an increased understanding of the stresses inherent in dealing with CF and alternatives for coping with these; and, the experience of universality.

As noted earlier, a family's involvement with a Cystic Fibrosis Clinic staffed by a multidisciplinary team (including physicians, respiratory therapists, nurses, nutritionists, social workers, and/or psychologists or psychiatrists) is essential for comprehensive care throughout the course of the illness. The mental health professional works to promote an enhanced quality of life for the patient and family affected by CF. Particularly for those who are members of the CF team, this role may assume multiple dimensions and capacities (such as inpatient and outpatient contact, community services, Miller, 1988). Clearly, mobility and ability to improvise are essential for making available the full ranges of services to families.

In summary, the mental health professional may contribute in a number of ways to the psychosocial adjustment of the family. This may take the form of direct service such as psychotherapy and counseling, or more indirectly through informal support. Educational services, such as clarifying misconceptions regarding the genetics and reproductive risks in CF, are also essential. The mental health professional may employ behavioral and stress management techniques for patients (e.g., Spirito, Russo, & Masek, 1984); monitor the coping of ill child, parents, and healthy siblings; and, provide marital or family therapy in cases of dysfunction (e.g., enmeshment) and/or difficulties in communication. Families at risk (such as single parents, families with an older CF member, those on limited income, those who have already lost one child to CF; cf, McCubbin et al., 1983) should be monitored as well.

In conclusion, it is unquestionable that cystic fibrosis presents numerous and major challenges for family adjustment. However, the future for these families is becoming increasingly optimistic. In the last few years, major breakthroughs have occurred in genetic research for this disease (Buchwald, Tsui, & Riordan, 1988). Similarly, research on the psychosocial sequelae of CF has become increasingly sophisticated (cf. Mrazek, 1985). Such work promotes a greater understanding of the family dynamics in CF, and provides clues for targeting individuals at risk for maladjustment as well as for the design of appropriate intervention strategies. In this way, the quality of life for families affected by CF continues to improve.

REFERENCES

Allan, J. L., Townley, R. R. W., & Phelan, P. D. (1974). Family response to cystic fibrosis. *Australian Pediatric Journal, 10,* pp. 136–146.

Barbero, G. J. (1973). The child, parent and doctor in death from chronic disease. In P. R. Patterson, C. R. Denning, & A. H. Kutscher (Eds.), *Psychosocial aspects of cystic fibrosis.* New York: Columbia University Press, pp. 76–83.

Begleiter, M. L., Burry, Y. F., & Harris, D. J. (1976). Prevalence of divorce among parents of children with cystic fibrosis and chronic diseases. *Social Biology, 23,* pp. 260–264.

Belmonte, M. M., & St. Germain, Y. (1973). Psychosocial aspects of the cystic fibrosis family. In P. R. Patterson, C. R. Denning, & A. H. Kutscher (eds.), *Psychosocial aspects of cystic fibrosis.* New York: Columbia University Press, pp. 84–92.

Blotcky, A. D., Raczynski, J. M., Gurwitch, R., & Smith, K. (1985). Family influences on hopelessness among children early in the cancer experience. *Journal of Pediatric Psychology 10(4),* pp. 479–493.

Boyle, I. R., di Sant'Agnese, P. A., Sack, S., Millican, F., & Kulczycki, L. L. (1976). Emotional adjustment of adolescents and young adults with cystic fibrosis. *Journal of Pediatrics, 88*(2), pp. 318–326.

Bronheim, S. P. (1978). Pulmonary disorders: Asthma and cystic fibrosis. In P. R. Magrab (Ed.), *Psychological management of pediatric problems (Vol. I): Early life conditions and chronic diseases.* Baltimore: University Park Press, pp. 310–344.

Brugman, S. M., & Taussig, L. M. (1984). The reproductive system. In L. Taussig (Ed.), *Cystic fibrosis.* New York: Thieme-Stratton, Inc., pp. 323–337.

Buchwald, M., Tsui, L. C., & Riordan, J. R. (1988, March). *The genetics of cystic fibrosis—mid 1987.* Paper presented at the Tenth International Cystic Fibrosis Congress, Sydney, Australia.

Burton, L. (1975). *The family life of sick children: A study of families coping with chronic disease.* London: Routledge & Kegan Paul.

Butler, J., Budetti, P., McManus, M. A., Stenmark, S., & Newacheck, P. W. (1985). Health care expenditures for children with chronic illnesses. In N. Hobbs & J. M. Perrin (Eds.), *Issues in the care of children with chronic illness: A sourcebook on problems, services, and policies.* San Francisco: Jossey-Bass, pp. 827–863.

Bywater, E. M. (1981). Adolescents with cystic fibrosis: Psychosocial adjustment. *Archives of Disease in Childhood, 56,* pp. 538–543.

Bywater, E. M. (1984). Coping with a life-threatening illness: An experiment in parents' groups. *British Journal of Social Work, 14,* pp. 117–127.

Canam, C. (1986). Talking about cystic fibrosis within the family: What parents need to know. *Issues in Comprehensive Pediatric Nursing, 9,* pp. 167–178.

Chase, H. P., Long, M. A., & Lavin, M. H. (1979). Cystic fibrosis and malnutrition. *Journal of Pediatrics, 95,* pp. 337–347.

Chesler, M. A., & Barbarin, O. A. (1987). *Childhood cancer and the family.* New York: Brunner/Mazel.

Cohen, L. F., di Sant'Agnese, P. A., & Friedlander, J. (1980). Cystic fibrosis and pregnancy: A national survey. *Lancet, 2,* pp. 842–844.

Cowen, L., Corey, M., Keenan, N., Simmons, R., Arndt, E., & Levison, H. (1985). Family adaptation and psychosocial adjustment to cystic fibrosis in the preschool child. *Social Science and Medicine, 20,* pp. 553–560.

Davis, P. B. (1984). Cystic fibrosis in adults. In L. Taussig (Ed.), *Cystic fibrosis.* New York: Thieme-Stratton, Inc., pp. 408–433.

DeFord, F. (1983). *Alex: The life of a child.* New York: Signet.

Denning, C. R., & Gluckson, M. M. (1984). Psychosocial aspects of cystic fibrosis. In L. Taussig (Ed.), *Cystic fibrosis.* New York: Thieme-Stratton, Inc., pp. 461–492.

DeWet, B., & Cywes, S. (1984). The psychosocial impact of cystic fibrosis. *South African Medical Journal, 65,* pp. 526–530.

DiMagno, E. P., Malagelada, J. R., Go, V. L. M., & Moertel, C. G. (1977). Fate of orally ingested enzymes in pancreatic insufficiency: Comparison of two dosage schedules. *New England Journal of Medicine, 296,* pp. 1318–1322.

Dinwiddie, R. (1983). The management of the first year of life. In M. E. Hodson, A. P. Norman, & J. C. Batten (Eds), *Cystic fibrosis.* London: Bailliere Tindall, pp. 197–208.

di Sant'Agnese, P. A., & Davis, P. B. (1976). Research in cystic fibrosis (first of three parts). *New England Journal of Medicine, 295(9),* pp. 481–485.

di Sant'Agnese, P. A., & Davis, P. B. (1979). Cystic fibrosis in adults: 75 cases and a review of 232 cases in the literature. *American Journal of Medicine, 66,* pp. 121–132.

di Sant'Agnese, P. A., & Hubbard, V. S. (1984a). The gastrointestinal tract. In L. Taussig (Ed.), *Cystic fibrosis.* New York: Thieme-Stratton, Inc., pp. 212–229.

di Sant'Agnese, P. A., & Hubbard, V. S. (1984b). The pancreas. In L. Taussig (Ed.), *Cystic fibrosis.* New York: Thieme-Stratton, Inc., pp. 230–295.

Drotar, D. (1981). Psychological perspectives of chronic childhood illness. *Journal of Pediatric Psychology, 6(3),* pp. 211–228.

Dunham, J. R., & Dunham, C. S. (1978). Psychosocial aspects of disability.

In R. M. Goldenson, J. R. Dunham, & C. S. Dunham (Eds.), *Disability and rehabilitation handbook*. New York: McGraw-Hill, pp. 12–20.

Dushenko, T. W. (1981). Cystic fibrosis: A medical overview and critique of the psychological literature. *Social Science and Medicine, 15E,* pp. 43–56.

Eiser, C. (1985). *The psychology of childhood illness*. New York: Springer-Verlag.

Falkman, C. (1977). Cystic fibrosis: A study of 52 children and their families. *Acta Paediatrika Scandinavia (Supplement), 269,* pp. 7–93.

Forstner, G., Gall, G., Corey, M., Durie, P., Hill, R., & Gaskin, K. (1980). Digestion and absorption of nutrients in cystic fibrosis. In J. M. Sturgess (Ed.), *Perspectives in cystic fibrosis*. Toronto: Imperial Press, pp. 137–148.

Freeman, R. D. (1968). Emotional reactions of handicapped children. In S. Chess & A. Thomas (Eds.), *Annual Progress in Child Psychiatry and Child Development*. New York: Brunner/ Mazel, pp. 379–395.

Gibson, C. H. (1986). How parents cope with a child with cystic fibrosis. *Nursing Papers, 18(3),* pp. 31–45.

Gibson, L. E., & Cooke, R. E. (1959). A test for concentration of electrolytes in sweat in cystic fibrosis of the pancreas utilizing pilocarine by iontophoresis. *Pediatrics, 23,* pp. 545–549.

Gortmaker, S., & Sappenfield, W. (1984). Chronic childhood disorders: prevalence and impact. *Pediatric Clinics of North America, 31,* pp. 3–18.

Grand, R. J., Park, R. W., & Stafford, R. J. (1983). Pancreatic disorders in childhood. In M. H. Sleisenger & J. S. Fordtran (Eds.), *Gastrointestinal disease: Pathophysiology, diagnosis, management* (3rd ed.). pp. 1436–1462.

Harder, L., & Bowditch, B. (1982). Siblings of children with cystic fibrosis: Perceptions of the impact of the disease. *Children's Health Care, 10,* pp. 116–120.

Harris, A., & Super, M. (1987). *Cystic fibrosis: The facts*. New York: Oxford University Press.

Hilman, B. C. (1973). Death and bereavement in chronic lung disease. In P. R. Patterson, C. R. Denning, & A. H. Kutscher (Eds.), *Psychosocial aspects of cystic fibrosis*. New York: Columbia University Press, pp. 95–97.

Hobbs, N., Perrin, J. M. & Ireys, H. T. (1985). *Chronically ill children and their families*. San Francisco: Jossey-Bass.

Hodson, M. E. (1980). Psychological and social aspects of cystic fibrosis. *The Practitioner, 224,* pp. 301–303.

Hymovich, D. P., & Baker, C. D. (1985). The needs, concerns and coping of parents of children with cystic fibrosis. *Family Relations, 34,* pp. 91–97.

Jessop, D. J., & Stein, R. E. (1985). Uncertainty and its relation to the psychological and social correlates of chronic illness in children. *Social Science and Medicine, 20(10),* pp. 993–999.

Johnson, S. B. (1985). The family and the child with chronic illness. In D. C. Turk & R. D. Kerns (Eds.), *Health, illness and families: A lifespan perspective.* New York: John Wiley & Sons, Inc., pp. 220–254.

Kalnins, I. (1983). Cross-illness comparisons of separation and divorce among parents having a child with a life-threatening illness. *Children's Health Care, 12,* pp. 100–102.

Kazak, A. (1987). Families with disabled children: Stress and social networks in three samples. *Journal of Abnormal Child Psychology, 15,* pp. 137–146.

Kerner, J., Harvey, B., & Lewiston, N. (1979). The impact of grief: A retrospective study of family functioning following loss of a child with cystic fibrosis. *Journal of Chronic Diseases, 32,* pp. 221–225.

Klass, P. (1988). Shattered dreams. *Discover, 6,* pp. 34–35.

Kulczycki, L. L., Regal, D., & Tantisunthorn, C. (1973). The impact of cystic fibrosis on the parents and patients. In P. R. Patterson, C. R. Denning, & A. H. Kutscher (Eds.), *Psychosocial aspects of cystic fibrosis.* New York: Columbia University Press, pp. 117–133.

Kushner, H. (1981). *When bad things happen to good people.* New York: Avon.

Kuzemko, J. A., & Heeley, A. F. (1983). Diagnostic methods and screening. In M. E. Hodson, A. P. Norman, & J. C. Batten (Eds.), *Cystic fibrosis.* London: Bailliere Tindall, pp. 13–30.

Kvalvik-Stanghelle, J. (1984, June). *CF patients in marathon.* Paper presented at the 9th International Cystic Fibrosis Congress, Brighton, England.

Lansky, S., Cairns, N., Clark, G., Lowman, J., Miller, L., & Trueworthy, R. (1979). Childhood cancer: Non-medical costs of the illness. *Cancer, 43,* pp. 403–408.

Lavigne, J. V. & Burns, W. J. (1981). *Pediatric psychology: An introduction for pediatricians and psychologists.* New York: Grune & Stratton, Inc.

Leventhal, J. M., & Sabbeth, B. F. (1986). The family and chronic illness in children. In M. W. Yogman & T. Berry Brazelton (Eds.), *In support of families.* Cambridge, MA: Harvard University Press, pp. 193–210.

Levison, H., Garner, D., MacMillan, H., & Cowen, L. (1987). Living with cystic fibrosis: Patient, family, and physician realities. *Comprehensive Therapy, 13(10),* pp. 38–45.

Lewiston, N. J. (1985). Cystic fibrosis. In N. Hobbs, J. M. Perrin, & H. T.

Ireys (Eds.), *Chronically ill children and their families*. San Francisco: Jossey-Bass, pp. 196–213.

Lippincott, C., Wery, K., & Stone, R. T. (1988, March), *CF teen girls support group*. Paper presented at the Tenth International Cystic Fibrosis Congress, Sydney, Australia.

Littlewood, J. M. (1980). The diagnosis of cystic fibrosis. *The Practitioner, 224*, pp. 305–307.

Lloyd-Still, D. M., & Lloyd-Still, J. D. (1983). The patient, the family, and the community. In J. D. Lloyd-Still (Ed), *Textbook of cystic fibrosis*. Boston: John Wright, pp. 433–445.

Lobato, D., Faust, D., & Spirito, A. (1988). Examining the effects of chronic disease and disability on children's sibling relationships. *Journal of Pediatric Psychology, 13(3)*, pp. 389–407.

Mabogunje, O. A., Wang, C., & Mahour, G. H. (1982). Improved survival of neonates with meconium ileus. *Archives of Surgery, 117*, pp. 37–40.

Maddison, D., & Raphael, B. (1971). Social and psychological consequences of chronic disease in childhood. *Medical Journal of Australia, 2*, pp. 1265–1270.

Masters, J. C., Cerreto, M. C., & Mendlowitz, D. R. (1983). The role of the family in coping with childhood chronic illness. In T. G. Burish & L. A. Bradley (Eds.), *Coping with chronic disease*. New York: Academic Press, pp. 381–407.

Matthews, L. W., & Drotar, D. (1984). Cystic fibrosis: A challenging long-term chronic illness. *Pediatric Clinics of North America, 31*, pp. 133–152.

Mattsson, A. (1972). Long-term physical illness in childhood: A challenge to psychosocial adaptation. *Pediatrics, 50(5)*, pp. 801–811.

McAnarney, E., Pless, I. B. Satterwhite, B. B., & Friedman, S. B. (1974). Psychological problems of children with chronic juvenile arthritis. *Pediatrics, 53*, pp. 523–528.

McCollum, A. T., & Gibson, L. E. (1970). Family adaptation to the child with cystic fibrosis. *Journal of Pediatrics, 77*(4), pp. 571–578.

McCracken, M. J. (1984). Cystic fibrosis in adolescence. In R. W. Blum (Ed.), *Chronic illness and disabilities in childhood and adolescence*. pp. 397–411.

McCubbin, H., I., McCubbin, M. A., Patterson, J. M. Cauble, A. E., Wilson, L. R., & Warwick, W. (1983). CHIP—Coping health inventory for parents: An assessment of parental coping patterns in the care of the chronically ill child. *Journal of Marriage and the Family, 45*, pp. 359–370.

McCubbin, M. (1984). Nursing assessment of parental coping with cystic fibrosis. *Western Journal of Nursing Research, 6(4)*, pp. 407–422.

McKeever, P. (1981). Fathering the chronically ill child: A neglected area in family research. *American Journal of Maternal and Child Nursing, 6,* pp. 124–128.

Meyerowitz, J. H. & Kaplan, H. B. (1973). Cystic fibrosis and family functioning. In P. R. Patterson, C. R. Denning, & A. H. Kutscher (Eds), *Psychosocial aspects of cystic fibrosis.* New York: Columbia University Press, pp. 34–58.

Miller, M. S. (1988, March). *Role of the mental health professional in cystic fibrosis.* Paper presented at the Tenth International Cystic Fibrosis Congress.

Mrazek, D. A. (1985). Cystic fibrosis: A systems analysis of psychiatric consequences. *Advances in Psychosomatic Medicine, 14,* pp. 119–135.

National Cystic Fibrosis Foundation (1987). *National Registry Statistics,* Bethesda, MD.

Nolan, T., Desmond, K., Herlich, R., & Hardy, S. (1986). Knowledge of cystic fibrosis in patients and their parents. *Pediatrics, 77*(2), pp. 229–235.

Norman, A. P., & Hodson, M. E. (1983). Emotional and social aspects of treatment. In M. E. Hodson, A. P. Norman, & J. C. Batten (Eds.), *Cystic fibrosis.* London: Bailliere Tindall, pp. 242–259.

Olshansky, S. (1962). Chronic sorrow: A response to having a mentally defective child. *Social Casework, 43,* pp. 190–193.

Orenstein, D. M., & Wachnowsky, D. M. (1985). Behavioral aspects of cystic fibrosis. *Annals of Behavioral Medicine, 7*(4), pp. 17–20.

Patterson, J. M. (1985). Critical factors affecting family compliance with home treatment for children with cystic fibrosis. *Family Relations: Journal of Applied Family & Child Studies, 34*(1), pp. 79–89.

Patterson, P. R. (1973). Psychosocial aspects of cystic fibrosis. In P. R. Patterson, C. R. Denning, & A. H. Kutscher (Eds.), *Psychosocial aspects of cystic fibrosis.* New York: Columbia University Press, pp. 3–12.

Perrin, E. C., & Gerrity, P. S. (1984). Development of children with a chronic illness. *Pediatric Clinics of North America, 31,* pp. 19–32.

Perrin, J. M. (1985). Introduction. In N. Hobbs & J. M. Perrin (Eds.), *Issues in the care of children with chronic illness: A sourcebook on problems, services, and policies.* San Francisco: Jossey-Bass, pp. 1–10.

Perrin, J. M., & Ireys, H. T. (1984). The organization of services for chronically ill children and their families. *Pediatric Clinics of North America, 31,* pp. 235–258.

Perrin, J. M., & MacLean, W. E. (1988). Biomedical and psychosocial dimensions of chronic illness in childhood. In P. Karoly (Ed.), *Handbook of child health assessment: Biopsychosocial perspectives.* New York: John Wiley & Sons, Inc., pp. 11–29.

Phillips, S., Bohannon, W. E., Gayton, W. F., & Friedman, S. B. (1985). Parent interview findings regarding the impact of cystic fibrosis on families. *Developmental and Behavioral Pediatrics, 6,* pp. 122–127.

Piersma, H. L. (1985). The family with a chronically ill child. In J. C. Hansen (Ed.), *Health promotion in family therapy.* Rockville, MD: Aspen System Corp, pp. 105–116.

Pless, I. B., & Perrin, J. M. (1985). Issues common to a variety of illnesses. In N. Hobbs & J. M. Perrin (Eds.), *Issues in the care of children with chronic illness: A sourcebook on problems, services, and policies.* San Francisco: Jossey-Bass, pp. 44–60.

Rosenstein, B. J., & Langbaum, T. S. (1984). Diagnosis. In L. Taussig (Ed.), *Cystic fibrosis.* New York: Thieme-Stratton, Inc., pp. 85–114.

Rosenstein, B. J., Langbaum, T. S., & Metz, S. J. (1982). Cystic fibrosis: Diagnostic considerations. *Johns Hopkins Medical Journal, 150,* pp. 113–122.

Sabbeth, B. (1984). Understanding the impact of chronic childhood illness on families. *Pediatric Clinics of North America, 31(1),* pp. 47–57.

Sabbeth, B. F., & Leventhal, J. M. (1984). Marital adjustment to chronic childhood illness: A critique of the literature. *Pediatrics, 73(6),* pp. 762–768.

Sabinga, M. S., Friedman, C. J., & Huang, N. N. (1973). The family of the cystic fibrosis patient. In P. R. Patterson, C. R. Denning, & A. H. Kutscher (Eds.), *Psychosocial aspects of cystic fibrosis.* New York: Columbia University Press, pp. 13–18.

Santulli, T. V. (1980). Meconium ileus. In T. M. Holder & K. W. Ashcraft (Eds.), *Pediatric surgery.* Philadelphia: W. B. Saunders, pp. 356–373.

Sargent, J., & Liebman, R. (1985). Childhood chronic illness: Issues for psychotherapists. *Community Mental Health Journal, 21*(4), pp. 294–311.

Schroder, K. H., Casadaban, A. B., & Davis, B. (1988). Interpersonal skills training for parents of children with cystic fibrosis. *Family Systems Medicine, 6*(1), pp. 51–68.

Schwartz, R. H., & Milner, M. R. (1984). Other manifestations and organ involvement in L. Taussig (Ed.), *Cystic fibrosis.* New York: Thieme-Stratton, Inc., pp. 376–407.

Seligman, M., & Darling, R. B. (1989). *Ordinary families: Special children.* New York: The Guilford Press.

Shapiro, J. (1983). Family reactions and coping strategies in response to the physically ill or handicapped child: A review. *Social Science and Medicine, 17*(14), pp. 913–931.

Solnit, A. J., & Stark, M. H. (1961). Mourning and the birth of a defective child. *Psychoanalytic Study of the Child, 16,* pp. 523–537.

Sourkes, B. (1982). *The deepening shade: Psychological aspects of life-threatening illness.* Pittsburgh: University of Pittsburgh Press.

Spinetta, J., Swarner, J., & Sheposh, J. (1981). Effective parental coping following the death of a child from cancer. *Journal of Pediatric Psychology 6*(3), pp. 251–263.

Spirito, A., Russo, D. C., & Masek, B. J. (1984). Behavioral interventions and stress management training for hospitalized adolescents and young adults with cystic fibrosis. *General Hospital Psychiatry, 6,* pp. 211–218.

Stein, R. E. K., & Jessop, D. J. (1982). A noncategorical approach to chronic childhood illness. *Public Health Reports, 97*(4), pp. 354–362.

Stein, R. E. K., & Jessop, D. J. (1984) General issues in the care of children with chronic physical conditions. *Pediatric Clinics of North America, 31*(1), pp. 189–198.

Stern, R. C., Doershuk, C. F., Boat, T. F., Tucker, A. S., Primiana, F. P., & Matthews, L. W. (1976). Course of cystic fibrosis in black patients. *Journal of Pediatrics, 89*(3), pp. 412–417.

Stewart, A. (1984). Cystic fibrosis. One: Supporting the parents. *Nursing Times, 80*(20), pp. 24–26.

Stullenbarger, B., Norris, J., Edgil, A. E., & Prosser, M. J. (1987). Family adaptation to cystic fibrosis. *Pediatric Nursing, 13*(1), pp. 29–31.

Taussig, L. (1984). Cystic fibrosis An overview. In L. Taussig (Ed.), *Cystic fibrosis.* New York: Thieme-Stratton, Inc., pp. 1–9.

Taussig, L. M., Lobeck, C. C., di Sant'Agnese, P. A., Ackerman, D. R., & Kattwinkel, J. (1972). Fertility in males with cystic fibrosis. *New England Journal of Medicine, 287,* pp. 586–589.

Travis, G. (1976). *Chronic illness in children: Its impact on child and family.* Stanford, CA: Stanford University Press.

Turner, J. (1984). Focus on children: II-Nursing care study: A parent's perspective. *Nursing Mirror, 159*(18), pp. 23–25.

Van Dongen-Melman, J. E. W. M., & Sanders-Woudstra, J. A. R. (1986). Psychosocial aspects of childhood cancer: A review of the literature. *Journal of Child Psychology and Psychiatry and Allied Disciplines, 27*(2), pp. 145–180.

Venters, M. (1981). Familial coping with chronic and severe childhood illness: The case of cystic fibrosis. *Social Science and Medicine, 15A,* pp. 289–297.

Whitaker's Almanack (121st edition) (1989). Detroit: Gale Research Company.

Williams, Y. B., & Rosenberg, G. A. (1981). The use of patients' drawings as an aid in diagnosis and treatment. *Cystic Fibrosis Club Abstracts, 22,* p. 167.

Wood, R. E., Boat, T. F., & Doershuk, C. F. (1976). State of the art: Cystic fibrosis. *American Review of Respiratory Disease, 113,* pp. 833–878.

Wright, B. A. (1960). *Physical disability: A psychological approach.* New York: Harper.

Wright, S. E., & Morton, M. E. (1968). Genetic studies on cystic fibrosis in Hawaii. *American Journal of Human Genetics, 20,* pp. 157–169.

Zach, M. S., Purrer, B., & Oberwaldner, B. (1981). Effect of swimming on forced expiration and sputum clearance in cystic fibrosis. *Lancet, 2,* pp. 1201–1203.

Zentler-Munro, P. L. (1983). Gastrointestinal disease in adults. In M. E. Hodson, A. P. Norman, & J. C. Batten (Eds.), *Cystic fibrosis.* London: Bailliere-Tindall, pp. 144–163.

CHAPTER TWELVE

Counseling Parents With Children With Disabilities
Rationale and Strategies

Peter Randell Laborde and Milton Seligman

Peter Randell Laborde, M.Ed., is director of Core Team Services for Hall-Mercer Community Mental Health/Mental Retardation Center of Pennsylvania Hospital, Philadelphia, Pennsylvania. Laborde is particularly interested in the use of applied behavior analysis in home settings and the preservation of at-risk families. He also maintains a private practice working with families who care for a family member with disabilities.

Laborde is principal author of the Pennsylvania Model Individual Written Program Plan for Vocational Rehabilitation Facilities *written for the Pennsylvania Department of Welfare and* Resource Manual: Information and Referral *written for the Pennsylvania Department of Education.*

Milton Seligman, Ph.D., is a professor in the Counseling Psychology Program at the University of Pittsburgh. He has edited or authored books and articles in the area of group psychotherapy and in the area of childhood disability and the family.

In addition to his administrative duties, Seligman teaches courses in individual and group therapy, clinical supervision and disability in the family. He maintains a private practice in Pittsburgh.

Disability strikes many children. The conditions that result in a disability are complex and diverse, and their manifestations are not always apparent. Some handicapping conditions are readily detected and can even be identified before birth. Others may not become known for months or years. It is estimated that over 4.3 million children and youth are disabled (United States Department of Education, 1987). Although accurate information of the actual incidence of disabling conditions is not currently available, it is certain that the number of children who are disabled in some way is quite high. It is our contention, however, that the effects of disability can be minimized, and these individuals should be helped to reach optimal levels of personal development. The success of disabled children to effectively participate in the everyday world is related to the ability of each child's environment to adapt to his or her special developmental needs. This means that the institution closest to the child, namely the family, needs to be flexible and able to cope with the crisis of disability.

Illness or physical trauma may result in disabling conditions occurring at any time in a person's life. Furthermore, as noted in this volume, not only is the person with the condition affected but their families are also affected. Parents whose children are identified as disabled are confronted with the need to make both short- and long-term adjustments. Often these adjustments are difficult to make and parents need help in making them.

Typical disabling conditions include deficits in cognitive functioning, perception, sensory acuity, neurologic functioning, expressive or receptive language, behavior control, and motoric functioning. A child may have one or more deficits that affect his or her ability to function adequately. Disabling conditions can vary markedly in the degree to which they impair functioning. The child who is disabled to a mild degree faces different obstacles than does the child who is moderately or severely disabled by the same condition (see Chapter 8 and Chapter 9). As a result of deficiencies in social supports, which may be compounded by dysfunctional family patterns, families may suffer serious consequences from a child's disability regardless of the type or severity of the condition. We believe that individual or couples' counseling with parents is a form of intervention that is well suited to helping parents of disabled children cope with their unique circumstances.

Counseling Is A Helping Process

It is essential that counseling be a helping process for parents. Misguided or ineffective counseling pursued for too long may make counseling unacceptable to parents in the future when it might be even more critical for their adjustment (Freeman & Pearson, 1978). Parents will exhibit a wide diversity of responses to receiving help, from welcoming it to angrily refusing it. Although providing information, emotional support, and counseling may be valuable, these supports may also place significant demands on parents, which can result in counterproductive outcomes. For example, parents with significant work and child-care demands may feel resentful regarding the time needed to attend counseling sessions that may be required in order for their child to participate in an early intervention program. Furthermore, parents of children with disabling conditions typically come into contact with a wide range of professionals and can develop a rather cynical view of those who offer help, particularly if they perceive their contacts with professionals to be negative. Some of the reasons for the tension that exists between parents and professionals are discussed by Darling in Chapter 5. However, several salient issues relevant to parent-professional relationships deserve attention here.

Professionals with varying backgrounds are called on to provide counseling to parents. Physicians who make the initial diagnosis of disability, pediatricians who provide medical services to families over many years, ministers who are consulted in an hour of need, therapists who attempt to intervene during periods of personal difficulties, and educators who teach the disabled child may be called on to provide counseling to parents. A broad range of professionals, then, function in a helping capacity to parents of disabled children. The need for trained professionals to help parents will become even greater in the future as the public policies of mainstreaming and normalization act to maintain disabled children in the community. Parents are now being told that their children are better off remaining at home rather than being placed in an out-of-home setting. Consequently, many families have older disabled members living at home for extended periods beyond the time when children generally become independent.

As medical science advances, more children born with severe disabilities are being kept alive. The efforts of neonatal intensive care units may be increasing the prevalence of individuals with severe, multiple handicapping conditions. As noted in Chapter 9, some of these children have severe and multiple disabilities that can place significant emotional and financial cost on parents. Advances in medicine has resulted in both a reduction in the number of deaths and an increase in the number of severely disabled people. Support for families whose severely impaired children survive must be planned for and provided by appropriate agencies.

There is a growing number of reports related to the training, experience, and attitudinal deficiencies of professionals who work with parents. Fox (1975) observed that "some parents react to [meetings with professionals] so strongly that individual meetings with professionals and group staffings become major traumatic events to be dreaded and avoided" (p. 36). Wolraich (1982) noted that physicians are often ill-prepared to work with parents. Some of the factors that impede physician-parent communication are (a) the physician's inadequate knowledge of developmental disabilities, (b) the physician's negative attitude toward disabled children, and (c) the physician's inept skills in communicating with parents. Wolraich believes that all three factors are interrelated: That is, deficiencies in one area affect the physician's abilities in other areas.

The areas of deficiency that Wolraich believes are important considerations for physicians can easily be attributed to other professionals as well. It should be noted, however, that the parent-physician relationship in particular has been under considerable scrutiny in recent years (Darling & Darling, 1982; Guralnick & Richardson, 1980; Howard, 1982; Jacobs & Walker, 1978; Powers & Healy, 1982), whereas in the 1970s the major emphasis was on the parent-teacher relationship (Chinn, Winn & Walters, 1978; Kroth, 1975; Seligman, 1979).

Seligman and Seligman (1980) noted the following issues that account for the adversarial relationship between parents and professionals.

1. Feelings of sympathy, pity, fear, or hostility toward parents.
2. A pervasive feeling of hopelessness or hostility about the parent's situation.
3. Overidentification with the parents' circumstances, which reinforces parental denial.
4. Viewing the parents' point of view as untrustworthy and of little value.
5. Viewing parents as emotionally unstable.

Ross (1964) stated unequivocally that professionals who work with parents should have certain qualities.

> A mental health professional may be able to develop these in the course of closely supervised experience but some people lack these qualities in sufficient measure that they should probably not enter a profession whose central task is helping other people. No amount of exhortation can make a rejecting person accepting, a frigid person warm, a narrow-minded person understanding. Those charged with the selection, educa-

tion and training of new members of the helping professions will need to keep in mind that the presence or absence of certain personality characteristics makes the difference between a truly helpful professional and one who leaves a trace of misery and confusion in the wake of his activities (pp. 75–76).

To be able to effectively engage in counseling with parents, it is essential that the professional's characteristics, attitudes, and biases be taken into consideration and that he or she be trained in the rudiments of counseling, at minimum. This view has gained the support of professionals representing several disciplines (Bissell, 1976; Kroth, 1975; McWilliams, 1976; Paul, 1981; Reynolds & Birch, 1982; Seligman, 1979).

DISABILITY AND THE FAMILY

Professionals who work with families must recognize the many complex and interacting variables that affect psychological adjustment. Many of these factors are discussed in other chapters in this volume. Those that are particularly amenable to counseling are the focus of this section.

The perceptions of others contribute to the degree of impact a disabled child has upon the family. A study of parents of children with cystic fibrosis found that half of the parents perceived community attitudes as negative and as a result felt some degree of social isolation (Meyerwitz & Kaplan, 1967). Walker (1971) found that mothers of children with spina bifida expressed concern about exposing their child to normal children and to more severely disabled children, because this might adversely affect their child. In Chapter 8, Fewell comments on the social stigma experienced by children and families with milder disabilities. The experience of stigma by family members adds considerably to the sense of handicap felt as a consequence of childhood disability (Seligman & Darling, 1989).

Parents also have differing perceptions about their child based on their experiences and expectations of disabled and nondisabled children. Indeed, Darling and Darling (1982) observed that parents of children with a disability often harbor negative attitudes toward deviance that resemble those held by the general public. As a result, parents experience a double shock when a disabled child is born. Not only must parents cope with their feelings about their disabled offspring, but they must also confront their previously held negative attitudes toward those persons they may have considered deviant.

Reaction to Diagnosis

Parents have a need to understand what happened to their child, what the condition is, why it occurred (this is not always known), how it can be treated, and the prognosis. Professionals should provide answers to such questions in a factual and compassionate manner, with the child's strengths and weaknesses both addressed. Fellendorf and Harrow (1969) reported that only one half of the parents they surveyed expressed satisfaction with the manner in which the diagnosis of their child's handicap was conveyed. Parents have reported incidents in which inaccurate information was presented in a harsh and uncaring manner. Springer and Steele (1980) reported that a majority of parents of children diagnosed as having Down Syndrome felt that physicians were unduly pessimistic in their assessment of their child's potential. Although professionals must be careful not to paint an unrealistically rosy picture regarding a child's future, they must be equally wary against burdening parents with negative prospects for their child's development, especially when the child's future development is unknown. Overly optimistic or pessimistic prognoses may lead to needless anguish.

As stated previously, not all disabilities are identified immediately. Parents may not become aware that their child is experiencing difficulties until months or years after birth. Some parents may not be knowledgeable about developmental milestones and thus may not realize that their child is experiencing delays in development (Jordan, 1971). When a disability is detected later, parents may experience difficulty in perceiving their child as disabled, having for some time perceived their child as normal. Bristol and Schopler (1984), for example, discussed the difficulties that parents experience with less obvious handicaps. These authors note that the child's disability may not only be less obvious to the parent and others, but the diagnosis may be ambiguous as well.

Barsch (1969) stated that parents with children with less obvious disabilities are presented with special challenges, because these parents must undergo gradual changes in their thinking about their child and about themselves. These changes often occur concurrently with the child's adjustment to new and, at times, traumatic experiences, such as starting school. Professionals should be aware of the confusion that parents experience in feeling that their child is not developing normally, while lacking information about the nature of their child's problem. This confusion, compounded by the normal, everyday problems of parenthood, can be distressing to parents. The professional can help parents at this time by being a source of emotional support as well as a provider and clarifier of information.

Accurate information is of paramount importance to the new parent of a disabled child. Parents do not expect professionals to have complete knowledge of their child's condition, although they do expect rudimentary knowledge (Schwartz, 1970). However, as already noted, parents are very concerned about how information is provided (Pueschel & Murphy, 1976). For example, Telford and Sawrey (1981) quoted a mother who characterized her professional conferences as "a masterful combination of dishonesty, condescension, misinformation and bad manners" (p. 143).

The mental health professional can help parents cope with the initial period of shock, confusion, and ambiguity regarding their child's disability. Information regarding diagnosis and prognosis, even if inconclusive, must be presented in a candid and compassionate fashion that conveys the professional's concern.

Shopping for Services

Once informed of their child's disability, parents sometimes seek further evaluations of their child. Professionals tend to view this behavior as a form of denial in which parents engage in an endless and fruitless search for a "cure" to their child's condition. This parental behavior may not, however, be as common as the literature suggests. Keirn (1971) investigated the prevalence of "shopping" behavior by parents and concluded that it is an overstated problem. Only 3 percent of the parents in Keirn's study were considered to be shoppers.

Seeking opinions from other professionals is an option that parents have a right and often a need to exercise. Indeed as Seligman and Seligman (1980) noted, parents may wish another opinion, or they may want to have the initial diagnosis or current problems reviewed, especially as the child achieves certain developmental milestones and the nature of the disability changes. Also, parents may "shop" because they feel they have been treated with little respect and dignity by professionals. They wish to confer with professionals who have the required expertise and who treat them compassionately. Keirn (1971) also found that parents who shop for services often are looking for evaluations that will permit their child to receive services provided to children with specific diagnoses.

On the other hand, Davidson and Schrag (1968) found that over half of the recommendations presented as part of a psychological consultation were not carried out by parents. This lack of follow-through by parents may be a consequence of parental denial. Alternatively, it may either be the result of misunderstanding on the part of the parents as to what is expected of them or reflect disagreement with the professional's judgment as to what is best for their child. Davidson and Schrag (1968) found that parents were much more inclined to follow recommendations that were mutually agreed upon. The mental health professional, acting as a broker, can help parents understand recommendations made on behalf of their child and can help parents negotiate more effectively with professionals. If agreement between parent and professional can be achieved, the likelihood of treatment implementation should increase.

Gorham, Des Jardins, Page, Pettis, and Scheiber (1975) surveyed 500 parents whose children were identified as disabled and found that 56 percent of the children had been provided with different diagnoses by different professionals. The authors indicate that this multiple labeling is a major source of parental frustration. Also, parents may shop for "good" diagnoses that may help their child obtain needed services so that they will not be denied entrance into highly regarded but limited-enrollment programs. Therefore, professionals must determine the parents' reasons for "shopping" before they conclude that denial is the motivating factor. If parents are in denial the professional can help them recognize this, especially if denial is having an adverse effect on the child.

Professionals must be wary, however, that parents may learn about treatments for disability that are considered to be out of the mainstream of generally accepted practice. Parents may be susceptible to faddish and unproven treatments. The professional may need to help parents sort through prevailing information and treatment approaches so that appropriate decisions can be made.

Related Factors Affecting Family Functioning

Parenting any child is a challenging endeavor. As noted previously, parents of disabled children experience challenges that other parents do not face. There are a number of factors, such as language difficulties, problems in child management, lack of play skills, social deficits, lack of emotional attachment, and poor self-help skills, that motivate parents of these children to seek help from professionals.

The lack of language is a particularly difficult problem for parents. For instance, parents may not receive cues or feedback from their child that provides them with reinforcement regarding their actions as parents (Hart, 1970). This lack of feedback may result in reduced parent-child interaction. Decreased interaction limits the opportunities the child has for developing necessary social skills that are typically learned from family members. The child may also experience a diminished sense of self-worth. A vicious cycle of limited parent-child interaction results — a cycle that is difficult to reverse. It is important for the sake of both the child and the parent to break this pattern as early as possible. Much progress has been made in providing early intervention and infant stimulation programs that can help facilitate parent-child attachments (Brassel, 1977, Dunst, 1990). Professionals can help support parents' efforts to take advantage of these programs.

Communication is also important in understanding the child's behavioral difficulties. Carr and Durand (1985) developed a model for assessing the communicative function of maladaptive behavior. They believe that most behavior problems are socially motivated and serve the purpose of garnering attention (even if it negative) or to escape from an unpleasant situation. By providing the child and the parent with alternative methods of communicating, the occurrence of disruptive behavior may be reduced. Properly trained specialists can help families with communication problems, behavior disorders, and maladaptive patterns of family interaction.

Marital Conflict

Although many families cope well, increased marital conflict may accompany the presence of a disabled child in the family. Ross (1964) believed that latent conflicts in the family may erupt with the added stress of providing for a disabled child. The child is often not the cause of these conflicts. That is, the potential for conflict may lie within the preexisting structure of family relationships. In terms of stress and conflict, Sabbeth and Levanthal (1984) found no difference in divorce rates between parents with chronically ill children and others; conflict was present in both groups of parents.

McCubbin, Nevin, Cauble, Larsen, Comeau, and Patterson (1982), writing about families with children with cerebral palsy, believe that families may have a need for counseling both for concerns specific to the child's disability and for other, nondisability-related sources of family stress. The professional can help parents distinguish family problems brought about by the family's characteristic interactional patterns from those arising from their response to their disabled child. Although it is true that a disabled child can disrupt family equilibrium, parents can be helped to become more aware of the causes of their frustration and to learn to diffuse it by changing their cognitions about their plight and/or by changing their behaviors. If parents intend to solely devote their lives to their disabled child, they should be helped to understand the source of their excessive attachment to their child and how it may hinder the child's development and the parents' independence. Parents may wish to explore how they can fulfill other unmet social, recreational, creative, or avocational needs.

Contrary to expectation, marital conflict may not be any greater in families with children with severe disabilities than in those with children with milder disabilities. Blacher, Nihira, and Meyers (1987), for example, found no differences in marital adjustment among groups of families with children with differing levels of mental retardation. Furthermore, they found no difference in the overall level of coping among these groups of subjects. These findings are supported by some of the research reported by Fewell in Chapter 8 and by Lyon and Lyon in Chapter 9.

Some have speculated that the type of disability (or the demand characteristics of the child's affliction) may contribute to stress within the family (Seligman & Darling, 1989). Goldberg, Marcovitch, MacGregor, and Lojkasek (1986) compared parents with children with Down Syndrome, neurological impairments, and mental retardation of unknown etiology and found that parents in the Down Syndrome group reported less stress than the other groups. These parents reported receiving more support from others but also reported that the child's impairment had the greatest impact on their self-image, which might possibly be related to feelings of responsibility for causing the genetic disorder.

Stress and Mothers

Mothers may feel special stress from raising a disabled child. Among other feelings, mothers of disabled children may experience guilt, anger, embarrassment, and jealousy toward other mothers who do not have a disabled child. Cummings, Bayley, and Rie (1966), for example, found that mothers with a mentally retarded child had significantly greater feelings of depression, were more preoccupied, and had more difficulty in handling anger toward their child than did a matched sample of mothers with no disabled children. Mothers of disabled children not only are reminded that their children are different from others but also anticipate prolonged periods as primary caregivers. If a disabling condition is severe, mothers generally perceive their caretaker role as perpetual, and their future may appear bleak as they anticipate increased hardship during their child's later years. This perception may indeed become fact for some mothers. Parents with a disabled child often do experience an extended role as primary caretaker of their child, often extending well into their child's adulthood. Peterson (1984) found a moderate relationship between the child's handicapping condition and the mother's health and marital adjustment. He found that the availability of emotional support and practical help moderated the effect of the child's handicapping condition on the mother. The perception of the mother's satisfaction with life in general and the social support she receives in caring for the child may play a significant role in the amount of stress she experiences (Bradshaw & Lawton, 1978). Although mothers may experience different levels of stress, depending on the child's handicapping condition or its level of severity (and we recognize that the issue of affliction, severity, and family adaptation continues to be debated), highly individual reactions probably account for most of the differences among mothers.

Single mothers may experience greater stress than do married mothers, especially poverty-stricken, single parent families. Beckman (1983) reported that single mothers reported greater stress than do other mothers when their infants had difficult temperaments, engaged in repetitive behavior, and had unusual or extraordinary caregiving demands. Single mothers who must care for a child with a disabling condition require both emotional and practical support in order to successfully negotiate the demands of their special needs child. Beckman's research also suggests that child characteristics (such as behavioral disorder) may contribute more to a mother's stress than type or severity of disability.

Stress and Fathers

As noted in Chapter 6 by Lamb and Meyer, fathers of disabled children also experience feelings of depression and low self-esteem. Cummings (1976), for example, reported that fathers indicated little enjoyment from their interactions with their mentally retarded child and found less enjoyment in their other children as well. Furthermore, fathers may be more disappointed with a mentally retarded son than daughter and tend to act in a more rejecting manner toward disabled sons. As a result, fathers may withdraw from the family, which weakens the mother's support system and increases her burdens as well as those of the siblings. Professionals need to appreciate the father's contribution to the instrumental and emotional well-being of the family. In regard to the research on fathers, it is important to note that existing speculation is based on only a handful of studies (Hornby, 1989).

Siblings and Stress

As noted in Chapter 7, siblings of disabled children have special concerns. Older sisters, for example, may display unfavorable attitudes and behaviors toward their disabled sibling and toward others when given the major responsibility of care for their disabled brother or sister (Fowle, 1968). Excessive responsibility combined with parental inattention and high achievement expectations can contribute to sibling problems. The female sibling in particular may fall victim to the "Cinderella Syndrome" (i.e., leaving home), because it may seem to be the most plausible escape from an intolerable situation. In attending to the needs of their nondisabled children, parents should facilitate communication between themselves and their children. For example, Grossman (1972) reported that adolescents found talking with their parents about their siblings' mental retardation to be as difficult as talking with them about sex.

Siblings may develop fantasies or dreams about their disabled sister or brother that greatly disturb them. They may fantasize about taking some unduly harsh or cruel action against the disabled person, which results in guilt and anxiety. They may also believe that they may catch or someday develop the condition that afflicts their disabled sibling. As a result, professionals must attend to the informational needs nondisabled siblings generally have. It seems that the less children know about their disabled sib, the more they have to cope with the ambiguity of the situation and, therefore, experience increased anxiety. As noted in Chapter 7, siblings may also become resentful about the inordinate amount of fiscal and emotional resources absorbed by the disabled child. Counseling should consider both the educative and emotional needs of siblings.

Responsibility of the Disabled Family Member

Coping with the effects of a disabled child is a challenge that needs to be shared by all family members if adjustment problems are to be held to a minimum. Although family members must generally contribute to the care of the disabled family member, they must also learn that the disabled child should also be given *reasonable* responsibilities for the management of the disability, the household and for providing support to other family members. Such responsibilities allow the child to achieve some measure of independence and to assume an important, contributing role in the family. This also allows the child to contribute to others' well-being and not be confined to only dependent roles in the family.

THE COUNSELING PROCESS

The counseling process can be viewed as having three main functions or components: educative counseling, facilitative counseling, and personal advocacy counseling. Although there will be some overlap in these functions, each component has unique aspects as well.

Educative Counseling

Parents typically have a need to be informed about their child's disability. Parents who receive complete and accurate information from the time they are first informed of their child's disability tend to seek out more information as their child develops (Burton, 1975). The professional must be prepared to explain salient information such as the type of disability, its prognosis, and its impact on the child and family to the parents to help reduce their sense of anomie and confusion. This information may need to be given to parents more than once so that they are able to digest its meaning and to ask questions for further clarification. As their child develops, the type of information parents need will change. Questions regarding education, placement, independence, and sexuality will arise as the child matures.

Parents often have little knowledge about disabling conditions until confronted by their own child's disability. Freeston (1971) found that fewer than one half of the parents of children diagnosed as having spina bifida had heard of the condition prior to the birth of their child. Only a few of the parents felt that they fully understood the initial explanation of their child's condition. Pueschel and Murphy (1976) found the same parental confusion regarding the communication of the diagnosis of Down Syndrome. They also found that some physicians delayed the disclosure of disability to parents, whereas others used inappropriate and outdated terminology, (e.g., Mongoloid and idiot). There is, then, a great need for professionals to help parents be better informed about their circumstances, about where they may receive additional information, and about available services. There is also a great need for professionals to be well informed and accurate about the language, diagnoses, and prognoses concerning childhood disability.

The professional cannot expect to be an expert on every disabling condition or even on all of the ramifications of any one condition. One can, however, refer parents to written materials, other knowledgeable professionals, and organizations with specialized information about disabilities. Often special education centers have libraries or media centers that have materials of value to parents. Professionals should review information and materials to which parents are referred to be sure that it is both accurate and appropriate (McWilliams, 1976). Some information can be so misleading that parents under- or overestimate the seriousness of their child's handicapping condition. Mutual exploration of appropriate materials by parents and professionals can ensure that accurate information is obtained, although as suggested above the professional should attempt an initial screening of such materials before recommending them. Materials of differing levels of complexity discussing the same information are often available.

Parents with children with disabilities often need to learn special teaching techniques to care for their children. They may also need specialized adaptive equipment to help their child perform activities of daily living. The physically disabled child, for example, may need to be fed differently than other children or may require equipment that encourages maximal mobility. The hearing impaired child may need to learn alternative communication techniques. Professionals can help parents become familiar with techniques that can facilitate their child's continued development. A word of caution: Well-meaning professionals, unaware of the "homework" other professionals assign to the family, may severely overburden the family system.

A number of professionals have produced materials aimed at helping parents learn specialized techniques (Berko, 1970; Caplan, 1972; Finnie, 1968; Pitt, 1974). As noted previously, such materials are generally available through special education centers and organizations such as the Association for Retarded Citizens and the Association for Children with Learning Disabilities. Organizations of professional and lay persons typically have a wealth of information for families with a child who has a specific disability. Such organizations, often specific in focus, concern themselves with particular handicapping conditions, such as epilepsy, retardation, autism, learning disability, arthritis, blindness, and deafness.

Parent Training

The professional must be careful how specific techniques are communicated to parents, because their application may be misunderstood and thus misused. For example, there are many procedures available that can be used to reduce the occurrence of inappropriate behaviors. If these procedures are used incorrectly, however, their potential effectiveness is lost and may become counterproductive. For difficult or complex behavior problems, it is advised that a referral be made to a behavior modification specialist.

Some parents have a need for parent training. The professional should assess whether parents have an understanding of normal child development, disciplining procedures, and growth promoting parent-child interactions. Parents who are confused about parenting skills may not provide a positive climate for their child's development, which may in turn lead to future difficulties. Parents who express or imply confusion regarding child-rearing methods may benefit from referral to parent training classes. General issues in child rearing may also be addressed in the counseling session.

Parents with disabled children may need special assistance in establishing clear, consistent, and positive methods of behavior management. Parents can learn basic skills in applied behavior analysis useful for reducing maladaptive behaviors. A wide range of materials are available aimed at increasing parenting skills in managing their child's behavior. It has been our experience that providing individual training in the context in which the behavior occurs is a particularly successful method of parent training. In-home consultation targeted to specific problem behaviors and generalized training aimed at more general parenting problems can help reduce family stressors.

In general, professionals can serve as interpreters of available materials and techniques and can encourage parents to carry through on suggestions that are described in the materials or are prescribed by other professionals working with their child. If the professional does not have the specialized skills necessary for training the parent adequately, a referral should be made to an appropriate specialist.

Parents may also need information regarding their rights for service and education. Laws such as Public Law 94–142 and Public Law 99–457, the Education for All Handicapped Children Act, have had a significant impact on the rights of disabled children and their parents. The Developmental Disabilities Bill of Rights Act of 1975 established mechanisms by each state to help developmentally disabled individuals and their families resolve disputes concerning needed services. Parents can be referred to other professionals who specialize in the rights of disabled individuals when legal issues emerge and provide support to parents if they decide to exercise their rights. Professionals should also be aware that they may be called on to help substantiate parental claims during legal challenges.

Parents need to know that not all available services are required to be provided. For example, in Pennsylvania, individuals with disabilities are not required to receive programming beyond school age. Many services are provided in Pennsylvania for the mentally retarded, whereas fewer are provided for the physically disabled. Similar situations occur in other states. Parents need to know that their child may be placed on a lengthy waiting list and may not obtain services for several years after graduation from school. Professionals can help prepare the family for life beyond school as noted by Lyon and Lyon in Chapter 9 in their discussion of "transitioning." Careful preparation can help assure that the child is placed in appropriate programs including ones that may lead to competitive employment and independent living.

One final word of caution. Ferhold and Solnit (1978), although strongly supportive of helping parents locate resources, believe that educative counseling should be facilitative, not advisory.

> The counselor is more a facilitator of learning and problem-solving than a teacher of facts or an instructor in child-rearing effectiveness. Although a counselor should be a competent source of advice and information, specific child-rearing practices are rarely advised. The counselor avoids too many specific directions, even when they appear to be helpful in the short run, if they dilute the process of enabling parents and child to be active on their own behalf. Optimally, the counselor helps with practical problems of child care by helping parents to be aware of alternatives from which they can choose what they prefer for their child and themselves (pp. 160, 161).

Ferhold and Solnit (1978) further make the intriguing statement that "the counselor needs to have faith that parents will make sound choices allowing for some mistakes along way; when the counselor can no longer accept the parents' decisions, he should withdraw" (p. 162).

Facilitative Counseling

In addition to providing information, professionals are often called on to provide support and to help clarify feelings parents may have toward their child or events in their lives. As noted earlier in this chapter, parents of disabled children may experience a variety of feelings. Parents have many different emotions as they struggle to come to grips with their disabled rather than their idealized child. This is a struggle that occurs over an extended period of time, resurfacing during various stages of the child's development. As trends in social policy have changed (e.g., from institutionalization to home care), disabled children now live for extended periods with their families. Because the availability of community residential programs has not kept up with demand, these prolonged periods may not be voluntary. Professional helpers need to be concerned with the needs of older, perhaps infirm, parents with disabled children who live at home.

When first told about their child's condition, parents cannot believe that they have a disabled child (see Chapter 3, "Initial and Continuing Adaptation to the Birth of a Disabled Child"). The professional can help the parents see their child in a realistic light by providing information the parents request and by being careful not to thrust too many realities on them before they are ready. The professional should acknowledge that the parent's dreams and plans for their child may be severely shaken while reminding them that they and their child can still, to a large degree, live a productive and comfortable life. Parents may initially fantasize that their child is perfect or that problems are momentary and will vanish in time. In any event, the professional needs to avoid being either unrealistically optimistic or overly pessimistic regarding the child's future.

Especially after a diagnosis has been communicated, information may bear repetition on several occasions so that parents understand both the possibilities and potential limitations inherent in their situation. Repetition may also be useful in that parents may feel overwhelmed especially at the early stage of first discovery, and, as a result, do not fully hear what is said. It is important for parents to hear optimistic, yet realistic, appraisals of their child's potential and that they be encouraged to seek help as soon as possible. In this regard, Pines (1982) reported that when some Down Syndrome children receive adequate infant stimulation, receive appropriate medical intervention for physical anomalies, and are monitored for imbalances (such as thryoid deficiency), the degree of mental retardation experienced by the child can be minimized. It is, therefore, incumbent upon the professional to be aware of existing early intervention programs in the community and be knowledgeable about the efficacy of such programs (Dunst, 1990).

Parents may blame themselves for their child's disability. Although an occasional condition, such as those that are associated with fetal alcoholism syndrome, is related to the behavior of the parent, most conditions are not. The professional can help parents in understanding that their child's disability is not their fault. Some parents nevertheless begin an endless search for the cause of their child's problem at this point. Feelings of guilt may center on past "misdeeds," as parents focus on events that cannot be changed and over which they have no control. The professional can explore guilt feelings with parents, help them understand their source, and help them accept that emotions such as guilt and anger are normal under the circumstances. In coming to grips with their situation, it is in the parents' best interest to work on those aspects of their lives, over which they do have some control (Prescott & Hulnick, 1979). The professional can empathize with the parents' feelings of guilt and also be sensitive to parental grieving but also can gently redirect the discussion to engaging in more activities to help develop a sense of mastery. Parents may be tempted to make up for supposed inadequacies by trying to be overprotective and not permit their child to experience the usual vicissitudes of childhood.

Parents may be tempted to throw all their energy into making up for their child's deficiencies. Careers may be ended or other drastic lifestyle changes may be made to the extent that all waking hours are devoted to the care and development of their child. Parents who need support and new perspectives may find it beneficial to become involved in a parent group with other parents who are facing similar problems. Such a group can help one to discover perspectives regarding their own needs and those of their child's. Although the disabled child may require more care for a more extended time period than nondisabled children, families need to find time to pursue other interests and to fulfill the needs of all family members.

Parents may have a difficult time providing appropriate parenting for their child. Feelings about the child and guilt about having such negative feelings may interfere with normal parenting responses. In addition, the child may not provide expected cues to the parent such as crying, cooing, visual tracking, or laughing. A lack of mutual cueing may result in a strained and awkward situation for the parent and child alike. The professional can help parents explore their feelings toward their child and to help them develop a more positive relationship. Parents can be helped to explore what cues they provide to their children and, vice versa, what methods of communication their children are using to communicate with them. Both parents and children may have legitimate communication styles that need to be understood by the other. On the other hand, parents may need to learn new techniques to communicate with their children.

Parents may withdraw from their child and attempt to disassociate themselves from the imperfections their child manifests. Some parents appropriately use counseling to help them separate from their child (Ferhold & Solnit, 1978). Generally, though, the professional helps parents in separating negative feelings toward the disability from their other, more positive feelings toward their child. Parents may need to express the hopes and dreams they had for their hoped-for normal child before they can work on developing new life goals that take the child's disabling condition into consideration. Expectations for the child may need to be modified but not necessarily totally abandoned.

Parents are confronted with many practical problems in raising a disabled child. Because of the special services the child may need, the family's financial resources may be strained, thereby limiting opportunities for other family members, such as college for other children. Family social and recreational patterns may be altered considerably owing to the added care required by the child or by the social stigma parents experience. Available time for parents to pursue personal interests may be markedly reduced. Sexual relationships may be hindered by negative feelings about oneself or one's partner or by the fear of producing another disabled child. It is important that parents find appropriate outlets for expressing negative feelings about the child's disability so that it is not directed toward the child, their other children or each other. Individual counseling is, of course, an appropriate vehicle for the expression of anger and the exploration of feelings of other emotions. Another excellent source of help is peer-conducted groups, where parents who share similar problems assemble for mutual support and practical help. The mental health professional should not overlook this potent resource for parents because it is an excellent adjunct to individual counseling and one that is gaining momentum as a viable mental health alternative (Seligman & Marshak, in press). Parent support groups are often sponsored by organizations that focus on specific disabilities. The professional may also wish to explore the possibility of forming a parent group. Recent developments have resulted in separate groups for fathers, siblings, and grandparents (Seligman & Darling, 1989).

Gordon (1970) wrote that parents of children with disabilities must deal with thoughts and feelings they find unacceptable. The professional can help parents explore disturbing thoughts and puzzling, unacceptable feelings. Depressive thoughts, such as wishing their child were dead or that they themselves were dead, may occur and need to be expressed and understood. Professionals can only be effective with parents during such emotionally charged moments when they themselves have come to terms with feelings often condemned by society.

The professional must be aware that a parent's feelings of rejection are not all-or-nothing emotions or a one-time occurrence. Parents may deeply love their child but may find one aspect of their child's condition difficult to accept. Also, feelings of rejection, similar to other emotions, tend to be cyclical, that is, they come and go over time. It is important for the professional to help parents realize that feelings of anger and occasional or limited rejection are normal and that their expression is acceptable. Hearing feelings of anger and rejection from other parents (say, in a self-help group) who have a child with a similar handicapping condition may prove effective at reducing guilt. Parents may feel that they alone have these feelings toward their child and thus they must be awful or sinful. Such thoughts are usually abandoned by sharing experiences with other parents.

Parents may withdraw from their child. They may pick up cues from family, friends, and neighbors that they are different from other people. Like parents, other people hold certain views of how children should look and act. Neighbors and friends may be perceived as acting in a more reserved manner toward the family. Kazak and Wilcox (1984) reported that the overall social support network of families with children with spina bifida compared to families with nondisabled children was smaller, perhaps because other family members provided more social support which reduced the need for other relationships, but perhaps also because of stigmatizing social encounters. In regard to others' reactions, Mark Twain (Clemens, 1963) once wrote, "There is something that he [man] loves more than peace — the approval of his neighbors and the public. And perhaps there is something which he dreads more than he dreads pain — the disapproval of his neighbors and the public (p. 344)." The social stigma parents often experience explains why family members may feel more comfortable with others who share a similar life situation. By associating with other parents in similar circumstances, they can feel reassured that they will be accepted.

Parents may feel that they have let others down, especially other family members such as a spouse or grandparent. In individual or group counseling or in a support group, parents can learn that their sense of being different in some fundamental way and feeling ashamed of their disabled youngster in certain social situations is typical and that they are not alone in suffering from such feelings. They can explore these emotions and learn not to feel shame over a situation not of their making and to feel pride in their accomplishments and those of their children.

Denial is a frequently cited phenomenon in the literature. Denial is a coping strategy that helps ward off excess anxiety (in this case the frightening reality that one's child is disabled). It is noteworthy that reality may serve the cause of denial to some extent. For example, a mildly disabled child may be an only child, making the opportunities for comparison of development limited. In addition, accurate intellectual evaluation of very young children with motor and sensory deficits is difficult, enabling parents and even professionals to believe whatever they want to believe about the child's true ability. As noted previously, in searching for a more favorable diagnosis and prognosis, parents may hop from one professional to another, often wasting time, energy, and money. For some parents this activity is essential, and unless it reaches the point of absurdity, professionals should be cautious about dissuading parents from seeking additional advice. Such behavior is not always caused by denial but may reflect parents' realistic appraisal of their situation and their need to behave in certain ways because of the nature of the disability or the quality of professional help available.

A general rule for professionals to follow is never try to force parents to cast aside a previously successful method of coping; the abrupt unveiling of what is being kept from conscious awareness can have a devastating effect. The strategy of encouraging parents to embrace the reality of their child's disability is necessary, but this step should never be attempted when parents are seen to desperately cling to their unrealistic view of their child. Denial that is chronic, however, requires attention. It is important to recognize that chronic denial can have severe consequences if parents fail to seek help and continue to make unrealistic demands on their child.

There is some danger in having only one parent involved in the counseling process. Additional strain is placed on the spousal unit when one parent begins to realize the seriousness of the disability and the other continues firmly to deny it. Sympathetic friends, relatives, and professionals may unintentionally support the parent's denial of the child's shortcomings by stressing assets and minimizing limitations. It is important that the professional provide encouragement and an atmosphere in which parents can recognize their child's special needs and not conspire with others to promote denial.

Some parents may never stop denying that their child is disabled. They may accept the diagnosis but reject its prognostic implications by holding onto the possibility of finding a miracle drug, a new operation, or a radically new diet. A parent may, for example, see her child as a "slow learner" rather than as mentally retarded and thus may place unrealistic performance expectations on the child. Parents may return to these feelings when their child seems to be making some progress and thoughts of the idealized normal child is again evoked.

It has been our experience that parents must be ready for help before the counseling process can be effective. If help is offered before parents are ready to accept it, they may enter into the therapeutic relationship only superficially. When their motivation to seek help is weak, it may be judicious to inform parents that counseling will be available in the future should they believe it would benefit them.

As the child grows older and passes milestones, such as beginning school or graduation from school, parents may reexperience many old feelings. The professional must recognize that the parents' feelings toward their child are cyclical and not be alarmed if parents need to cover "old territory" at different times of their child's development. Indeed, the professional should be aware of four major turning points in the developmental cycle of families with a disabled child.

1. When parents first learn about or suspect the existence of a disability.
2. At about age 5 or 6, when a decision must be reached regarding the child's education.
3. When the time has arrived for the child to leave school.
4. When the parents become older and may be unable to care for their child.

Opihory and Peters (1982), employing a stages model, provide a useful guide to interventions with parents who have recently given birth to a disabled newborn. Stage theory holds that parents generally follow a fairly predictable series of feelings and actions after a child's diagnosis has been communicated to them. The stages are shock/denial, anger, bargaining, depression, and acceptance.

During the *shock/denial* stage, the professional should gently provide an honest evaluation of the situation that the parents are confronting. Simply describe the child objectively and indicate that some special care is needed. The professional should not remove the parent's hope or interfere with their coping style unless it is inappropriate or dysfunctional to the family.

When parents reach the *anger* stage, the professional must create an open and permissive atmosphere so that parents can vent their anger and pain. The professional must be accepting of the parents' criticism, even if it is directed toward him or her, and not personalize their remarks or defend other professionals or himself or herself. It is important to keep in mind that projected anger reflects the parents' own anxiety and stress in the face of a situation that will significantly change their lives. On the other hand, the helper needs to be mindful that some parents have been treated so atrociously by professionals that their anger and frustration are genuine. The distinction between real and projected anger can be difficult to evaluate. It helps to be knowledgeable about the quality of service provision offered by local agencies and personnel so that appropriate referrals are made to competent professionals. It is important at this stage for professionals to allow parents to express their feelings and to avoid diverting or suppressing their anger.

Opihory and Peters (1982) recommended that professionals discourage parents from dwelling on a review of the pregnancy during the *bargaining* stage. During this phase, parents feel that they can reverse their child's condition by engaging in certain redemptive activities. Opihory and Peters advise that the professional should point out a child's positive characteristics, encourage involvement, and remain optimistic without giving guarantees about the child's potential progress. It is also essential that parents continue to establish warm and loving relationships with their disabled child and balance their life with personal goals that may be fulfilling. Professionals need to be wary of parents who fill their lives with a variety of outside activities at the expense of their child or of parents who are so involved with the child that their lives becomes severely restricted.

The *depression* stage can be characterized by mild or severe mood swings. The professional needs to be able to distinguish between clinical depression and milder forms of disphoria. Mild, situational, and time-limited depression is common, and parents need to be reassured that what they are experiencing is normal. Feelings of depression do not occur just once but can emerge at various stages of the family's life cycle. Opihory and Peters (1982) and Olshansky (1962) stated that professionals should not be critical of the parents' feelings of depression but should continue to show concern for their welfare. They believe that professionals need to be especially alert to signs of regression to earlier stages, although we do not necessarily view this with alarm. Anger and mild denial, for example, can resurface and should be considered normal unless these feelings become chronic and are held on to rigidly.

During the *acceptance* stage, the professional should continue to reinforce the positive aspects of the parent-child relationship. This stage is typically characterized by family relationships that are fulfilling because a realistic adjustment to the disabled family member has been achieved. Therefore, the need for professional help and support is more likely not crucial at this stage.

As the child matures into adolescence and young adulthood, parents may have difficulty allowing their child to move away from home, either to a community residential treatment setting or to independent living, even when such a living arrangement is indicated and available. Parents may be so invested in their child that they may find it exceedingly difficult to "let go." Letting go is especially difficult for overprotective parents who view their son's or daughter's growing independence with apprehension. In such instances the professional can empathize with their apprehension and feelings of loss and help parents redirect their desire to nurture. It may also be useful to remind parents that contact between them and their child will not cease. Furthermore, for willing parents, it can be beneficial for them to explore the genesis of their overprotective behavior toward their child.

On the other hand, parents may have the desire for their children to achieve independence. They may be tired of the long-term nurturance that has been required of them, they may wish to experience the freedom of a childless home, or they may see independent living as a natural and age-appropriate development for their child. Placement may be desired but may not be obtainable. It is not unusual for community residential programs to have long waiting lists where only placements of an emergency nature occur. Public agencies may not show great empathy for the need for placement for families who have lovingly cared for their children. Ironically, those families who have provided for their children may be the ones denied residential placement, whereas other, less caring families gain greater access to this service.

Concurrently, children who have reached adulthood and who no longer receive special education may not be sufficiently in need of services to qualify for adult day programming. Parents need to be prepared for this possibility and to be ready to have their child home during the day. Parents need to be aided in making plans for their children beyond graduation from school so that developmental gains are not lost and so that behavioral difficulties do not begin or increase. Parents need to be encouraged to support and seek out newer, nontraditional vocational programs such as supported work that can help their child become situated into meaningful work environments. The alternative may be having their child at home all of the time, which reduces the freedom parents can look forward to in mid to late life.

The fact that a disability exists is not as important as how the disability is perceived. Phenomenologically oriented professionals argue that identical events are perceived differently by different people, a point of view that must not be lost on those who work with parents. The discovery that one has an ulcer may be taken in stride by one person and may throw another into a chronic state of depression. According to the phenomenological point of view to which we ascribe, it is possible that parents with a severely disabled child may be considerably more accepting and exhibit better coping behaviors than another set of parents who have a moderately or mildly disabled child. These individual differences make it imperative that the professional look at the parents' circumstances from *their* point of view. Although many factors contribute to highly individualized reactions to a crisis, the accumulated experiences of family members predispose them to respond in certain ways to specific life events.

As previously mentioned, parents may have difficulties that are a response to dysfunctional family interactions or they may suffer from a mental health disorder that is not the result of the presence of a disabled child. The professional can explore these difficulties with parents, helping them separate these concerns from problems more clearly associated with their child. The professional can also help parents become aware of how the child aggravates preexisting difficulties. Providing help to a parent who is mentally ill or mentally retarded poses unique problems. It has been our experience that such parents can respond to specific, concrete aid in the form of in-home programming where both modeling and ongoing support is provided. Assistance is, by necessity, likely to continue to be needed over an extended period. Also, the professional should be aware of signs of neglect and abuse and be prepared to respond as required by law. Even families displaying a high degree of dysfunction can learn to cope more effectively with the difficulties of rearing a disabled child.

Disabled children share a number of developmental milestones, childhood diseases, and personality changes that their nondisabled counterparts undergo—a point of view that the professional may wish to share with parents. The professional can help parents assess their child in terms of normal child development, which may help them focus more on similarities than on differences. As noted earlier parents may become so overprotective that the child is not given the opportunity to learn by experimenting, trying and failing, trying again and succeeding, a normal requisite of child development. Wolfensberger (1972) referred to "the dignity of risk" in asserting that the taking of risks is crucial to the development of all people; individuals learn through both their successes and mistakes. The professional can help parents decide what are reasonable risks for their child and encourage parents to support their child's positive efforts and generally promote early cognitive and socioemotional parent-child experiences.

Child rearing is a challenging task for any parent, yet parents of special needs children are generally burdened by additional stressors. The professional can help these parents cope by providing the support and understanding they need to see that their child has value and potential and that the family can achieve many of their goals.

Personal Advocacy Counseling

Parents have the ultimate responsibility and authority for the welfare of their children unless this responsibility is removed by legal means. Parents typically want what is best for their children, yet they may not know how to obtain it. Furthermore, parents of a disabled child may become involved with professionals from many different agencies who provide them with advice and recommendations that may be conflicting or confusing.

Parents may therefore be puzzled after receiving well-meaning, yet confusing and conflicting advice from several sources.

Personal advocacy counseling refers to the process of aiding parents to actively and purposively work for their own and their child's welfare by obtaining the support and services they need. This model of counseling helps parents become their own case managers. Parents learn about their personal power to make positive changes and use that power to do so.

Families often need a combination of both "hard" and "soft" services (Bubolz & Whiren, 1984). Hard services such as respite care, in-home aid, and other family support services can reduce the family's level of distress. Soft services such as counseling augment other essential services and help families cope with emotional, relationship, and practical issues. Personal advocacy counseling can help families use hard services more effectively.

Providing help to disabled individuals and their families can be a formidable task. Conflicting opinions exist as to which treatments or courses of action are most beneficial. For example, one educator may recommend a self-contained classroom, whereas another may recommend mainstreaming. Conflicting professional opinions leave parents in a quandary: Who should they believe? How do they decide which method is likely to achieve the best results?

In addition to differing opinions of their child's diagnosis, prognosis, education or rehabilitation, parents may have to juggle advice from a variety of sources, such as a health agency, a mental health/mental retardation center, a school, a child welfare agency, a respite care service, and others. Each may have its particular perspective regarding what is in the best interest of the child. It is little wonder that parents seeking appropriate and adequate care for their child find the maze of professional services so confusing (see Chapter 4). One of us has had the experience of working with one family that was involved with 22 different service providers at the same time. This wealth of services may be as detrimental to the family as not having enough support.

Each service may require parents to be involved in developing an individualized plan of action. These planning meetings, often conducted by a professional team, can be intimidating to the parent. In such instances, personal advocacy counseling can assist parents by helping them clarify what it is they wish for their child, helping them prepare what they want to communicate at such meetings, and supporting the notion that their ideas and input are an important part of the team planning process.

Brewer and Kakalik (1979) found that, although many services are available for children and their families, parents often are not aware of them. These researchers found that even when parents knew of services they often did not know how to access or coordinate services to meet their own and their children's needs. Although parents must shoulder most of the responsibility for their child, they may not have the knowledge to decide what services are best or most appropriate. They therefore need help in deciding which problems require their attention and what services will best meet these needs. The professional can help parents in becoming their own case managers by carefully sifting through goals for the child and the family and by being educated about which services/agencies can meet identified goals.

Many states are now making specific services available to families with disabled children. These services, often called family support services, may help the family in maintaining their disabled child in the home (Castellani, Downey, Tausig, & Bird, 1986). Important support services such as transportation, respite care, and information and referral may be lacking or may only be available to families with children with specific disabilities. Furthermore, investigation into what services should be made available and in what manner they should be provided needs to occur. These support services become especially critical as the availability of out-of-home placement options declines.

The professional must become familiar with general referral procedures and must be knowledgeable about how the various human services available to parents and their disabled children operate. For example, finding financial services may be most critical for the well-being of a particular family. McCubbin et al. (1982) wrote that the financial burdens carried by a family with a child with cerebral palsy is a source of continual family stress. For example, a child with cerebral palsy may need expensive adaptive equipment, architectural modifications, and medical and rehabilitative treatment.

Professionals should not be expected to become familiar with all of the specific services available. However, they should be generally knowledgeable about the community and what it can provide for families in terms of supportive services. One of us found that over 800 human service providers were extending services to individuals living in an area with fewer than half a million people (Laborde, 1979). He also found that services changed rapidly, with at least one significant change (moved, new programs added, old programs deleted, new phone number) occurring in one fourth of these services every 3 months. With such rapid change, the professional cannot be expected to keep abreast of the details of all specific services. Even so, as already noted, professionals who work with parents should be generally aware of available resources.

Professionals must be wary of referring parents to the same few agencies. Agencies that are well known to one professional are most likely well known to others. These agencies are often overutilized, whereas other agencies with similar services and comparable expertise may remain underutilized.

Brewer and Kakalik (1979) proposed that direction should be provided to parents with disabled children for the purpose of aiding them in their search for appropriate services. Professionals should be familiar with several resources within their community that can perform this function, such as information and referral services, associations concerned with specific disabilities, and municipal or county human service consortia. The professional may act as a broker of these services by helping the parent formulate a clear idea of which needs are most pressing and deciding where to receive services. The professional, for example, may contact information clearinghouses to obtain complete, accurate, and up-to-date information on available services to meet specific needs. With such information in hand, the professional can help the parent develop a plan of action for obtaining needed assistance. This type of help can be an important component of personal advocacy counseling and decision making.

The primary goal of personal advocacy counseling is to assist parents experience a sense of control over their life. Parents, by experiencing this sense of potency, may act with greater confidence and purpose when confronted with choices or situations not to their liking. Personal advocacy counseling can help parents work for their family's welfare in a positive, determined manner.

For more socially and politically minded parents the professional can help in encouraging them to advocate for issues that are important to them. Individuals with disabilities need the help of all concerned people. Parents are a group that legislators listen to, and it is our view that professionals must support parents in their efforts to make their voices heard so that the social conditions for all people with disabilities continue to improve.

REFERENCES

Barsch, R. H. (1969). *The teacher-parent partnership.* Arlington, VA: Council for Exceptional Children.

Beckman, P. J. (1983). Influence of selected child characteristics on stress in families of handicapped infants. *American Journal of Mental Deficiency, 88,* pp. 150–156.

Berko, F. (1970). *Management of brain damaged children: A parent's and teacher's guide.* Springfield, IL: Charles C Thomas.

Bissell, N. E. (1976). Communicating with the parents of exceptional children. In E. J. Webser (Ed.), *Professional approaches with parents of handicapped children.* Springfield, IL: Charles C Thomas.

Blacher, J., Nihira, K., & Meyers, C. E. (1987). Characteristics of home environment of families with mentally retarded children: Comparison across levels of retardation. *American Journal of Mental Deficiency, 91,* pp. 313–320.

Bradshaw, J., & Lawton, D. (1978). Tracing the causes of stress in families with handicapped children. *British Journal of Social Work, 8,* pp. 181–192.

Brassel, W. (1977). Intervention with handicapped infants: Correlates of progress. *Mental Retardation, 15,* pp. 18–22.

Brewer, G., & Kakalik, J. (1979). *Handicapped children: Strategies for improving services.* New York: McGraw-Hill.

Bristol, M. M., & Schopler, E. (1984). A developmental perspective on stress and coping in families of autistic children. In J. Blacher (Ed.), *Severely handicapped young children and their families.* Orlando, FL: Academic Press, pp. 91–142.

Bubolz, M. M., & Whiren, A. P. (1984). The family of the handicapped: An ecological model for policy. *Family Relations, 33,* pp. 5–12.

Burton, L. (1975). *The family life of sick children: A study of families coping with chronic childhood disease.* London: Routledge & Kegan Paul.

Caplan, F. (1972). *The first twelve months of life.* New York: Grosset & Dunlap.

Carr, E. G., & Durand, V. M. (1985). Reducing behavior problems through functional communication training. *Journal of Applied Behavior Analysis, 18,* pp. 111–126.

Castellani, P. J., Downey, N. A., Tausig, M. B., & Bird, W. A. (1986). Availability and accessibility of family support services. *Mental Retardation, 24,* pp. 71–79.

Chinn, P. C., Winn, J., & Walters, R. H. (1978). *Two-way talking with parents of special children.* St. Louis, MO: Mosby.

Clemens, S. L. (1963). What is man? In C. Neider (Ed.), *The complete essays of Mark Twain.* Garden City, NY: Doubleday.

Cummings, S. T. (1976). The impact of the child's deficiency on the father: A study of fathers of mentally retarded and chronically ill children. *American Journal of Orthopsychiatry, 46,* pp. 246–255.

Cummings, S. T., Bayley, H. C., & Rie, H. (1966). Effects of the child's deficiency on the mother: A study of mothers of mentally retarded, chronically ill, and neurotic children. *American Journal of Orthopsychiatry, 36,* pp. 595–608.

Darling, R. B., & Darling, J. (1982). *Children who are different: Meeting the challenge of birth defects in society.* St. Louis, MO: Mosby.

Davidson, P. O., & Schrag, A. R. (1968). Prognostic indicators for effective child psychiatric consultations. *Canadian Psychiatric Association Journal, 13,* p. 533.

Dunst, C. (1990). Discerning the implications and future of early intervention efficacy research. Paper presented at the University of Pittsburgh, School of Education.

Eyman, R. K., & Call, T. (1977). Maladaptive behavior and community placement of mentally retarded persons. *American Journal of Mental Deficiency, 82,* pp. 137–144.

Fellendorf, G. W., & Harrow, I. (1969). If I had to do it over . . . *Exceptional Children, 36,* pp. 43–44.

Ferhold, J. B. & Solnit, A. (1978). Counseling parents of mentally retarded and learning disordered children. In E. Arnold (Ed.), *Helping parents help their children.* New York: Brunner/Mazel.

Finnie, N. R. (1968). *Handling the young cerebral palsy child at home.* New York: United Cerebral Palsy Association.

Fowle, C. M. (1968). The effect of a severely mentally retarded child on his family. *American Journal of Mental Deficiency, 73,* pp. 468–473.

Fox, M. A. (1975). The handicapped family. *Lancet, 2,* pp. 400–401.

Freeman, R., & Pearson, P. (1978). Counseling with parents. In J. Apley (Ed.), *Care of the handicapped child.* London: Laverham Press.

Freeston, B. M. (1971). An inquiry into the effect of a spina bifida child upon family life. *Developmental Medicine and Child Neurology, 13,* pp. 456–461.

Goldberg, S., Marcovitch, S., MacGregor, D.. & Lojkasek, M. (1986). Family responses to developmentally delayed preschoolers: Etiology and father's role. *American Journal of Mental Deficiency, 90,* pp. 610–617.

Gollay, E., Freedman, R., Wyngaarden, M., & Kurz, N. (1978). *Coming back: The community experiences of deinstitutionalized mentally retarded people.* Cambridge, MA: Abt Books.

Gordon, T. (1970). *Parent effectiveness training.* New York: Wyden.

Gorham, K. A., Des Jardins, C., Page, R., Pettis, E., & Scheiber, B. (1975). Effects on parents. In N. Hobbs (Ed.), *Issues in the classification of children.* San Francisco, CA: Jossey-Bass, pp. 154–188.

Grossman, F. K. (1972). *Brothers and sisters of retarded children.* Syracuse, NY: Syracuse University Press.

Guralnick, M. J. & Richardson, H. B. (Eds.). (1980). *Pediatric education and the needs of exceptional children.* Baltimore, MD: University Park Press.

Hart, N. W. (1970). Frequently expressed feelings and reactions of parents toward their retarded child. In N. R. Bernstein (Ed.), *Diminished people: Problems and care of the mentally retarded.* Boston: Little, Brown, pp. 47–72.

Hornby, G. (1989). Effects on fathers of parenting a child with Down's syndrome. Paper presented at the Annual Conference of the British Psychological Society, Bournmouth, England.

Howard, J. (1982). The role of the pediatrician with young exceptional children and their families. *Exceptional Children 48,* pp. 316–321.

Jacobs, F. H., & Walker, D. K. (1978). Pediatricians and the Education for All Handicapped Children Act of 1975 (Public Law 94–142). *Pediatrics, 61,* pp. 135–137.

Jordan, T. E. (1971). Physical disability in children and family adjustment. In R. L. Noland (Ed.), *Counseling parents of the ill and handicapped.* Springfield, IL: Charles C Thomas, pp. 16–26.

Kazak, A., & Wilcox, B. (1984). The structure and function of social support networks in families with handicapped children. *American Journal of Community Psychology,* pp. 645–661.

Keirn, W. C. (1971). Shopping parents: Patient problem or professional problem? *Mental Retardation, 9,* pp. 6–7.

Kroth, R. L. (1975). *Communicating with parents of exceptional children: Improving parent-teacher relationships.* Denver, CO: Love.

Laborde, P. R. (1979). *Annual report,* (Pennsylvania Direction Service, Contract No. 300–77–0458). Washington, DC: U.S. Department of Health, Education and Welfare, Bureau of Education for the Handicapped.

McCubbin, H. I., Nevin, R. S., Cauble, A. E., Larsen, A., Comeau, J. K., & Patterson, J. M. (1982). Family coping with chronic illness: The case of cerebral palsy. In H. McCubbin, E. Cauble, & J. Patterson (Eds.), *Family stress, coping and social support,* Springfield, IL: Charles C Thomas.

McDowell, R. L. (1976). Parent counseling: The state of the art. *Journal of Learning Disabilities, 9,* pp. 614–619.

McWilliams, B. J. (1976). Various aspects of parent counseling. In E. J. Webster (Ed.), *Professional approaches with parents of handicapped children,* Springfield, IL: Charles C Thomas.

Meyerwitz, J. H., & Kaplan H. B. (1967). Familial responses to stress: The case of cystic fibrosis. *Social Science and Medicine, 1,* pp. 249–266.

Olshansky, S. (1962). Chronic sorrow: A response to having a mentally defective child. Social Casework, 43, pp. 191–194.

Opirhory, G., & Peters, G. A. (1982). Counseling intervention strategies for families with the less than perfect newborn. *Personnel Guidance Journal,* 60, pp. 451–455.

Paul, J. L. (Ed.). (1981). *Understanding and working with parents of children with special needs.* New York: Holt, Rinehart & Winston.

Peterson, P. (1984). Effects of moderator variables in reducing stress outcome in mothers of children with disabilities. *Journal of Psychosomatic Research, 28,* pp. 337–344.

Pines, M. (1982, November). Infant-stim: It's changing the lives of handicapped kids. *Psychology Today,* pp. 48–53.

Pitt, D. (1974). *Your Down's syndrome child: You can help him develop from infancy to adulthood.* Arlington, TX: National Association for Retarded Citizens.

Powers, J. T., & Healy, A. (1982). Inservice training for physicians serving handicapped children, *Exceptional Children* 48(4), 48, pp. 332–336.

Prescott, R., & Hulnick, P. (1979). Counseling parents of handicapped children: An empathetic approach. *Personnel and Guidance Journal, 58,* pp. 263–266.

Pueschel, S. M., & Murphy, A. (1976). Assessment of counseling practices at the birth of a child with Down's syndrome. *American Journal of Mental Deficiency, 81,* pp. 325–330.

Reynolds, M. C., & Birch, J. W. (1982). *Teaching exceptional children in all America's schools* (Rev. ed.). Reston, VA: Council for Exceptional Children.

Ross, A. O. (1964). *The exceptional child in the family: Helping parents of exceptional children.* New York: Grune & Stratton.

Sabbeth, B. F., & Leventhal, J. M. (1984). Marital adjustment to chronic childhood illness: A critique of the literature. *Pediatrics* 73, pp. 762–768.

Schwartz, C. G. (1970). Strategies and tactics of mothers of mentally retarded children for dealing with the medical care system. In N. R. Bernstein (Ed.), *Diminished people: Problems and care of the mentally retarded.* Boston: Little, Brown, pp. 73–106.

Seligman, M. (1979). *Strategies for helping parents of exceptional children.* New York: Free Press.

Seligman, M. (Ed.). (1982). *Group psychotherapy and counseling with special populations.* Baltimore, MD: University Park Press.

Seligman, M., & Darling, R. R. (in press). *Ordinary families, special children: A systems approach to childhood disability.* New York: Guilford Press.

Seligman, M., and Marshak, L. (Eds.). (1990). *Group Psychology: Interventions with Special Populations.* Boston: Allyn and Bacon.

Seligman, M., & Seligman, P. A. (1980). The professional's dilemma: Learning to work with parents. *The Exceptional Parent, 10,* pp. 511–513.

Springer, A., & Steele, M. (1980). Effects of physicians early parental counseling on rearing of Down's syndrome children. *American Journal of Mental Deficiency, 85,* pp. 1–5.

Telford, C. W., & Sawrey. J. M. (1981). *The exceptional individual* (2nd ed.). Englewood Cliffs, NJ: Prentice Hall.

United States Department of Education. (1987). *To assure free appropriate public education: Ninth annual report to Congress on the implementation of the Education of the Handicapped Act.* Washington DC.

Walker, J. H. (1971). Spina bifida—and the parents. *Developmental Medicine and Child Neurology, 13,* pp. 462–476.

Wolfensberger, W. (1972). *Normalization: The principle of normalization in human services.* Toronto: National Institute on Mental Retardation.

Wolraich, M. L. (1982). Communication between physicians and parents of handicapped children. *Exceptional Children, 48,* pp. 324–329.

CHAPTER THIRTEEN

Family Therapy

Nancy S. Elman

Nancy S. Elman, Ph.D., is an associate professor in the Psychology in Education Department, School of Education, University of Pittsburgh. She teaches introductory and advanced courses in family systems and family therapy and serves as coordinator of practicum and internship training for the Program in Counseling Psychology. In addition, Elman serves on the faculty of the Family Therapy Certificate Program in the School of Social Work and is a psychotherapist in private practice in Pittsburgh.

Over the past 25 years, family therapy research and practice has evolved into a full-scale and well-accepted approach to dealing with human problems. It is one of the newest strategies, following well-entrenched psychodynamic approaches to individual and group treatment that developed in the early twentieth century and flourished in the years immediately after World War II. Models of family therapy typically credit general systems theory, developed in the 1940s by biologist Ludwig von Bertalanffy, with the basic framework for studying complex interaction in living systems (Hoffman, 1981). Several models of family intervention, such as the psychodynamic, structural, and strategic models, have each in their turn been embraced as the most promising approach to the practice of family therapy, but there is now a movement toward a synthesis and integration of the best of these approaches (Nichols, 1984).

369

Only in recent years have there been efforts to apply family therapy models specifically to families with a disabled member (Berger & Foster, 1986; Kaslow & Cooper, 1978; Powers & Bruey, 1988). Therapeutic interventions have progressed from a focus on the child, to the mother-child dyad, and lastly to others in the family, particularly fathers and siblings (Houser, 1987; Seligman, 1983). Most recently, attention to the interactive functioning within the total family system and between the family and other systems has been seen as crucial in helping families with a disabled member (Coppersmith, 1984; Turnbull, Summers, & Brotherson, 1986). One image of the family that conveys its interconnectedness is that of the mobile. Like a huge cast steel Calder mobile, or a small one hanging over a baby's crib, each piece in the structure is connected to every other. Movement in one part of the mobile necessarily sets off change in each other part until the entire structure inevitably reestablishes a balance, a homeostasis, and comes to rest. It may be useful to think of the family as structured like a mobile, set in motion by a shift from within or without, seeking a balance appropriate for its particular structure, while needing to be flexible and capable of movement.

The goal of this chapter is to describe family systems theory as it applies to therapy with families with a disabled child. A family systems perspective and several key dimensions of family systems functioning are described here. This is followed by an overview of systemic family therapy interventions with families with a disabled child and also presents what is *generally* understood about families with a disabled child. The therapist is cautioned to make a careful assessment of the structure and dynamics over time of a particular disability in a specific family context before planning interventions (Crnic, Friedrich, & Greenberg, 1983).

Most studies of family dynamics have been either case study or cross-sectional designs. They have often lacked control groups and groups of families with children with different disabling conditions. Furthermore, they have considered only a few of the myriad intervening variables, although it is clear that families as functioning systems are intricate and complex. In addition to these methodological weaknesses, it must be kept in mind that many family therapy interventions have not been carefully evaluated for families with children with specific disabilities.

In sum, there is little at this point that can be said definitively about *the* family with a disabled child. From both research and clinical points of view there are deficiencies in our application of family systems theory in this area. To date, therapists applying this knowledge to families with a disabled child have been the exception. The family therapist about to engage a family with a disabled child would be well to remember Tolstoy's famous introduction to *Anna Karenina:* "Happy families are all alike; every unhappy family is unhappy in its own way."

THE FAMILY SYSTEM AND THE THERAPIST

Families initially come in contact with a family therapist in one of two ways. They may be referred by any number of other persons or agencies such as friends, family, physicians, school, or a social agency. Alternatively, the family may come for help on their own, hoping or believing that their intolerable discomfort or pain can be alleviated (Kaslow & Cooper, 1978). In either case, the family that appears for treatment with a therapist typically feels hopeless, perhaps helpless, and family members believe that they have failed utterly in their efforts to cope. Therefore, the therapist about to engage a family with a disabled child needs to not only understand the family dynamics and be able to apply appropriate therapeutic interventions, but must recognize the family's desperate need for support and affirmation. The fact that they have sought help, however resistant or defensive they may initially appear, is a step toward the family's investment in improved functioning and is an indication of positive motivation. The family does not wish to continue to suffer!

If the family was referred to the therapist, the referring person(s), particularly if medical or school based, may have made family members feel that they are to blame for their plight. The decision to make a referral may have been determined by a perception that the family has failed to cooperate or comply with the agency's plan for treatment of the child. Therefore, the therapist must be sensitive to the reason for the referral, and care must be taken not to create or maintain a dysfunctional triangle between the agency, the therapist, and the family (Selvini-Palazzolo, Boscolo, Cecchin & Prata, 1980). The therapist must be perceived from the outset as someone who supports the family and who can help them mediate the relationships among family members and between the family and others. If the therapist is perceived to the colluding with the agency in blaming the family, the therapist's effectiveness will be undermined.

Baird and Doherty (1986) referred to this complex relationship in health care as a therapeutic rectangle composed of the patient, the family, the health care team/agencies, and the therapist. From either perspective, the *treatment system* needs to be seen as incorporating and responding to each of these components, rather than merely to comprise the immediate family system members.

The message conveyed by the institutional position of the family ther-

apist suggests that even before meeting with a family, the therapist must assess the potential role conflicts, or constraints, the professional affiliation
may represent. For example, a therapist on the staff of a school or mental
health agency will have a different contextual relationship with the family
than will a therapist employed by a hospital. This may determine how the
therapist is perceived by the family and some of the ways he or she can be a
helpful resource to the family (Berger & Foster, 1986; Coppersmith, 1984).

Although the therapist may not have specific knowledge about the
handicapping condition and the agencies that provide services, some knowledge of disabilities and community services is helpful. Most important, the
therapist needs to understand and assist family members in negotiating the
family's boundaries and exchanges with those systems.

Family systems theory infers that problems in the family are not
caused by the child with a disability nor by the behaviors of any single family member. The assumption that a particular member is to blame for the
family's woes is the view that the family typically presents when they first
appear. In many families, the perceived source of the family's difficulties
will be the disabled child, the identified patient (Wikler, 1981). When all of
the family's pain or dysfunctions are blamed on the child, he or she can
acquire the role of the scapegoat* or patient, when indeed the family is the
patient.

Rather than identifying or placing blame, the family therapist takes
what is called a *systemic* view of the problem. That is, the problems the
family experiences are viewed as resulting from the interaction and reciprocal patterns of structures and functioning among members of the family
system and between the family and other systems with which it interacts —
recall the analogy of the family as a mobile.

Thus a family systems perspective shifts the focus from the identified
patient to the family; the family's problems are the result of members' dysfunctional interactive patterns. This contextual view of family functioning
further emphasizes broader systems or networks (Kazak, 1986), within
which the family interacts and which have such a powerful reciprocal influence on the family system. Especially important are the reciprocal interactions of family members with extended family (grandparents and others in
the parents' family of origin), the medical and educational systems, and the
world of work or school of family members.

This emphasis on reciprocal interaction in the family system is consis-

---

*The notion of the scapegoat is derived from an ancient Hebrew tradition. The sins of
the community were heaped symbolically on the head of a single goat, which was then sent to
wander and die in the desert, cleansing the community of its sins (Hoffman, 1981). It should
be remembered that the goat was not a particularly sinful goat before being chosen for its sacri-
ficial task!

tent with Bronfenbrenner's (1979) approach to the ecology of development, in which the interaction across levels of the individual, the family, the community, and the culture are seen as the interlocking context for both understanding and intervention. From a family systems perspective, interactive effects are viewed as having circular explanations (Hoffman, 1981). Circularity assumes that dysfunctional behavior is maintained in ongoing or redundant cyclical patterns of interaction. Intervention is aimed at modifying or adapting that interaction rather than determining, in a linear fashion, which came first or what caused the problem.

A caveat seems in order before proceeding. The notion of therapy itself usually assumes the presence of pathology. Certainly some familes with chronically handicapped children were or have become dysfunctional before they present for family treatment. Many are normal families struggling with the expectable difficulties of an already complex world that has become severely exacerbated by the specific needs of a chronically disabled child. This is a social issue, and families have become more active in recent years in defining their situation as a positive adaptation and in confronting negative professional attitudes and other stigmatizing and demeaning viewpoints (Darling, 1979; Featherstone, 1980). The assessment of the extent of dysfunction is, as well, a substantive diagnostic issue for the therapist (Harris, 1984).

Each therapist who works with a family with a disabled child must confront whatever biases he or she may hold regarding those who are disabled and the extent of pathology in their families. The first assumption that a therapist makes may well be that the family has a major pathology, particularly if the family is attempting to cope with the aftermath following the child's diagnosis. At this point, the family will be reacting to both the enormous emotional overload and the high demand for action to care for the child and obtain appropriate professional services. This view of pathology is also likely to have been inculcated in the therapist, since the language of pathology, and skills for detecting it, were typically part of professional training (Karpel, 1986).

The alternative view is that the family is attempting to cope with a critical situation that interferes with normal development. The family will continue to grow and evolve as it gains strengths and skills to cope with stress and to reorganize to meet the needs of both child and family. Therapy in this view is designed to assist the family, in an educative or supportive way, to proceed with its developmental work and deal with the often unpredictable course of the child's disabilities. The work in recent years that has focused on developmental stages and transitional processes, as well as the understanding of stress and coping processes, is particularly useful to a developmental approach to family therapy. In large part, this is why these perspectives are reviewed in this chapter as key conceptual models for approaching family therapy.

To some extent the view of the family as pathological, or alternatively as essentially normal, involves an attitudinal problem for the therapist to recognize and address. In addition, some determination must be made regarding the functioning of each particular family that relates directly to goals and intervention strategies. This assessment is central to all further work. Leahey and Wright (1985) delineated a number of conditions in a family coping with chronic illness in which intervention would be recommended. These seem to be useful criteria by which to evaluate the level of dysfunction in a family. These criteria include whether:

a. a family member's physical or mental condition is having an obvious detrimental impact upon the other family member,

b. family members are contributing to the symptoms or problems of an individual,

c. one member's improvement leads to symptoms or deterioration in another family members,

d. an important individual or family developmental milestone is missed or delayed (pp. 64–65).

Developmental phases of a child's condition or illness that might help identify the extent or lack of pathology include the following elements: diagnosis, marked deterioration in the child's condition, movement from hospital or rehabilitation center to home or community (or vice versa), or confrontation with death and dying.

Finally, a number of characteristics of the family's organization and structural dynamics will be useful in assessing the developmental/ pathological continuum of difficulties. These include the following: the extent to which the family and subsystems within the family are overinvolved and/or isolated from supports and resources; the extent to which functional roles have become split, rigid, or redundant; and the extent to which parental or marital issues are regularly being deflected or detoured through the symptomatic child. These and other dimensions of family structure and function are discussed in the following sections.

MODELS OF FAMILY FUNCTIONING

Family Life Cycle Development

Life cycle theories have been well-established as models for describing and understanding development and change in families and individuals. In addition to well-known intrapsychic models of development such as those of Erikson (1963) and Piaget (1963), which have been applied to individuals, several key stages of both family and marital life cycle have been described (Carter & McGoldrick, 1980; Duvall, 1977; Scarf, 1987).

Most life cycle models emphasize the increasing capacity for autonomy and differentiation, without loss of the capacity for intimacy, relatedness, or connectedness. Developmental models posit that both dependent, or relational, and independent capacities need to be enhanced and imply that transitions require reorganization or restructuring of the individual's relationships to others and to work.

From a family systems perspective, it is important to assess the extent to which family distress may be expressive of developmental tasks and transitions appropriate to the stage of the family. In traditional families, life cycle models typically describe six or eight distinct stages of family development. Most have to do with the modifications associated with the growth and changing needs of children. Duvall (1977) provided a widely used eight-stage model of family life.

1. Married couples without children
2. Childbearing families
3. Families with preschool children
4. Families with schoolchildren
5. Families with teenagers
6. Families as launching centers as children leave home
7. Middle-age parents (empty nest)
8. Aging family members.

A family stage in this model is usually determined by the age/tasks of the oldest child, so a family might be dealing with more than one set of developmental tasks.

Any disruption from a traditional pattern, such as divorce, death, or remarriage, adds new subphases and additional developmental tasks to the cycle. Across the life cycle, change and transitional processes become normal and expectable sources of stress for any family. Understanding family life cycle theory helps both the therapist and the family avoid a pathological interpretation when the experienced stresses are due to life transitions.

The family with a disabled member faces both normative and atypical developmental tasks. Researchers on disability and chronic illness are beginning to study the reciprocal impact of these normative and disability specific developmental tasks and processes (Rolland, 1987; Turnbull et al., 1986). Turnbull et al. (1986) are particularly helpful in identifying stresses of families with mentally retarded members that arise during each developmental stage of the family and intersect with normative developmental needs of other family members. They suggest that anticipation and preparation for both on-time and "off-time" transitions mitigates their difficulties.

Rolland (1987) also developed a model of the interaction of the family life cycle with the course of the illness. Rolland organized illness or diseases from a psychosocial perspective and over time: from the onset of the illness or diagnosis and the crisis it may provoke, through the chronic or "long haul" phase, to a terminal phase dealing with death and dying, mourning, and loss. Categories for assessing the developmental context of the disease include (a) onset, (b) course, (c) outcome, and (d) extent of incapacitation. Particularly helpful in Rolland's typology is an emphasis on the interpersonal and family involvement at various stages and with various modes of an illness. Thus, he is able to identify the flexibility required of a family to make the transition from the close, involved, emotionally loaded crisis phase to a more stable, chronic phase. Such flexibility will be evident, for example, in fostering the child's increasing responsibility for appropriate self-care. Rolland defines as a crucial task of the chronic phase of illness the maintenance of maximal autonomy for all family members in the face of a pull toward excessive mutual dependency and caretaking. Thus, for example, the boundaries around a close, involved family caring for one disabled child will need to be loosened to assist an adolescent sibling to develop healthy relationships with peers and the wider social world. These boundaries also need to be loosened to ensure that the parents are able to accomplish their developmental tasks in the middle adult years.

Another useful distinction made by Rolland is between an illness or disease that is chronic yet stable or progressive, and one that is episodic and characterized by periods of relapse. Recognition of the strain on the family system caused by the frequency of transitions between various states of the illness, as well as the uncertainty of when a relapse may occur, are key developmental transitions to which a family therapist must attend.

Whether one considers a normative family transition or one that is atypical but adaptive to a child's affliction, each developmental transition creates a certain amount of stress and requires shifts in the family's roles, functions, and relationships. A transition may also reawaken emotional issues of loss and of grief over the permanency of the handicapping condition of a child (Black, 1982). A number of authors have commented, for example, on the developmental shifts in the family when children are enrolled in school (Turnbull et al., 1986). The normative family restructuring necessitated at this time is likely to be exacerbated by the recognition of the differences, compared to normal children, in the child's abilities, appearance, or potentialities and in the available educational resources. The school-age years also bring the family into contact with a wide variety of educational and community professionals with whom they must find a way to work and relate.

If the parents are expected by teachers to also be educators, a new role emerges. This role has been much debated in the literature (Seligman, 1979; Turnbull & Turnbull, 1986). From a developmental family systems perspective, the important question may be whether the family is able to sustain appropriate boundaries *as* a family, without role strain or overload, while still engaging productively in the tasks and roles of the educational system. For example, mothers who assume the role of teacher may not be able to experience the freedom from daily care of a school-age child that other mothers can anticipate after the preschool years.

Although little research has been forthcoming on the family with a disabled adolescent, indications are that this phase can be one of the family's most difficult periods (Blum, 1984; Frey, 1984; Mitchell & Rizzo, 1985). A family systems therapist must attempt to determine the extent to which issues of sexuality and independence, which characterize adolescence in general, are interactive with the particular difficulties and needs of the disabled adolescent.

The family therapist must also be sensitive to the family's other life cycle issues at this point. In addition to the developmental needs and tasks of the adolescent, the system may also be adapting to the developmental needs of parents who are facing the possible disappointments and losses of middle age. Elderly grandparents may have the parents feeling sandwiched as caretakers in the new role of parenting their parents. In addition to these predictable stresses, the family must also deal with health, career, and financial resources, which are ongoing family tasks, along with planning for the continued needs and care of a disabled adolescent. Many families with a disabled member believe that there is no future beyond the adolescent period. This lack of hopefulness can seriously interfere with the family's planning and problem-solving capacities to meet the needs of the child and the rest of the family members.

Family therapy at this point needs to address the potential discrepancies among the developmental needs of various members of a family with a disabled member, and to assist the family to not become stuck at this stage. A developmental perspective that may be useful for the family therapist is the comparison with the normal stresses for families that are associated with this period. Olson and McCubbin (1983), for example, reported from their national samples of normal families that there is an increase in stress and discomfort throughout the childhood and adolescent years. A substantial improvement in quality of life and adaptive family relationships was reported at the end of that period.

Thus, attention to the family life cycle, and its interaction with specific developmental requirements of the child's illness or disability, is a major perspective for organizing family therapy. This perspective helps the therapist to plan and select interventions designed to facilitate that development.

Family Stress and Coping

The recognition of stress, and strategies for its amelioration, as a crucial variable in the functioning of a family system provides a second key perspective for conceptualizing family therapy interventions. As suggested earlier, such models are especially helpful in limiting the assumption of pathology in the family's adaptation to the complexity of life with a disabled child.

The identification of stressors, that is, events that require a family to change and adapt, is evident throughout this book. The family therapist needs to have an awareness of specific components of stress as well as a recognition of an emphasis on the resources and coping strategies available to the family. Facilitation of and support for the family's strengths and capacity to use and engage resources may be one of the most significant tasks of the family therapist (Karpel, 1986).

Probably the most complete and well-researched model of stress and coping for the family therapist is the Double ABCX Model of adaptation developed by McCubbin and Patterson (1983). This work is an extension of the Hill family crisis model, in which a crisis (X) was defined as the product of a stressor (A), which interacts with the family's crisis-meeting resources (B), which interacts with the definition the family makes of the event (C). The double ABCX Model is an attempt to describe the continuing cycle of adaptive and adjustive responses of the family beyond the original stress/crisis. A key variable in this model is the recognition of the "pile-up" of stressors and demands in the aftermath of a major stressor.

The Double ABCX Model emphasizes the acquisition, enhancement, and use of resources over time as well as the changing definitions and meaning given to events and the resultant coping strategies. Hill's model is especially helpful in understanding the ongoing adaptive requirements of the family with a disabled child. As with Rolland's model for the developmental phase of illness, the Double ABCX Model emphasizes that various coping responses and resources are useful during different phases of distress. It enables the therapist to identify factors important in the continuing needs of the disabled child over time, as well as the stresses and coping attendant to other normative developmental events in the life of the family (Bristol & Schopler, 1984; McCubbin & Patterson, 1983).

The stress and coping perspective on family systems also emphasizes the identification and availability of the family's resources. Resources can be defined as those capacities of the family that prevent a change from creating a crisis or disruptiveness in the system. A family's resources include (a) the family members' individual personal strengths, (b) the family system's internal resources, (c) family coping strategies, and (d) social supports.

The family therapist must assess and work with individual and utilitarian family resources, such as personality (i.e., ego strength), health, financial resources, and extended family support. The perception of and meaning attributed to events and responses by both individual and family will also be crucial in determining the impact an event will have. Regardless of the particular definition the family gives to an event, research on coping converges on the notion that the following elements — (a) a capacity for optimism in the face of stress, (b) along with a sense of self-efficacy (that it is possible to master the situation rather than simply be victimized by it), and (c) some belief in a higher purpose or religiosity — are central to the adaptive meanings attached to stressful situations (Bristol, 1984; Crnic et al., 1983). Therefore, such strategies as "normalizing" and "reframing," as meaning-giving interventions in family therapy, are particularly useful in helping families cope. These interventions are widely used by family therapists attempting to influence the latent resourcefulness of family response.

Pratt (1976) synthesized one description of the family that successfully manages stress in calling it the "energized family." The energized family has a "fluid internal organization characterized by flexible role relationships and shared power, which promote personal growth and member autonomy." The Circumplex Model of balanced cohesion and adaptability developed by Olson and the Minnesota group (Olson, Sprenkle, & Russell, 1979) identifies more specific components of the well-functioning family that are useful to the family therapist. Family cohesion is the emotional bonding that family members have toward one another. Family adaptability is the ability of a marital or family system to change its power structure, role relationships, and relationship rules in response to situational and developmental stress. A basic assumption is that families in the middle ranges of these two dimensions will cope most successfully. That is, they will be neither rigid nor chaotic in organization and task functioning, nor too close or too distant and unavailable emotionlly.

Reiss and Oliveri (1980) contributed additional concepts of families that are coping well with stress. From extensive research on family problem solving, they identify three paradigms or processes that characterize the "energized family" described by Pratt. A paradigm is the enduring conception each family holds about the fundamental nature of the social world and its place in that world. Although these paradigms change during serious or disabling crisis, "energized" families have some fairly enduring characteristics that include the following:

Configuration   A concept held by the family that the social world in which they live is ordered by a coherent set of principles that they can discover and master through exploration and interpretation. These families can work together to discover patterns in problem-solving tasks that lead to successful conclusions.

Coordination   The care with which each member dovetails problem-solving efforts with others in the family. This is similar to Olson's definition of cohesion, but it reflects specifically the family's belief that they share the same experiential world and can communicate about it.

Closure   The capacity of the family to delay closure or final decisions until they have the needed and available evidence. Delaying closure reflects a family's search for input from the environment. It assures current openness to new experience rather than quickly assuming or requiring a repetition of the past. Again, a parallel can be drawn with Olson's notion of family adaptability.

The task in family therapy of increasing the family's capacity for effective problem solving may be handled through a variety of educative strategies, as well as through restructuring efforts, communication skills, supporting the capacity for effective leadership or "executive" functioning, and encouraging greater appreciation for differences.

McCubbin et al.'s (1980) research on coping styles and strategies of families is of particular use to the family therapist. McCubbin identified five coping strategies by which the family manages interactions within the family and transactions between the family and the community. Two of these are *internal* family coping strategies (ways family members use resources within the family). The two internal strategies are (a) reframing — the family's ability to redefine stressful experiences in a way that makes them more acceptable and manageable, and (b) passive appraisal — defining the problem as one that the family cannot or need not control or something that will take care of itself.

Three are external strategies (behaviors family members use to acquire resources outside the famiy). The external strategies are (a) acquiring social support, (b) seeking spiritual support, and (c) mobilizing the family to acquire and accept help from others. Studies using this model have indicated that different combinations of the strategies are effective, but most indicate that the capacity for reframing, some spiritual orientation, and the capacity to make use of outside resources or social supports are the most critical in distinguishing well-functioning from maladaptive families.

In regard to external coping strategies, studies indicate that the availability and capacity to use social supports and networks are contributing factors to family success in coping with the stress of living with a disabled child. Among important social supports in dealing with families are neighborhoods, family, and kinship networks (multigenerational family systems); self-help and peer groups; and of course, the professional health care delivery system (Kazak, 1986; McCubbin et al., 1983).

Family Organization and Structure

The model of the family system as having a structure or organization to meet its needs is the third key perspective for understanding normal families, as well as those with dysfunctional adaptations to developmental or life cycle tasks or to coping with stress. Perhaps the most useful structural model of family functioning is the one developed by Salvador Minuchin (1974) and his colleagues (Minuchin & Fishman, 1981; Minuchin, Rosman, & Baker, 1978). Not only is this model comprehensible, it has implications for therapeutic interventions that can be readily drawn and enacted by the family therapist.

Two central concepts in the model of family structural organization are (a) the family is hierarchical in nature, and (b) the nature of the boundaries determines a great deal of what goes on within and across family subsystems. In seeking a balance of emotional and functional relationships in the family "mobile," families often either violate appropriate hierarchical relationships or establish dysfunctional boundaries.

Key subsystems within the structure of a family system include (a) the parental subsystem, (b) the spousal subsystem, (c) the sibling subsystem, and (d) the individual subsystem (Minuchin & Fishman, 1981). It is significant that the first two, the parental and the spousal subsystems, include the same membership (mother and father; husband and wife). This is one way of indicating that subsystems are functional as well as membership-defined. Mother and father have different needs and opportunities when they function as husband and wife that are distinct from their parental tasks with the children. Lack of recognition by both adults and children of these two subsystems is often a factor in family difficulties. Occasionally, others play a role in the parental system, such as a "parental child" or a grandmother. Their limited functioning in this subsystem is highlighted by the fact that they do not belong in the spousal subsystem as well.

The concept of hierarchy emphasizes generational roles and responsibilities. It suggests that healthy well functioning families will be maintained by appropriate leadership, decision making, and family management accomplished by the parental generation. The family structure is in difficulty when the parents are in charge only overtly, and there is at work a powerful cross-generational coalition that, in reality, is more powerful. Such is the case in the coalition of one parent and child against the other parent. From a hierarchical point of view, the most significant boundary to maintain is the generational boundary. Parents should parent, and children should do what children do. As a quick rule of thumb, one of the first diagnostic questions in a family session is to determine whether the generational boundary is being violated. One family therapy wag, for example, suggests that whenever a family is seemingly controlled by the needs of a too-powerful, manipulative child, that child can be understood to be "standing on the shoulders" of one of the adults. When adults in the family cooperate in firm leadership and guidance of the family, a child is not able (and probably does not need) to have so much control or influence.

Boundaries are the rules that define membership in a system or subsystem. They determine who participates in the system and how. In any family system, each individual and each subsystem has boundaries. A spatial model helps to understand this dynamic process (Nichols, 1984). Boundaries that are rigid look like this:

Or they can be clear and functional and look like this:

Or, they can be diffuse and look like this:

· ·

Looking at these representations of boundaries, it is possible to imagine what entry into or exit from a subsystem can be like. If the boundaries around a system or subsystem are rigid, it is probably very difficult for anyone else to get in or out. If a mother and her sick child are locked tightly into a rigidly bounded dyadic subsystem, the father and other family members cannot access or aid that subsystem, and neither mother nor child can exit readily to engage with other members of the larger system. Isolated families with disabled children have a rigid boundary between the nuclear family and the outside world. In either case, these rigid boundaries are too exclusive to allow the family members sufficient flexibility and access to each other or to outside resources to meet varied needs.

If the family boundaries are excessively diffuse, family subsystems might be poorly defined. It may not be clear who belongs in which subsystem, or who is responsible for what, and the family may appear to be underorganized or even chaotic. Under stress, families with diffuse boundaries may be unable to organize appropriately to accomplish necessary tasks. In this case, the needs for care of a disabled child may go unmet, or they may be met in a capricious or unpredictable way.

Minuchin's structural model of families describes a continuum of family emotional functioning along the dimension from enmeshed to disengaged. Midway between these two extremes lie flexible families whose boundaries are clear and the subsystems identifiable, but where there is enough openness to allow access to others and to allow the members to participate in other subsystems without abandoning their primary identity.

What is predictable in many families with a disabled child, particularly where the family is having persistent difficulty in adapting, is that the family is too enmeshed or overinvolved in response to the child, the disability, and the required care and treatment. It is perfectly normal and expectable that parents of young disabled or ill children are somewhat overinvolved in their care. In fact, healthy involvement and bonding, at least between mother and child, provides the emotional glue that ensures the survival of the child. Developmentally, however, it is appropriate for that overinvolvement to decrease over time. The boundary around the unit should not be so exclusive that both the mother and child are prevented from successful functioning in other subsystems or from independent or autonomous functioning outside the family.

Enmeshed or too-cohesive family systems tend to be emotionally overreactive within the family, and conversely, to have overly rigid boundaries between the family system and the outside world. This in part explains or describes the limited functioning in families that remain isolated from outside social supports. Isolated families also exhibit the properties of a closed system in which there is too little exchange of information with the outside world. These negative outcomes are called entropy, the tendency of a closed system to yield to disorder or disorganization. Paradoxically, then, the enmeshed family closes its boundaries and protects itself while that very process creates new problems.

In enmeshed families, emotions are contagious: If one person is depressed, the others in the subsystem are depressed. Or, if a child is not doing well, someone else doing well in the family can be perceived as an act of disloyalty in some families! Because emotions are contagious, members of the family do not feel that the full range of their feelings and needs can be expressed, particularly if they cause pain to others. The children in this type of family may, for example, learn that anger or sadness is not acceptable because it triggers similar anger or sadness in others.

In terms of family adaptability, families with the most flexibility are most likely to accomplish the changing tasks and needs of the family over time. Families most likely to be dysfunctional, then, are families that are stuck in the same pattern and repeat it over and over, regardless of whether it is appropriate to an event or crisis. A clear example is the family attitude toward food, eating, and nourishment. It is appropriate for the mother of a

6-month-old baby to carefully monitor the foods given to the child to make sure the meat is cut up in digestible portions, temperatures are not scalding, and so forth. When the mother of a 16-year-old teenager who is capable of self-feeding devotes the same kind of attention to food and to the eating behavior of that child, there is clear evidence of the redundance and overinvolvement characteristic of dysfunctional and enmeshed families. Developmentally, it impairs appropriate attainment of the autonomy and independence of which the child is capable.

In many ways, a dysfunctional family with a disabled child resembles the psychosomatic families described by Minuchin et al., (1978). Although a family with a disabled child is not necessarily a psychosomatic system, many dysfunctional families function under stress in similar ways. These interlocking patterns have been shown by Minuchin to exacerbate illness episodes and otherwise influence appropriate care in families with diabetic, epileptic, and anorexic children.

The four interacting transactional patterns that Minuchin identifies in psychosomatic families include:

1. enmeshment, the extreme form of proximity and intensity in family interactions and emotionality.
2. overprotectiveness, which shows in an excessive degree of concern of family members for each other's welfare.
3. rigidity, evidence in a commitment to maintaining the status quo and a high vulnerability to external or unplanned events.
4. lack of conflict resolution, resulting in patterns of avoidance, denial, and the detouring of conflict.

It is in the avoidance of conflict that some families become overinvolved with a disabled child. In such cases, the child's illness or need for care becomes a part of the regulation of the emotions in the family system. An inappropriate focus on the child (perhaps where it is not necessary) detours the direct expression of conflict. Children who function in a coalition with one parent against the other or who serve as a detour for parental stress or difficulties find that, paradoxically, their illness contributes to the protection of the family and its apparent stability. Again, the child caught this way in the family process is inappropriately involved across a generational boundary.

Although additional research is needed to determine the parallel between variously disabled children and those with psychosomatic illnesses, there is some evidence that this model is appropriate for families with mentally retarded children (Berger & Foster, 1986) and with many forms of adolescent and young adult disabilities (Strax & Wolfson, 1984). Family structure and adaptability is thus responsive to and influences both developmental progress and the family's resource for coping with stress.

DEVELOPMENTAL ASSESSMENT AND THERAPEUTIC INTERVENTION

As suggested earlier, most families seek family therapy when they feel hopeless and/or helpless and believe that their efforts to mend themselves have failed. To allow the family to experience hope and support, it is imperative that the family therapist first join with the family and acknowledge their pain and their struggle (Minuchin, 1974; Minuchin & Fishman, 1981). It is only with a sense that the therapist believes in them and in their efforts and capacity to function well that trust can be established to allow the therapeutic work to proceed. The initial joining phase of family therapy thus resembles the first phase of individual therapy where a therapist attempts to develop rapport and a good working relationship.

A second characteristic of most families entering therapy is that they have defined the problem and the cause, however erroneously. Their perception may be that if only the therapist could fix the problem as they envision it, things would be better. The family may not understand that their beliefs about the problem, and the efforts that they have made to solve it, may in fact be making the situation worse. Keeping a stiff upper lip, for example, may be preventing family members from expressing emotional needs within the family, thereby making it difficult to utilize therapy.

Families suffering from chronically high levels of stress and judging themselves to be coping poorly can be expected to have a more limited repertoire of responses than would well functioning families. That is, in addition to feeling as badly as they do, these families are apt to have adapted to distress by using a number of redundant communication or relationship patterns that are quite rigid, restrictive, and dysfunctional. When stressed, creative solutions to problems are much harder to put into operation. As noted earlier, some families with disabled children have severely restricted social worlds, interacting less with extended family, friends, or other enriching community groups (Kazak, 1986). Often medical, educational, or social service professionals have replaced more normal social encounters.

It is highly likely that stressed families will restrict their social repertoire within the family in much the same way that they have withdrawn from other relationships. Each time the alternatives have been restricted it surely will have been for a good reason—the avoidance of a real or supposed pain or discomfort, such as not hurting someone's feelings. Unfortunately, the outcome of constricted behavior is usually to increase the very stress or discomfort that was being avoided. Thus the family therapist must be prepared to join or empathize with a family whose sense of discouragement and limited range of relationships make them least open to be joined. The family needs to be seen as trying to do what seems best in this situation at this moment. It is this family that the therapist must join, affirm, and begin to establish a trust that will let the family work with him or her (Anderson & Stuart, 1983).

Initial joining of the therapist with a family also requires that a specific assessment be made of the family's functional and emotional situation. One of the most serious limitations of the research on families with disabled members has been to overgeneralize across a wide variety of handicapping conditions (Kazak, 1986). Before interventions are attempted, the family therapist should work with the family to assess their specific developmental situation. The assessment, incidentally, may have a therapeutic effect in itself.

The family is liable to be overgeneralizing in its own appraisal, which may in turn be inhibiting clear decision making and problem solving, as well as further contributing to emotional turmoil and a sense of being overwhelmed. In other words, the family may be catastrophizing, inadvertently heightening anxiety, and contributing further to stress. A careful assessment of specific actions and descriptions of exact sequences of events surrounding a particular problem, elicited by a calm, non-anxious therapist, may help the entire family focus on more concrete, manageable aspects of the situation.

A number of specific aspects of the disability and the disabled child must be assessed. For example, is the limitation primarily a chronic physical illness with no accompanying mental limitations, or is there a primary mental retardation or mental illness? Has the disability been present from birth or was the onset later? If later, how did it occur and what explanations or beliefs does the family have for the onset? To what extent is the problem likely to be life threatening? Another major factor is the family's view of the extent to which they feel stigmatized. The family's experience of social stigma may be the most handicapping aspect of their situation (Seligman & Darling, 1990).

Other questions that need to be answered: Is the child capable of some emotional reciprocity with family members? How does this capacity for emotional connectedness encourage the involvement of other family members or, conversely, increase their pain regarding the child's limitations? (Vine, 1982). To what extent does the disability impair the child's functioning, especially in the areas of learning, mobility, self-care, and responsibility?

The extent of a child's dependency throughout the life cycle of the family is a salient feature in assessment. Although the research is conflicting on this point, McCubbin, Cauble, and Patterson (1982) and Crnic et al. (1983) have indicated that the severity of the disability is related to the level of family stress and to the extent of reported marital dissatisfaction in families with older children. To the extent that the diagnosis of a disability is ambiguous and the course of treatment uncertain, emotional stress for the family can be expected to be high as well (Berger, 1982, McCubbin & Patterson, 1983). The stress will be mitigated by the requirement that even more energy and resources be expended in the search for information or answers (where perhaps there are none that are clear anyway), as well as the inevitable tendency to attempt to locate the source of blame and responsibility.

In addition to the specifics of the disability itself, the family therapist will need to pay attention to other characteristics of the child and the family. Some research suggests, for example, that the child's sex may be a factor in the family's reaction and that handicapped male children impact family stress levels more dramatically than do female children (Bristol & Schopler, 1984; Farber, 1968), possibly more for fathers (Lamb, 1983). Probable explanations offered for this are the concerns for independent living and autonomy that families expect from boys, even in today's "liberated" society.

The effects of the age and sibling position of the disabled child is equally important to include in an assessment. As the child approaches or negotiates successive developmental milestones, the family may face an increasingly wide discrepancy between their disabled child and other children (Gallagher, Beckman, and Cross, 1983). Renewed or chronic grief and mourning at the lack of developmental accomplishments may accompany these periods (Wikler, Wasow, & Hatfield, 1981). In addition, the age of the child influences to some extent the involvement of family members with others, notably school personnel and peers. The need to cope with dilemmas of social stigma can be expected when the family "goes public" (Fewell, 1986).

The age of the disabled child has been found in some studies to be related to the amount of reported marital distress or conflict, but highest amounts have been reported in both the older years (Gallagher et al., 1983) and with the youngest children (Kazak, 1986). Caution must be exercised here, however, in not inferring specific cause and effect. The relationship of stress in the marriage and family to the age of the children has been shown to increase in a normal sample through the adolescent years, as the dilemmas of both the child and the family's needs intersect (Olson & McCubbin, 1983).

Little research has focused on the family with an adolescent or older disabled offspring. It is to be assumed, however, that in most cases the adolescent period will be a difficult one for the family. The question of the "launchability" of the disabled child and the potential thwarting of parents' aging life cycle movement, resulting in their perpetual parenthood, will impact the entire system. Struggles over responsibility for self-care, especially around medical compliance for some adolescent difficulties, such as diabetes, can be expected to be exacerbated at this stage (Mitchell & Rizzo, 1985), as will the effects of the disabled adolescent's search for a sense of identity, competence, and self-esteem (Strax & Wolfson, 1984).

In summary, during the initial assessment and joining stages of family therapy, whatever difficulty the family is experiencing should be viewed in the context of the specific factors of the disabled child's capacities and limitations, as well as the child's circumstances within the family constellation.

Along with the specific inquiry about the child's disabling condition, it is important to inquire about and observe specifically the structure, functioning, and other processes of the family (Harris, 1984). Communication patterns, problem-solving skills, and coping styles are especially important. Structural family therapists call this process of inquiry and observation "tracking."

A mistake in family therapy at this point would be to overgeneralize about the family's functioning. It is important that the family therapist inquire and observe as specifically as possible about *who* participates *with whom, when, where,* and *in what ways.* The therapist can only find out about dysfunctional interpersonal patterns by asking specific questions and then by tracking that information through a whole sequence. For example, the family may simply report that there is too much fighting, everyone is stressed, and they are wondering whether the family can survive. In examining specific interactions it may be that a certain sequence in fact occurs. Perhaps the mother and the disabled child are frustrated in their interaction. Each time the stress reaches a certain level, the father is activated to respond. Any number of behaviors might follow this sequence until the interaction is somehow completed. Other members of the nuclear or extended family, for example, another sibling or a grandparent, might also be activated to become involved, either escalating or reducing the tension.

One way to track a specific type of family functioning is to ask what are called "circular questions" (Penn, 1982). Circular questions are designed to elicit patterned relationships of family functioning. The therapist might ask questions about differences or comparisons to other aspects of family functioning (e.g., What is happening now? How is the interaction different from before the problem began? How will it be different when the problem is resolved?). Other questions ask the family what they *do* when a problem occurs (e.g., Who is the first to notice, or who gets most upset? If the father is activated, who talks with whom about his behavior? Who takes responsibility for communication with other children or grandparents?) Circular questioning thus allows the therapist to track a sequence, to "gradually enlarge the field of observation" (Selvini-Palazzoli et al., 1980). This approach suggests that the patterned sequence that was originally a solution to the family's problem has itself become the problem. It further provides a clearer picture of points in the structure and function of the family where the therapist might usefully intervene to alter the pattern of interactions and, hopefully, the outcome.

Throughout an initial session with a family, one of the tasks is to determine whether family therapy is actually the indicated treatment. If it is, then the *goals* of the work need to be specified. The therapist will want to arrive at a contract with the family, even if it is an informal one, about agreed upon goals and the strategies for meeting them. As indicated above, one of the most significant early joining tasks for the therapist is to begin to convey a sense of hopefulness to an otherwise discouraged family. In negotiating the plan for ongoing family therapy, the therapist also needs to join with the family in establishing that returning for future sessions is worthwhile.

The therapist must also convey to the family that he or she is not intimidated or overwhelmed by their problems. Therapist competence to tolerate the strength of the family's emotional and relational needs must be evident from the beginning, to encourage the family to trust in the anticipated work.

Another way of insuring a balanced view of the family is to be certain that the therapist has a "systemic map" that allows a wider lens for organizing thinking about families. One of the most useful maps devised in family therapy is the genogram (McGoldrick & Gerson, 1986). The genogram provides the therapist and the family a framework for conceptualizing the nuclear family in a broader multigenerational and extended family perspective. It allows the family and therapist to identify patterns of coping and the construction of family roles and functions that influence the current family situation. The family therapist is urged to use the genogram as an aid to assessment and early treatment planning.

In addition to goals for healthy, adaptive functioning, there are some specific goals of family therapy with families with a disabled child. Powers and Bruey (198) outlined a set of treatment objectives developed to "assist in the development and maintenance of a normal family process across the lifespan" (p. 27). The goals include:

1. Facilitating a healthy response to initial diagnosis.
2. Facilitating functional forms of organization within the family sys-

tem, especially addressing boundary problems, subsystem functioning, and cross-generational coalitions.

3. Facilitating the development and maintenance of social networks including both extended family and community-based support systems.

4. Facilitating service access and coordination, including educating the family about available resources for service and functioning as a liaison to coordinate services.

5. Facilitating the development of advocacy skills, and empowering the family in the method and process of advocacy, perhaps including assertiveness skills.

In addition to formulating goals for therapy, the therapist also needs to estimate the length of treatment necessary and to determine whom to include in the treatment. The length of family therapy treatment will depend on the service setting, the family's current level of functioning, and their expectations and motivation.

During the contracting period, the family therapist should suggest an approximate number of sessions to work on a particular problem. The more resistant a family seems to treatment, the briefer the initial contract may need to be. It is sometimes better to engage a family in agreeing to three or four sessions to see what can be accomplished, than to suggest that therapy will require months of intensive treatment. Often the success of the early sessions and the establishment of a dependable therapeutic relationship with the therapist will allow the family to set a second contract to do more intensive work.

It may be important for the family therapist to be clear about setting initial or intermediate goals. It is helpful, for example, to say something like:

> Let's meet for the next 4 weeks. We will try to resolve Problem A, and we'll see what might be helping or not helping the situation. At our fourth meeting, on (*date*), we'll decide together how much we've accomplished. If we need more work on Problem A, or if there are other things to be addressed, we'll decide at that time how to proceed.

This style of contracting is partly effective because it includes the family in the planning process as well as in the work of the sessions. Collaborating with family members to attain the least amount of change that will meet their needs is far more likely to elicit their trust and helpfulness than a demand for a number of sessions whose usefulness may not seem clear to the family.

The question of whom to include in the family sessions is partly a matter of appropriate structure and therapeutic strategies and partly a practical matter of availability and willingness. Although some family therapists refuse to see the family unless everyone is present, most therapists will begin to work with those who are willing to come, with the potential goal that other family members may join later.

It is not unusual in family therapy for one or more members to refuse initially to come to the sessions. The reluctant members are sending a message that it is not their problem or that they do not think they can help to change the situation. Each case is different, but many family therapists will make some effort to try to involve those persons in later sessions, if they do not appear on their own. It can be appropriate for the family therapist to invite the missing family member directly, emphasizing that the person's view and understanding of the problem might be especially helpful.

Some therapists will write letters or send messages to missing family members, paradoxically encouraging them to stay away from the sessions because they are, in that way, helping others to work at solving the problems. These strategies need to be used with extreme care but they do have an interesting no-lose feature. That is, if the family member stays away, it might, in fact, allow the others to work better. If the missing member does decide to appear to "lend expertise" to the problem, the therapy will be aided by wider inclusion of family membership.

Each family therapist needs to develop strategies for joining with the disabled child as well as other members of the family. In cases of multiple and severe disabilities or where the child is too young to participate, it may be advantageous to not include the child in regular sessions. It will be crucial, at some point, however, to see all members of the family together. The nature of their interaction, communication patterns, and other nonverbal behavior can be clarified only by observing the family in action together. Where possible, a home visit early in therapy or a session conducted in the family home may reveal behaviors and system patterns that are not observed in the therapist's office.

Scheduling of family sessions is also important. It is often true that if the clinic or office of the family therapist does not operate on flexible hours, interested family members may not be able to attend if it interferes with work. A major deterrent to successful family work has been the resistance of agencies to accommodate schedules, fee structures, billing practices, and room arrangements or other structural elements necessary to work with families. If the therapist is in an agency where family work is regularly practiced, this will not be a problem. If the therapist is venturing into new areas by working with the entire family, it will be crucial to address these questions before the therapy begins (Anderson & Stuart, 1983).

ROLES

In attempting to determine the extent to which family structure and functioning are dysfunctional, it is useful to consider the way in which roles are
assumed and enacted in the system. As noted previously, roles can be relatively functional and flexible, or they can be rigid and limiting and probably, over time, dysfunctional (Koch, 1985). Families, like all other groups,
use roles to accomplish necessary living tasks. In well-functioning families,
roles are appropriate to the needs of the individual and the family, and they
can be adapted over time as the needs and capacities of family members
change. In highly stressed or dysfunctional families, role behavior often becomes polarized and complementary. That is, one person enacts only one
part of a role, and someone else enacts the other parts of the role. A common example in family therapy are the roles of the spender and the saver, or
miser. Although it is appropriate for each person to spend some of the family's resources, and for all to be concerned about saving for the future, roles
in dysfunctional families appear to be completely isolated at one or another
end of the "utilizing resources" spectrum. Furthermore, each person tends
to believe that the behavior (spending or saving) of the other is reflective of
inherent characteristics of that person and to believe that if only the other
would change, things could be worked out. Each individual blames the
other for starting the polarization and both feel stuck.

In families with a disabled child, the literature describes several such
polarized roles. The most obvious of these would be the helper/helpless
roles enacted by one parent (usually the mother) and the disabled child. Because the caretaker-parent/ill-child coalition is functional to an extent
(Walker, 1983), it sometimes happens that the roles become rigidified and
overgeneralized, perhaps to situations in which the parent does not have to
be the helper (either because it is not needed or because someone else can do
it). Furthermore, the disabled child does not need to be helpless in situations in which the disability does not limit ability. The coalition between the
caretaker-parent and the medical or educational systems on behalf of the
child may further isolate them from the remainder of the family. For example, mothers attend most medical appointments alone with the child, which
can contribute to the father's further isolation. Similarly, one child (usually
the oldest and most often a girl) may adopt the helping, caretaking role
known as the parental child (Minuchin, 1974). Although at times her
strength and assistance to the family is an invaluable asset, the role may de-
prive this child of appropriate self-expression and growth. In turn, it can
encourage the dependence and lack of self-sufficiency of other children and
further inhibit the family's normal developmental progress. Other siblings
in the family may also feel unattended or unappreciated (see Chapter 7, Siblings of Disabled Brothers and Sisters).

Major polarized roles in dysfunctional families with a disabled child may involve the caretaking parent and the indifferent one, or the demanding, pushy parent and the overprotective one. An initial interview with the family often reveals that roles that they have been rigidly anchoring in the system are perceived by the parents to be needed in reciprocity to compensate for the other's role behavior. The outcome, of course, is to limit and restrict the possibilities for all involved.

One effective intervention is to encourage parents to reverse roles (Papp, 1983). If the person who has been overfunctioning (e.g., assuming the caretaking role) can be directed to "do less" in order to facilitate the other doing more even for a brief period, it is possible to begin to initiate changes in rigidly maintained role behavior. For example, in considering an overfunctioning mother in the family, the task of the therapist would be to support the mother's doing *less* either for the child or the father, so that the child and/or father can do *more*. Fathers sometimes report, by the way, that they have previously withdrawn and refrained from doing more because they have *believed* that the mother did not wish to have her overfunctioning interrupted. If the family therapist can initiate *some* change or a reversal in the enacting of rigid reciprocal roles, more appropriate sharing and shifting of the roles and even the development of new and creative solutions to the accomplishment of the family's goals can be achieved.

NORMALIZING AND REFRAMING

Second only to the importance of *joining* by the family therapist is the therapist's skill in assisting in the determination of the meaning that the family attaches to the reality of having a disabled child. A number of reports of well-functioning families with a disabled member suggest that their belief in the meaningfulness the child brings to their life is a significant factor in maintaining effective family organization and behavior (McCubbin et al., 1983).

To the extent possible, a family therapist strives to *normalize* (Minuchin, 1974) the difficulties that have brought a family to treatment. There will be aspects to the situations encountered by the family in treatment that are similar to experiences in most families. Normalizing suggests that the difficulty, struggle or feeling being experienced by this family is not only normal for the circumstances, but actually expectable. The process of normalization of difficulties can help reduce both feelings of stigma associated with having a disabled member and the sense of isolation. It identifies that others, even if personally unknown to the family, are struggling in similar ways. The risk here, of course, is of trivializing the family's problems as being so common as to be unimportant. When conveyed with care by the therapist, the normalization of the family's feelings and efforts can greatly assist in reducing anxiety and the sense of catastrophe. Another resource for families that believe that they suffer alone is peer and self-help groups.

The second component of assisting the family with the meaning it attaches to its situation is the strategy of *reframing.* Reframing is often one of the most powerful and immediately effective strategies employed by a family therapist. When a therapist reframes a problem or behavior, it begins to change the context or the meaning of the behavior, and it therefore represents a first step in the direction of change in the family system. It is also an additional means of joining with the family in a supportive way and of reducing distress by normalizing the family's situation.

To reframe a behavior or an interaction involves simply reinterpreting the behavior, putting it into a new "frame." The most useful reframing in family systems therapy is to redefine a behavior as (a) benignly motivated and (b) capable of being changed (Hoffman, 1981). Most often family members will have ascribed malevolent intentions to the parent or child whose behavior they cannot change, and they will have decided by now that the behavior is intractable and they are helpless to change it.

When a behavior is defined for the family as benign and under the control of the person exhibiting the behavior, an entirely different context for understanding and responding to the behavior can be elicited. For example, if a mother is defined as overinvolved and intrusive, the family therapist can respond empathically to how much she cares for her disabled child and how hard she has tried to find ways to help the child to grow as successfully as possible. The therapist can further comment on the difficulty of knowing how to change in the face of the child's and family's changing needs.

This basically simple reframe of the mother's behavior, from intrusive to caring, concerned and confused about change, alters the perception of and meaning attributed to the experience. The mother probably feels more understood than she has in the past and feels that continuing effort is worthwhile, even if it has not always worked. The rest of the family also views the mother in a different perspective. An underinvolved parent or relative may feel more able to choose alternative responses when the behavior is framed as one that encourages self-care or independence.

Rather than being angry, then, other family members might be elicited to encourage or assist the mother's solid intentions. The family and the therapist can discuss ways to effectively care for the child. This movement beyond the reframing itself capitalizes on the tone of the reframe to suggest collaboration and gathering information to make decisions as appropriate to helping well-intentioned family members.

Reframing also allows the family to adapt its view of the disabling condition itself. DeShazer and Lipchik (1984) gave several examples of reframing a handicap from being perceived as a crippling condition to one with strengths. A young woman ashamed of her crutches was helped to choose brightly colored or decorated ones in order for her to emphasize her strengths rather than discount herself as a cripple. Blindness has been reframed as facilitating competence in sound or kinesthetic perceptions (Webb-Woodard & Woodard, 1982). Perhaps the most important reframe a family can make is to shift from a view of the disabled or ill child as being overly helpless to one in which the child's capacities that are not affected by the disability are highlighted. Families that are able to see those strengths in the child are less likely to be frozen in dysfunctional, overinvolved patterns that are detrimental to the growth of the child and other members of the family.

Unfortunately, one simple or even elegant reframe will not by itself alter the redundant negative course of blaming responses in dysfunctinal families. The reframe can, however, become a metaphor that continues to provide new views or coloration for the meanings the family attributes to behaviors.

Family therapists often wonder whether it is safe to reframe a behavior because it might not be accurate. In general, there are two cues to the relative accuracy of a reframe and, therefore, of its usefulness. An accurate reframe can generally be recognized in the initial response of the family members to the therapist's statement. Often, if the mother has been accurately reframed as caring, she will sigh, or smile, or otherwise convey her sense of having been accurately understood. Other family members will also indicate that the frame seems to "fit," although they had not actually thought of it that way.

The second way in which a reframe is recognized as accurate is pragmatic: Does it work? A reframe of the mother's behavior that allows the family to approach the problem in fresh ways and to look for new solutions must have some degree of fit or accuracy or the family will not accept and continue to work within that perspective.

Finally, a reframe must seem at least partially believable to the therapist. That is, the therapist who reframes the mother as concerned and confused about ways to change must genuinely believe that this is true. In part, the therapist's ability to use this frame to see the family is known immediately and intuitively by the family, and they will feel tricked or mistreated if they suspect it to be an artificial technique. More important, it is probably true that a therapist who cannot believe that the mother is caring and capable of change probably will not help the family much. The therapist who holds to a negative frame and blames the mother for her overinvolved intrusiveness is likely to end up agreeing with the family that the situation is hopeless and that nothing can be changed.

THE ONGOING PROCESS OF FAMILY THERAPY

Once the initial contract for family therapy sessions is established and the assessment of the family's situation and goals has been determined, the actual work of the therapy sessions can proceed. In most families with a disabled child, it is probably predictable that there will be some degree of enmeshment or overinvolvement among certain members of the family system, possibly with a concomitant distancing and disengagement from others. In addition, it is highly likely, as discussed above, that there is "stuckness" or rigidity in the family patterns and responses, and that the family would benefit from expanding its capacity to respond flexibly to members' needs. From a developmental perspective, it can be assumed that the rigidity and the enmeshment will impair the family's ability to make developmental transitions and adaptations appropriate to members' needs for growth and autonomy.

Most family therapy interventions will be designed to modify overinvolvement and to increase the family members' capacity for flexible adaptation (without introducing the threat of chaos). In the face of the stressful situation that a disabled infant can introduce into the family, it is essential that members adapt flexibly so that other family functions and relationships do not suffer unnecessarily.

From a structural perspective, a major portion of the work in family therapy is addressed by *restructuring*. Restructuring essentially refers to changes in the hierarchical and boundary organization of the family system (Berger & Foster, 1986). The family therapist attends to the leadership, power, and decision-making function of *hierarchical* relationships and the nature of the *boundaries* among the subsystems in the family and between the family and the outside world. The nature of these boundaries have been described earlier in this chapter as varying from open and clear to closed and rigid. The hierarchical focus emphasizes appropriate generational subsystem relationships: grandparents, parents, children.

In families where boundaries and generational hierarchies are not clear (e.g., when there is a coalition between one parent and a child), the functioning of the parental and spousal systems, necessary to the organization and leadership of the family, may be interfered with. If there is overinvolvement of one parent with a child, or if a grandparent intrudes into decisions about the marriage or child rearing, or if a child functions too frequently in a parental role (e.g., a nondisabled sibling), then appropriate family structure is contravened. The boundaries around a subsystem need to be strengthened if they are weakened by one of these relationships or loosened if there has been too rigid an exclusion. For example, the family therapist may use and devise strategies that enhance the spousal/marital relationship by excluding the involvement of either the disabled child or others. A parental child, although often filling a useful and necessary role in family functioning, is given the opportunity to also have an appropriate role in the sibling subsystem for his or her own sake as well as for the clarity it affords the rest of the family.

A useful way to understand the operation of a cross-generational and therefore hierarchy-violating coalition is to use the model of the *triangle*. In the typical overinvolved mother-child dyad so often reported in families with a disabled member (Walker, 1983), one or more of the other children and/or the father are excluded from the relationship. A search for the role or position of the third party or subsystem in detouring or defusing a relationship is often a simple way to identify dysfunctional family relationships. Understanding of the triangled relationship also suggests tasks to effect the needed restructuring. Information included in the genogram as well as actual interactions during the therapy sessions are the clearest ways to identify triangles.

Boundary violations and subsystem imbalances might be noticed in the seating arrangement during therapy sessions. For example, does the disabled child (or some other child) regularly sit between the parents or next to one parent but closer than the other parent/spouse. Minuchin (1974) and other structural therapists suggest simply changing the seating arrangement within the session as a first step toward realigning relationships. The therapist may extract the child who has crossed the generational boundary, by inviting the child to join the therapist in observing mother and father talking together. Occasionally, children may be excused from part of a session so that the mother and father can discuss adult topics not relevant to the children. Or, the children may remain for part of a session from which the parents are excused, to highlight the importance of respecting the sibling subsystem and its capacity to work without being regulated by the parents. Each of these interventions are ways in which the boundary around either the parental/spousal subsystem, or between the parents and the children, can be supported and affirmed. It also demonstrates yet another key principle of family therapy, namely the importance of enactment.

The principle of *enactment* is that any change the therapist wants to initiate in the family's functioning must be initiated and supported within the family therapy session before it can be excepted that the family can accomplish the change outside. Asking the parents to talk without the interruption of one or more children, for example, may elicit anxiety because of their own communication difficulties, which, in turn, invariably elicits involvement of one or more of the children. If the therapist cannot see how that sequence occurs and does not intervene to support the change *in the session,* the instruction to the family to make such a change when they go home has little likelihood of being successful.

In addition to underlining structural boundaries by varying seating and family composition, the family therapist will need to pay careful attention to typical communication patterns. Enmeshed and stuck families are typically characterized by communication patterns that are redundant (e.g., having the same argument pattern each time a topic is introduced) and by a variety of communication disturbances, such as one person speaking for another, one person who is regularly silenced or enjoined from speaking, someone whose role it is to speak or change the subject to reduce the anxiety when the emotional level in the family becomes "too hot."

A number of tasks in family therapy can be used to improve these communication patterns. One of the least complicated for the family therapist is simply to direct clear communication through to completion. When one person interrupts or speaks for the disabled child (unless the child really cannot communicate his or her own feelings and observations), the therapist must frame the interruption as an effort to help, and assist the helper to wait, on the grounds that it is really important to help the child's view be presented.

When the assumption or projection of similar feelings (e.g., "You're angry with me") is automatically made by members of the family, it is important for the therapist to elicit and reinforce differences. Families that are overinvolved or enmeshed are usually afraid, in some way, of the negative consequences of acknowledging differences. Given the stress of working together and coping with a disabled child, it is little wonder that families have often colluded to deny that there are important differences in needs and styles of coping. Hearing those differences and realizing that they can add fresh alternatives to the experience of endless unsatisfying interactions can bring the proverbial breath of fresh air to the family's emotional life and sense of possibilities.

As noted earlier, in an effort to solve a problem, families often do "more of the same" (Watzlawick, Weakland, & Fisch, 1974) when a solution or intervention does not work in the first place. Nagging is a good example of this phenomenon. A parent asks a child (or a spouse) to do (or not to do) something and the child fails to comply. In response, the mother asks in a louder voice, or more frequently, or implies that failure to comply will result in further difficulties for her (guilt!) or for the child (fear!). A coercive and dysfunctional cycle of nagging and resistance becomes established. Each person will blame the other for starting the cycle. The interpretation of blame, or cause and effect in the cycle, is often a function of "punctuation," assuming a beginning and end in a cycle of interpersonal behavior that is really repetitive. The key issue is to redirect or interrupt the pattern; to break the familiar vicious cycle and allow healthier, more adaptive patterns to emerge. For example, in the above illustration, the mother might be helped to find a positive reinforcement for the child's desired behavior.

Frequently, the reduction of enmeshment and inappropriate involvement across generational boundaries hinges on the quality of the interaction between the parents. Dysfunctional families with a disabled child frequently report difficulties in the marriage with intimacy, sexuality, communication, and a sense of shared value. Conversely, some studies report that the strongest correlation with successful family adaptation was perceived support from the spouse (Bristol & Schopler, 1984).

There are enough reports of marital discord and dissatisfaction in intact families with a disabled child to suggest that family therapy must support or strengthen the marital bond. If one parent is missing as a result of either divorce or death, the adult needs of the remaining parent must still be attended to as well as the special adjustment of the family dynamics and processes attendant upon the loss of one parent or the acquisition of a new one through later remarriage (Wikler, Haack, & Intagliata, 1984).

In intact families, however, increasing the capacity to work together as spouses and as parents may require careful effort on the part of the family therapist. In part, the care required in this part of the work may evolve from the family's denial of problems or conflict in the marriage. Therapy with a family with a disabled child needs to be distinguished from marital therapy with and for the parents. In many cases of family therapy, the recognition that a primary problem is within the marriage may result in an offer of marital therapy at the conclusion of the family work. Within the family context, however, the attention to the marital/parental relationship is toward the goal of improving the family's overall functioning.

One way for the family therapist to address this issue is to recall that the adults in the family represent two distinguishable subsystems: spousal and parental. Although these subsystems involve the same two people, the parental subsystem is related to their functioning as parents to the children and the spousal subsystem to their adult relationship and to their needs for intimacy.

One of the most efficient ways to assess and perhaps improve family functioning is to attend to the amount of time that the parental/spousal subsystem devotes to itself. The simple question "When was the last time you two spent an evening out alone together?" may elicit sufficient information to design a plan with the parents for such private times. In such an instance, some therapists prescribe that the parents not only go out together but that they do not tell the children when they are going or where they have been. Although this strategy may work with some families in which the children are capable of self-care during the parents' absence, this strategy is not as likely to be workable in families with very young or with some disabled children.

A useful homework assignment is to encourage the parents to take more time for themselves and to spend planned time together away from the rest of the family. Lack of time for the marriage is a problem in almost any busy family with small or school-age children; it is often a primary source of stress in families with a disabled child. This will be partly the result of the child's needs for special care and the lack of others who can or will provide respite.

In some cases, however, the parents will not have made appropriate efforts to obtain other care (e.g., respite care) for the child and time for themselves. Some of this will be the result of the guilt they feel over their disabled child and a reluctance to enjoy themselves and have a normal life in the face of the child's perceived deprivations. There are, too, cases in which the overinvolvement in the care of the child seems to be a way to avoid an unhappy marital relationship. In families in which this is the case, as in many families with children with psychosomatic illnesses (Minuchin, et al., 1978), the child expresses needs or demands for care at exactly the moment when tension in the marital relationship might appear. In either case, the appropriate care and development of a disabled child is most likely to be facilitated when the relationship of the parents is distinct and has clear boundaries from the child's problems.

A final intervention in some family therapy might take the form of a *ritual*. All families have rituals and celebrations of marker events such as birthdays to underscore the emotion of a developmental shift or transition. Families under severe stress however, often forgo those celebrations, and many nonnormative events have no anticipated ritual. Imber-Black (1988) hypothesized that families with a disabled child are especially likely to be confused about how to use celebrations and rituals because they feel so stigmatized and unlike other families.

The family therapist may help the family experience both enrichment and more successful transitions if appropriate celebrations are developed, rather than passing them up altogether. Imber-Black describes the rather elaborate celebration and gift-giving developed with one family around the placement of a severely retarded 20-year-old daughter into a group home. By encouraging satisfying exchanges of gifts and a family party to mark this event, the family was able to have an experience of their daughter moving on to a next appropriate arrangement for herself. The family could also acknowledge that there would be changes and losses as they adapted to her leaving. In this way, a ritual enabled a family to successfully cope with a difficult situation by participating in a process of celebration of the "launching" of an adolescent. It also helped the family anticipate its other developmental needs at that point in the life cycle of the family.

TERMINATION

Family therapy is generally briefer than individual psychotherapy, as mentioned earlier, and the process of termination is often less remarkable (Hoffman, 1981; Nichols, 1984). Therapy with a family with a disabled child may terminate much the way it does with other families. Not all of the needs of the family will have been met nor all the problems resolved. The work of the family therapy will not be complete and may well not be for several years, but the crisis or immediate distress will have been reduced to manageable proportions.

There are, in addition, two barometers of family functioning that help the therapist anticipate and plan for termination. These two barometers are the developmental and structural shifts that begin to develop in the family as the therapy proceeds. From a developmental perspective, family therapy is an effort to help a "stuck" family get "unstuck" and be able to continue forward with its own resources to accomplish current and future tasks. The family with a disabled child is faced with both normative and atypical life cycle events. A number of these have been highlighted in this and other chapters in this book: the school-age transition to the educational system, the onset of adolescence, the question of perpetual parenthood of the family with middle-aged parents. Family therapy, then, usually stops when the family is beginning to change and to proceed with accomplishing developmental tasks.

The second indicator of progress is the appearance of structural or functional changes. Usually, if a symptom has been structure-maintaining, the symptoms will begin to abate, even though the disabling condition of the child has not. For example, the therapist may notice that more functional problem-solving or instrumental behaviors are being enacted. There may be less emotionality or other resistance, less violation of generational boundaries in inappropriate coalitions, or less distress in the family's relationship with extended family, health care, and other community social systems. Communication will be clearer when there are fewer instances of silencing or interruptions, and differences of opinion can be expressed and valued; and an "executive" parental system will be operating but will not autocratically exclude the input of relevant members.

Part of what makes termination in family therapy relatively uncomplicated is that in addition to the brevity of the therapy (perhaps as much as a dozen sessions), the therapy probably has focused all along on the family's functioning outside the therapy sessions. Enactment and homework assignments have addressed how the family modifies its situation without the presence of the therapist, and the therapy is largely construed as an aid to real-life functioning.

During the termination phase the family is given credit for changes that it has accomplished. It is appropriate also at this point to specifically review the strategies the family has learned and preview ways that they can use these strategies in the future as new and expectable developmental difficulties arise.

One additional way to make the termination of family sessions more natural is to begin to space sessions farther apart. As the family begins to improve and to work actively at solving its problems, it is beneficial to schedule sessions less often. Attendance at therapy sessions will probably feel less essential to the family as well. It thus affirms the family's strength and resources to begin to come less often as the negotiated changes appear rather than to search about for additional problems to solve or goals to attain. If meetings have been weekly, a shift to meeting every 2 weeks and then to 1-month intervals is a useful increment. It gives the family the clear sense that they are doing the work on their own with the knowledge that the therapist is available to troubleshoot. For some families, saving issues or questions for the therapist is also one way of defusing and normalizing conflicts.

Scheduling a follow-up session 2 or 3 months after the last formal session is often a useful idea. This, too, encourages the family to proceed on their own, while assuring them of the therapist as an available backup. It is also helpful to encourage the family to call if they feel a need or if something unique arises. Even after this follow-up session, it is important to let families know that they can always return for a session or two. Transitions during the termination phase of family therapy help to define for the therapist and the family that the work is developmental, that the family can and is proceeding forward, and that there is no stigma if a future dilemma should require a consultation with the therapist.

REFERENCES

Anderson, C., & Stuart, S. (1983). *Mastering resistance: A practical guide to family therapy.* New York: Guilford Press.

Baird, M., & Doherty, W. (1986). Family resources in coping with serious illness. In M. Karpel (Ed.), Family resources: The hidden partner in family therapy. New York: Guilford Press, pp. 359–383.

Beavers, J., Hampson, R., Hulgus, Y., & Beavers, W. R. (1986). Coping in families with a retarded child. *Family Process, 25,* pp. 365–377.

Berger, M. (1982). Predictable tasks in therapy with families of handicapped persons. In A. Gurman (Ed.), *Questions and answers in the practice of family therapy* (Vol. 2). New York: Brunner/Mazel, pp. 82–87.

Berger, M., & Foster, M. (1986). Applications of family therapy theory to research and interventions with families with mentally retarded children. In J. Gallagher & P. Vietze (Eds.), *Families of handicapped persons: Research, programs and policy issues.* Baltimore, MD: Paul H. Brookes, pp. 251–260.

Black, D. (1982). Handicap and family therapy. In A. Bentovim, G. Barnes, & A. Conklin (Eds.), *Family therapy: Complementary frameworks of theory and practice* (Vol. 2). London: Academic Press, pp. 427–439.

Blum, R. (Ed.) (1984). Chronic illness and disabilities in childhood and adolescence. Orlando, FL: Grune & Stratton.

Bristol, M. (1984). Family resources and successful adaptation to autistic children. In E. Schopler & B. Mesibov (Eds.), *The effects of autism on the family.* New York: Plenum Press, pp. 289–310.

Bristol, M., & Schopler, E. (1984). A developmental perspective on stress and coping in families of autistic children. In J. Blacker (Ed.), *Severely handicapped young children and their families.* Orlando, FL: Academic Press, pp. 91–141.

Bronfenbrenner, U. (1979). *The ecology of human development.* Cambridge, MA: Harvard University Press.

Carter, E., & McGoldrick, M. (Eds.). (1980). *The family life cycle: A framework.* New York: Gardner Press.

Coppersmith, E. (Ed.). (1984). *Families with handicapped members.* Rockville, MD: Aspen Systems.

Crnic, K., Friedrich, W., & Greenberg, M. (1983). Adaptation of families with mentally retarded children: A model of stress, coping, and family ecology. *American Association of Mental Deficiency, 88,* pp. 125–138.

Darling, R. (1979). *Families against society.* New York: Sage.

DeShazer, S., & Lipchik, E. (1984). Frames and reframing. In E. Coppersmith (Ed.), *Families with handicapped members.* Rockville, MD: Aspen Systems, pp. 84–97.

Duvall, E. (1977). *Marriage and family development* (5th ed.). New York: Lippincott.

Erikson, E. (1963). *Childhood and society.* New York: Norton.

Farber, B. (1968). *Mental retardation: Its social context and social consequences.* Boston: Houghton Mifflin.

Featherstone, H. (1980). *A difference in the family.* New York: Basic Books.

Fewell, R. (1986). A handicapped child in the family. In R. Fewell & R. Vadasy (Eds.), *Families of handicapped children: Needs and supports across the life span.* Austin, TX: Pro-Ed, pp. 3–34.

Frey, J. (1984). A family/systems approach to illness-maintaining behaviors in chronically ill adolescents. *Family Process, 23,* pp. 251–260.

Gallagher, J., Beckman, P., & Cross, A. (1983). Families of handicapped children: Sources of stress and its amelioration. *Exceptional Children, 50,* pp. 10–19.

Harris, S. (1984). Intervention planning for the family of the autistic child: A multilevel assessment of the family system. *Journal of Marital and Family Therapy, 10,* pp. 157–166.

Hoffman, L. (1981). *Foundations of family therapy.* New York: Basic Books.

Houser, R. (1987). A comparison of stress and coping by fathers of mentally retarded and nonretarded adolescents. (Unpublished doctoral dissertation, University of Pittsburgh). *Dissertation Abstracts International.*

Imber-Black, E. (1988). Celebrating the uncelebrated. *Family Therapy Networker, 12,* pp. 60–66.

Karpel, M. (Ed.). (1986). *Family resources: The hidden partner in family therapy.* New York: Guilford Press.

Kaslow, F., & Cooper, B. (1978). Family therapy with the learning disabled child and his/her family. *Journal of Marriage and Family Counseling,* pp. 41–49.

Kazak, A. (1986). Families with physically handicapped children: Social ecology and family systems. *Family Process, 25,* pp. 265–282.

Koch, A. (1985). A strategy for prevention: Role flexibility and affective reactivity as factors in family coping. *Family Systems Medicine, 3,* pp. 70–81.

Lamb, M. (1983). Fathers of exceptional children. In M. Seligman, (Ed.), *The family with a handicapped child: Understanding and treatment.* New York: Grune & Stratton, pp. 125–146.

Leahey, M., & Wright, L. (1985). Intervening with families with chronic illness. *Family Systems Medicine, 3,* pp. 60–69.

McCubbin, H., Cauble, E., & Patterson, J. (Eds.). (1982). *Family stress, coping and social support.* Springfield, IL: Charles C Thomas.

McCubbin, H., & Patterson, J. (1983). The family stress process: The double ABCX model of adjustment and adaptation. *Marriage and Family Process, 6,* pp. 7–37.

McCubbin, H., Patterson J., McCubbin, M., & Wilson, R. (1983). Parental coping and family environment. In D. Bagarozzi et al. (Eds.), *Marital and family therapy.* New York: Human Sciences Press, pp. 107–136.

McGoldrick, M., & Gerson, R. (1986). *Genograms in family assessment.* New York: Norton.

Minuchin, S. (1974). *Families and family therapy.* Cambridge, MA: Harvard University Press.

Minuchin, S., & Fishman, C. (1981). *Family therapy techniques.* Cambridge, MA: Harvard University Press.

Minuchin, S., Rosman, S., & Baker, L. (1978). *Psychosomatic families: Anorexia nervosa in context.* Cambridge, MA: Harvard University Press.

Mitchell, W., & Rizzo, S. (1985). The adolescent with special needs. In M. Mirkin & S. Korman (Eds.), *Handbook of adolescents and family therapy.* New York: Gardner Press, pp. 329–342.

Nichols, M. (1984). *Family therapy: Concepts and methods.* New York: Gardner Press.

Olson, D., & McCubbin, H. (1983). *Families: What makes them work.* Beverly Hills, CA: Sage.

Olson, D., Sprenkle, D., & Russell, C. (1979). Circumplex model of marital and family systems. *Family Process, 18,* pp. 3–28.

Papp, P. (1983). *The process of change.* New York: Guilford Press.

Penn, P. (1982). Circular questioning. *Family Process, 21,* pp. 267–280.

Piaget, J. (1963). *The origins of intelligence in children.* New York: Norton.

Powers, M., & Bruey, C. (1988). Treating the family system. In M. Powers (Ed.), *Expanding systems of service delivery for persons with developmental disabilities.* Baltimore, MD: Paul H. Brookes, pp. 17–41.

Pratt, L. (1976). *Family structure and effective health behavior: The energized family.* Boston: Houghton Mifflin.

Reiss, D., & Oliveri, M. (1980). Family paradigm and family coping: A proposal for linking the family's intrinsic adaptive capacities to its response to stress. *Family Relations, 29,* pp. 431–444.

Rolland, J. (1987). Chronic illness and the life cycle: A conceptual framework. *Family Process, 26,* pp. 203–222.

Scarf, M. (1987). *Intimate partners: Patterns in love and marriage.* New York: Random House.

Seligman, M. (1979). *Strategies for helping parents of exceptional children.* New York: Free Press.

Seligman, M. (1983). Siblings of handicapped persons. In M. Seligman (Ed.), *The family with a handicapped child: Understanding and treatment.* Orlando, FL: Grune & Stratton, pp. 147–174.

Seligman, M., & Darling, R. (1989). *Ordinary families, special children: A systems approach to childhood disability.* New York: Guilford Press.

Selvini-Palazzoli, M., Boscolo, L., Cecchin, G., & Prata, G. (1980). The problem of the referring person. *Journal of Marital and Family Therapy, 6,* pp. 3–9.

Strax, T., & Wolfson, S. (1984). Life–cycle crises of the disabled adolescent and young adult: Implications for public policy. In R. Blum (Ed.), *Chronic illness and disabilities in childhood and adolescence.* Orlando, FL: Grune & Stratton, pp. 47–57.

Turnbull, A., Summers, J., & Brotherson, J. (1986). Family life cycle: Theoretical and empirical implications and future directions for families with mentally retarded members. In J. Gallagher & P. Vietze (Eds.), *Families of handicapped persons: Research, programs and policy issues.* Baltimore, MD: Paul H. Brookes, pp. 45–65.

Turnbull, A., & Turnbull, H. (1986). *Families, professionals and exceptionality: A special partnership.* Columbus, OH: Merrill.

Vine, P. (1982). *Families in pain.* New York: Pantheon.

Walker, G. (1983). The pact: The caretaker-parent/ill-child coalition in families with chronic illness. *Family Systems Medicine, 1,* pp. 6–29.

Watzlawick, P., Weakland, I., & Fisch, R. (1974). *Change: Principles of problem formation and problem resolution.* New York: Norton.

Webb-Woodard, L., & Woodard, B. (1982). A case of the blind leading the "blind": Reframing a physical handicap as competence. *Family Process, 21,* pp. 291–294.

Wikler, L. (1981). Family therapy with families of mentally retarded children. In A. Gurman (Ed.), *Questions and answers in the practice of family therapy* (Vol. 1). New York: Brunner/Mazel, pp. 129–132.

Wikler, L., Haack, J., & Intagliata, J. (1984). Bearing the burden alone: Helping divorced mothers of children with developmental disabilities. In E. Coppersmith (Ed.), *Families with handicapped members,* Rockville, MD: Aspen Systems, pp. 44–62.

Index